Surviving the Planet X Tribulation

There is Safety in Numbers

Surviving the Planet X Tribulation

There is Safety in Numbers

Marshall Masters

Your Own World Books
Nevada, USA

yowbooks.com

COPYRIGHT

Surviving the Planet X Tribulation: There is Safety in Numbers

No part of this book may be reproduced or transmitted in any form or by any means, graphic, electronic, or mechanical, including photocopying, recording, taping, or by any information storage retrieval system, without the written permission of the publisher.

Your Own World Books
An Imprint of Knowledge Mountain Church of Perpetual Genesis, NV, USA
Author: Marshall Masters

Third Edition — July 2021
ISBN: 979-8-53393-499-2
yowbooks.com

Notice: Every effort has been made to make this book as complete and as accurate as possible, and no warranty or fitness is implied. All of the information provided in this book is provided on an "as is" basis. The authors and the publisher shall not be liable or responsible to any person or entity with respect to any loss or damages arising from the information contained herein.

Fair Use: This book contains copyrighted material and is made available for educational purposes, to advance the understanding of Planet X research and related survival issues, etc. This constitutes a "fair use" of any such copyrighted material as provided for in Title 17 U.S.C. section 107 of the US Copyright Law. In accordance with Title 17 U.S.C. Section 107, the material in this book is made available for non-profit research and educational purposes.

Trademarks: All terms mentioned in this book that are known to be trademarks or service marking have been capitalized. Knowledge Mountain Church of Perpetual Genesis cannot attest to the accuracy of this information and the use of any term in this book should not be regarded as affecting the validity of any trademark or service mark.

Related Titles

Win-Win Survival Handbook: All-Hazards Safety and Future Space Colonization

Everything we are taught about surviving the "end-of-life-as-we-know-it" is wrong, according to Win-Win Survival Handbook author Marshall Masters, and here is why:

The conventional Plan A is about building to fail and playing the odds. When the odds do not pan out, Plan B is about huddling in a box in the ground, eating dead food, and wondering what comes next.

With a Win-Win, you build for continuity of life so that you are going over speed bumps when others are hitting walls. Your Plan B is the noble and life-affirming mission to prepare your progeny to colonize distant worlds.

This book guides you through the development process with detailed instructions for designing, building, and shielding communities for self-sufficiency, survival, colonization, and profit.

In a country blessed with Win-Wins, there will always be hope for the future – no matter what comes our way.

Radio Free Earth: The Complete Beginner's Guide to Survival Communications

Radio Free Earth shows you how to select and use a wide range of affordable consumer and amateur two-way radios for long-range and short-range communications.

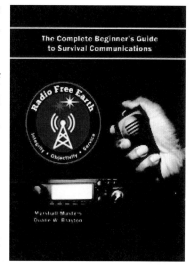

Written for non-technical readers, it demystifies the world of amateur radio with simplified, building-block explanations. Ideal for survivalists and hobbyists alike, it reduces months of personal study down to a matter of days. Topics include:

- Radio basics such as frequencies and desirable features
- Long-range and short-range communication strategies
- Choosing the right radio for any survival mission
- Shopping for affordable and reliable radios and equipment
- Protecting your radios from artificial and natural events

When you finish this book, you will know where to begin, what to buy, when to buy it, and who uses it – fast!

Acknowledgments

This book represents a culmination of over fifteen years of research and publication. Along the way those who have followed my websites, Your Own World USA, and the Planet X Town Hall, have contributed vast amounts of information, observations, and ideas. They are also in it for the species, and like me, they hold dear a vision of what life can be in a Star Trek world following the tribulation.

To Vice Steward, Joseph Lewis thanks for his wonderful assistance in the production of the 2nd edition of this book; a good and true friend, he is always there for me.

To J. P. Jones, my mission brother, I offer warm thanks, not only for his help with this book, but for all the research, help, and support he has given me over the years. Without his help my previous work, *Being in It for the Species: The Universe Speaks,* would not have been possible.

To Doug Abramson my sincere thanks for his assistance with the Communications for Civil Rule and Incident Command System chapters.

To Guild Steward, Duane Brayton, my heartfelt thanks for his support and assistance with refining the site reconnaissance evaluation strategy described in this book.

To David B. South, founder of Monolithic Dome Institute and a man with many demands on his time, he graciously granted me an interview for my *Cut to the Chase* podcast which aired in September of 2015. Before, during, and after that interview he answered all of my technical questions regarding the use of domes for survival shelters.

To Barbara Lou Townsend, the administrator for my Planet X Town Hall online community and to all of our other volunteer moderators, my special thanks to each one for their many years of Planet X research efforts in service to others.

Above all my deepest thanks is for all of you who have supported my work through the years. This work would not have been possible without your kind assistance and words of support.

Table of Contents

Marshall's Motto

Destiny comes to those who listen,

and fate finds the rest.

So learn what you can learn,

do what you can do,

and never give up hope!

1

You and Me

As I write this, my hope is that you are reading these words now because someone who knows you, respects you, and seeks your leadership has put this book into your hands because of what you are now seeing in the sky.

You, standing out on the street with your friends, loved ones, and neighbors, are pointing up at the heavens with a dark sense of mystery about what you see. The so-called experts on television are assuring everyone that this will pass with only a minor inconvenience. But there is something deep within you clutching at your soul with a kind of fear you seldom have felt in your life. Not the fear of what you see, but fear from knowing that you are unprepared for what you see. All of this is because, despite the false assurances, you know it's happening on your watch, and deep inside you, your connection to Creator is resonating with this simple, repetitious message, "It's time to get your flock to safety."

As a published Planet X researcher since 2002, I have anticipated this date with destiny. Through all these years the only thing that has mattered to me has always been one question, "How can I be of service to you?" "What can I do to help you and those who depend on your leadership and your love to survive what will become a long tribulation of a decade or perhaps more?"

This moment, as you are reading this book, has haunted me for years because this moment represents the last window of opportunity. This is an opportunity and should not be squandered with pontification and granularity. Rather, this is a time for leadership.

While all those about you have the luxury of speculation and disagreement, you have no such luxury. What you have is the responsibility to get your flock to safety, and it is a very weighty responsibility, indeed. Therefore, permit me the opportunity to be of service to you by helping you to shoulder that responsibility with greater confidence in yourself and the future.

As I sit here now, composing this work in a before-time well in advance of your reading it, I have two choices: I can propel myself forward in time as I write this book to the tension, fear, and uncertainties of your present circumstances. Or, I can ask you to come back in time with me to this very moment. I can invite you to a time when we can talk about this as old and dear friends in a relaxed setting — where you will have the time to contemplate and to meditate upon the knowledge I can share with you.

In the coming tribulation you and those you trust most are going to make impossible decisions — not just each day, but many times each day. Only in the evening when you lay your head down to sleep will you have the luxury of time to question the wisdom of your decisions. For this reason I am choosing not to propel myself forward in time to your moment. In doing so I would only add to your current sense of dread with information that you know is late in coming — perhaps too late to make a difference, though I pray you never believe that.

No my friend, and I do call you my friend even though I will never know your name, recognize your face, or hear your voice. Through my connection to Creator I feel our bond. Years ago a learned man once shared his definition of the word Namaste with me.

He explained that Namaste is a polite form of greeting in the Hindu custom which means, "That little bit of God in me greets that little bit of God in you." So, in my heart my little bit of God is telling me I need to be in service to you and your little bit of God as well. We are all in this together. And at this moment as I pen these words, I am overwhelmed with the new magnificent sense of connection to you, and the enormous burden you face in the years to come.

With this in mind I now share with you what, as a leader, must be your eternal message of hope to those who will entrust their lives to your care. I say to you now as you must say to them time and again:

- We will survive.
- We will prevail.
- We will thrive.

At every gathering you must repeat these words. At the close of every meeting you must repeat these words. With every teaching opportunity you must repeat these words.

Now my friend, I'm going to ask you to embark on a time journey back to this time; to a magical place where I can meet you like an old friend. When you arrive, you will find yourself in a large private summerhouse overlooking a picturesque lake. The house is large with large windows that flood the interior with a pleasant light.

It is a place where you and I, our families, and our close friends have gathered for summer retreats over the years. During the day there is the business of making meals and tending to children who are always running about laughing and playing. They like swinging into the lake off a large rope hanging from an old tree and just enjoying a carefree time.

At night, there come the quiet times when the children, exhausted from a day's play, sleep peacefully in the downstairs bedrooms, of which there are many. On a large veranda an old golden retriever by the name of Sheba, who just seems to have adopted the place, sleeps with one eye open just to be sure the night passes without incident. This is the place where we will meet. It is far from where you are, and where I now sit and write.

Imagine, before you a silvery, egg-like machine just appears. It is the time machine that you will use to come back in time to join me here at the lake. To make it work, you must recite a motto I have shared with those who have followed my work for well over a decade. I call it, "Marshall's Motto."

So dear friend, please leave the disturbing reality of your moment behind as you step into the time machine. As you do so, you will hear the hatch close with a soft hiss behind you, and beneath your feet there is a whirring of machinery as you settle into a comfortable chair in the center of the machine. Before you there is a stark panel that has only a microphone in its center. The time machine is awaiting your command, and when it is given, the next thing you'll know — you'll be there. Are you ready? Then repeat after me:

"Destiny comes to those who listen, and fate finds the rest."

"So, learn what you can learn, do what you can do, and never give up hope!"

Now the machine hums with life and dances with light. Your journey is about to begin. So close your eyes and relax, for when the journey is complete, and you open your eyes, I'll be there waiting for you.

2

The Big Picture

Your eyes open, and there you are in bed next to the one you love. Odd, how your last memory is of being in a time machine, and yet, here you are without any sense of having gotten here. You know you are at the lake house, and that you are in a downstairs bedroom.

It is all too familiar. Even so, surreal ideas are buzzing around in your head like a swarm of bees that keep you from a well-deserved slumber.

Across the pillow you hear a sleepy voice, "Thinking about those dreams again? You know, the ones you keep having each morning before you wake up?"

"Yes," you admit reluctantly, "I can't get over how real they are."

"Before you toss and turn all night, why not go upstairs and make yourself a glass of warm milk? We'll both sleep better for it."

You slip your hand across the bed into a gentle clasp. "You're right." You agree as you pull the covers off with your other hand. Letting go, you slide out of bed slowly as the creak of old oak beneath your feet reminds you of the history of this majestic old home.

Donning the robe you left dangling on a bedpost, you step into a pair of slippers that should have been replaced years ago. But you didn't have the heart to because they're just so darn comfortable. Making your way down the hall, a plug-in nightlight at the foot of the stairs guides your steps, and leads you up towards the kitchen and dining room above.

Passing by one of the bedrooms you see bunk beds in the dim light, and each is filled with slumbering children. Most sleep as serenely and picturesquely as a Norman Rockwell painting. Many are contorted in ways only Houdini could imagine; the children sleep without a care in the world — a deep sleep you've long forgotten in your adult years. As you quietly paddle down the hallway towards the stairs, you wonder if there will ever be a time in your life when you will be able to sleep like that again.

The wooden steps of the stairway creak as each step and riser adjusts to your weight. Careful to be quiet, you see a bright light at the end of the stairwell. Perhaps you're not the only one who can't sleep.

Tea and Camaraderie

Entering the second floor with its large kitchen, dining, and living room areas, you see me at the stove boiling some water for tea.

"Couldn't sleep, huh?" I ask with a wistful smile.

"Well, you know what they say; misery loves company. You seem to be having the same problem."

We both chuckle. In all of the years that we've known each other, our repartee is rooted in love and friendship, which is a touchstone of the camaraderie in our convoluted journeys through life.

"I'm making chamomile tea. What do you say we fetch up some cake to go along with it and sit out on the balcony?" A massive deck runs the full length of the house. It is dotted with chairs, tables, and brightly colored patio umbrellas.

The offer is appealing and you eye one of the cakes on the center station. Everyone brings something from home, and this cake was served earlier that evening during the first dinner. So, everyone is now free to enjoy. "What do you think about that exquisite-looking chocolate cake in the center?"

"You read my mind. It's clear to see the kids already found it."

"Oh yes, that's quite a crime scene, which tells me two things: first, it's the good stuff, and second, this could probably be our last chance to have some." I reach into a cabinet and pull out two plates and hand them to you. "If you would be so kind, dear friend, and do the honors, and cut us two thick wedges of that sumptuous-looking cake."

I pour the hot water into the teapot, being sure to cover it with a cozy, "By the way, do you remember where we keep the dog biscuits for Sheba?" You point to a cabinet, and I remove a few biscuits from the box and slip them into a side pocket in my robe.

With that we head out to the wide balcony on the second floor and settle into a couple of chairs at a table near the outer railing. We have a good view of the night sky above and the lake below. What a perfect night it is. The air is sweet and comfortable; the stars are so thick one could imagine stepping from one to the next.

As we settle into the plump cushions of our redwood patio chairs, Sheba, the golden retriever guardian of this beautiful lake house, ambles up to see what we're up to and if there is a treat for her.

I take the biscuits out of my pocket and hand them to you. "Remember, Sheba is a bit long in the tooth, so it helps if you break them up for her." With a nod you take the biscuits and break them up.

Sheba is soon gleefully crunching away on her treats, and we talk about the day and pass the time with idle conversation while our chamomile tea steeps. I lift the cozy and lid off of the teapot and say, "Looks like it's time for tea and cake," after which we both dig in with great relish."

The cake is so sumptuous we hardly say a word until finally, when you are scraping up the last bit of frosting, you say, "Can I talk to you about a disturbing dream I'm having?"

"You can talk to me about anything. You know that. But before you tell me about the dream, tell me when did it occur?"

"In the morning, you know that twilight zone time between sleep and wakefulness."

"You say it is disturbing. Why is this so?"

You collect your thoughts as you set down your plate. Quiet and reflective you pick up your mug and roll it in your hands feeling its warmth against your palms. Finally, you say, "It's because I always see the same thing again, and again, and again. It always starts in the same place and ends in the last place."

Now I set my plate down, "So, tell me, what do you see each time, from the very beginning to the very end?"

Taking a sip of tea to mask a pained expression, you mutter under your breath, "I hope you're not going to think I'm strange."

"You're my friend, and I love you. Dreams, such as these, are never strange; for to all things there is a purpose. Tell me."

Squirming in your chair, you take a deep breath, because now in your mind, you see it again, "It always begins with me looking out to sea. I can smell the salt air, and I feel the sand beneath my feet. The shoreline is bare and naked a good ways out, and I can even see old sunken fishing boats long hidden offshore. It is a macabre scene. That is when it comes. A massive vertical wall of turbulent water and the sound of it is deafening. Behind me, I hear the terrified screams of people fleeing, and I turn around. When I do, all I see are the backs of those running away from the approaching monster and it strikes me as a rather futile gesture. That is when I spy an old couple looking out to sea and holding onto each other tightly. I can see in their faces that they know the final seconds of their lives are ticking away, but there is no panic. I know that all they want is to be together, and to comfort each other. They hope that if they clutch tightly enough, they will die in each other's arms. Then, snap! I wake up. Bless my soul; it always starts this way, and it always ends this way, and I don't want to think about how many times it's happened. It's quite maddening, you know."

Feeling your emotional pain, I reach across the small table between us and put my hand on yours, "I've lost count of how many times I have heard others describe prophetic dreams just like yours. Most are about tsunamis, earthquakes, and volcanic eruptions. A few are about something seen in space. However, no matter what the dream is, the dreamers always beg me not to think of them as being strange. So know this, you are not alone, and what you have experienced is very real."

You eyes seek mine, "So what is the meaning of all this?"

Staring out at the lake I answer, "I bet you feel like someone has just slapped you in the face with a dead salmon, and there you are spitting scales and not knowing why." With that I rise and lean on the railing, and look at the lake below, and you join me.

"OK. You've heard this before from a lot of other people. Here's what I want to know: Are you going to coddle me? Or are you going to tell me what the meaning of all this is?"

That makes me chuckle, "Fair enough. For starters, you've had what I call an awareness-wakening dream. The reason you're having it now is that before you were born you made a promise to God, and now your obligation has come due. Mind you, many make such promises before they are born, but few have the courage to make right on them because doing so is very difficult. Very difficult indeed."

Sheba starts to muzzle my hand in search of a treat. She smells that one last biscuit in my pocket, and she's not about to let me go back into the house with it. I take it out of my pocket and begin breaking it into small pieces for her as I warn, "Are you truly ready to go down this rabbit hole, dear friend? If so, what I am about to share with you will change your life forever."

"Are you talking, red pill or blue pill, like in the movie, 'The Matrix'?"

"No, I'm talking about real 'burning bush' stuff, and if you ask me to share this with you right now, one of two things is going to happen. You make good on your promise, or you will live the rest of your life with the shame of knowing you were too weak to keep your promise, and God will know it too. So, there will be no going to sleep with a blue pill and all of this is forgotten. There is no forgetting, and while you're chewing on that, I'm going to go back into the kitchen and add some water to the pot. I think we can squeeze a couple more cups out of this chamomile."

Walking back into the kitchen, I feel your eyes on my back, and I know what is going through your mind. I've seen it many times before and there is no way around it. If it is to have meaning, this kind of truth must be grasped.

With the teapot refreshed with boiling water, I amble back out onto the balcony and find you sitting in your redwood chair and deep in contemplation. You notice me settling back into my chair, and looking over say, "I've never run away from anything in my entire life, and I'm not going to run away from this. For better or for worse, I must know the meaning of it. Don't coddle me."

Your courage makes me smile, "Well, let's begin with this. I am the chief steward of a church that I founded, and you are the pastor at yours. Yet, you know I was never a spiritual man until late in my life."

To which you respond, "You were always a self-defined and born-hard geek. You've always marched to the beat of a different drummer. This is why I never spoke to you of my faith, nor asked you about yours. It has always been an unwritten understanding between us that each of us would find God in our own way, and in our own good time."

I nod appreciatively, "Dear friend, your respect for this boundary has been one of the most sacred aspects of our friendship, and it has always endeared you to me. So, with this in mind I will share with you how the understanding of this coming tribulation has brought me to God — but not in a fearful way mind you. You know that I have always thought science is the most magnificent way to appreciate the handiwork of a divine being. However, you also know that I would always deny this belief to others. Looking back, I regret that."

"Yes, I've always seen that in you, that one day you would come to find God in your own way and on your own terms. But now that we're talking, I am curious as to why you sought God?"

"Why? Why? Why?" I set down my fork and point upwards at the starry night above us, "We are facing a tribulation of a decade or more, and I understand the science of it, but that scientific understanding has only one destination — fear — the fear you realize when you reach the limitations of science. When I reached this point, I came across an article about some Nobel laureates who had come to the same juncture. Then, unwilling to live within the confines of what science cannot do, they went beyond science to what some would call the paranormal, or to matters of faith.

That article was the first step for me, and where it led me was to a profound question, 'Where does God live? And what is God's mission?' Clearly, for all things there is a purpose;

God is no different. Perhaps, I could have turned to you at that point, but I didn't because yours is what I call a terrestrial faith.

Perpetual Genesis

With earthly beliefs a people's worldview encompasses their community, their church, their country, and the earth. Everything beyond that line of sight is considered 'God,' and they leave it at that. As a man of science, I could not accept such a limited terrestrial view. No. What I wanted was a cosmic view without limitations."

"This is pretty bold stuff," you observe.

"Yes, but only for those with a terrestrial view of our relationship with God. I found that beyond our line of sight is God, but what is beyond God? I'll tell you — the void — the endlessness of the space-time continuum wherein God created us and wherein God resides. Ergo, God does have a mission which is not limited just to our species and planet. That's terrestrial egotism. Rather, as I see it, God's mission is something I call perpetual genesis. That is the perpetual creation of life from the lifelessness of the void. This is not to say that the void is without substance. Rather, the void is filled with substance such as the dark matter and dark energy which our scientists have recently discovered. In comparison with that, what we know as substance is but a minuscule percentage. Therefore, God does not create life from the lifelessness of the void by turning nothing into something. Rather, it is through intention that God creates universes from the very soup of the void with each universe having its own unique laws of physics."

You rub your chin wistfully, "OK, leaving this as a possibility, what does it have to do with my prophetic dreams?"

"Bingo!" I gleefully exclaim, "Now we come to the crux of the matter. That being, before you and I were ever born, we each, as eternal beings, made an eternal promise to God to be in service to God's mission of perpetual genesis. In other words, this is not a promise we make as physical beings like a scared soldier in his foxhole bargaining with God for a chance to survive the battle. Rather, this is an eternal promise we make as eternal beings. So how does it work? Here you and I are in these bodies, in this species, at this time, and on this planet. And when our eternal job here is done, like good soldiers, we'll go where God sends us next — to the next planet, to the next species, and to the next time. This now brings us back to the question, 'What does this have to do with your prophetic dreams?' As I said before, your dreams are happening to remind you that your eternal promise is now due."

Taking it all in, you move your head side-to-side, "Assuming for a moment you're right about this perpetual genesis theory, what will be the outcome of this eternal promise you say I've made?"

"You will help to facilitate a spiritual and intellectual evolution of our species that is initiated by a catastrophic tribulation."

"You know, many of my faith would call you a raving lunatic," you say as I feed the last bit of biscuit to Sheba.

"And what do you say?"

"For now, all I'm saying is that I'm not walking away from this conversation." Then, you pause and think for a moment, "But I am going to walk back into the kitchen and get us another slice of that delicious cake. And when I get back, I want you to stop talking to me like I have rubber knees and cut to the chase."

"Then make mine a thick slice," I jest, as you turn on your heels and walk to the kitchen with Sheba in tow. Watching the old golden retriever following closely in your steps, I cannot help but think she's learned that conversations such as ours come with the bribery of treats. A thought which makes me wonder how many times she has done the same with other visitors to this beautiful lake home.

You return, and we settle in again with hot mugs of chamomile tea and thick slices of chocolate cake. I begin with a question, "Have you ever heard of catastrophism?"

"Is that like uniformitarianism or Darwinism?"

"Good question, but no. Before uniformitarianism or Darwinism catastrophism was the prevailing view of science. What catastrophism tells us is that life is not solely ordered by a long gradual process of evolution, but cycles of quiescence punctuated by catastrophe. Ergo, we have long cycles of relative quiescence with minor catastrophes, but nothing on a massive global scale. However, these long periods of relative quiescence are punctuated by very brief moments of extreme catastrophe in which life on our planet is reordered."

"So if I follow you, what you are saying is that my prophetic dream is a harbinger of an imminent catastrophic period that will reorder life on our planet?"

I'm delighted by your answer, "Exactly! For the last fifteen years I have been talking about and writing about a dark cloud coming, and it is coming. We stand at the threshold of a series of catastrophic events that are about to punctuate the relative quiescence of our existence. However, as an eternal being, you knew this was coming long before you were ever born. Long ago you made your promise to God, that you would find the silver lining in this dark cloud, and that you would help bring a positive future to fruition."

"Why?"

"Because, survival only for the sake of saving your own skin leads to darkness and de-evolution. We are facing a tribulation of a decade or more, and the only thing that we can depend upon to bring us through that without losing our humanity is hope for the future. The same kind of hope that poor European immigrants had when they purchased steerage passage on ships bound for America — the hope of making a new and better life for themselves, for their children, and for their children's children. Hope that helped them to endure harsh lives in cold water flats and the exploitation of sweatshops; so that, in time their children could become professionals, and their grandchildren would then have the freedom to bring the joy of art to what is often a bleak world."

You shake your head in disbelief, "But I'm just the minister of a small church, not a Moses. Isn't your vision of finding a silver lining in this cloud a bit grandiose?"

"Before I answer that; where's Sheba?"

"Last I saw, she was going down the stairs; I suppose to make her rounds. After all she is the matron of the house. Don't worry; she'll be back." You pat your pocket, "and when she returns, I've got a few biscuits for her."

Bunker Bunnies

With that we both pick up our plates and work on our second portion of cake. "Good for Sheba. But as for my vision of what is about to come, no, it is not grandiose. Not in the least, because over the years I have consulted with many wealthy people, and all they ever wanted from me was to know if the approximate location of their bunkers was survivable. In fact the locations they chose always were. That's all they wanted to know because they would spend at least a half a million dollars to build and equip their underground bunkers. In each and every case their planning was in service to self; just themselves, their own, and no one else. In fact, the further away other people were from them the better."

"Given that I can't afford to build a bunker, how can I hope to compete with them or do what they do?"

"You don't understand. They're what I call 'bunker bunnies.' They all have about two years' worth of food set aside. While those on the surface suffer, they will be eating healthy meals in their hot tubs and watching '*The Sound of Music*' on their big-screen TVs. Then, one day they'll have to surface to forage, and that's when their best-laid plans will fail them. The minute they step out onto the surface, the dregs of humanity will smell their healthy bodies from up to a mile away. After that they'll die, and they'll die badly. So, in spite of all their money, and all their cleverness, and all of their selfishness, they will have only planned themselves into becoming banquet feasts for cannibals."

The mental image I've painted makes you shiver, "If that is what is going to happen to them, wouldn't it just be better for my loved ones and me to find a ground zero location, set out some lawn chairs, and wait for it all to end?"

"Absolutely not," I answer, "Because, surviving the coming tribulation is not about holding onto things; it's about holding onto each other; it's about being someone who walks humbly with God on a spiritual path. This is the most valuable thing for survival — not money — what is most valuable is your connection to God as a spiritual person. When you think about this only in material terms, all that you are doing is behaving like a good little consumer robot. When you have a problem, you go shopping. On the other hand, as a spiritual person, you first go to your relationship with God. There you will find your eternal promise of perpetual genesis and make good on it."

You shake your head, "But I'm just one person!"

"No, you are the leader of a faith-based organization, the pastor of a church. As a person, your connection to God is your advantage, not your ability to build a million-dollar bunker. However, as the leader of a faith-based organization, your organization has four considerable and compelling advantages — advantages that cannot be understated or measured in financial terms during what is to come."

You hold up a finger, "Hold that thought." Having made her rounds, Sheba returns for another treat. This time you take the dog biscuit out of your pocket and hand it to me. "Your turn. Since my church has four considerable and compelling advantages, as you say, I want you to break this biscuit up into four parts, so Sheba and I can get the good news, one piece at a time."

Faith-Based Advantages

Given that Sheba's tail is wagging with excitement, it's unanimous, "Ok," I agree and break off the first piece and feed it to Sheba. "Advantage one — chain of command. The number one reason secular collectives fail is not that they are unable build bunkers or stockpile food and defensive weapons. It is, absent an external threat, they become divided by political machinations and power grabs, and the collective inevitably fragments and fails. On the other hand you have a respected and established chain of command. Sure, all organizations are political, and yours is no different, but when it comes to a respected chain of command, you do have an advantage."

"You'd better get to point two real fast. Sheba is licking her chops."

"Yeah, yeah," I break off the second piece and Sheba lunges for it. "Advantage two — mobilization. As a faith-based organization, it can take you thirty years to build a library for your church, but when it comes to responding to a disaster, you'll be up and running in three days or less."

Sheba is just finishing the last piece as I break off the next one and hand it to her, "Advantage three — diversity of related skills. If you go to a software company, most of the people there will be software engineers. In other words, for-profit organizations are only as diverse as their business model requires. As a church, there is no such limitation. When you pray together on Sunday, the person in front of you could be a lawyer, to the right of you a sanitation worker, to the left a nurse, and behind you an accountant. You never know because everyone is there to pray together — not to do business."

Sheba is eyeing the last piece intently, "Okay girl, here you go," and I shake the crumbs off my hands to let her know that she's gotten the last of her treats. "Advantage four — related skills networking. Let's go back to the previous advantage. Everyone who prays in your church not only brings a unique skill of their own, but most have hobbies with additional skills, and they also bring connections to other people, that also have unique skills. For example, the lawyer is also a ham radio operator who knows many other local hams that volunteer for ARES. The ham shack in his house contains thousands of dollars of equipment and has a roof covered with antennas of all sorts. The sanitation worker is not only incredibly valuable to your efforts, but he also knows several water treatment engineers. You'll need those, for sure. And it turns out the nurse assists in a volunteer hospice program. She can attract trained volunteers to render hospice and palliative care. And finally, you learn that the accountant is a retired master sergeant with combat experience and that he is also a volunteer instructor in a national nonprofit that teaches marksmanship."

Now you're nodding your head, "So this is why you say that surviving the tribulation is not about holding onto things but holding onto each other?"

"Now, you're cooking with gas."

Still not quite convinced, you shake your head, "OK, I get it on one level, but on another, I'm still having a hard time wrapping my head around this. However, the big question in my mind now is that given you've been writing about this, and authoring about this, and giving radio and TV interviews on this topic for fifteen years, why tell me this now? Why didn't you tell me all of this before?"

"Because, I didn't want you to become an oyster."

You raise your eyebrows, "I hate to ask, but what the heck do you mean?"

Turning People into Oysters

After the last bite of cake on my plate I take another sip of tea, allowing the silence to focus your attention, "If I had come to you to share this information before you had your awareness-waking dreams, I can tell you exactly what you would have said. You would have said, 'It's all nonsense; nothing is going to happen; and I don't want to hear about it.' Then, if I were to be so rude as to force this knowledge of awareness on you, you would have become like an oyster making a pearl. In other words this knowledge would have been like an irritating grain of sand that you could not expel. You would have then begun to wrap it with one successive layer of nacre after another until you created a hard pearl to insulate yourself from it. The result of all of those layers of nacre around this truth would make it infinitely more difficult for you to come into awareness, and it would be unlikely that we would have this conversation at all. This is what I mean by turning people into oysters — pushing awareness on them when they're not ready for it."

As the conversation winds down, you stand and stretch, "To be honest, I do not know if I'm ready for it as you describe it. It is a bit overwhelming."

Nodding in agreement, I reply, "If you're not ready for awareness, then you're not willing to shoulder the burden. Granted, we've had an interesting broad-brush conversation this evening, but the day-to-day reality of leading a faith-based organization through a decade of tribulation is not going to be chocolate cake and dog biscuits. It will be a brutal existence; each and every day you will be faced with impossible decisions — not just once a day but several times a day. Keep this in mind; you knew this when you promised God that you would serve the mission of perpetual genesis. If you decide to make good your promise and shoulder this burden, then you'll need to understand the full measure of it. To this end I will do all that I can for you, but first, you must decide if you have the courage to shoulder the responsibility of the promise you made to God before you were born. In other words it's fish or cut bait time."

Looking down at the patio floor, you put your hands in your pockets, "I... I...," you stutter, "I just don't know about this eternal promise thing. I'm not sure if I can accept this burden, let alone do it." You hesitate, "And what about these miserable dreams? Will they continue to haunt me?"

I give you a tight hug and promise, "You will know the answers to all these questions when you wake up in the morning."

With an uncertain smile you say, "In that case, I'm going to turn in. How about you?

"No, not yet, I still have a few things I need to do this evening; you go on and get some sleep. I'll see you in the morning."

With that you turn and walk back into the house, and down the stairs to your bedroom. The sound of gentle snoring tells you to slip gently under the sheets, and you do. Laying there in the night, above your head a faint sliver of light casts itself across the ceiling, making a broken field of gray shapes. As you study them, sleep overtakes you, and for the first time in a very long while you sleep like a child.

3

Impossible Decision

One of the most delicious things in life is a good night's sleep. You awaken to a day that is brighter, with equally brighter spirits. And so you're awake earlier than usual this morning. Bouncing out of bed, you climb the stairs to find the other guests engaged making breakfast. You volunteer to work the griddle. Besides wanting to help, you enjoy running the griddle. Throughout the early part of the morning, you've been flipping up stacks of happy-face pancakes for the kids and watching them wolf them down along with tall glasses of fresh fruit juice. It's the kind of morning that just makes the world feel right.

The griddle is cooling, and the children have scampered down to the lake. They're busy running about, burning off their breakfasts. Sheba is running with them and having the time of her life. It's one of those living memories you know you'll treasure for the rest of your life.

While you pick at homemade muffins and drink coffee, the conversation with the other parents around the table is pleasant and distracting. About this time I come up from downstairs rubbing my eyes, not looking as rested as I should. "Don't tell me; you pulled an all-nighter?"

As I pour myself a glass of orange juice, I rasp out, "You could say that."

You turn the griddle back on, "What's your pleasure?"

"To be honest, I'm still full of chocolate cake, but a few of those potato pancakes and some sour cream would be nice. Then I think I'll just go back to sleep for a few more hours."

"Let me make you a few fresh ones," you offer. "These have been sitting here for a while." I nod gratefully and sleepily begin sipping my juice. The conversation at the table resumes, though much of it is a blur to me. Part of me wants to chime in, but another wants to slip back into a slumber.

Keeping Your Promise

The time passes in a fuzzy way, and after a while you bring me a plate with a tidy pile of warm, golden potato pancakes with a side of sour cream. As you set the plate before me, you lean over and whisper in my ear, "How do I keep my promise?"

It's good to hear you say that and to be honest; I never doubted you would. "Good, but this is not the right time or place to begin," I answer softly.

"I figured as much," you agree, "So how about this for a plan? I'll come down around noon and shake you out of bed. While you shower and shave, I'll load the boat down at the dock with fishing gear, a cooler, and a picnic basket packed with tasty treats. There's a small cove at the far end of the lake I've wanted to fish. What do you say we go and try our luck over there?"

"Why not? It sounds like a good plan to me. Make sure we have a fully charged battery for the electric trolling motor. I can't remember if someone put it on the trickle charger yesterday or not. I know I didn't."

You smile, "It was one of the first things I did after we got here yesterday, so no worries. Eat up and get your forty winks. I'll take care of the rest." I nod with a mouth full of potato pancake, "I didn't think I was that hungry, but you've made them so tasty I can't have just one — or two, or three. It's like they're saying to me, 'Forget the chocolate cake, there's a new sheriff in town!'"

On the Lake

As promised, it's noon and you're shaking my shoulder, "Come on sleepy head, you're burning daylight. Get yourself together and meet me down at the dock."

Yawning, I grumble, "Right. Got it." Feeling rested I stretch, get out of bed, and ramble into the bathroom to start the shower.

It is a beautiful summer afternoon with blue skies and fleecy white clouds. Ambling down the stone steps to the dock, I see the kids lining up at the barbecue pit. One of the parents is making hot dogs and hamburgers on the grill, and another is setting out buns and goodies on a covered picnic table.

Beneath the table lies Sheba. She's had a good morning running around with the kids, and now she's a little tired. She's getting a little "me time" for herself, but she is watching me intently. She slowly gets up and trots up towards me, and I pat her on the head, "Sorry sweetheart, I forgot the biscuits." Instead of returning to the shade beneath the picnic table, she trots alongside me as I continue to the dock.

"Well, I see you brought company," you say with a laugh. I shrug my shoulders and step into the boat. I observe that you've got everything well organized, and there is that large picnic basket you promised. It makes me feel a bit of a tickle in my tummy. I sit down in the center with you at the stern and a steady hand on the steering handle of the electric motor. It's a performance thrust motor with a big, freshly charged, 24-volt battery — more than fast enough for the day. "Cast off the line. Let's get going."

I throw off the line and just as you power up the motor, Sheba jumps into the bow of the boat. "Whatcha gonna do?" I look at you and shrug my shoulders, "She's the boss around here. So who are we to tell her she can't go fishing?" We laugh, and with that, we slowly work our way into the lake, watchful for any stray swimmers. Thankfully all the kids are lined up for a bounty of hot dogs, hamburgers, and cold sodas.

We both silently settle into the activity, feeling the boat move through the clear, blue waters of the lake. Neither of us talks much until we reach the center of the lake. As for me, I'm waiting to see which one of us is going to start the conversation. I'm wondering if you are truly ready to honor your promise, or perhaps you whispered that question to me with some reservation in your mind.

You break the silence, "I didn't have that dream this morning. In fact for some reason that I can't quite put my finger on, I know I will never have it again. I also have made my decision to keep my eternal promise to God."

"And how do you feel about that promise and the concept of perpetual genesis? Do you think that you are going to play a role in the evolution of our species through, and beyond, the coming tribulation?"

"On an intellectual level I feel a strong urge to say, 'balderdash!' and leave it at that. But life has taught me that faith doesn't work that way, and this is a commitment of faith. Either you have it, or you don't. It's just that simple. I feel it; it calls to me; and I sense that I'm ready to go the distance."

"So did this come to you this morning in the shower?"

"No. It was all there just as natural as life itself when I opened my eyes this morning. Just like you said it would."

"Then you are ready."

You nod in agreement, "So, where do we begin — beans, bullets, and bunkers?"

I ignore the question for a moment, "Have we got any cold drinks?"

"There is a small cooler behind the picnic basket."

"Thanks," I reach behind me and pull out a cold can of brewed tea. Popping it open I answer, "Beans, bullets, and bunkers are important; I will not understate that. However, every man, woman, and child in your community are going to be thinking about beans, bullets, and bunkers every day. So, if you're doing the same thing, what are you thinking about? And how are you thinking about it?"

You lean forward a little, "I'm not following you."

"Okay, let's look at it this way. If all you're thinking about are beans, bullets, and bunkers, then you see your situation through shortages and limitations — the very same reason why we consumers robotically run to the store at the drop of a hat. Yet, during the tribulation, there will be nothing in the stores, nothing but desperate people hoping to find something — anything. So this is a dead end. If, as a tribulation leader, all you think about each day are beans, bullets, and bunkers, you're not leading; you're just a tally keeper. People will come to tell you what the community does not have each day and trust me; you'll get an earful of that each day. If all you can do is say, 'Thank you for informing me about the shortage,' you're nothing more than an overrated shopping consultant."

You nod your head appreciatively, "In other words I'd just be an echo of the problem and not a source for a solution."

Taking a long sip of cold tea I give you a wink, "You catch on quickly. I like that about you."

"So, as a leader, how do I become a part of the solution?"

The Three Precepts

"What I teach is what we call 'The Three Precepts of Perpetual Genesis.' These are the three things you must always preach and focus on providing as a tribulation leader:

- First, self-sufficiency knowledge,
- Second, hope for the future,
- Third, the knowledge that you are not alone."

"As for the beans, bullets, and bunkers, this comes under the category of self-sufficiency knowledge. So, instead of cataloging what the community doesn't have, you look for moments to inspire. The Three 'I's: Invention, Insight, and Initiative."

"Are you also telling me that as a leader, I must never see the glass as half-empty — that I must always see it as being half full?"

"In a manner of speaking, yes, as long as you remember there is a difference between being optimistic and being a Pollyanna. That being said, necessity is the mother of invention. An unfortunate aspect of our current society is that corporations protect their intellectual property rights by convincing us we are incapable of having an original thought beyond getting a new credit card to buy more things we do not need. Worse yet, when someone has the gall to have an original thought that competes with their interests, they're brutishly smashed down and suppressed."

"Like those urban legends about engines that run on water, or get 500 miles on a gallon of gas?"

"Urban legends! Now you're thinking like a corporate patsy." You shake your head in disbelief as I say, "Yes, you are thinking like a corporate patsy because those are not always urban legends. Rather, many of these kinds of inventions do pop up on a regular basis. What most people don't realize is that corporate operatives sit at the front door of the patent office, waiting to spy out innovative ideas that need to be suppressed. They protect the financial interests of a vested few at the expense of the many. What the public does not see is government goons marching on the orders of elites to unlawfully arrest inventors, seize their assets, and then intimidate them into silence. It happens all the time, believe me."

"Hmmm…I guess I'm a little naive here," you say sheepishly.

"No, you're not. All you know about this is what our corporate media wants you to know. The fact is, a handful of corporations control the media in our country, and what little you do know serves their interests, not yours. Remember to do your homework. Dig deep. There are reliable voices out there beyond the eye-candy and glitter of the readily accessible ones. There are good people out there who do care about the truth."

"I'll keep that in mind. And thanks for giving me a Mulligan on this one. The question in my mind right now is how will all of this suppression by corporate interests impact the survival chances of my community during the tribulation?"

I clap my hands in celebration. A bit startled, Sheba lurches up in the bow. "Now you're thinking like a leader, so let me give you the answer. One of many benefits of the silver lining in this dark cloud of the tribulation is that the chaos will unleash the inventive powers of common folk — in ways, we could never imagine. For example, think of Nikola Tesla. His nemesis was Thomas Edison, a man world-renowned for his many inventions, and he certainly did help to shape life as we know it today. Yet, many of us today remember him more as a greedy, self-interested man who ruthlessly suppressed the insightful gifts of Nikola Tesla. Nonetheless, Tesla never faded away. In fact, he is revered today for one simple reason — he was in it for the species. His passion in life was not greed, as was the case with Edison. Tesla's passion was to better the lives of the common man and woman. This is not to say Edison was not effective in providing useful inventions for humanity. But for a substantial portion of his life, Edison used his fortune and fame to suppress and humiliate Tesla. Once Edison passed away, so did his legacy of suppression. That's when Nicholas Tesla's heritage of service to others re-emerged from the darkness of suppression, inspiring new passions in the hearts of many young and inventive souls."

"It reminds of what they say about artists — you never get rich until you're dead." With that, you throttle back the boat's motor and point to the cooler, "Could you pass me one of those cans of iced tea? And do go on."

The New Nikola Teslas

I pull out a cold can and hand it to you, then spread my arms wide, "Open your mind and consider this. During the worst of the tribulation, the control mechanisms of these corporate interests and their government goons will be shattered. They'll be too busy hunkering in their bunkers to meddle in affairs on the surface. And they'll soon learn that nothing ever goes according to plan. However, on the surface, people like us, from one end of the country to the other, will witness a whole new generation of Nikola Teslas rising. They will each have a unique brand of genius, and they'll be happy to share their inventions in service to others. In return, all the compensation they'll need is to be acknowledged, to have a valued place in an enlightened community, and for us to celebrate their inventiveness, as we must. Think about the magic of it all. We need new ways to power our survival communities. Without the restraint of suppression, a new generation of Nikola Teslas will find ways to achieve that very thing. During the dark times remember this, my friend: a tribulation is much like a forest fire. It clears the forest floor of dead fuel so that vibrant young trees can climb toward the light of the sun in a rapid and unfettered celebration of life."

"I get it," you beam, "Always be on the lookout for invention and ways to inspire it."

"Bingo! But of equal importance for you as a leader is to inspire insight and initiative. You will not only need inventors; you will need critical thinkers as well — those with the patience to calmly study a situation or problem until they find an epiphany within a moment of clarity. The effective solutions these innovative thinkers will bring will greatly enhance the survivability of your community and others.

The one thing that more important than even invention and insight is initiative. If you have to order people to be creative thinkers, the first thing they'll create are reasons why what you want is impossible. On the other hand, those who have the initiative to take creative, effective action to solve problems and get things done on their own will be precious beyond belief. These are the very people you must cherish, nurture, and protect as a leader."

With that, you throttle up the motor and the boat picks up speed, "And what about the people I do not cherish, nurture and protect as a leader?" you say with a sigh.

Again, your grasp of new ideas tickles me. Unnoticed by me, Sheba has been watching me out of the corner of her eye. Before I can clap, she moves quickly, nudging her muzzle against my side, perhaps to remind me that theatrics are unnecessary. I reach around and scratch her behind the ears and she gives me an, "OK mister, you've got 1,000 years to stop that," look.

The Ego-Driven

"So, who do I not cherish, nurture, and protect as a leader? That's simple — ego-driven people. As survivors, they'll be easy to spot. They'll be the ones who say, 'I don't know what I'm doing, but I do know I have to be the boss.' Then there will also be the ones who flip in and out of ego. They're not as easy to spot as the strongly ego-driven, but they're just as dangerous, if not more so."

You nod in agreement, "I deal with ego-driven people all the time in my church. They're often some of my biggest contributors."

"Correct me if I'm wrong, but they'll donate money to something like a library. Then in exchange for that donation, they want to sit behind you as you lead Sunday services and to be celebrated in an opening ceremony for the library. And let's not forget the big bronze plaque with their name on it or the name of someone else they want to honor."

"You've got their number, all right."

"Well, in times like these, folks who've made their fortune by sticking their hands into other people's pockets are looking for someone like you. For a measly 10% of their ill-gotten gains, they can buy recognition for their goodness with a contribution to your church. They hope that when you sing their praises God will be fooled into forgetting the ill-gotten gains that they've kept, along with their continued questionable business behaviors. So do you think you are such a great orator that you can fool God?"

That one gets a stern glare from you, "Of course not! But we need donors to fund our work, and so we tolerate these ego-based behaviors and comply with their requests for public recognition."

"Point taken, however, if that donor were a truly spiritual person, he or she would have sat down in your office and simply asked how much it would cost to build the library. Then once you named a sum, the check would be written and given, the library would be built anonymously, and that would be that. The right hand would not know what the left hand had done. The lesson here is that wealth is neither good nor bad. It is how that wealth is acquired, and how it is used. If wealth is used as an expression of ego, then you are nothing more than a tool in service to their selfish desires. By the way, these selfish desires are the reason ego-driven people are a danger, and they will imperil the survival of your community."

"How so?"

"In several ways but remember this about ego — not all ego-driven people are sociopaths, but all sociopaths are ego-driven. Unleash one of these monsters upon your community, and like virulent cancer it will metastasize and destroy everyone. Very likely you know why this is, but as a teacher, I know that the first failure of communication is the assumption. So, let me be clear."

You hold up a finger, "I want to hear this, but we're about to round the bend into that cove. Do me a favor and keep an eye out."

"Aye, aye, Skipper," I say as I spin around in my seat, pulling Sheba close to me. We all study the cove, which is incredibly beautiful. To one side is a small beach lined with graceful trees, and opposite it, a tall rock cliff with vines growing on it, casting deep shade into the water. "I bet we'll have some luck next to that cliff. Why don't you motor over there and we will set our lines."

You throttle down the motor and the boat gracefully glides to a stop as we admire this secluded, magical spot on the lake. "This should do just fine for starters," you say with satisfaction, "But before we bait our hooks and set the lines, I want to hear what you have to say about ego-driven people and why they are dangerous to my community."

I swivel back around and smile. I admire the way you are staying on point, and how quickly you grasped the important things. I feel a swelling sense of pride for you as a tribulation leader, and it doubles my resolve to counsel you as wisely as I can.

"I want you to imagine that you're standing in a paint store. On the wall to your left is a black paint chip sample which represents the cool, inky blackness of oblivion. On the opposite wall, to your right, is a white paint chip sample which represents the warm, radiant, golden-white light of God's love. Furthermore, these chips also represent the two absolute human emotions. The black chip is fear, and the white chip is love. With this in mind, we now see a myriad of paint chips of every imaginable color stretching across the walls of the paint store. No matter how many thousands of shades there are, each one is nothing but a shade of the two absolutes — black or white. Black is the oblivion of fear, and white is the divine white light of God's love. Then, directly in the center, half way across this cornucopia of colors we see two paint chip samples. One is slightly to the black side and the other to the white side."

"Not to jump the gun," you say, "but am I to assume that ego begins at that slightly black paint chip sample in the center? Then ego increases as we follow the darkness back to the pure black of fear and oblivion?"

"I couldn't have said it better myself. Now let's take this one step further. As eternal beings there are only two directions we can travel — towards the blackness of fear and oblivion, or towards the light and love of God. For those who choose oblivion, it is an easy ride, like coasting downhill on a bicycle. For those who choose to travel the other direction towards God, it's all an uphill climb. This is why being a spiritual person is about being spiritual without exception, each and every day. If you are not moving forward toward God, you are moving backward, toward oblivion. There is no saying, 'I will pedal uphill for now, but if I see something I really want, I'll take it and then resume peddling uphill as a spiritual person.' Here is where people of ego backslide and take their first slippery step toward oblivion."

"Because, as the Bible tells us, we cannot serve two masters," you chime in. "We will end up loving one master and hating the other."

"Absolutely, yet those in ego always think they're more clever than the rest. So as the leader of a community, there will be those among you who will be clearly spirit-driven. Likewise, there will be those who are so ego-driven that their descent into darkness seems almost irreversible and you will know them instantly. They will come to you as the worst sorts — arrogant sociopaths, murderers, rapists, marauders, warlords, gangs, cannibals, and those who engage in any form of inhuman horror. As a tribulation leader, you will come to be able to quickly recognize who your community can survive with, and those who will cause its doom."

You rub your chin reflectively, "I love your metaphor of the paint chips. If you don't mind, can I use that one for a sermon? However, I do not see a clear answer to my previous question, 'and what about the people I do not cherish, nurture and protect as a leader?' Or have I missed something?"

Your question is perfectly timed. I hold Sheba's head with my two hands and say, "What do you think Sheba? Is this the right question?"

"Woof, Woof!" the old retriever happily barks, "Woof, Woof!"

"Well, I agree with Sheba. By the way, you didn't happen to pack a few dog biscuits did you?"

With a warm smile, you point to the picnic basket, "You know me, Scouts' motto, 'Always be prepared.' Look for a small red tin. They're in there."

Taking out a biscuit, I break it into small pieces, feeding each one to Sheba. "To answer your question, let's go back to our paint store color chip example. Remember the two paint chip samples at the dead-center of the display? And how one was slightly to the black side and the other to the white side

"Yes."

"In our congregations, we each have those who hover around these two central paint chip samples, not fully embracing one side or the other. Many like to see themselves as spiritual people devoted to the noble virtues of the white side of the equation. Then they have their moments of lust and greed when they jump to a paint chip on the black side of the equation. Or as the comedian Flip Wilson used to say, "The devil made me do it." This is why I call them 'flippers.'

Flippers

Flippers can smile brightly as they greet everyone on Sunday and sing the loudest. Then on Monday they go out and cheat widows and orphans merely because they can easily line their pockets that way."

"You're not telling me something I don't know. On the other hand isn't it our job to encourage them toward God; to help them understand how and why to stay solidly on the white side of the equation? Not to judge them or to feel morally superior to them?"

"Yes, in this present time but in a tribulation survival community the needs will be different. During the tribulation, flippers are the ones who will bring death to your community in the most stealthy and insidious of ways. I've learned this on a personal level as a consequence of my efforts to bring truth to people. Each time I author a major book or produce a major video documentary, I invariably lose a friend. As I start my project, out of the blue, they will do something irrational and destructive. Something unusual for them, but which seriously and negatively impedes my efforts. This has happened over and over again. At first, I did not understand what was happening, but over time a pattern emerged. As you well know, I am a keen student of patterns and trends."

You gesture excitedly with your hands, "Someone could derail you? This I've got to hear. Tell me more."

"Yes, and they do sometimes derail me. You see, people like you and me are light workers in service to God's mission. We, therefore, possess a tremendous amount of life force energy within us. Some call it prana, chi, or other names, but in the final analysis, it is the energetic light of God's love within us. Each corporeal being either has that light or does not. Spirit entities on the path to the blackness of oblivion do not possess, nor can they create this life force energy. That being said, I will be the first to agree that I'm oversimplifying this, but for the sake of preparing for survival, we need to work with a simple framework. After the tribulation, we can return to our libraries and more subtle studies. For now, all we need to know is that evil is parasitic and poisonous and that beings on the path to oblivion, whether incarnated or not, need life force energy to exist. Without it, they sink rapidly into the blackness of oblivion, and what awaits them there is death eternal, and they know that. Likewise, because they are ego-driven, each believes they are more clever than those who have come before them. They believe they can beat the system."

"But what about the ones who realize that regret their destructive course, and then change direction by redeeming themselves once again onto the path towards the light of God's love?"

"Here we are in agreement, my dear friend. If we are to say that God has a passion for something, clearly that passion is for redemption. In fact, in a future conversation, we are going to talk about that in a very special way. But for now, we just need to talk about the relationship between ego and a parasitic need to feed on the life force energies of spirit-driven tribulation survivors. You see, there is only one motive for dark spirits on the path to the blackness of oblivion — to feed on the life force energy of others. The greater your life force energy, the more forceful and persistent the attacks will be against you by dark spirits, both directly and through those susceptible to their influence. People like you, and I, and the spiritually-driven members of our congregations will be the nexus of a perpetually attempted feeding frenzy during the tribulation."

You put your hands up, "The only thing you need to add to all these explanations is, 'But wait, there's more!'"

"Well, there is," I chuckle, "and don't be so glum because this is not as hopeless as you may think. The first thing you need to understand is where you are vulnerable — namely, those close to you who are flippers who dance back and forth between the dark chips and the white chips. When they land on a dark chip, it is by way of their ego, and there is where the access point for malevolent dark spirits lay. Like evil fishermen in the shadows, ego is where the dark spirits set the hook in their jaws. But what you must always remember is that a flipper hooked by a dark spirit through ego never feels the hook dig in. Consequently, their egos can never accept what has happened, and that prevents any positive resolution for whatever destructive situation the dark spirits have cooked up through them."

"You know, that reminds me of something you told me about propaganda a few years ago."

That comment lights a smile on my face, "Yes, and that point is well taken, because the insidious thing about modern propaganda is that it does not deny itself. Rather, it subtly manipulates the ego with what is known as neuro-linguistic programming or "NLP" to give the gullible a false sense of confidence. The result is that while the gullible always acknowledge that the world is full of propaganda, deception, and manipulation, in the same breath they'll confidently assure you that they are too clever to be susceptible to any of it. Blinded by their egos, they are hooked by the propagandists. But they never feel that hook dig in."

You rap on the side of the boat with a grin, "Now you've hooked my attention. As they say, even a blind hog can find an acorn. So let me see if I understand what you're saying. People, who are weak and vacillate between the dark and the light, 'flippers' as you call them, are therefore susceptible to manipulation and will not perceive it when they stray to the dark side?"

"Exactly! Now let's take it to the next level. Once a flipper has been hooked by a dark spirit, the dark spirit's agenda is to feed off their life force energy — and yours. However, this parasitic feeding can only occur when the flipper and the target are in some state like fear, anger, or another negative emotion. Therefore, to create this parasitic milking state, if you will, the dark spirit must embroil your flipper friend and yourself into a negative confrontation of some sort, based on fear, or anger, or another negative emotion. There is no philosophical, political, theological, or any other form of "-ology" goal in this. If you delude yourself with such thinking, you will miss the point of how simple this is. The simple parasitic goal of the dark spirit is to milk life force energy, and the process works no differently than cows being led into a milking machine stall. Getting the milk, or the life force energy, in this case, is about the ends justifying the means, and nothing more. Consequently, once this parasitic process begins, you will unwittingly become embroiled in an illogical and sticky conflict with a flipper close to you. Worse yet, the conflict will be irreconcilable. The flipper will continually turn petty molehills into angry mountains, and there will be no rational path to resolution. In fact, the more you try to work things out, the more you will exacerbate the parasitic process. It is a classic 'tar baby' scenario like the old stories of Brer Fox and Brer Rabbit."

I can see this clicking together in your mind, "So in a practical sense, when you see this happening the only way to deal with it is to terminate your relationship with the flipper, and thus end the parasitic access. It's the only way to stop a parasitic attack, both for you and for the other person. What gets me is that while I see how this works, I do not perceive a complete answer here."

"Excellent observation, my friend. You're batting a thousand today because sometimes it's just not about parasitic feeding. Sometimes these dark spirits are so malevolent that their intention is not just to feed, but rather, it is to cause suffering and even death, which they can also feed upon.

In this case, instead of provoking a confrontation between you and this other person, they may take a more subtle tack, one that is much difficult to see coming. For example, we all hate going to a public toilet and finding that the person who used it before us left the toilet clogged so it might overflow a flood of dangerous microbes onto the floor, which may then spread contamination and illness. Worse yet is seeing that someone is leaving a bathroom without washing their hands, in which case we must hope they will not be spreading fecal matter to surfaces or items they touch or food they are preparing. Or, we may have a situation where someone is coughing all over their hands then touching things in a public area, and sneezing without covering with the crook of their arm or with a tissue. They will be spreading illness rather than acting courteously and responsibly to protect those around them.

In our present time, these low-life behaviors are an annoyance and not a serious threat because we have access to good medical care, antibiotics, and disinfectants. But let's assume that now we're in the tribulation and this person goes deep into ego and a dark spirit gets a hook into them. Now you could have a deadly health crisis on your hands.

Consider this, if everyone in the world had clean and safe water to drink, half of the hospital beds in the world would be empty. And most viruses are spread in offices by contact — touching doorknobs, elevator buttons, coffee pot handles, and other items or surfaces contaminated with the virus. In other words, communicable diseases can quickly spread through entire communities, causing horrible misery and even death with terrible rapidity.

Further, consider what any water treatment engineer will tell you — the tiniest bit of fecal matter can unleash a very deadly plague into a community. Remember, there was once "the age of cholera" where many people would fall ill and die within a few days, and it could return through poor hygiene and contaminants in the water supply. This particular plague would cause great suffering and death, and perhaps even the community's collapse. A minor illness that spreads rapidly can seriously hamper productivity needed for the community's survival. So if you have someone practicing questionable hygiene and sanitation in your congregation while also showing a lack of regard for others, during the tribulation a dark spirit could turn them into a Typhoid Mary."

Parasitic Milking Machines

Your head sags as you visualize the threat in your mind, "Good God, this is insidious. Are you telling me that my community could be targeted for extinction by illness this way?"

"Yes. A spiritually-based community will look like the mother of all parasitic milking machines to the dark spirits, and they will surely come to take a spoil of your life force energy, without mercy. Their eyes will be as cold as that of the shark, and their poisons as sharp as their teeth, and they will milk you to extinction — if you let them.

As to the weak flippers manipulated by dark spirits in this stealthy way, they will not understand why they're doing what they do. It will just be a vicarious anonymous thrill like forcing others to deal with their toilet filth or skipping necessary hygiene steps like washing their hands. They are hooked, and so they will act out of a deeply rooted character flaw. After the harm is done, they will realize what they did, and you can depend on them to deny any responsibility for their acts. Even if they do offer a sincere apology, the damage will have been done, and the dark spirits will have long since taken their spoil. And now the strength and viability of your community may be in question."

The thought of it all gives you a shiver, "Well, I sure hope you've got some solution or defense for this, because what you've just told me makes me feel like I'm bare-assed and buck naked."

I reach over and pat you on the arm and say, "This is why you and I are having this conversation today, and yes, there is good news. You don't need to be bare-assed and buck naked because shielding yourself and your community from dark spirits is simpler than you can imagine. So be of good cheer, my friend."

"The first and most obvious step is to offer prayers and affirmations for the protection of yourself and your community and to encourage others to do the same — daily. It is always wise to pray as if everything depended on God, but to act as if everything depended on you."

"That brings us to the second step, trial by fire. I'm not talking about making somebody prove themselves by walking across hot coals, or seeing if they have the courage to stand and fight alongside their comrades in the heat of battle."

"So what kind of fire are you talking about?" you ask.

Now I lean forward and gently press my index finger into the middle of your sternum, "The light I'm talking about is within you. It is the light of God's love that burns brightly within you because you are spirit-driven and in service to God's mission. It's brighter than most, which is why dark spirits are always looking for new ways to get at it and milk it."

"Well, if you're looking for weaknesses of character or sociopathic tendencies," you reply, "then that is a matter of extended observation. You have to observe someone over time so as to see if they are exhibiting these behaviors or tendencies. In the case of an anonymous poor-hygiene poop-spreader, that could be ugly."

I shake my head impatiently, "You're talking to me about science, and I am a born-hard geek. Remember, you do not have the luxury of time to come at this like a scientist. Besides, in my opinion many scientists like to think that they're the only ones who have the right to be wrong because you're too stupid to figure it out for yourself. This is exactly what they'll say here. Forget that. Wakey, wakey! You're not a scientist. You're a Spirit-driven leader in service to God's mission, and there is a faster, easier, and equally reliable way to make a conclusive determination."

"I'm all ears; tell me more."

The Fire of God's Light

"With science you observe the subject over time. With faith you observe yourself from within," again, I gently press the center of your sternum, "Here is where the fire of God's light and love resides within you. Now let me ask you, do you see us both as being spirit-driven?"

"Of course."

"Good. Now think inwardly about the divine fire of God's light within you. When you and I are together, does it burn more brightly? Is it a bit warmer?"

You blink a few times and say, "Come to think of it, yes. I feel it now, and it feels natural. It feels good."

"But does it feel safe?"

"Yes."

"Now I'll share something I've recently observed. Have you noticed that each time you and I get together, Sheba stops whatever she's doing and immediately comes and joins us treat or no treat?"

"Yes. Oh, my gosh. Are you telling me that she senses this inner fire that is burning brighter?"

At this point, I just can't help myself. I take another dog biscuit out of the picnic basket and break off a piece as Sheba scrambles to her feet, "Tell me, girl, can you sense our fire?

"Woof woof!" She barks, her wagging tail thumping against the side of the boat like a bass drum mallet.

I feed her a piece of biscuit, "OK; maybe I'm a little melodramatic, but the point here is that Sheba does sense it. For her, it is natural and visceral. Likewise, when someone of questionable character comes around Sheba has a pretty mean growl."

"You have a point there."

"So this is what the test of fire is. Something as simple as Sheba's natural ability to sense what is within each of us whether it is the fire of love or the darkness of evil, fear, or hate. With this in mind, let me now explain the trial by fire."

"First you easily eliminate those who are ego-driven as well as those who are clearly evil and well on their way to the blackness of oblivion. If someone is Spirit-driven, you'll know it by how bright the fire within you glows and by its warmth. If someone is a dark spirit whether incarnated or not, their presence will have the opposite effect, because those of the darkness do not feed your fire, they feed on it. Ergo, surround yourself with those who feed your fire. Conversely, with those who seek to feed on your fire, keep as far away from them as possible. Or at the very least keep them at arm's length."

You are nodding your head appreciatively, so I know it's starting to make sense to you, "Don't tell me, we're going back to the paint store with the two paint chips in the center. The one is a little bit on the black side, and the one that is a little bit on the white side."

"Precisely, the tendency in our present society is for others to go along with the flippers to get along. Ergo, in the absence of conflict we let them sit around our divine fire, so to speak. While this can inspire some flippers to become spiritually-driven in every sense, most will maintain their place by doing little things to feed your fire and will also seek to ingratiate themselves to you. That is until one day a dark spirit hooks them. Then the next thing you know, they're throwing buckets of inky black water on your fire and creating outrageous, insoluble conflicts and drama in your life."

The 30 Minute Test

"With suspected flippers who are already causing community difficulties you can perform what I call, 'The 30 Minute Test.' Find a quiet time of the day and a contemplative setting, then focus your thoughts solely on that person and their past actions, behaviors, and their interactions with you and others. If by the end of that thirty-minute time span you:

- ♦ Do not feel the fire within you grow brighter and warmer,

- ♦ Do not have a confident feeling about this person's acting consistently in service to others with good character and good intentions,

- ♦ Have persistent concerns about their attempts at inappropriate control over others,

Then you must exclude them. If they are in your community, it is best to expel them immediately because their inability to remain spirit-driven will make them vulnerable to manipulation for both parasitic and poisonous reasons."

"Either way, if you allow someone who fails the thirty-minute test to remain close to you or in your community, then, do not be surprised when they cause terrible harm to befall you or those who depend upon your wise leadership. Also keep in mind that these weak, marginal characters will come with inducements, gifts, favors and flattery to establish and maintain their position. No matter how small or how great the benefits they bring are, the eventual price of these 'benefits' will be hard, if not impossible, for your community to bear. This is why no matter what they offer to maintain their position or access, it will be something you did not need or want, and you will find that it was not worth it in the end."

"But if I do that, it could cost us a great deal of valuable materials that we will need in a tribulation situation," you object.

I shake my head, "No. Remember what history teaches us about the Trojan horse subterfuge. How it carried within it the demise of the entire city of Troy. In other words, you need these inducements and gifts as much as you need a Trojan horse. Besides, if you think this way, you'll deny yourself the benefits that can come through the law of attraction and synchronicity. This is something we will discuss later on, but not today, because right now it's about time we started fishing! Don't you think?"

"Well, I've got a plan then. First, let's get our hooks in the water and then let's get our hooks into that picnic basket because I'm pretty darn hungry." With that, you reach over and pick up the two fishing rods tucked along the side of the boat. "I have a Styrofoam cup there with some fresh red wigglers in it, down by your feet. While I get our rods ready, pick us out a couple of plump, lively wigglers."

"Aye, aye, Skipper!" I answer, and picking up the container I begin to sort through it for a couple of likely candidates. The tackle is set on the fishing rod, and almost immediately I have two worms in hand, "You know I always feel a bit guilty about jabbing a hook through a live worm," I wistfully observe as I impale my unfortunate bait.

You shrug your shoulders, "Well, if you want to come home with fish this is what you have to do." After baiting your hook, you suggest, "Let's start with a short cast in the shade of the rock cliff. That seems like it should be a good start. Then we can work backward from that."

A few moments later our bobbers are floating on the still, blue waters of the lake close to the rock cliff. We settle in to see if a nice, fat, gullible fish will take the bait. With our poles resting on the oar hooks, we set the picnic basket and cooler down on the bottom of the boat between us. "I've got some fried chicken in here. It's the best thing you've ever tasted, I guarantee."

Sure enough, the fried chicken is simply splendid. Maybe it's because were sitting in a boat in the middle of a beautiful cove with our lines in the water. Who knows, but it sure does taste good. From time to time we each toss a small piece of chicken to Sheba, who wolfs them down with great relish.

"So tell me," I ask as I strip a leg bone clean, "Would you say that making the decision to expel a flipper from your community is a good example of what I call an impossible decision? The kinds of decisions you're going to have to make each and every day as the leader of a community in the midst of a horrific tribulation?"

"Well, I could see how in some ways that, yes, it would be an impossible decision."

Your answer demonstrates an anticipated lack of clarity because present-day America is far more forgiving of nihilistic, destructive, and self-interested behaviors than America of the past — an America that was vibrant, energetic and growing. "Well, my friend, it's time for you get a good bead on what an impossible decision will look like in the coming tribulation. I call this, 'The Infant in the Road Scenario,' and it will tax your ability to lead and at the same time preserve your community's noble virtues. Are you game for the test?"

You reply with a cocky grin, "Yup, here we go again with…'but wait, there's more!' OK, fire away."

The Infant in the Road Scenario

"OK, hot dog," I point at our red and white bobbers floating in the water, "What are we doing at this very moment?"

"We're fishing."

"And what is our strategy?"

"To see if a big fish is hungry enough and stupid enough to gobble our bait."

With that, I lean forward and narrow my eyes, "In this impossible decision test you're the fish, my friend, and it's called, 'The Infant in the Road Scenario.'" Now I see a more serious look drawn on your face.

"Here is the beginning scenario. The time is well along into the tribulation, long after a complete collapse of law and order. It is the first light of day, and on the road leading up to your armored front gate someone has left a helpless infant in the middle of the road, about one hundred yards away and close to some abandoned vehicles alongside the road. Your sentries report their observations, and word of the infant's plight begins to spread throughout the community. Initially, the infant is silent and many fear that the child is dead, but as the sun rises over a nearby hill, the infant awakens and begins kicking and screaming incessantly. Now the situation takes a turn for the worse."

"Keep in mind the following, depending on conditions; we humans can begin to hear loud noises up to city block away, or about 300 yards. So at 100 yards, this abandoned infant is quite audible. Also keep in mind that a baby's scream can reach our pain threshold of 120 dB, much like a rock concert. But unlike a rock concert, a baby's scream targets a very sensitive frequency range of the human ear, between 1,000 Hz and 5,000 Hz, typically around 3,500 Hz. Why? Mother Nature has hard-wired us to respond to a baby's cry. In fact, we can't help ourselves, because these cries activate primitive fight-or-flight responses that are deeply embedded in our brains. Worse yet, people with children of their own are much more strongly impacted, because they're more tuned in, so to speak."

"Consequently, every parent in your community becomes torn with emotional pain and some will begin to demand against all logic for the gate to be opened so the infant can be rescued. However, you've ordered the gate to remain closed because you can see something is wrong with this situation. For example, is the baby a plague carrier? If so, should you put the lives of everyone in your community at risk for the life of an infant abandoned by an outsider for mysterious reasons? Another thing, assuming someone is still alive to love this child, why would they leave the child so far away from your front gate? And why would they not seek to contact you about this personally, and hand the child directly into someone's arms?"

"As you ponder these concerns, a tormented young woman with excellent hearing comes to you and begs for permission to go outside the front gate to rescue the infant. She tells you that she is willing to risk her life to save the infant and no one else has to go into harm's way." I hold up my index finger, "Now the test begins with one simple question. As the leader of this community, what will you do?"

You rub your chin, pondering the situation, and hesitatingly answer, "Well, if she only wants to place her life in harm's way to save the infant, I suppose it is worth the risk. I'd let her go."

If you had military combat experience, this would not have been your answer. Again, I lean forward with my index finger pointed at the center of your sternum, but this time I punch it hard enough to make you flinch, "You just killed your entire community!"

"What, how can that be?" you exclaim.

"I have another question. This woman knows your defensive strengths and weaknesses very well, as does every other member of your community. So now you've decided to let her walk out there 100 yards away all by herself to rescue this infant. Have you stopped to think that there may be someone lying in wait behind those abandoned vehicles? It could be soldiers of the local warlord. Ergo, this is likely a ruthless leader who wants to capture your community and its resources and facilities. They will probably kill your men, the young, the old, and then rape your women however they want before they kill them as well. Your weapons, facilities, and supplies will then be used to strengthen their ability to inflict more damage on others in the area, and the cycle of suffering is intensified."

"When your courageous volunteer is 100 yards away from you and picking up the baby, she won't notice the warlord's soldiers coming up from behind her to snatch her until it is too late. How long do you think it will take when they torture her in terrible ways for her to give them all the intelligence she has on your offensive and defensive capabilities, and where your food stores and medicines are hidden?"

Now you look horrified, "Oh, I didn't even think of that possibility. Capture and torture!"

"Let's move on. I've got another question for you. While your enemy is torturing the intelligence out of your young volunteer, what's going on in your community? Do you think by now people are becoming divided as to what to do about a young woman being tortured for intelligence, and an infant still at risk, all because you made that particular decision to let the volunteer go?"

"This is getting deep."

"Yes. But I need a better answer than that from you."

"Well, what if I assign an all-volunteer security detail to escort her out to retrieve the infant?"

"Okay, let's take that one on. First, you have to call for security volunteers. So now you not only have a young woman who is ready to put her life in harm's way, but you also need to find two or three other people to do the same. Your volunteers will likely be some of your best and brightest, who sincerely want to help. Let's say you have your woman who originally volunteered and three security detail personnel going out there to get the infant. You think this is the smart thing to do?"

"Well, I think it solves the security problem, and it should work? Yes, I think I would do that."

"Fine, they walk out there to pick up the child; suddenly all three security personnel fall to the ground like limp rag dolls. Then, two seconds later you hear the rifle reports from the hill opposite your compound telling you that the warlord's snipers have just eliminated three of your best security people. Meanwhile, the woman is still snatched, and once again she is being tortured for intelligence about your community. Okay, hot shot, what are you going to do now that three people are dead, one is being tortured, and the infant was still not rescued? On top of that, how is this going to instill confidence in your leadership abilities within your community?"

Now you're completely taken aback, "I had no idea this was going to be so complicated, and treacherous, and complicated!"

"Excuse me, but this is what's called an impossible decision. You do not get a second chance for your experimental ideas once people are dead. In fact, all you've done is to show your community that you are incompetent to lead. So not only do you have three security team members dead and a young woman being tortured for intelligence, now people in your community are starting to question your leadership abilities and demand a change. This, in turn, will rip apart the cohesion of your community as people inevitably take sides."

"So yes, I do need to be hard on you, because this hypothetical scenario is likely a piece of cake compared to other situations that you, as a leader, will face in the coming tribulation. If you don't figure out what you're going to do now, you will fail and your people will die. There are no second chances!"

You wipe your hand across your forehead, "You're right, I don't know what I'm doing here. I don't even think at this point I'm the right person for this job. After all, I have no military experience, and it's hard for me to even imagine such cruelty," you hang your head, "I don't know what to do to solve this scenario. I just don't know what to do."

This time instead of poking you hard in the chest, I gently place my hand on your shoulder, "My dear friend, you've just said the first intelligent thing, if not the most important thing of the day. A fool will follow a bad decision with more bad decisions out of ego alone. However, a wise person knows when to accept responsibility for what they do not know, and that is what you have done. Now you are ready for your first lesson on tribulation leadership. That is, if you want it."

"Of course I want it. Help me."

"That is exactly what I am here to do." I look over at the picnic basket and see a couple of slices of apple pie at look mighty tasty, "I'm sorry I pushed you on this. It is necessary so you will feel the impact and difficulty of the situation. Now you are ready for the knowledge of how to prevail. Let's relax with a couple of cold drinks and those rather inviting-looking slices of apple pie. After that we'll get into the lesson. When we are finished with this lesson you will know what it takes to be an effective leader, bringing your community safely through seemingly impossible challenges."

A faint smile comes to your lips, and I'm grateful that we did not wind up in an argument. I get out the pie and one more dog biscuit for Sheba, and soon we're all happily munching away. This "*Infant on the Road Scenario*" is always hard, especially for those who have never been trained for such things.

Tribulation Leadership

You glance over at our bobbers, "Not even a nibble. Our voices echoing off that rock cliff have probably scared the fish away, so much for our bait."

"Bingo! You just said the magic word, 'bait.' Let's start from there. I remember watching an underwater nature film, and in it, a pod of dolphins tracks down a large school of anchovies. They organize themselves and then launch their attack. The objective was simple. All they needed to do was to break up this large school of anchovies into several smaller bait balls. After that, feeding on the stragglers was easy. While they attacked, other predators came from both air and ocean to feed, and in very little time almost nothing was left of that once large school of anchovies. To put it simply, it was the time-tested tactic of divide and conquer. Now let's apply that to this situation."

"So, you're thinking about the warlord?"

"Exactly, never forget that 100% of what you do not know can hurt you in some way or another. Therefore, the first thing you need to do is to start working on what you do not know. If you are going to defeat your enemy, you must learn to think like your enemy, or you will never be able to anticipate their attacks. As a tribulation leader, you must always see the battlefield from your enemy's point of view, and through their ambitions."

"So, back to the scenario, in this situation could you assume the infant has been abandoned by a desperate family member? Perhaps, on the other hand is this infant being used as bait no differently than the red wigglers on our hooks? It's not a tough call. When in doubt, err on the side of caution. If a warlord is using this infant as bait, then he or she has defined the field of fire as well as the timing of the attack. In other words, your enemy has the initiative. But only if you respond emotionally, hastily, or irrationally, which is exactly what your enemy is banking on. Think about it, if a big fat fish swimming around in this small cove decides to nibble at our bait, we may see one of our bobbers dance a little bit. However, it's only when we see it suddenly plunge that we've hooked a prize fish that is careless, impulsive, and hasty."

"So what you're saying is that the warlord is the fisherman, the infant is the red wiggler, and we are the fat fish, so to speak. And when the warlord sees the bobber plunge, it's because we've acted hastily and irrationally?"

"I couldn't have said it better myself. So with that, let me give you a couple of leadership principles that will help you. Then you tell me how you would apply those principles to this situation. The first is timing. As a spiritual person, you know how God handles timing when it comes to options. All options are in play, but only in the 11th hour, once others' free will choices have run their course, will the best option become obvious. It's like a bingo game; the wheel goes around, and around, and around, until finally, one ball falls out. Now, you tell me how you would use that principle in this scenario?"

You take your time before you answer this one, tapping your lower lip as you have a habit to do. Finally you say, "While the infant's cries will be problematic, as long as the baby is crying I know the baby is alive. While it might appear cruel, I can begin to turn the tables on my enemy by doing nothing and not taking the bait, thereby denying my enemy a hasty and irrational response. The question is for how long?"

"Bravo. Good answer. Remember, there are no absolutes in the universe except for one — change. All things change over time. By denying your enemy a hasty and ill-thought-out response you've begun to change the situation in your favor. Granted, not by much, but a positive change is still a positive change."

"Next is the combat principal of spiritual leadership. You must never draw blood by your own hands, save for the most extreme circumstances such as your compound being overrun. Now how does that apply to this situation?"

You begin tentatively, "I think I understand what you're asking. What this means is that while I am the leader of the community, there must be someone I trust and to whom I have delegated the responsibility of security command. And to be honest, that could be a 13-year-old with a big slingshot for all I know."

"David killed Goliath with a slingshot and God's help, and don't forget it!" It's good to see you chuckle as I continue, "You're right, you will need an incident commander. Later on, I'm going to teach you about something called the Incident Command System, or ICS, and how you can use this Federal first-responder system to manage situations such as this. But for now, let's keep it simple."

"Let's just say you have a competent security chief, provost marshal, sheriff, or whatever you choose to call him or her. The next principal is command clarity. I remember hearing a story about General George Washington from the American Revolutionary War. He had just arrived with his troops to a new area and called for the camp to be made. When General Washington was asked how he would like the camp to be laid out, he left all of the arrangements to the discretion of his staff. Washington was asked why he did not give specific orders on the camp arrangements. He said that once you give orders on a specific subject, you will always be required to give orders on that specific subject. If you are to be effective as a leader, issue as few commands as possible and do so in writing so that they are clearly understood. Many, many examples of General Washington's written orders to his troops have been preserved. Now, I want you to apply the principle of command clarity to this scenario. How does it apply?"

"Well, whatever I'm going to do," you begin confidently "I will give my orders in writing."

"And what are those orders; assuming you have the time to write them down?"

"Well, I guess I would order my security chief to organize a recovery team of sufficient size to rescue the infant."

I shake my head, "No, wrong answer. Strategy and tactics is the domain of your security chief, who in this case is your incident commander. Therefore, such an order would mean you are micro-managing your security chief when he or she understands such circumstances better than you do and has the capability to form a more effective plan. Remember, when it comes to security strategy and tactics, these are the domain of your incident commander. Your incident commander should be chosen because they have the expertise required to handle this particular situation."

"So if I'm the community leader, am I just a bystander?"

"Don't get frustrated; you need to see this as a tribulation leader. As I said before, in this circumstance strategy and tactics is not your domain. Let me tell you what is. What you need to give to your security chief or incident commander, in this case, is three things:

- First, give a vision of what success looks like,
- Second, state the objective(s),
- Third, provide resources."

"I call this a mission directive. Now, I want you to create a mission directive for your incident commander."

Now you're tapping your lower lip a little faster, "Well, umm, my vision is that nobody dies. The objective is to save the infant. And as to resources, I suppose whatever the incident commander has on hand."

I lean forward, "If I were your incident commander and I received this as a mission directive from you, I'd be polite to your face, but behind your back, I would tell those that hold my private confidences that your leadership abilities and intelligence are extremely questionable."

"What?!" you rub your forehead, "How on Earth can I be the right person for this job?"

"You have the humility to ask the right questions. Now let me give you the right answer. We will examine the mission directive your incident commander needs. First is the vision. In other words, what does success look like? And this has absolutely nothing to do with the infant. Remember, the vision in your mission directive is always about your community. All you see is them. If you see yourself in that vision, then you have gone into ego, and you will fail. Step down and let someone else run the show."

"In this case your vision of success is that no matter what the outcome is, your community remains safe, unified, and confident that all that is humanly possible has been done, and the actions taken were wise and carried out well. If you inflict heavy damage upon your enemy, but the infant's life is lost, the community will mourn the infant's death, but they will remain cohesive knowing leadership has consistently acted in their best interests. Thus, while the safety and the cohesion of the community are what matters most, saving the infant, as cruel as this may sound, is secondary."

"As to the objectives, you have two. The most important are not the infant. You are facing an attack by what is most likely a superior armed force. Not only is your enemy using this infant as bait to provoke a rash response, but your enemy is probing your defensive and offensive capabilities. So remember the pod of dolphins. They broke up a large school of anchovies into bait balls so they could feed on them. This is exactly what your enemy wants to do to you in this scenario. Therefore, your first objective is to destroy, or at the very least severely debilitate, your enemy to discourage future incidents. After that, the second objective is to rescue the infant, but only if you can do that without putting your responders in harm's way. In a world with no 911, you cannot afford heroics."

"Now, concerning resources, what you have here is an extraordinarily dangerous situation. So leaving your incident commander to work with whatever resources he or she may have access to on a routine basis is not enough. This is an incident where you are facing a powerful adversary. Give your incident commander full access to all of your resources so he or she can decide which resources are to be deployed, and which are to be held in reserve. This is your mission directive."

A big Cheshire cat smile comes across your face, "Now I get it! No doubt there is more for me to learn, but I get it."

"And what do you get?"

"I can't let my emotions get in the way. I need to always keep a clear focus on the outcome as it relates to the security and cohesion of my community. To that end, I must give my incident commander a clear mission directive along with whatever resources are needed to accomplish the task."

"Excellent! Now how do you feel about yourself as a tribulation leader?"

"A lot better, but I know I've still got a way to go. That being said, can I throw you a curve ball question?"

"Sure."

"Let's assume it's sometime around noon. The infant is still crying and kicking, but not as much. Now a pack of feral Dobermans is observed stalking the infant. Clearly, they are interested in a meal. Now, would you let the dogs attack the infant? Or would you order your incident commander to immediately rescue the infant?"

"I would do neither."

You answer with surprise, "Neither!?"

"That's right, neither."

"So what would you do?"

"Well just look around because the answer is obvious. In all of this time, we been here neither of us has seen any sign of movement on our two bobbers."

"No doubt, we scared off the fish. After all we've been talking loud enough to wake the dead."

"Okay, so let's assume that you and I have been sitting here like good stealthy fisherman and we haven't made a peep. In fact, Sheba has been sound asleep all this time as well. In addition to that, let's assume we still feel there's a strong possibility that there are some prize fish in this cove."

"Hmm, so you're looking for a little wiggle room. Fair enough. I suppose in that case, at some point, we will have to reel in our lines to check our bait."

"Precisely, now, let me apply that to your curve-ball question, and why I would do neither."

"This I have to hear."

"I would not let the dogs eat the infant, nor would I launch a rescue. Rather, I would expect my incident commander to order our snipers to shoot the dogs. I'd wait a short while first, to see if my commander will order that. If not, I will order it done myself."

"Would you be doing that to save the infant's life?"

"Yes, partially, but it could be that what we're seeing is really not a pack of feral dogs. In fact, they could belong to the warlord, who is using them to see why we're not biting on the bait. Yes, there is a good possibility of that. By shooting the dogs and not allowing ourselves to be tricked into a hasty response, we will send a message to the warlord. We have teeth and brains, and we will not be stampeded."

I am pleased that your curve-ball question has presented me with a teachable moment, and these should never be squandered, "Never forget that the greatest weakness of ego-driven evil people is their tendency to overreach. They lack the humility to be perceptive of their own limitations, which can give you unique opportunities to painfully 'explain' their weaknesses to them, on your own terms. Therefore, assuming that these dogs were set upon the infant by the warlord, by killing them we gain a small fraction of the initiative. Moves and counter moves, my friend, moves and counter moves."

"Overreach. That is a very valuable lesson. I'll remember that for sure, "you say thoughtfully as you begin to reel in your line, "I also think it's time to try another spot on the lake. What do you say we get our gear in order and go find us another fishing spot?"

Sensing that we are about to do something different, Sheba stands up at the bow, looking out from the cove to the opposite shoreline. "I think Sheba is telling us where to go look for fish," I say as I began reeling in my line. A few minutes later everything is shipshape, and we're on our way, with you at the helm, and Sheba pointing the way.

As we motor out towards the middle of the lake, you ask, "Just out of curiosity, if I were to study any three people from history to help me prepare to be a tribulation leader, who would you suggest?"

"Well, that gives a lot of room for preference."

"I know, but still the same, who would you suggest?"

Standing at the bow, Sheba looks back at me. It makes me wonder, is she interested in knowing the answer to this question as well? And what is it about this dog that makes her so different? After all, Golden Retrievers are beautiful, loving dogs, but they're not renowned for being the most intelligent. Yet, there's just something about this dog, something that I just can't put my finger on. Oh well, for now, I'll just put that mystery in a glass jar on the shelf and wait for the universe to fax me a label.

"Well," I respond, "the three I would suggest are Sun Tzu, General George Patton, and Winston Churchill. This is not to say that there aren't others, but these are the three I would suggest as most useful to study regarding the tribulation."

"Thanks, I'll keep that in mind the next time I go to the library. So, what's next?"

"As far as today goes, the class is out and in recess for the rest of the day. The sun is getting low in the sky. Meanwhile, I don't know about you, but I've got a serious hankering for some fresh fish tonight."

"Yessiree, that works for me," you gleefully respond, "but just one last question — what's on tap for tomorrow?"

"Well, that's why I had a late night last night. Tomorrow you and I are going to a fair. Specifically, we are going to the Planet X World's Fair. So wear a good pair of walking shoes."

4

Planet X Orbitarium

It was another late night for me but not quite as late. This time I find you with a hot breakfast and the flapjacks are flying high. You do get a kick out of seeing how high you can flip a pancake into the air before it falls back on the griddle, nice and neat as you please. Yes, it's your thing, and when you're not busy flipping pancakes, you're always looking around the table for a hungry eye. That's when you spy me nursing a mug of hot coffee.

"It's going to be a big day ahead, how many pancakes you want, Mr. Walking Shoes?" you tease.

All I can manage is a weak smile as I hold up four fingers. Everyone around the table is singing our praises, and I'm quite happy about that. After our lesson yesterday we did some serious fishing and motored back with a heavy stringer full of small mouth bass. Then we grilled them up into an unforgettable fish feast with Sheba as the guest of honor.

As we regaled everyone with our exploits, they were amazed to learn that even the most expensive and sophisticated electronic fish finders on the market couldn't compare with Sheba's ability to sense where the fish are biting.

At first they seemed a bit doubtful, when we explained that while finding the best fishing spots, we learned that Sheba has a very distinct lexicon. One bark for "no," two barks for "yes," three barks for "maybe," and when she's really confident about something, she'll bark twice for "yes" and repeat it again, for a total of four emphatic barks.

That was when things got fascinating. We slipped a nice chunk of grilled bass into her dog bowl, but Sheba wouldn't have anything to do with it. However, when we fed her a piece of fish by hand, she'd snap up each piece with great relish. And so that night, as everyone enjoyed grilled bass, we took turns asking Sheba if she wanted a treat. Each time she would bark twice when anyone held out a piece of grilled fish and asked if she wanted it. It was a remarkable night. The morning conversation was about Sheba's lexicon and a fish feast that we would never forget.

Like Sheba with the fish, I tore into my pancakes with great relish. Using the last piece of pancake to mop up the last of the egg yolk on my plate, I washed it down with a long slug of coffee.

I was so busy eating I hadn't noticed you watching with satisfaction as you shut off the griddle and hung your apron over the chair. "Well all," you announce, "We've got a long day and a big walking adventure ahead; so, we must bid you all adieu until this evening."

Feeling satisfied, we go out onto the balcony. There, next to the outside stairs, Sheba is waiting for us. She has an eager glint in her eye and a happy wag in her tail. You bend over and pat her on the head, "Sorry old girl. Where we're going today, they're not going to allow you to join us."

"What on earth gave you that idea?" I exclaim. "As the creator of the Planet X World's Fair, that is for me to say. I will have you know that I have designed my park to be Sheba-friendly. So she comes right along."

You laugh, "That reminds me of that great line from Mel Brooks' movie, *History of the World: Part I.*'It's good to be the king." as we start down the long flight of stairs.

Half way down I stop and turn around to look at Sheba, "Well girl, what do you think? Is it good to be the king?"

"Woof woof," she answers quickly.

"Well, now it's unanimous. So, off we go to the time machine."

Far out of sight from the house and the lake, we walk into a stand of tall trees. I remove a remote control device from my pocket and point it at athick, brushy area. Moments later the brush vanishes. "The brush is a hologram I used to cloak the time machine," I explain.

"I was wondering where you parked that thing," you chuckle. "Got a question, Given that the two of us are spending a lot of time together, how come nobody, including our spouses, has voiced any complaints? Not that I'm complaining, mind you."

As the time machine hatch opens, I explain, "This is not just a time travel machine; it does other things as well. It's why I call it the Swiss Army knife of imagination. There's a tool for just about everything." This time there are two chairs in the machine, and I gesture toward one. "If you will, please." As we settle in, Sheba curls up on the floor behind us and the hatch closes.

"Are you ready?" You nod affirmatively, and I lean forward and speak into the microphone, "Planet X World's Fair." With that the machine begins to hum, and I look back over my shoulder to check on Sheba. Completely unfazed, she's licking a paw.

Welcome to the Planet X World's Fair

A flash of light fills the machine. In the next moment, we're all standing at the entrance to the fair. Above our heads is a large, colorful, arched sign. It reads, "Welcome to the Planet X World's Fair."

You look at me with 1,000 questions in your eyes. "All in good time," I assure you.

Just inside the entrance is a kiosk with a map of the park and all of its exhibits. You go toward it like a kid in a candy shop. As you eye the many options, I reach over and point to the Planet X Orbitarium. "Here is where we will begin."

With a simple, "Woof woof," Sheba starts walking in the right direction, and we follow.

This exhibit is not far from the entrance, and as we walk along, I explain that there are two parts to the Planet X Orbitarium. The first is the Hall of Heroes. This is an important exhibit because for years there has been a propaganda lie repeatedly trumpeted that the search for Planet X was an Internet hoax. The second part is the Orbitarium, where we'll see how the Planet X System orbits our sun.

As we approach you note, "This whole place looks like it was made in the 1960s."

I nod, "Yes, I based this fair on the historical archives of the 1964 World's Fair in Queens, New York. It's amazing what you can find on the Internet these days."

"Why that particular fair?"

"Now I'm showing my age, but as a young boy, I was there. I remember how it filled me with a powerful sense of awe and wonder. It was the very first time I saw a video phone. It had a touch tone dial pad. It was not exactly like the ones we have today, because it didn't have an asterisk and a pound sign key, but the tones were the same. I'll never forget that instant of seeing someone from another part of the exhibit and having that video phone conversation with them."

"It was a magical time in America, wasn't it?"

"Oh my, yes! In May of the previous year, I had watched on my mother's old black and white TV set when "Gordo" Cooper took the last flight of the Mercury program, just as I had all of the previous launches. It was an exciting time to be alive. It made me feel like I was witnessing the emergence of a new civilization with hope for the future."

"And then came the 70's," you add wryly.

"Disco, Ugh…Dumb luck," I lament as we approach a grassy area. I look at Sheba and point to the grass, "This will be your last chance for a while." With a keen sense of knowing she trots off to the grassy area and begins sniffing for a good place to take a squat.

"Did you bring a baggie?"

I shake my head, "No, but remember, it's good to be the king. Watch this."

Sheba finishes her business and trots towards us.

"And..." You quip with mild annoyance.

"And…watch this." With that a little machine with large rubber wheels and bristling with antennas rolls out onto the grass. "This is my super duper poop remover," I proudly explain as the little machine deftly sweeps Sheba's scat into its canister.

You shake your head, "Don't tell me they had that in 1964!"

"Okay, creative license, like Mel said, 'It's good to be the king.'" With that I point to the exhibit entrance.

A few other people are in line in front of us. We're soon greeted by a pleasantly-smiling young woman with large brown eyes, dressed in a smartly-styled blue suit, and pointy-toed, kitten-heeled pumps. Her dark hair is swept up into a French twist with bangs dangling to her cheek on one side which rounded out an impressive picture of a very competent and well-trained presenter.

"Gosh, she looks familiar," you observe with a puzzled voice, "Where have I seen her face before?"

"It's Audrey Hepburn; similar to how she looked in the 1961 movie, *Breakfast at Tiffany's.*"

The presenter gracefully gestures, stretching out her hand to indicate the way, "Welcome to the Planet X Orbitarium. Please walk to your right until you find an open booth in the Hall of Heroes. You will see a panel with a "start" button. When you press it, you'll see a brief presentation of the notable figures in the centuries-old search for Planet X. Once the presentation has finished, another door in the booth will open which will lead you into the Orbitarium. We hope you enjoy your visit. Now, please step to your right..."

The first several booths are closed, with a little red "occupied" light above each door. Soon we find one with a green light and an open door, inviting us to enter. It is a long narrow room with a door on the opposite side. To our right is a large screen with a narrow control panel on the front.

We stand to face the screen as Sheba edges between us. Putting her front paws up on the control panel to get a good view she looks up at me as though to say, "So push the button already," but before I can, you do it for us. With that the room goes dark, and the door closes automatically. Seconds later the widescreen rear-view projection screen on the panel in front of us begins to flicker to life.

Hall of Heroes Presentation

The presentation begins with a simple slide showing the Planet X World's Fair logo. During the first few minutes of the presentation the narrator immerses us into the topic by explaining that the search for Planet X is centuries old. In a moment where he pauses, you press the pause button.

"He sounds a lot like James Earl Jones, but in a magical way," you observe.

"It took a lot of research for me to create this park, but especially to create the right kind of feeling. In other words what I want you to take away from here is not just facts, figures, and possibilities. What I want you to learn from this visit and the others that we'll make, is that, but also much more. At the end of all this I want you to understand what you are preparing for — not the end of this civilization but a clean slate for the beginning of the next. I want you to feel that magical hope and unbridled optimism that can once again inspire us to accomplish things that cynical doubters would label as unimaginable."

"So where did you get the inspiration for this narrator?"

"Well, you know me; I've probably seen Field of Dreams a hundred times over the years. The first time was in and I was mesmerized by a scene at the end of the film. It's where the character Terence (James Earl Jones) gives Ray (Kevin Costner) a dreamy prediction to defy the threat of the foreclosure of his farm. It begins with Jones saying, 'People will come, Ray; they'll come to Iowa for reasons they don't even fathom.'"

It brings a smile to your face. "Yes, I remember, 'People will come, Ray.'"

"I'm glad you do because the time will come when you will face your congregation, and they will have fear etched on their faces and in their hearts. A fear that is worse than the threat of an eviction notice that much I can assure you. So remember, when this time comes, do not speak in a stern or patronizing voice like someone threatening foreclosure. No, my friend, this is when you will need to draw on the memory of this memorable scene and use it to help you set a proper tone. This will be the 'peace that they need.'"

"'People will come, Ray.' I got it," you say warmly as you prepare to resume the presentation. "Thanks for that." As though she'd been waiting for that revelation to happen,

Sheba found a comfortable spot near the opposite wall. The important thing had happened, and the rest would be mere context. You press the play button and the presentation resumes.

"For countless generations, we have gazed up at the night sky with a sense of awe, and we have marveled at the majesty of God's handiwork. So that our children could teach their own children one day, we explained the stars to them with shapes familiar to them, (even though one would have to use a tremendous amount of imagination to visualize such celestial creatures).

"For those who observed the skies for signs of things to come, it was a never-ending quest to understand these night sky harbingers. these celestial creatures foretold difficult times. So we today, like those who came before us , also observe the night sky for insight. While our ancestors had clearer viewing skies, we have the advantage of technology.

"In the past the furthermost planet visible to the unaided eye was Saturn, and it stayed that way for tens of thousands of years. Then something magnificent happened that would begin to change our entire understanding of who we are and where we fit in the universe.

"In 1774 Frederick William Herschel, British astronomer and composer of German origin, constructed his first large telescope after which he spent nine years surveying the sky. He achieved considerable results. He imaged thousands of stars, but on March 13, 1781, he made a discovery unlike any other in the history of humankind. During his observations, he noticed that one celestial body was not a star; it was different.

"Consequently, on March 13, 1781, William Herschel discovered the Planet Uranus, a frigid, featureless gas giant, roughly 4 times the size of Earth, and the very first planet in our solar system to be discovered with a telescope.

"Following Herschel's discovery, French astronomer, Alexis Bouvard, observed perturbations in the orbit of Uranus. In other words something beyond Uranus was tugging at it each time the gas giant crossed before it —a tiny gravitational zigzag if you will.

"If one were to choose a father of Planet X research, it would be Alexis Bouvard. He rightly deduced that the perturbations in the orbit of Uranus were being caused by a yet-unknown planet beyond the orbit of Uranus. This planet would come to be known as Uranus's perturber and regrettably Bouvard died before the coordinates of this unseen perturber could be mathematically determined.

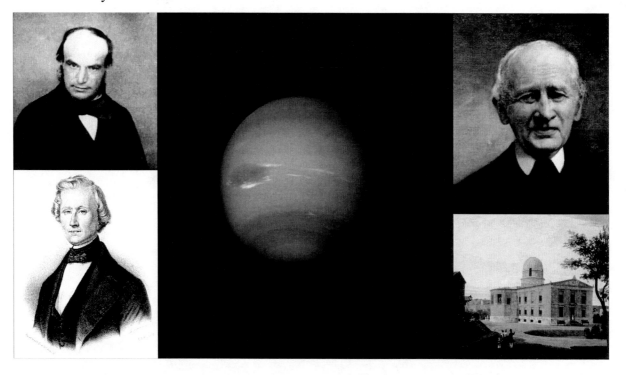

"Over half a century later those calculations would come to fruition when British mathematician, John Couch Adams (seen in the upper left) and French mathematician, Urbain

Le Verrier (seen in the lower left) used Bouvard's observations to mathematically determine the location of Uranus's perturber.

"Both men did excellent work, but Verrier received the official credit because he relayed those coordinates to Johann Galle of the Berlin Observatory. Galle observed Neptune five days later on 23 September 1846, which made Neptune the first planet to be discovered by mathematical prediction.

"After the discovery of Neptune astronomers were able to observe the planet, and to their surprise they discovered a perturbation in the orbit of Neptune like that of Uranus. At this point astronomers knew that there was still a large, undiscovered planet beyond the orbits of Uranus and Neptune and it was causing these orbital perturbations. It was called Neptune's perturber, and this is when the search for what we presently call Planet X languished for more than half a century until that search moved a continent away.

"In 1894 Percival Lawrence Lowell, a wealthy Bostonian, businessman, mathematician, and astronomer, took up the gauntlet. Leaving the comfort and opulence of Boston for the clear skies and pine forests of Flagstaff, Arizona, he established the Lowell Observatory. He chose this location in the belief that it would be ideal for viewing the planet Mars and to continue the search for Neptune's elusive perturber.

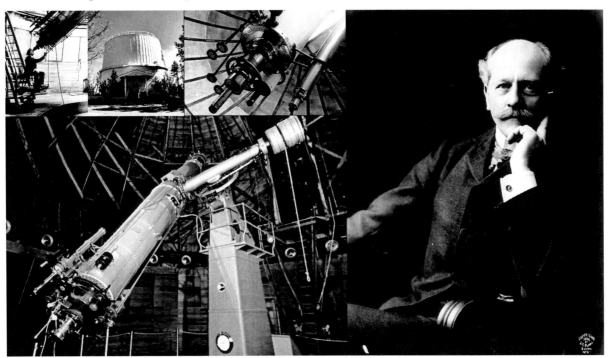

"Sometime between 1903 and 1908 Lowell coined the phrase, "Planet X," which does not mean the 10th planet, as some people might assume. Rather, "X" implies a celestial unknown, similar to when an algebra teacher asks you to "Solve for X."

"Sadly, Lowell passed away without finding Neptune's perturber. Though interestingly enough, a year before he passed away, he did photograph Pluto, in March and April of 1915. He failed, however, to recognize it as a planet, but the search for Planet X would not end there.

"In 1929 a young astronomer, by the name of Clyde W. Tombaugh, was hired by the Lowell Observatory to continue the search for Planet X. On February 18, 1930 Tombaugh discovered the planet Pluto.

"'Oh my,'" the astronomers of the time must have thought. Neptune's elusive perturber would no longer elude them because Tombaugh had finally observed the mysterious Planet X. Consequently, the topic of Planet X languished after Tombaugh's discovery. As with most things, it was the same old song — problem solved and time to move on to something new. And that's how things remained until 1978.

"In 1978 the discovery of Pluto's moon Charon would bring astronomers back to the search for Planet X, Neptune's perturber. This is because it was determined that Pluto, which is roughly 60% the size of our own moon, is not big enough to trifle with Neptune. Why we have a fondness for something so distant, lifeless, barren, and cold as Pluto amazes many. Yet, this fondness boiled furiously when the International Astronomical Union demoted Pluto to the status of a dwarf planet in 2006.

"Poor Pluto, it had its days of fame as the elusive Planet X, but they came to an end because it simply wasn't big enough to disturb a gas giant that is roughly four times the size of the Earth. At least that was the story north of Earth's equator. South of the equator Pluto had long been discounted as a candidate for Planet X."

Carlos Muñoz Ferrada, astronomer, scientist and seismologist.

"In 1940 Chilean Astronomer Carlos Muñoz Ferrada, a man of great passion and insight, was the first to forward an explanation of Planet X. He called it Hercolubus, a name given it by the ancient Atlanteans. It was a massive object that they claimed brought about the demise of their civilization."

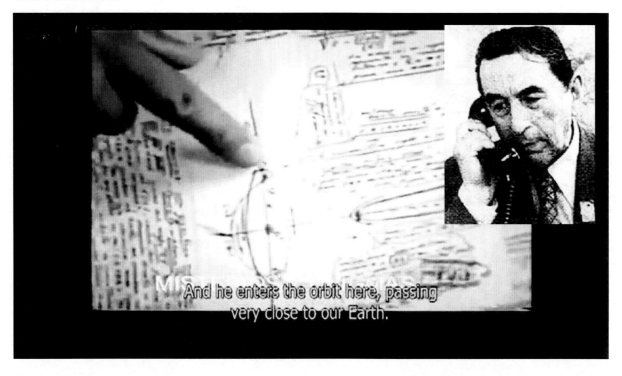

And he enters the orbit here, passing very close to our Earth.

"Where Ferrada differed dramatically from Lowell and Tombaugh was that he proposed not one, but two objects. One was a black and mysterious small star; the other was a planet several times the size of Earth. Another way in which he was different was that he described a long elliptical orbit for these objects. Here you see him pointing to an illustration of his own making, which interestingly would be corroborated some 36 years later. Not by astronomers but a man burning with a passion for finding the answer to an ageless question, "How did we as a species come to be?"

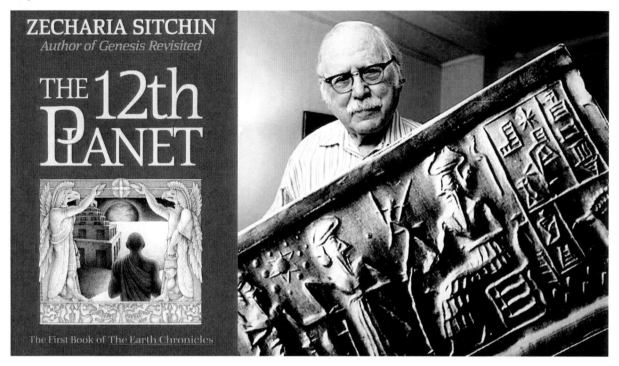

"This man was Zecharia Sitchin, a Russian-born American who in 1976 published the first of his many Earth Chronicles books titled, The 12th Planet. According to his translations of ancient Sumerian texts, a race of beings living on a planet the Sumerians called Nibiru bio-engineered humankind. They spliced their genes with those of our early hominid ancestors to create modern man as slaves to mine gold for them. Perhaps this explains a particular affliction we call "gold fever."

"These beings that genetically altered us for their purposes are called the Annunaki. What we call Planet X today, according to the Sumerians, orbits our sun every 3,600 lunar years. While some flybys of the Planet X System are uneventful, others can cause devastating global cataclysms on Earth.

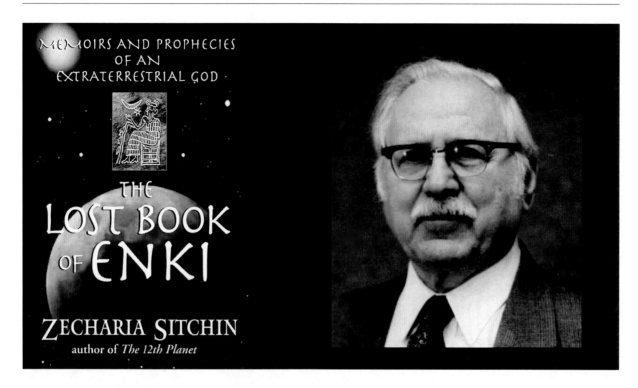

"It is important to note that while Sitchin wrote several books on Nibiru over the course of his life, one that was especially interesting was the Lost Book of Enki, published in 2002. Enki was the Annunaki lord who created modern man. In this autobiography he explains in precise detail how those of Nibiru came to Earth for gold to repair the atmosphere of their home planet and how he was instrumental in the creation of our species as it exists today.

"Undoubtedly, this is where Sitchin sparked the ire of religious fundamentalists because according to Enki, our species, as we know ourselves, came from his loins. Since then, the topic has been plagued by agenda-driven attacks, slander, and outright disinformation.

"Nonetheless, a mystery is still a mystery. Now, not only could Planet X present us with a future possibility of catastrophic events on Earth; it could also radically change how we think of ourselves."Yet, the search for Planet X remained a vibrant one as evidenced by this 1983 article in the New York Times titled, "Clues Get Warm in the Search for Planet X." In fact the 1980s were a time of great curiosity and speculation about Planet X by mainstream science and the media alike. That was until NASA launched the Infrared Astronomical Satellite (IRAS) on January 25, 1983, to map the sky using infrared imaging.

"At first things went exceptionally well; then, suddenly NASA announced that IRAS was no longer able to complete its mission due to a failure in its super cooling system.

"It was in fact a convenient cover story because this critical event was not a failure of technology. It was a failure of leadership, and one that would be the first of many untruths according to several military whistle-blowers with access to secret documents. Each has said that the IRAS failure was a cover-up. What actually happened was that it had successfully imaged Planet X. Yet, the search for truth can still find its way to the light on rare occasions.

"In a Victoria Advocate article published on June 14, 1988, NASA astronomer, Dr. John D. Anderson, was quoted as saying that telemetry from the Pioneer 10 spacecraft indicated the existence of Planet X. All of the whistle-blowers corroborated this fact.

"However, like a crumb that had fallen off the table, Anderson's groundbreaking announcement remained unnoticed until the March 2012 publication of an expose titled, "The Planet X Cover-up in the Mainstream Media," on the Your Own World USA website. No doubt the lights burned through the night in NASA offices following the publication of that article. Soon thereafter the entire June 14, 1988, edition of the Victoria Advocate was deleted from the Google News Internet site. Forever gone was Anderson's Planet X announcement that "We have a 90 to 99 percent confidence that Uranus and Neptune are being disturbed, and by one candidate for that is a single Planet X."

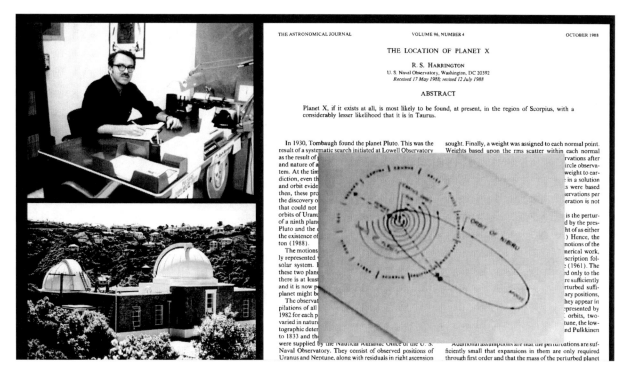

"In October of 1988, Dr. Robert Sutton Harrington, the chief astronomer of the U.S. Naval Observatory, published his paper, "The Location of Planet X in the Astronomical Journal.""

"Then, in 1991 Harrington upped the ante by commissioning a special telescope to be used for a Planet X sky survey, and that survey was completed at the Black Birch Observatory in New Zealand. It was a southern station of the US Naval Observatory that was eventually closed in 1996.

"Up to this point the government could bury the truth of Planet X with small moves. That was until Harrington's own pursuit of the truth went beyond the government's ability to suppress the truth as it had with the 1988 Victoria Advocate interview with NASA astronomer, Dr. John D. Anderson.

"This turn of events would occur in 1990; one year before the 1991 Black Birch observations were swept under the carpet by NASA. It was then that Harrington unwittingly steered into treacherous waters.

"In 1990 Zecharia Sitchin filmed an interview with himself and Robert Harrington. The completed documentary titled, "*Are We Alone in the Universe*," first aired in 1992. It contained three politically explosive elements. Some believe these were what led to the assassination of Robert Harrington in 1993 because two of them came from none other than Harrington himself in that 1990 interview.

"In that 1990 interview Harrington speculated that Planet X, or Nibiru as the ancient Sumerians called it, could possibly sustain some form of life. In other words Harrington, a United States government astronomer, publicly acknowledged the possible existence of the Annunaki as described by Zecharia Sitchin in his many books on Nibiru.

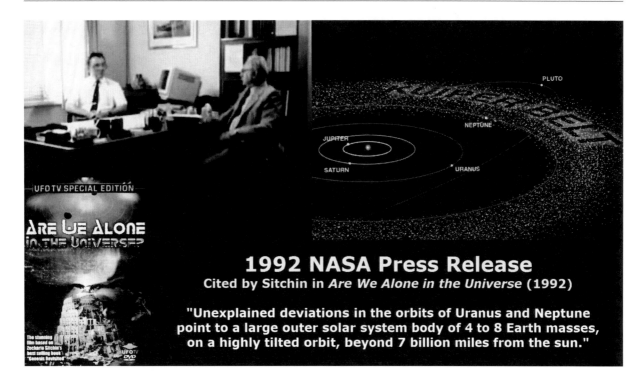

1992 NASA Press Release

Cited by Sitchin in *Are We Alone in the Universe* (1992)

"Unexplained deviations in the orbits of Uranus and Neptune point to a large outer solar system body of 4 to 8 Earth masses, on a highly tilted orbit, beyond 7 billion miles from the sun."

"In this same interview Harrington further stated the opinion that the planet Pluto once orbited Neptune and it was dislodged by Planet X into its present orbit. This theory was groundbreaking because it put a whole new twist on the story of Pluto.

"These two revelations by Harrington were powerful enough to put him in the cross-hairs of those seeking to suppress the truth. But even more dangerous was something Sitchin added to the end of the documentary before its release in 1992. This last minute addition may have pulled an ugly trigger so to speak.

"What Sitchin added at the end was a 1992 NASA press release that said, "Unexplained deviations in the orbits of Uranus and Neptune point to a large outer solar system body of 4 to 8 Earth masses, on a highly tilted orbit, beyond 7 billion miles from the sun."

"Consequently, the implications of this documentary were profound. This is because Sitchin's last minute addition of the 1992 NASA press release at the end of Are We Alone in the Universe was smoking-gun proof that what he and astronomers Robert Harrington and Carlos Ferrada were saying about Planet X was the truth.

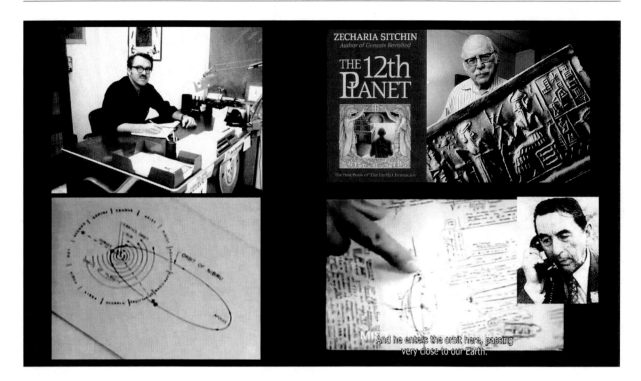

"Then, in 1993 Harrington suddenly died from a type of rapid-onset cancer known to be used by intelligence agencies for targeted assassinations. The mysterious death of this healthy astronomer in the prime of his life quickly silenced the Planet X topic with the mainstream media and the science community alike. In a sense, it was a veiled threat, "Tamper with this at the risk of your career, or perhaps even your life."

"What made it both mysterious and ominous was an obituary written about Harrington by Charles E. Worley of the U. S. Naval Observatory. In it he wrote about Harrington's search for Planet X, "Late in his career Bob seemed quite skeptical of such an object." A claim nobody since has corroborated. Yet it sent a clear signal — Planet X was now a third rail topic. Touch it and you die. It's sad to say, but the signal was broadly received and acted upon; then came the cover-up.

"Immediately following the mysterious death of astronomer Robert S. Harrington, government spin-meisters launched an aggressive media disinformation campaign to bury and discredit Planet X research.

The Planet X Cover-up in the Mainstream Media

Yowusa.com, 18-March-2012
Justin Braithwaite

Page 2 of 2

Harrington's Death Unleashes Cover-up - 1993

There is no other explanation for the stunning reversal of Planet X reporting in the mainstream media than NASA, the US Naval Observatory, and ultimately the US Government launching an all-out cover up and disinformation campaign.

Lakeland Ledger - Jun 6, 1993
Researcher: Planet X Isn't There

"erroneous observations and calculations"

The Times-News - Jun 27, 1993
Analysis Questions Existence of Planet X

"apparent death blow to the Planet X theory..."

Discover - September 1, 1993
Planet X is Dead

"no planet fitting Planet X's description"

This was fully described in a 2012 article by Justin Braithwaite published by Marshall Masters on the Your Own World USA website.

In that article, Braithwaite notes,

"By analyzing an extensive amount of publications relating to Planet X, in chronological order, not only does the cover up of Planet X become extraordinary, but one gains a unique perspective of the evolution of the Planet X discovery.

Planet X transformed from almost certain existence to the evaporation of Planet X evidence in a mere six months and immediately following the death of Harrington.

There is no other explanation for the stunning reversal of Planet X reporting in the mainstream media than NASA, the US Naval Observatory, and ultimately the US Government launching an all-out cover up and disinformation campaign."

"After decades of impartial reporting, the mainstream media suddenly flipped to the negative after Harrington's death with headlines like, 'Researcher: Planet X Isn't There,' 'Analysis Questions Existence of Planet X,' and, 'Planet X is Dead.'

Surviving the Planet X Tribulation

Did Planet X / Nibiru Kill The Dinosaurs?

YOWUSA.COM, 28-January-02
Marshall Masters

There is a growing interest in finding planet-sized object in long period orbit that brings through the core of our solar system on a regular basis, and causing huge mass extinctions with each flyby of Earth.

The names Planet X and Nibiru are heavily mentioned on web sites like Zeta Talk and by talk radio personalities like Art Bell, along with the next flyby date of 2003. If Planet X really exists, then we have to assume that it has passed this way before and

"A former CNN science features field producer during the 1980's and a retired Silicon Valley systems analyst, Marshall Masters, began writing on the topics of space threats and Earth changes in 1999.

"In 2001 he became interested in the topic of Planet X because it explained, in part, the deterioration of the Arctic ice that he had witnessed during Aeroflot polar flights from Moscow to San Francisco.

"All this led to the first Planet X article that he published on his Your Own World USA website in January of 2002 titled, *Did Planet X / Nibiru Kill the Dinosaurs?*" This article was based on a theoretical analysis he had conducted with Dr. Brian Marsden, then Associate Director of the Smithsonian Astrophysics Observatories.

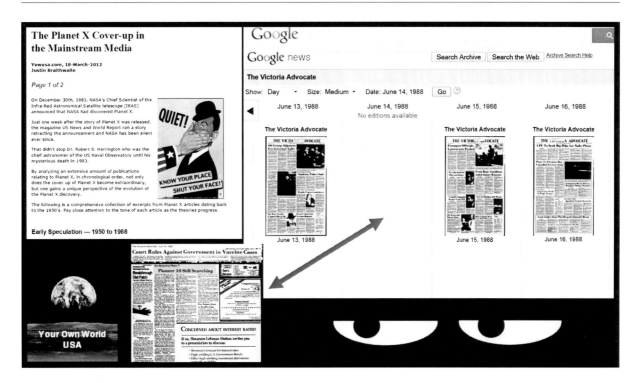

"A self-defined seeker of truth, he and his many contributing citizen journalists have exposed several cover-ups over the years. An example is the 1988 cover-up of NASA astronomer Dr. John D. Anderson's interview published in the Victoria Advocate on June 14, 1988. They also exposed the manner in which the whole field of Planet X research was maliciously suppressed following the 1993 mysterious death of the chief astronomer of the U.S. Naval Observatory, Dr. Robert S. Harrington. Your Own World USA would break other news stories, as well.

"In April of 2006 Marshall, along with Dutch physicist and Your Own World USA co-founder, Jacco van der Worp, broke the news story of the South Pole Telescope. Referred to as the SPT, their article was titled, "*South Pole Telescope (SPT) — America's New Planet X Tracker.*" At the time the SPT was still being constructed.

"The massive 10-meter telescope is now located at the Amundsen–Scott South Pole Station in Antarctica. To put it simply, it is the perfect instrument to observe the Planet X System in the southern skies.

"While the reasons for locating the SPT are complex, Dutch Physicist Jacco van der Worp determined that the very same science could have been conducted in southern Chile for a fraction of the cost.

South Pole Telescope (SPT) — America's New Planet X Tracker

Yowusa.com, 26-April-2006
Jacco van der Worp
Foreword by Marshall Masters

America is now spending huge sums to deploy the massive The South Pole Telescope (SPT) in Antarctica. The final installation will be the size of a mini-mall and will require a massive C-130 airlift effort to transport pre-assembled modules and a large staff to the most desolate, inhospitable and inaccessible region of the world. Why? Because Planet X / Nibiru was first sighted in 1983 and this discovery spurred the USA to build the SPT — humanity's new Planet X tracker.

Amongst independent researchers like us at YOWUSA.COM and the equally committed researchers with whom we share data, the 1983 IRAS observation of Planet X / Nibiru has always been a hot topic. On a private level, we often discuss how the NASA's IRAS spacecraft first captured infrared images of it back in 1983 with the same lament. Given the lack of corroboration, how can you publish a story that can easily be shot down as a rumor? That was then.

Now we have the corroboration we've lacked for years, The South Pole Telescope (SPT). Far more powerful capable and survivable than the 1983 IRAS spacecraft and Hubble Space Telescope put together, this manned observatory will soon begin tracking Planet X / Nibiru from the pristine skies of Antarctica.

Why is America spending a massive fortune to transport this massive facility with massive C-130 airlift to the most desolate, inhospitable and inaccessible region of the world to track this massive inbound? Because this is where astronomers will find their ultimate Kodak moment and this is good news. Their resulting multi-spectrum observations will translate into life-saving data.

"However, the position maintained by Masters and van der Worp was that the real purpose for the SPT would be Planet X observation, once it became operational.

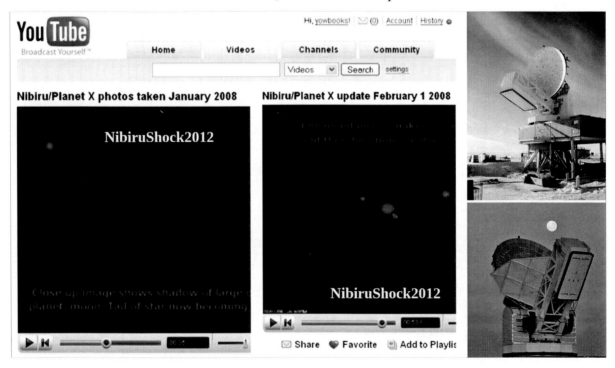

"One year after the SPT went online whistle-blowers posted highly credible disclosure videos of SPT imagery on YouTube. The first SPT disclosure pictures were anonymously posted under the YouTube channel name of NibiruShock2012. It was titled, "*Nibiru-Planet X photos taken in January 2008.*"

"Then on March 3, 2008, NibiruShock2012 posted a second video titled, "*Nibiru-Planet X update with February 1, 2008.*" In that video he stated that the Planet X System was approaching from the south at an extremely shallow angle which is consistent with what astronomers Carlos Ferrada and Robert S. Harrington had theorized. This was the first time the public ever saw Planet X imagery.

"In the March video, NibiruShock2012 showed us that Planet X is actually a system, not just a single planetary object. It is a mini-constellation of planets and moons orbiting around a brown dwarf star which is a smaller binary twin star to our sun.

"After these two videos were posted, Marshall Masters contacted the original Nibirushock2012 through YouTube and then was able to establish him as a credible source. Shortly after that, the Nibirushock2012 channel was hijacked by paid disinformation operatives who implemented a deceitful cover-up campaign to discredit those first two videos which had been anonymously posted by the original Nibirushock2012. Despite this setback another SPT whistle-blower would show up later that same year.

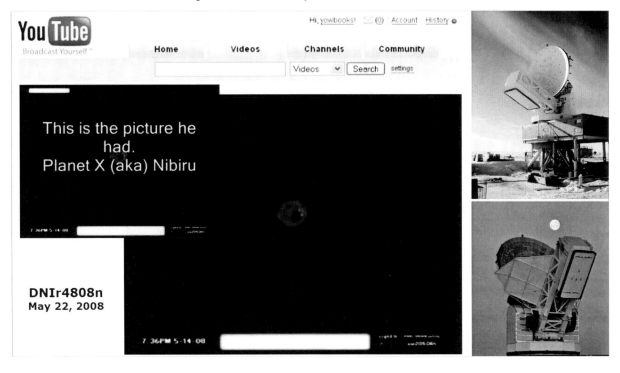

"On May 22, 2008 Marshall Masters received an anonymous tip about a new SPT disclosure video that had been posted minutes earlier on the YouTube channel, DNIr4808n. Marshall immediately downloaded the video. This was fortunate because within a few hours the channel was closed and the video removed. Fast close-down or removal response times such as this are customary when a government agency has ordered it.

"Furthermore, when you compare the images in the DNIr4808n with NibiruShock2012 videos, it's obvious that both are the same object, which also happened to be in the southern sky beneath us.

"In the video DNIr4808n explained that a personal friend working at the SPT, whom he named, had sent him this image of Planet X captured by the SPT on May 14, 2008. Because he mentioned his friend's name, DNIr4808n triggered the rapid removal of this vital disclosure video from YouTube.

"However, a few days later the DNIr4808n channel was restored along with pornographic video advertisements to discredit it. It was a further proof of government suppression. This was especially so when the rapid take-down of the channel and the obscene smears by impostors are taken into account.

"But the real question was why the government was so sensitive about the **NibiruShock2012 and DNIr4808n SPT disclosure videos? What was driving the government's mean-spirited and ugly take-downs of these YouTube channels? The answer would come a few months later.**

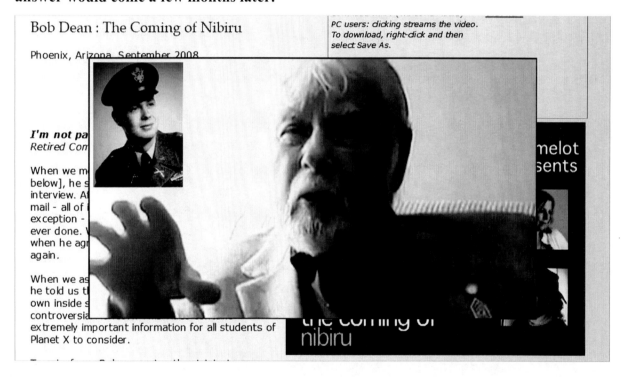

"Founded by Kerry Cassidy, the Project Camelot site is a gathering place for whistle-blower testimony. In September of 2008 Project Camelot posted an interview titled, "Bob Dean: The Coming of Nibiru or Planet X."

"Bob Dean is a whistle-blower and also part of a group called, "The Old Boys Club." This group is composed mostly of retired military officers, non-commissioned officers, and government officials with high-security clearances who have come forward to reveal what they know about extraterrestrials and Planet X.

"In his 2008 interview with Kerry Cassidy, of Project Camelot, Bob Dean offered a clear warning. This coming flyby of the Planet X System will be a worst-case scenario like that of Noah's flood, as opposed to that of the Hebrew Exodus from Egypt, a best-case scenario. The difference between the two is where Earth is situated relative to the Planet X system as it begins the downward leg of its orbit towards aphelion, the most distant point from the sun in its orbit. During the Exodus, Earth was on the opposite side of the sun when this occurred, making that a best-case flyby. However, this coming flyby will be a worse-scenario because like during the flyby of Noah's flood, Earth will be on the same side of the sun as the Planet X system, as it heads back into the southern sky beneath us The possible death toll of a worst-case scenario is staggering to comprehend because, according to some estimates, up to 90% humanity will perish during this coming flyby.

In that 2008 interview, Bob Dean explained all of the harbinger signs. Then at 1:37:43 he answers Cassidy's question about when the Planet X flyby would begin. His answer, "No later than 2017," then he added, "I'll throw 2017 out, and you can take that to the bank."

"It is important to note that all of the harbinger signs Dean predicted in 2008 are happening now. Therefore, knowing a little more about a man who has foreseen our future is in order.

"Husband to Marcia Schafer, Robert O. Dean, is a retired U.S. Army command sergeant major with a 28-year career filled with top-secret assignments. While stationed in France in the 60's, he was given top secret clearance to work in an area known as "The War Room." Dean read a COSMIC Top Secret NATO Study called, "The Assessment" while serving in the Operations Center of NATO's Supreme Headquarters Allied Powers in Europe (SHAPE).

"The purpose of this NATO military study was to analyze the implications of the alien presence here on Earth. It was a document that changed his life and which compelled him to come forward.

"He did so in 1991. This was about the time astronomer Robert S. Harrington was organizing the Black Birch Observatory Planet X sky survey in New Zealand. Now retired, Dean was disgusted with the paranoid hiding of this knowledge — knowledge he believed all citizens have a right to know. So he decided to break his security oath and go public about Planet X and the existence of aliens.

"His first public appearance in 1991 was at the world's first UFO conference in Arizona where he stated that extraterrestrials pose no threat whatsoever and that they have been visiting and landing on Earth for centuries.

"In a personal conversation with Marshall Masters, publisher of Your Own World USA, Dean confirmed the statements he made in his September 2008 Project Camelot interview. In the years following that conversation, Masters was able to independently corroborate Dean's 2008 statements, and for this reason regards him as a reliable and highly-credible Planet X whistle-blower.

"Another group held in high regard by Masters is the Skyview Team. They are a group of anonymous astronomers who posted ground-breaking observations made with their own telescopes of the Planet X System onto YouTube.

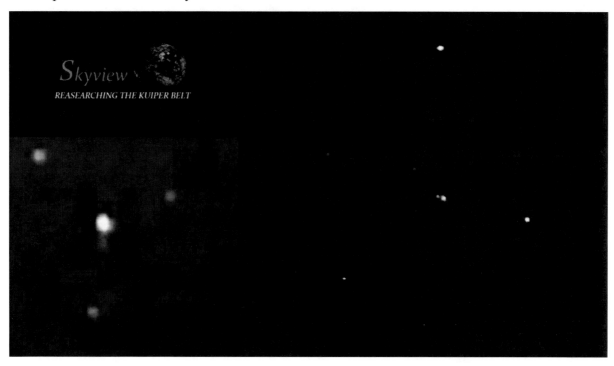

"A frequent target of government hackers and paid disinformationalists, they were continually under attack on YouTube. Their channels were hijacked so that valuable videos could be removed and replaced with demeaning sex videos and other nonsensical trivia to humiliate and demean the group.

"However, by creating new channels on YouTube they were able to continue publishing their videos until May of 2014 when the group finally announced, that having been harassed for so long, they would cease their efforts.

In 2016, two years after the original Skyview Team Youtube channel went dark, it resurfaced again. While the original Skyview Team was secretive in nature, Marshall was in direct contact with leading members of the original team. Based on this experience, Masters, believes this second incarnation of the Skyview Team to be a group comprised of newly formed impostors.

"The successful suppression of the original Skyview Team was a loss for all seekers of truth. They were actively observing and reporting the Planet X System as seen in an early video they posted which fully corroborated the January 2008 SPT disclosure video by NibiruShock2012 with similar wide-field views.

"Not only did their observations support what was being observed at the SPT; they also corroborated other observations as well.

"In late December of 2012 a Yowusa.com reader contacted Marshall Masters to report an unidentified object near the sun. Residing in Costa Rica on the foothills of the Turrialba volcano and concerned about possible eruptions, the reader regularly monitored the volcano's surveillance camera mounted on the Eastern rim of the Turrialba volcano.

"Operated by a Costa Rica University the volcano camera's location is at nearly 11,000 ft and the imagery was compelling. Marshall quickly identified an object in the real-time feed and dubbed it "Bluebonnet." It would appear each day near sunset. The object was persistent and natural which prompted Marshall to assemble a research team of volunteers under the direction of Barbara Townsend.

"Beginning in January of 2013 the team monitored the volcano feed on a daily basis. In the process they collected hundreds of Bluebonnet observations both with motion and still studies. The observation data was then reported in several articles and YouTube videos which came to the attention of the original Skyview Team because Masters first observed Bluebonnet in the constellation Ophiuchus.

"In late 2013 the original Skyview Team posted a video on YouTube corroborating the Your Own World USA team's observations of the object Marshall named "Bluebonnet" in the constellation Ophiuchus.

"The object they designated as a KBO, a Kuiper Belt Object, is actually the Nemesis brown dwarf star at the core of the Planet X System. In the image they captured with their own telescope in the infrared spectrum, they identify Marshall's Bluebonnet showing it in the constellation Ophiuchus.

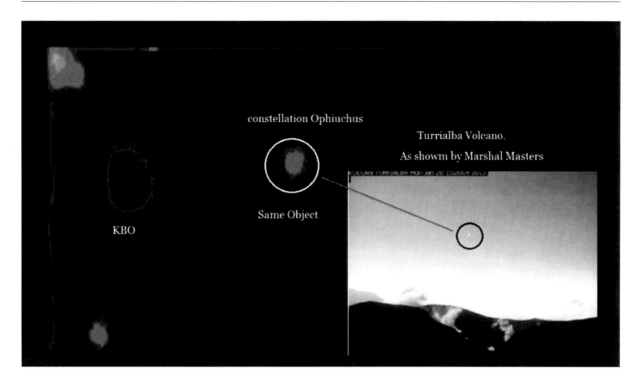

"What Marshall would later learn was that what he named Bluebonnet is actually the Planet Nibiru, the outermost object in the Planet X System.

"The name Nibiru comes from the ancient Sumerian texts as translated by Zecharia Sitchin and means "Planet of Crossing." The term is quite apt because it is coming our way, as you will see next in the Orbitarium.

"This concludes the Hall of Heroes presentation. After the lights come back up, please exit through the door to your left and follow the corridor to the Orbitarium."

The Orbitarium

As Sheba follows from behind, we stroll through a curved, softly lit corridor leading from the Hall of Heroes to the Orbitarium. I notice a sad and bewildered look on your face, "You OK?"

"Ugh...I...I..." your voice trails off, "I can't believe it."

"Can't believe what?"

"Oh sure, everyone knows our government lies to us, but with something like this, they would have to level with us. Wouldn't they?"

I gently pat you on the shoulder, "There's your first mistake."

"What?"

"You heard me," I answer softly, "Yes, and that was your first mistake. You used the phrase, 'our government.' There is no 'our government,' nor has there been an 'our government' for quite some time. It's just 'the government,' and the faceless people who own it."

Your head swivels slowly in my direction, "And if 'we, the people' do not own it, who does?

"The same people who own the printing presses that make our money. Start there and whoever is pulling their strings is where you'll find your answer, but not today."

"That doesn't make sense."

"Of course it makes sense," I answer patiently, "Think about it. You can drive across the breadth of our country, and it's most likely you'll see more American flags on the sides of chemical plants than you will on t-shirts. It's because the people know, or at least they sense it."

You stop mid-stride, and your eyes drill into me, "My God, it's true. That does make sense."

I look at Sheba behind you, "Well girl, should I tell him today?"

"Woof," her answer is no.

I look at you and nod for us to continue walking, and we resume our short journey down the corridor. "You need to see what you're going to see next, before what you'll learn tomorrow will make sense to you. Can you trust me on this?"

"I…I…suppose so."

Now neither of us utters another word. It's one of those pregnant moments when you know deep emotions are welling within, and the wrong word, intentional or otherwise, could unleash a flood of regrettable emotion. Following the curve of the corridor we see it open outward into the oval-shaped room of the Orbitarium.

In the center is a black stage with a circular pedestal in the middle. To both sides of it, following the length of the room, are rows of stuffed chairs like those you find in a modern theater. There is just enough space to walk between the folding chairs and the polished aluminum railings bordering the stage.

Behind and above us the shell of the Orbitarium is just as black as the stage and set back several feet behind the seats. Above are the fixtures that brightly light the room with a soft incandescence. The feeling of the place is that you can imagine yourself far away from home — detached, yet comforting in a way that seems natural.

We make our way along one side to the middle, fold down our seats, and settle in. I nod my head at Sheba as I fold down another seat next to me. Without hesitation she jumps into the chair and curls up.

As the other members of the audience filter in to take their seats, you lean over and in a half-whisper say, "I never knew that you were involved in such a challenging and long struggle with your work. You never said anything to me."

"We all have our own promises to keep, and keeping them is something we each do in our own way."

"But if the government is willing to kill people to keep this secret, why are you still alive?"

"If I answer that question, will you promise to focus your attention on this presentation?"

"Agreed."

Out of habit, one I suppose I've recently acquired, I glance over at Sheba. She is looking at me with gentle eyes that seem to say it's my call. At least that's what I sense, so why not?

"In a manner of speaking you can say that my life is like a Louis L'Amour western novel. I love reading them because they're simple. The good guys wear white hats, and the bad guys wear black hats. They all carry six shooters, ride fast horses, and in the end, the white hats always win."

It brings a smile to your face, "Yep, that's Louis L'Amour."

I nod appreciatively, "What you need to remember about the government is that it has white hats and black hats as well. And truth be known, there are more white hats, but the real power resides in the hands of the black hats.

"What both white and black hats have in common is that when it comes to dealing with honest seekers of truth, both must work in the shadows. Consequently, when the black hats do their worst, the white hats intervene, provided they can do so without exposing themselves."

"So in essence, the white hats are anonymously running interference for you to shield you from black hat attacks?"

That comment draws a Cheshire cat grin across my face. "Exactly! That is when I provide them with the opportunity to do so, which means no boastful arrogance or egotistical quips. It is why I always tell the truth as I know it, without unnecessary embellishment.

"This is not to say that I have one hand tied behind my back, either. As you know, when I come across someone who is confusing people with self-serving bombast and lawyerly prevarications, I have been known to hoist them with their own petards, as the old saying goes. After all, there is nothing sweeter than to turn a liar's lies against them. Now, have I answered your question? And will you pay attention to the presentation?"

Before you can answer me, the lights begin to dim as the presenter enters the room. Walking straight to the small circular pedestal in the center of the stage, she gracefully steps up.

You elbow me in the side and in a slightly jovial voice say, "Your Audrey Hepburn is here. You know the one that greeted us when we came into the Pavilion?"

"The very same one," I reply, "That's how they work it here. Each presenter gets to meet their audience face-to-face. It makes the experience more real for the presenters and creates more of a bond between them and the audience." With that, I put a finger to my closed lips, and you nod in agreement.

A series of spotlights that dot the walls begin to softly light the young woman as she stands with her head lowered toward her chest and her arms by her sides. Small gleaming metal discs glint from her fingertips along with the thin silver wire harnesses that hold these sensors on. Standing in the center of the pedestal her glossy, dark, up-swept hair gleams slightly in the soft light. Her head is just level with the audience's seats, much like the conductor in the orchestra pit of a Broadway theater — Noticeable, but not obtrusive.

With a graceful gesture of her arms, she announces, "Ladies and gentlemen, welcome to the Orbitarium. Today you are going to learn about the orbit of the Planet X System. For those of you who already enjoy astronomy, the terms I'm going to use today will be very familiar. For those of you who are new to the topic, we use these terms because they are essential to forming a universal understanding of how the Planet X System orbits our sun. Also, to illustrate the relationships between objects and distances, the holographic representations you are about to see in this presentation are not to scale."

The other lights in the Orbitarium fade to black save for those spotlighting the presenter. On the side where everyone entered the Orbitarium, two large doors slowly swing shut, sealing the corridor. Aside from the familiar red exit signs, all the audience can see is the presenter standing in the blackness.

"Now I want you to imagine that we are all floating in space beyond the orbit of Jupiter. It is here, from this point of view, where we shall begin.

Sol and Nemesis

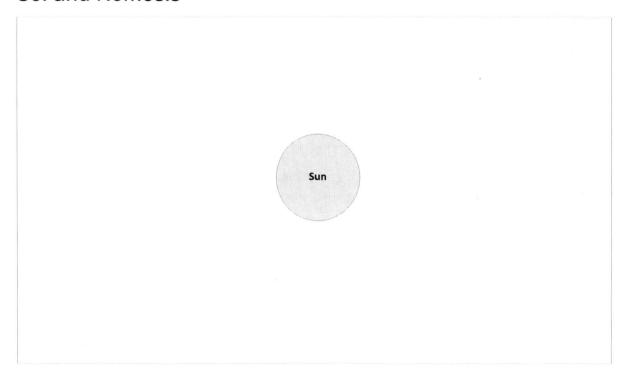

Reaching up toward the center of the ceiling, holding her hand's shoulder width apart, she brings them straight down in a flowing motion, coming to a stop just above her head. In response to her hand directions, a holographic image of our sun descends straight down above her head.

"This star in the center of our solar system is called a yellow dwarf. It is 4.5 billion years old, and in about 2.5 billion years, it will slowly begin to balloon into a red giant, spelling doom for our planet. Our yellow dwarf sun is not the most common type of star in our galaxy, nor is it alone."

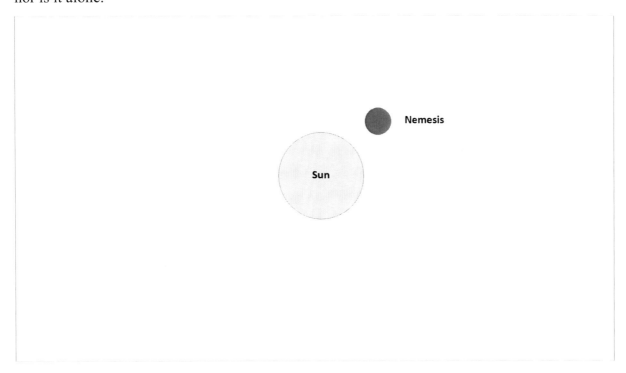

Raising her right hand, she uses two fingers to draw down another object from the ceiling. This time a small red orb lowers next to the sun at its 2 o'clock position.

"Our sun's smaller twin is Nemesis, a brown dwarf star. Interestingly enough, we've recently discovered that brown dwarfs are more common in the galaxy than previously thought. But unlike our star, they are very difficult to see in the visible light range until they are relatively close.

"Our two stars do not orbit each other, but rather the smaller, Nemesis, orbits the larger, Sol. Today you will see the journey Nemesis takes from its closest point relative to Sol out to the furthest reaches of our solar system.

"When Nemesis is far away it is not a threat to our planet, but when it is near, that is when our troubles begin. Therefore, to understand how Nemesis moves around Sol, our sun, we need a common point of reference for both stars."

The Ecliptic and Skies

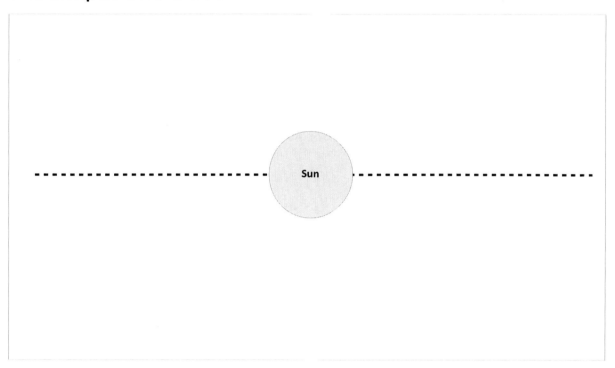

She pushes her right hand up and away, and the orb representing Nemesis fades to black.

"What I'm going to show you next is something called the ecliptic. To do that we will begin with an imaginary point in the very center of the sun."

Extending the index fingers of her two hands, she brings them together and points them at the center of the sun, and a centered, small black dot appears.

"Now I'm going to create a thin disk emanating from the center of the sun all the way out to the edge of our Orbitarium."

Spreading her two index fingers horizontally apart until they are facing in opposite directions, a thin plane of holographic light extends outward from the sun to the wall of the Orbitarium. As thin as a playing card, it is perfectly level with the tops of the seat backs. Adults are now seeing it from above, and children from below. The holographic light is gentle and does not strain the eye. It is more like climbing a tall mountain above the clouds to see a whole new horizon.

"We also call this the plane of our solar system, and I'll bet many of you enjoy passing some free time by reading the horoscope about whatever astrological sign you were born under."

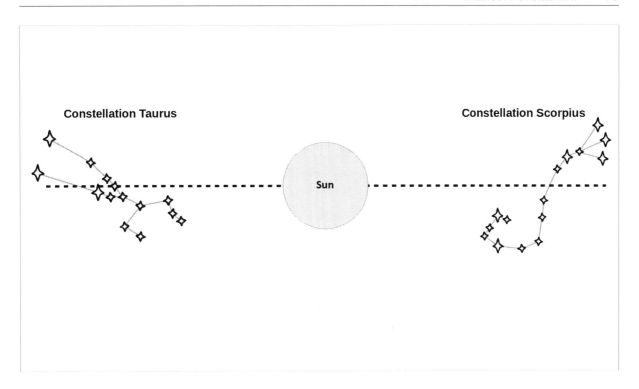

Clenching both outstretched hands to into gentle fists she extends her fingers upright, palms facing the walls and all around the Orbitarium. We begin to see holographic images of the twelve constellations of the zodiac, all centered on the ecliptic. To her left is the constellation Taurus, and to her right, the constellation Scorpius.

"As you can see, the ecliptic, or the plane of our solar system, extends from the center of the sun outward to the twelve constellations of the zodiac."

She lowers her hands to her side and all of the constellations disappear. Then, raising her hands once again, only Taurus and Scorpius appear.

"As you can now see, Taurus is to my left and Scorpius is to my right. So let's talk about these two constellations for just a moment."

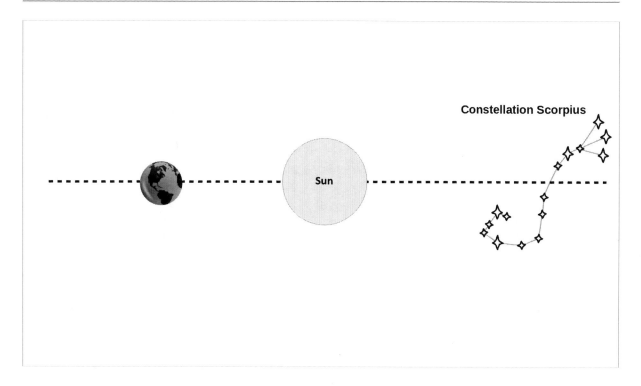

Next, she raises her left hand, and as she does the constellation Taurus disappears. Then as though she is taking hold of something, she brings her arm back down level with the ground and an orb representing the earth appears.

"Here we see our Earth to my left. Our planet, like most of the other planets in our solar system, orbits our sun at, or very near, the ecliptic. When we see the sun between Earth and the constellation Scorpius, we say the sun is in Scorpius."

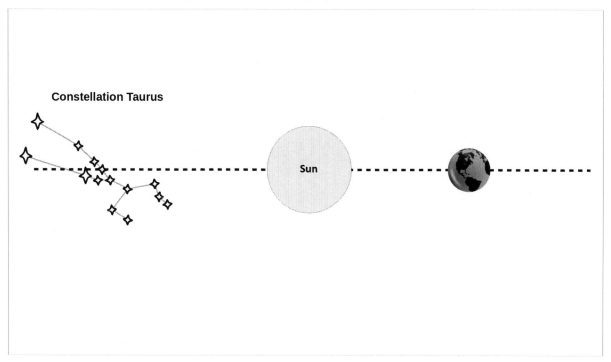

Keeping her arms and hands in the same alignment, the round pedestal she is standing on begins to pivot 180 degrees. As it does the constellation Scorpius is now replaced with the earth, and the constellation Taurus appears where the earth was.

"Conversely, when we see the sun between the Earth and the constellation Taurus, we say the sun is in Taurus. Now, let's bring it all together so we can add two new terms."

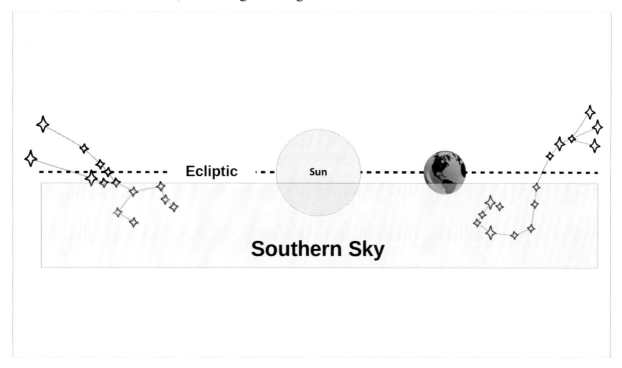

She curls both hands into loose fists and extends her fingers turning her hands palm down. Now all of the twelve constellations of the zodiac and Earth appear along with the ecliptic. Then, directly beneath the ecliptic, the entire Orbitarium is bathed in a gentle green light.

"The skies below the ecliptic are referred to as the southern sky. This is the region of space where the Planet X System spends most of its time, and thankfully it is of little concern to us when it is transiting this region of space."

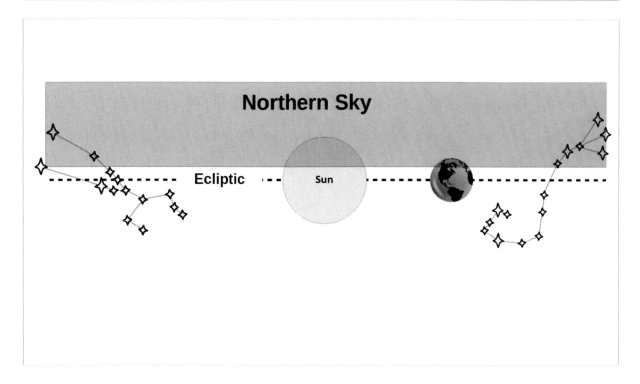

Turning her hands palms up, the gentle green light of the southern sky fades to black, and above the ecliptic, the entire Orbitarium is bathed in an eerie, reddish light.

"The sky above the ecliptic is referred to as the northern sky. This is the region of space where the Planet X System spends relatively little time in its overall orbit, but where it can cause great hardship for us as it transits through this region of space."

She claps twice and lowers her hands to her side. All of the holographic images disappear, and all we see is her standing alone on her pedestal which is lit by the soft spotlights in the Orbitarium ceiling.

"What is important for everyone here to understand is that the right perspective must always be used when contemplating the orbit of the Planet X System around our sun. This means you must always see objects in our solar system where they area relative to the ecliptic.

"For those of you who are new to this, it can be easy to confuse the ecliptic with the horizon as seen from your back yard. This is because Earth is oriented to the ecliptic which is an ever-changing thing. On the other hand, when seen from space, the ecliptic is always the ecliptic."

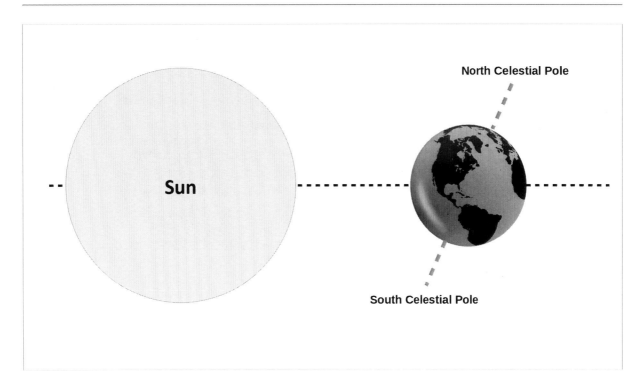

She raises her hands and with her left hand pulls down a holographic image of the sun. This one is much larger than those used before, and with her right hand she brings down a holographic image of the Earth. Then like a child finger painting, she redraws the ecliptic and then draws a line through the Earth representing the north and south celestial poles.

"As you can see here, we have a line representing our physical north and south poles. Keep in mind, these physical poles are not the same as the north and south magnetic poles used by our compasses. In fact those of you who know how to read a compass with cross-country navigation understand that our magnetic poles do move; whereas, our physical poles are permanently aligned with the center axis of our planet. It is also important to note, that while our physical north and south poles are permanently aligned with respect to our equator, they are also tilted 23.5° with respect to the ecliptic of our solar system. In other words, while the sun's equator is level with the ecliptic, ours is not. Our equator is inclined at an angle to the ecliptic."

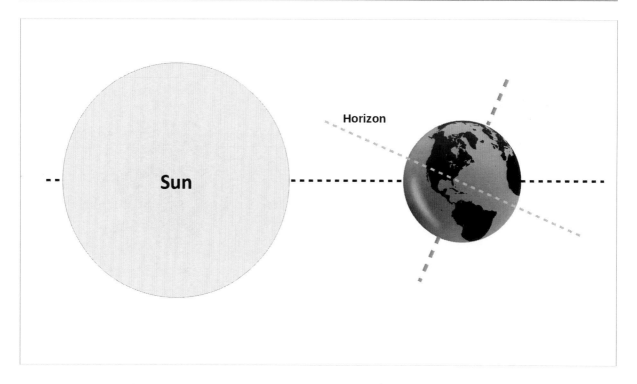

Using the index finger of her right hand, she draws a line passing through the Earth's equator.

"This line passing through the equator represents the horizon we see when we stand out in our backyard at night to observe the sky. However, this is not the ecliptic because our physical poles are tilted with respect to the ecliptic. Therefore, what we think are the northern and southern skies continually change depending on the time and season of year. Consequently, if we are using our view of the horizon in our back yard instead of the ecliptic to understand where the Planet X System is at any particular time, we will mistake its true location."

With a pleasant smile, she points her index fingers straight ahead, with the left above and the right below as the pedestal begins to swivel 180° in the opposite direction. As she turns, all of the holograms in the Orbitarium fade to black, and a magnificent night sky view of the Milky Way paints itself all along the walls.

"The Milky Way is the galaxy that contains our solar system. It happens to be a convenient way to see the ecliptic with your own eyes."

Going from upper left to lower right she paints a line with her index finger, that superimposes itself on the center of the Milky Way.

"What you see with this red line is the ecliptic, the plane of our solar system. This will help us to see how the Planet X System orbits our sun relative to the ecliptic."

She claps her hands twice and again the entire Orbitarium goes dark. The spotlights lighting her intensify and illuminate her fully as the pedestal beneath her begins turning slowly.

"Before I introduce you to the Planet X System, we need to talk about the profound differences between this small mini-constellation and our own solar system. Up to this point you have learned about the ecliptic or the plane of our solar system. All of the major planets in our solar system orbit the sun on or near the ecliptic in counterclockwise orbits.

"Interestingly, all of the major planets in the Planet X System are in counterclockwise orbits around Sol's Nemesis. However, unlike the major planets that orbit our star, the major planets orbiting Nemesis each have their own orbital plane, and each is significantly different from the others. "This is because our solar system formed differently from that of the Planet X System. The planets in our system follow a counterclockwise orbit around the sun, near or on the ecliptic, because this process began with the very birth of our solar system.

"What makes the Planet X System different is that it was not created with the birth of our solar system. but It was created elsewhere in the galaxy. Traveling through the vast distances of space, it gathered its own planets and moons until it was eventually captured by the gravity of our sun. This is why the Planet X System's orbit around our sun resembles a comet more than anything else.

"Consequently, the Planet X System plays by its own set of rules. So, if we are to truly understand it, we must do so understanding that it has its own unique set of rules. Instead of comparing the behaviors of its objects with those of our own solar system, ladies and gentlemen, we could say that the Planet X System marches to the beat of a different drummer. With that in mind let us now identify the major objects of the planet X system."

Major Objects of the Planet X System

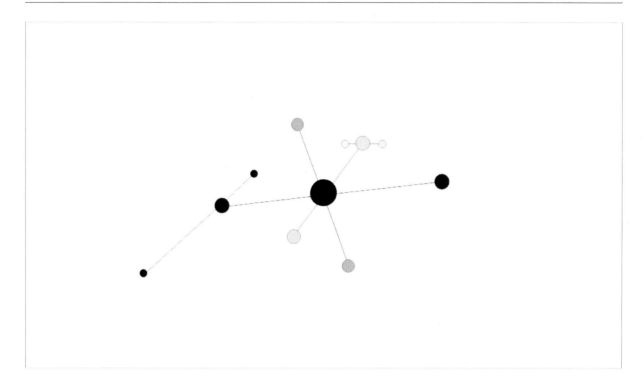

She claps her hands again and reaches upward with her hands in a cupped position and lowers them straight down. Near the ceiling a new hologram begins to form as it slowly lowers to hover directly before the audience. All the major planets and moons are tracking in their respective orbital paths around Nemesis at the center of the hologram.

"As you can see, at the center of the Planet X System is the small brown dwarf star called Nemesis. Around Nemesis orbit planets, and some of them have moons that orbit in ways that seem haphazard when compared with the planets and moons of our own solar system. As we said before, The Planet X System marches to the beat of a different drummer.

"In the Hall of Heroes, you learned about the story of the planet Pluto. When Pluto was discovered in 1930 by Clyde Tombaugh, it was thought to be Neptune's perturber or Planet X. That was until 1978 with the discovery of Pluto's moon Charon. Pluto was determined to be only 60% the size of our own moon, and therefore it lacked the mass to perturb the orbit of Neptune.

"There are more planets in the Planet X System than the three we are going to show you today. By some estimates there are seven, but we're only going to focus on the planets with sufficient mass to perturb Earth as they pass by us —— the planets larger than Pluto. So, with that in mind, let's begin by introducing the major objects in the Planet X System."

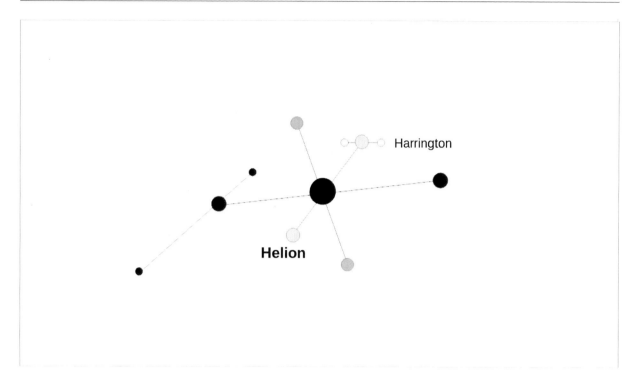

She points her finger at Helion. It begins pulsing and glows more brightly, as does its moon, Harrington.

"Helion is the innermost major planet to Nemesis, and it has one moon approximately the size of our own moon. This moon is named Harrington in honor of Robert Sutton Harrington, the U.S. Naval Observatory chief astronomer, who many believe was assassinated in 1993 for sharing his work on Planet X.

"If we were to use the face of a clock as our reference, we would see Helion orbiting Nemesis between the 2 o'clock and 8 o'clock positions.

"Helion is a bright, gaseous planet approximately 3 1/2 times the size of Earth which makes it somewhat comparable in size to Uranus. If we were to see it from another one of the planets orbiting Nemesis, it would look like a smaller second sun in that system."

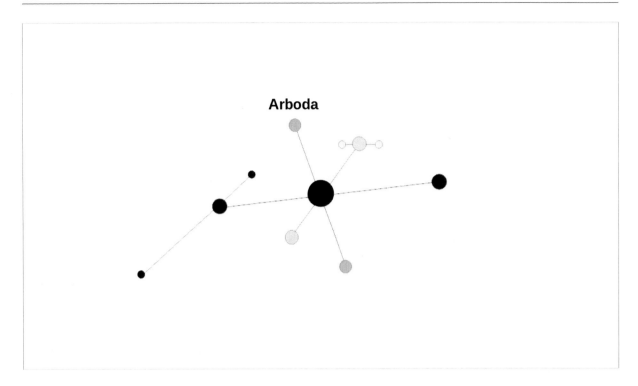

Arboda

She snaps her finger and points at Arboda. Helion returns to its previous state, and now Arboda begins pulsing and glows more brightly.

"Arboda is the second innermost major planet to Nemesis and has no moon. If we were to use the face of a clock as our reference, we would see Arboda orbiting Nemesis between the 11 o'clock and 5 o'clock positions. Arboda is a rocky planet approximately 2 1/2 times the size of Earth."

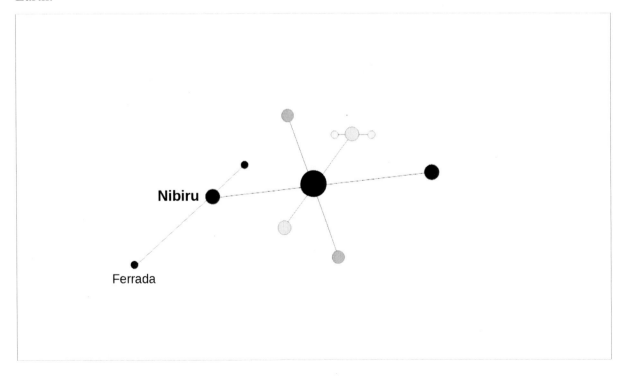

Nibiru

Ferrada

She snaps her fingers again and this time points to Nibiru. Arboda returns to its previous state, and now Nibiru and its moon Ferrada begin pulsing and glowing more brightly.

"This is the Planet Nibiru. It is a rocky planet made famous by the translations of the Sumerian texts by Zecharia Sitchin. Nibiru translates to 'place of crossing' or 'planet of crossing,' which is an apt title because Nibiru is the outermost major planet from Nemesis in the Planet X System.

"If we were to use the face of a clock as our reference, we would see Nibiru orbiting Nemesis between the 8 o'clock and 2 o'clock positions. At six times the size of Earth it is the largest major planet in orbit around Nemesis. Its moon, Ferrada, named after Chilean Astronomer Carlos Muñoz Ferrada, is approximately the size of our own moon."

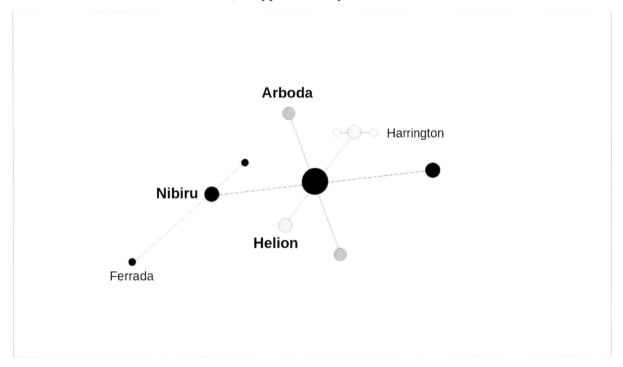

She snaps her fingers again and Nibiru, and its moon, Ferrada, return to their previous state. Now the system appears as it first did.

"And there you have it ladies and gentlemen, the major objects in the Planet X System: Helion with its moon Harrington, Arboda with no moon, and Nibiru with its moon Ferrada.

"Earlier I told you that we only the presented major objects which have enough mass to perturb our own planet as the Planet X System flies through the core of our own solar system. When our presentation here in the Orbitarium is finished, we invite you to visit the Tribulation Carousel Theater to learn exactly how these objects will move through our solar system during the flyby.

"Now let's see exactly how the Planet X System orbits our Sun."

Orbital Path of the Planet X System

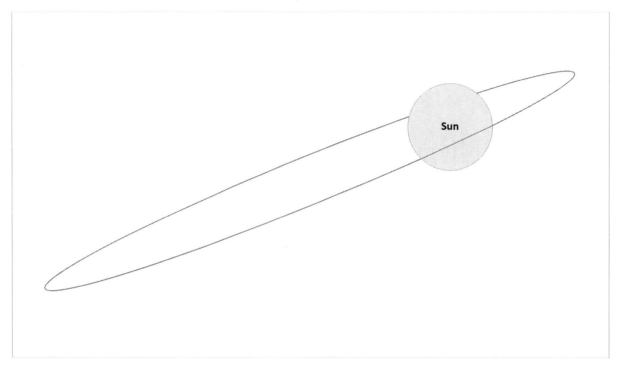

She snaps the fingers of both hands the Planet X System hologram fades to black. Stretching her hands outwards mid way from the top of the Orbitarium, she partially cups her hands, pulling them toward her, and brings down another hologram of the sun. It comes to a stop above her head halfway between the floor and the ceiling.

Then, with her fingers outstretched and her palms facing to the side, she makes a small pushing motion, and the sun begins turning slowly. Closing her right hand into a loose fist, she points her index finger and makes a sweeping elliptical motion around the sun, as an orbital path, shown as a red line, appears around the sun.

The furthest point of the orbit is below the sun and nearly reaches the audience's seating area. With the sun revolving in the center, the orbital path circles it in a synchronous movement to give the audience a 360-degree view of the orbital path.

"Here you see the orbital path of the Planet X System. While we're very familiar with the orbits of our own planets around the Sun, the Planet X System itself orbits the sun much like a long-period comet. According to Kepler's Second Law the closer the Planet X System is to our Sun, the stronger the Sun's gravitational pull on it will be, and the faster it will move. Conversely, the farther the Planet X System is from our Sun the weaker the Sun's gravitational pull on it will be which is where the Planet X System slows down in its orbit. Ergo, what we have is an orbital path that has variable speeds, depending on the location."

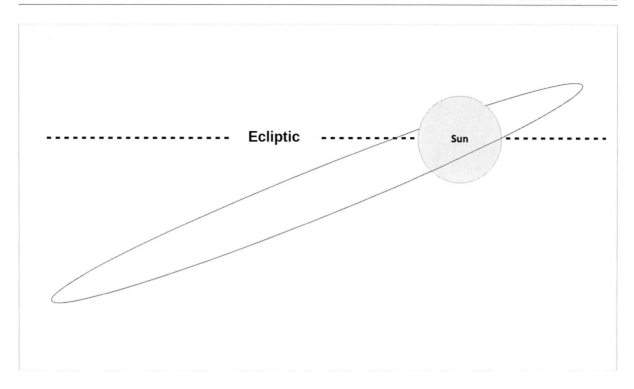

She brings her two index fingers together, and then in a single sweeping motion, points horizontally apart in opposite directions. As before, a thin plane of holographic light extends outward from the center of the sun to the walls of the Orbitarium.

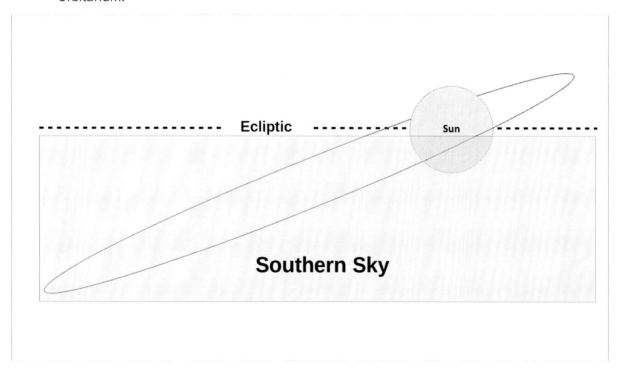

"Here as before, we see the ecliptic. What is immediately obvious is that the better part of the Planet X System's orbit is below the ecliptic."

She points her right hand to the left and just under the ecliptic, and then sweeps it to the right. From the ecliptic, the hologram shows a transparent green overlay.

"As you recall, the southern sky is where the Planet X System spends most of its time, and where it causes us little concern while it transits this region of space."

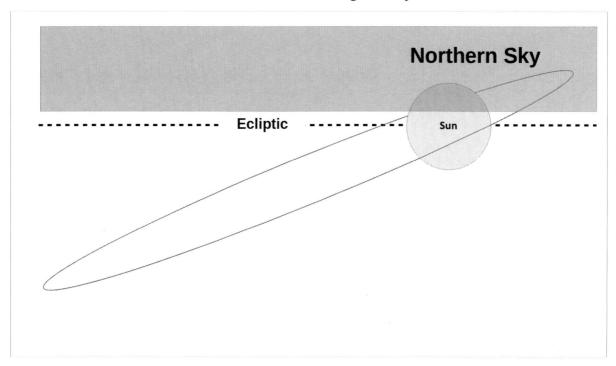

She points her left hand to the right and just above the ecliptic and snaps her finger. As she sweeps her hand to the right, the transparent green overlay fades as a transparent red overlay appears above the ecliptic, leaving the hologram with only a transparent red overlay above the ecliptic.

"Conversely, the northern sky is the region of space where the Planet X System spends relatively little time in its overall orbit, but it is where it can cause us great hardships. So, the first step in understanding how the Planet X System orbits our sun is to see what the Planet Uranus and the brown dwarf star at the heart of the Planet X System have in common."

Planet Uranus and Nemesis

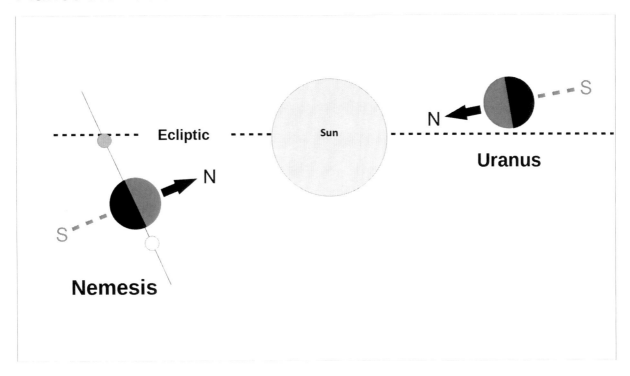

She claps her hands twice, and the entire hologram fades away. Bringing her hands together with loose fists, she twists them in opposite directions, her left hand down and her right hand up. Then she draws them apart until they are pointing in opposite directions. Above her, the familiar hologram of the sun appears, and then the ecliptic swells outwards in all directions to the walls of Orbitarium as red and blue objects appear on either side of the sun. The one to the left of the sun and below the ecliptic is Nemesis with its planets. The one without planets above the ecliptic to the right of the Sun is Uranus.

"What we see here is Uranus above the ecliptic and Nemesis below it. These holographic objects are divided into two hemispheres, blue for Northern Hemisphere and red for Southern Hemisphere. As you see here, Uranus is tipped on its side with its north pole pointing towards the sun. This is because it has an axial tilt of approximately 98° which makes it a bit of an odd-ball in our solar system.

"It is believed that Uranus's extreme axial tilt is the result of being struck by a large object a long time ago — a case of cosmic hit-and-run if you will. Could the culprit be an object in the Planet X System? That's a good question. As you can see, the axial tilt of the Nemesis brown dwarf star is also approximately 90° which makes its north pole point at the sun, just like Uranus.

"The point, we must always remember, is the Planet X System is tilted with its north pole always facing the sun. So for the remainder of this presentation, we will continue to use this two-color representation for Nemesis to help you visualize its polar orientation as it orbits the sun."

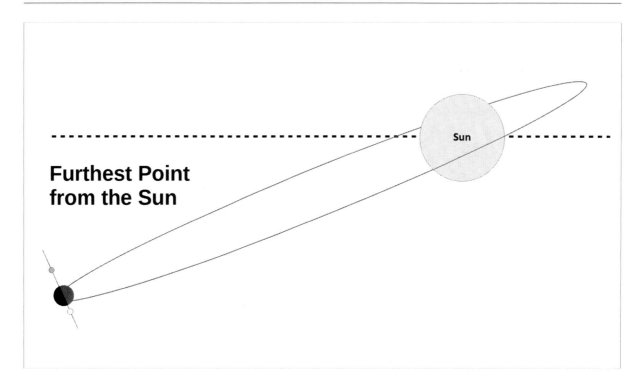

**Furthest Point
from the Sun**

She points her right hand at Uranus, snaps her fingers, and the planet fades away leaving the Sun, Nemesis, and the ecliptic. With that, she pushes the sun to the side, and using her right index finger, paints the Planet X System's orbital path as before. She then uses the thumb and index finger of her left hand to reduce the holograph of the Planet X System and moves it to the furthest part of its orbital path in the southern sky.

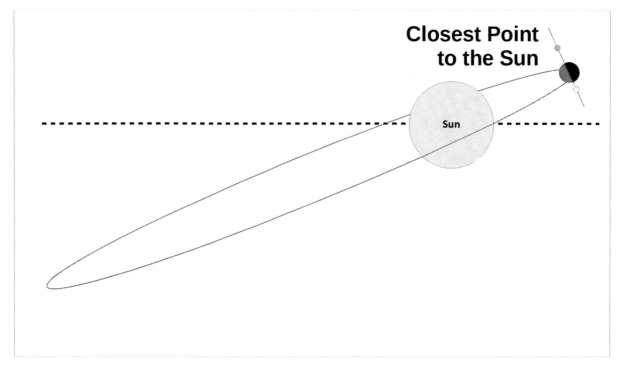

**Closest Point
to the Sun**

Keeping her left thumb and index finger on the Planet X System holograph, she moves it to the opposite side of the orbit.

"Here we see the Planet X System at its nearest point to the sun. This point in its orbit is called perihelion, and it is important that you remember this term. This is because this is the point in the Planet X System's orbit where things can become very difficult for us. With that we're ready to see a complete orbit of the Planet X System around our sun."

3,600 Lunar Years

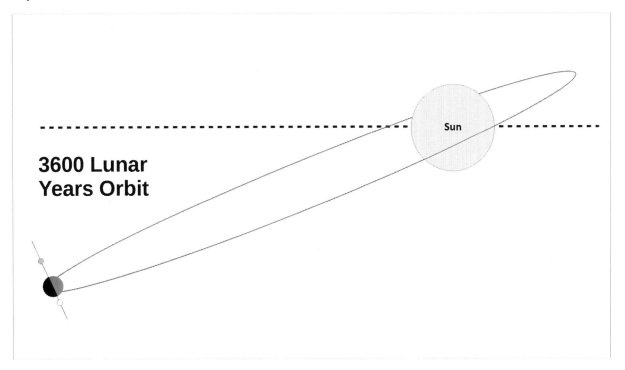

3600 Lunar Years Orbit

Keeping her left thumb and index finger on the Planet X System holograph, she moves it back to the point of aphelion in its orbit.

"The Planet X System has a 3,600 lunar year orbit. This means it takes 3,600 lunar years for the system to leave its point of aphelion and to return there. It is important to understand the distinction of a lunar year because we use the Gregorian calendar which is solar-based. The lunar year is based on the cycles of the moon's phases; the Gregorian calendar is based on our planet's orbit around the sun. This results in a lunar year of about 354 days, and a Gregorian year of about 365 days.

"Is the difference significant? Absolutely, the last flyby of the Planet X System occurred during the time of the Hebrew Exodus from Egypt. When you calculate the orbit using lunar years, the orbit of the Planet X System matches perfectly with historical records. Now let's move forward to the next point in the orbit."

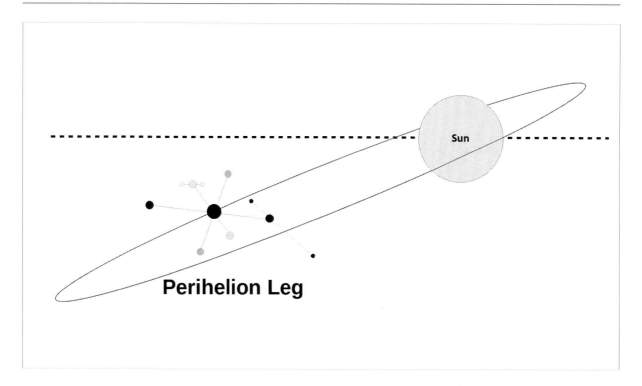

Perihelion Leg

Keeping her left thumb and index finger on the Planet X System holograph, she advances it along the orbital path along its inbound path towards our Sun.

"Like some comets, such as Comet Halley, the Planet X System follows a clockwise orbit around our sun. Here we see it rising up from the southern sky towards the northern sky on its perihelion leg."

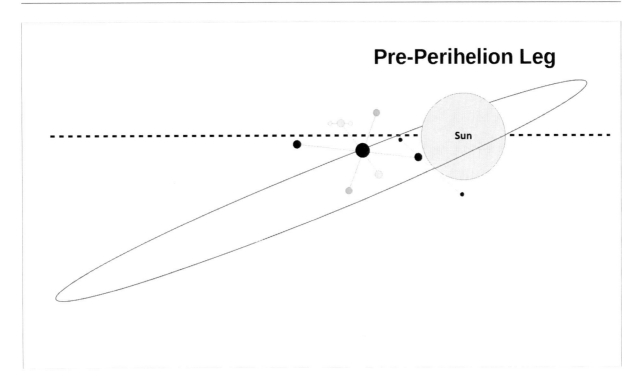

Pre-Perihelion Leg

Keeping her left thumb and index finger on the Planet X System holograph, she advances it along the orbital path from its inbound path to a point near the ecliptic.

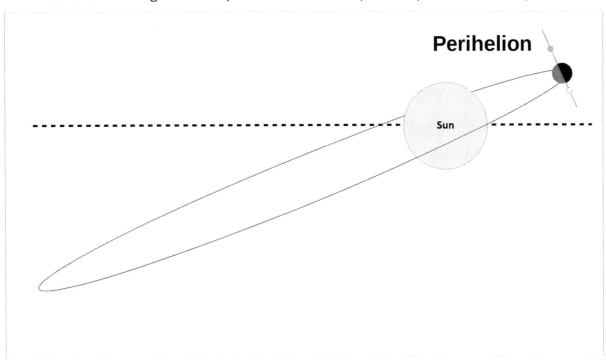

Perihelion

"As the Planet X System approaches the ecliptic, it enters its pre-perihelion leg where it begins accelerating towards its point of perihelion, and the closer it comes to the Sun, the stronger the Sun's gravitational pull on it becomes."

Keeping her left thumb and index finger on the Planet X System holograph, she advances it along the orbital path from its inbound path to its point of perihelion.

"When the Planet X System reaches its point of perihelion, it will accelerate even more quickly as it whips around our sun. Perihelion is also the point where the Planet X System is at its closest distance to our Sun, and here is where the real danger to earth can begin."

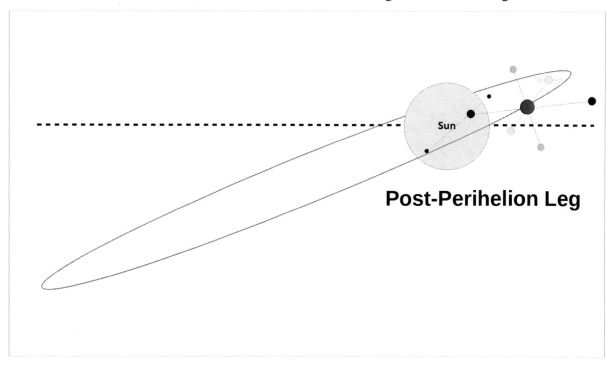

Keeping her left thumb and index finger on the Planet X System holograph, she advances it along the orbital path from its outbound path to its point of post-perihelion.

"Here we see the Planet X System in its post-perihelion leg, between perihelion and the ecliptic. When you visit the Tribulation Carousel Theater, you will learn why we call the post-perihelion leg, from perihelion to the ecliptic, "the kill zone." That's when you'll learn the bad news."

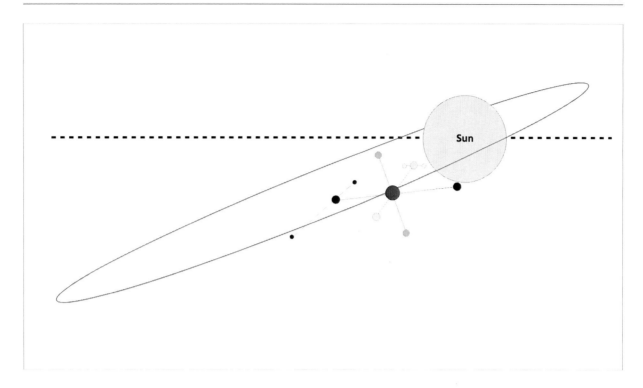

Keeping her left thumb and index finger on the Planet X System holograph, she advances it along its aphelion leg in the southern sky.

"The good news is that as the Planet X System passes its point of perihelion, it will whip around our sun. It will begin to go faster as it heads towards its outbound aphelion leg, towards the southern sky, where it eventually slows again. This is the opposite of the inbound leg because the further the Planet X System is from our sun, the weaker its gravitational pull becomes on it. It moves more slowly in its orbit when it is farther away."

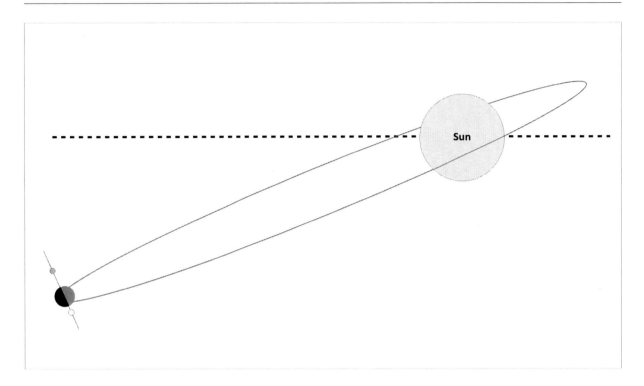

Keeping her left thumb and index finger on the Planet X System holograph, she advances it along the orbital path back to its point of aphelion in the southern sky.

"But do not begin celebrating until you've visited the Tribulation Carousel Theater."

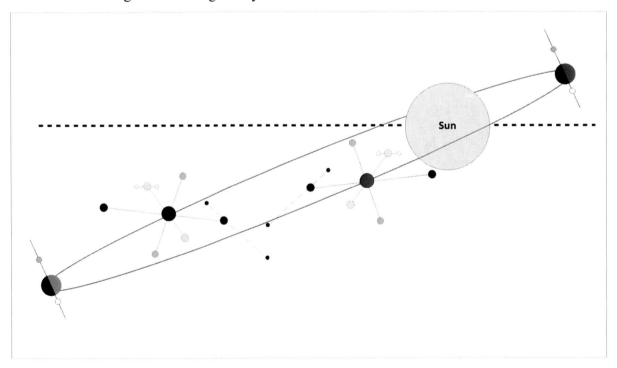

Now she snaps her fingers three times along the previous points of the orbit, creating copies of the Planet X System holographic image at each point.

"Here we see the Planet X System at its point of aphelion in the southern sky, then again where it is on its inbound leg towards the northern sky, then at its point of perihelion where it is at its closest distance to the sun, and finally it is on its outbound leg in the southern sky back to its point of aphelion.

"I'm showing you these four points because earlier you saw how the north pole of Nemesis and the north pole of the planet Uranus face the sun due to the extreme axial tilt of both bodies. So here you see that not only is the Planet X System tilted on its side, its North Pole always faces our sun. This is especially important when it is in the northern sky. You'll learn why when you visit the Tribulation Carousel Theater."

> She claps both hands, and the complete holograph fades to black as the ceiling spotlights illuminate her more brightly. On the opposite side of the Orbitarium where everyone entered earlier, two large doors now swing apart to reveal an illuminated exit corridor.

"This concludes our presentation. We hope you enjoyed it. As you leave, please be sure to pick up one of our color brochures with representations of the holograms used in this presentation. Thank you."

The entire audience claps loudly. It has been an excellent presentation, and the presenter smiles appreciatively as folks begin to file out of the Orbitarium.

I stroke Sheba's head, "I think I see someone who needs some time on the grass."

"She's not the only one," you chime in.

"Well then, that makes it unanimous."

As we enter the corridor with large images on the wall from the presentation you ask, "So what's next, the Tribulation Carousel Theater?"

"Nope," I answer, "School is out for the day. Tomorrow we're going somewhere else, but we'll come another day for the theater. That's for sure. In the meantime the plan for the rest of today is; first, we take the pause that refreshes. Then, I suggest that we hit the food court for a hearty meal, and afterward, take a spin on the overhead monorail so that we can scope out the park."

"Works for me," you beam.

"And what do you say, old girl?"

"Woof woof! Woof woof!"

5

What's at Stake

This morning I find you at the griddle as usual, but this time you're making buckwheat pancakes. That's a new twist.

"Well, there you are!" you call out to me, "Another late night tinkering away no doubt. Pull up a chair and enjoy some gluten-free pancakes this morning."

"Gluten-free?"

"Yup, the conversation yesterday was about Celiac disease and kids with ADHD. You know Attention Deficit Hyperactivity Disorder. So while you and I were out on our adventure, everyone else decided it was time to experiment with some gluten-free recipes and see which ones the kids will like."

"And buckwheat pancakes are your secret weapon?"

You flip a cake in the air with the grace of a Cirque du Soleil performer. "That and my homemade blueberry syrup," you reply to a round of praises from the breakfast table.

"Well then, I'd love a stack of those tasty-looking buckwheat pancakes. Could someone please pass the secret syrup?"

The pancakes were amazingly good, and I couldn't bear to leave a crumb on my plate. Everyone began to clear the table and in a few minutes the kitchen was in order. One of the others said, "We know, we know. You two need to go on your adventure for the day. See you later."

"Thanks, everyone," I say as we bid our farewells and head off in the direction of the caretaker's cottage and workshop, about fifty yards from the main house towards the woods.

As usual, Sheba spots us on the move and follows alongside as we ramble along the path to the cottage. "So, what's the lesson today? And does it have something to do with the Tribulation Carousel Theater?" you ask.

"We'll do that tomorrow. Today you need to learn what's at stake?"

"Why so?"

"Because what you will see tomorrow in The Tribulation Carousel Theater will be very disturbing, unless you're prepared for what you will learn. Remember, this is not about fear-inducing 'ghost stories.' It's about leadership, and this is the point of what you will learn today. To be effective you must shape your survival paradigm. Then, and only then, will be you ready for what you see tomorrow. Meanwhile, we need to check on something. And oh, by the way," I say as I unlock the large sliding door on the front of the small cottage, "Can you keep a secret?"

"You know I can."

"That's good," I say as the door slides open, letting the morning sun pour in. On the opposite wall, the light casts small shadows on the many tools hanging in orderly rows on metal hooks on the pegboards above the workbench.

On the center of the workbench is an old television, the kind with vacuum tubes and mechanical tuners with their large knobs. You point to it and ask, "So is that old television your latest tinkering project?"

"As a matter of fact, it is. Do me a favor. Shut this door behind us," I turn on the lights and fire up that old TV as you slowly pull the door closed with an expectant look on your face.

"It's tough to find old vacuum tubes these days. Thankfully all of the tubes in this set work just fine," I note as I switch on the set, "Just needed to clean the contacts on the tuner dials a bit. I would have had to, anyway, as I needed to make a special modification. You'll see in just a moment."

The television flickers to life as a few bars pass up along the screen. After a few moments, the picture settles in.

"Wow!" you comment as you pull up a stool and sit down, "I haven't seen clothes like that since..."

"Since the 1980s?" I interject.

"Come to think of it, yes."

"Well, what you see here is the very first broadcast of the Cable News Network on June 1, 1980."

"You're right," you add, "and there is Ted Turner dedicating CNN in a speech that day, which begs the question, why do I see this?"

"An excellent question, the reason is that two things happened in 1980 in Georgia that would have long-lasting ramifications. Obviously, CNN was launched. There is something else, something many people do not know. It was dedicated in late March of that year before a group of a few hundred onlookers. Today we know it as the Georgia Guidestones, but some call it the American Stonehenge. And yes, some call it the Illuminati Ten Commandments for the 21st century, while others believe that CNN founder Ted Turner had a hand in its making because he is such a strong environmentalist."

"All of which is speculation, of course."

"I am delighted to hear you say that because most folks who visit the monument arrive filled with predetermined notions and prejudices. However, to understand the Georgia Guidestones as a faith-based tribulation leader, you need to visit it with an objective, open mind and that's exactly what we're going to do today. We are going to use the time machine to visit it in-situ as the archaeologists say, as it was on the afternoon of June 1, 1980. There we will talk about what is really at stake in the coming tribulation."

"Is this the secret you are talking about?"

"No," I answer with a big grin. "I have been working on a treat for everyone, and I'm saving it for the big farewell dinner." I nod my head towards the corner of the cottage, "See that old refrigerator over there?"

"Yup."

"An old friend of mine is an avid home brewer. Not only does he make fantastic ales and porters, but he also has a passion for good, old-fashioned homemade root beer. The other day, he shared a bottle with me, and it was amazing. It made me understand what it should taste like, and why what we buy in the store today is just a cheap artificial knock-off, for the most part. I asked him about serving his root beer for everyone on the last night of our getaway here at the house, and he agreed to set me up with the concentrate and gadgets. I've been making it right here in this cottage from day one."

"What's in the concentrate?"

"All he told me is that it's an old recipe with mishmash of roots and bark, flowers, leaves, berries, and what-not. The recipe dates back to Early America when root beer was a staple in the American diet. And here's the interesting thing, after you make it you leave it in the refrigerator for a few days to improve the flavor even more, and the very first batch I made is just about ready. Care for a taste?"

Your face lights up, "I never thought you'd ask."

I open the refrigerator and inside are rows of blue glass soda bottles with French wire and gasket caps, all filled with root beer. I pull out two bottles and hand one to you, "Just keep in mind, I'm an amateur, so no promises here. By the way, the secret is that nobody is to know about this until the last day of our visit here."

You take your bottle in hand and open the cap and clink it on mine, "To the secret," you toast as you take a small sip. Your eyes light up, and so you take another sip and then, to my delight, you gulp down half the bottle. "Wow! This is amazing stuff," you exclaim, wiping your lips.

I take a drink from my bottle and find myself equally pleased that my efforts have borne such wonderful fruit, "That, it is!"

Placing a small tin on the floor, I pour the rest of my bottle into it, and Sheba laps it up happily. It appears she appreciates an excellent home-made root beer as well.

"So, what do you say we put some ice and some bottles of root beer into that little cooler over there in the corner and go for a visit in the time machine to the Georgia Guidestones?"

"Wherever the root beer goes, I go," you say with a grin. So we clean out the cooler, fill it with ice and bottles of root beer, close up the cottage, and hike out to the time machine.

Settling behind the control panel, Sheba curls up on the floor behind us as the hatch automatically closes. With that, I instruct the machine to take us to 34°13′55.40″N 82°53′39.80″W in Elbert County, Georgia, and set the time for late in the afternoon on June 1, 1980. The machine begins whirring; moments later there we are.

Before us is the large granite monument. Nineteen feet, three inches tall, its ten guidelines for the 21st century are inscribed in English, Spanish, Swahili, Sanskrit, Hebrew, Arabic, Chinese, and Russian.

"By the way," you note, "You mentioned that some call it the Illuminati 10 Commandments, which is completely wrong. Only God can give us commandments, as he did with Moses. As to this monument, you can call them guidelines, but certainly not commandments."

I pat you on the back, "I think we're going to have a fantastic conversation." Looking down at Sheba I ask, "What do you think girl?"

"Woof woof!"

Intermediary Wyatt C. Martin of the Granite City Bank (right), and Charlie Clamp, sandblaster on **The Georgia Guidestones** project look over one of the stones after the message had been inscribed. This the English version, is one of eight languages used on the stones.

"Well, there it is. Let's take a walk around the monument as I fill you in on a few details." As we walk around the monument, I explain that it was commissioned by a man called "W. C. Christian." A curiously unknown person, most believe he was a member of a secret society like the Rosicrucians or Freemasons because of the precise astronomical viewing ports built into the monument.

Pointing at the slits, often referred to as mail slots and a channel, I explain how each one is used to observe different aspects of the sky. For example, one channel is used to find the celestial pole. I also explain that people occasionally report feeling strange energies near the monument, similar to the energies experienced by those who visit crop circles in England. However, neither of us is sensing this today.

"So what do you think is the real story about this monument?" you ask with a puzzled expression, "Is it the elites telling us that this is how they want to reorganize the world? In which case, I can see why a lot of people would hate it."

I nod in agreement, "It's why I chose this day. The monument is still obscure and only the locals know about it at this time. Those interested have already come by to see it, and so we'll have it to ourselves for the afternoon without being disturbed. On the other hand, if we were to make this trip in your present time surveillance cameras would be monitoring us, because in 2008 when Barack Obama was elected president, angry protesters defaced the monument with polyurethane paint and graffiti."

"So do you think they were justified because this monument was erected by elites who want to treat us like slaves?"

"Well, there is an argument for that given that it's talking about a massive, 90% plus reduction of the world population, a one-world government, and a new form of spirituality based on, 'Rule passion — faith — tradition — and all things with tempered reason.' Would that even allow a free expression of faith at all?"

I stop walking for a moment and turn to face you, "If you make an uninformed decision about the significance of this monument and leave it at that, then as a faith-based tribulation leader you will fail the community you are destined to lead for the first time." You raise your eyebrows at me.

"Today I'm going to offer you an interpretation of this monument that is not discussed anywhere else because there is a connection between this monument and what the Planet X System is about to do to our planet."

"Which, as I gather, is what I'll learn tomorrow in the Tribulation Carousel Theater."

"Now you're catching on," I point to a slab a few feet west of the monument, "That's the flagstone, and it has some useful information about the monument, its celestial alignments, languages, and so forth. Go over there and study it while I get the cooler out of the time machine. Then meet me over by the English-language slab."

"Sure enough, and don't forget Sheba's tin. I'm sure she'll want some more root beer as well."

"Woof, woof!"

"You got it; see you at the English slab." As I walk back to the time machine, I notice Sheba is following you to make sure she'll get her root beer instead of following me. Odd thing that. What is it about this dog? Oh well, that's a mystery for another day.

I return with the cooler and Sheba's tin to find you leaning up against the Russian-language slab, studying the ten guidelines in English on the opposite slab.

"If you ask me, it looks like a Malthusian New World Order monument," you observe dryly.

I sit down on the ground with my back to the Russian-language slab and put the cooler to my left side, "Or some Agenda 21 plan by elites to control all life on Earth, beginning with a massive reduction in the human population."

You nod in agreement as I pat the ground next to me, "Sheba, come sit beside me."

As you slide down the granite slab to sit beside me, Sheba rambles up beside me and muzzles the cooler. "OK girl, it's time for root beer." I place her tin pan on the ground next to me and take two bottles out of the cooler. Opening both, I pour a little from each into her tin, then hand one to you.

Sheba laps up her root beer with relish as you take a few sips from your bottle, "I never asked you if you've got a name for this root beer."

"I call it 'Backside Root Beer.'"

You choke a little bit on your drink and shake your head, chuckling, "Why would you name it after a part of the human anatomy that every parent comes to know while diapering their firstborn?"

"There you go; you've jumped to a premature conclusion. A mistake most people make, and it's why they do not understand the real significance of this monument as it pertains to surviving the Planet X tribulation."

You lean your head back, "So what does the backside have to do with Planet X?"

"For years you've heard me say to audiences, 'I'll catch you on the backside.' So then, what is the backside, you may ask? It's what happens after the tribulation when we once again see blue skies and taste sweet water. That's what I mean by the backside. Each time I take a sip of this root beer I'm thinking of a new beginning for humankind. The coming tribulation is not about the end of this civilization for me; it is about a clean slate for the beginning of the next civilization."

You tap your bottle on mine and say, "I'll drink to that." Taking a long slow drink, you finally set your bottle down. "OK, no more premature conclusions. Now, tell me about these ten guidelines."

"Fair enough, here is what we'll do. You'll read them one at a time, and then I'll give you my explanation for each one. Keep in mind, what I'll tell you are reference points and nothing more. You still have to sort this out on your own. So let's begin. Read the first one at the top."

"Maintain humanity under 500,000,000 in perpetual balance with nature."

"Now tell me, what is missing from this first guideline?"

You take your time, and I see you whispering to yourself at times. Finally, you say, in a tentative voice, "It doesn't tell us how we get to less than half a billion souls on the planet."

"Brilliant! I couldn't have said it better. Now I'll tell you how we arrive at a half a billion souls on the planet. The vast majority of humankind lives on or near an ocean shoreline. If you're an elite, the fastest way to dramatically reduce the global population is to trick people into ignoring the signs of a clear and present danger, so they will die in place. That way the tsunamis created by earthquakes, impact events, and the pole shift will drown billions of people."

"This is why there is so much disinformation, propaganda, and cover-up on the Planet X topics. Setting people up to fail by keeping them in ignorance has long been the agenda of the elites. As to the few that do survive, they will be severely weakened and in smaller, more manageable numbers for the elites to control."

Sadness fills your face, and you shake your head, "It is unbelievably inhumane. It is practical in a way only evil, sociopathic minds could contemplate."

"I know. It's a hard one to get your head around, but that is the way it is. Now, read the second guideline."

"Guide reproduction wisely – improving fitness and diversity."

"And what is missing from this guideline?"

This time you answer more quickly, "It doesn't say who is guiding the reproduction, or how."

"Bravo! In other words, one man's eugenics is another man's concentration camp. The open-ended aspect of this particular guideline is disturbing, to say the least. Now, read the third guideline."

"Unite humanity with a living new language."

Now I smile, "This third guideline presents us with an intriguing possibility as to the nature of those who created this monument. A living new language can only be a language not currently in use, and not a dead language like Latin. Ergo, the secret society that created this monument is probably not affiliated with the Roman Catholic Church, which is not to say their hands are clean, either. Now, read the fourth guideline."

"Rule passion — faith — tradition — and all things with tempered reason."

"Keeping the words 'rule' and 'tempered' in mind, what do you think is the message of this guideline, not for us as societies, mind you, but as individuals."

"Thank you for that last clarification, because for society, it reeks of thought police and totalitarian control with 'reason.' But on a personal level..." your voice trails away as you ponder what you're going to say next.

Patiently waiting for you to continue, I look over at Sheba's tin. She has licked it clean. So I pour a little more of my root beer in it while making a mental note to myself that she's had her limit for the day.

You shift your position on the ground, look over at me, and finally say, "Keeping the words 'rule' and 'tempered' in mind, my guess is that this fourth guideline is a piece of advice about balance. That ruling with reason is the best way to keep all things in a satisfying proportion."

"Wow, I'm impressed. You did better than I did the first time. Now let me add something. This fourth guideline specifically mentions passion, faith, and tradition with a general reference to all other things. Ergo, what it says is that we each must balance our passion, faith, and tradition in proportion to all other things. Ergo, passion, faith, and tradition must not be allowed to solely govern your thinking to the exclusion of more intellectual attributes. This is a very important guideline, so please keep it in mind as we'll come back to it later. Now read the fifth guideline to me."

"Protect people and nations with fair laws and just courts."

"Now, what could have possibly prompted the creators of a monument erected here in America to say such a thing?" I grin.

"You must be kidding!" you answer wistfully. "My God, look at what Washington, D.C. has become, a cesspool of unfair laws favoring special interests. As for the courts, how can there be just courts with all these unfair laws? But that's old news. What I really want to know is with all this greedy insanity dispiriting the country, where is the seed of this? From where did all this originate, assuming there is one place?"

Sheba eyes me intently as I hold up the blue bottle to see how much root beer is left. About two good swigs, I guess. So I take one swig, set the bottle down to save the second for later, and fish a dog biscuit out of my shirt pocket. "No more root beer for you girl, how about a little treat?" I break off a piece and hand it to her.

"What, you're thinking about your answer?"

Leaning my head back against the granite, I sigh, "So you want to know the seed of the evil that has overtaken our country?"

"Yes."

"Get in line. Better yet, slap that question in a search engine and it seems there are about as many answers today as there are people interested in answering it."

"Let's not talk about how people see it today," you hold up your bottle of root beer, "Imagine that I am a backside survivor drinking my bottle of Backside Root Beer around the campfire with other survivors. How will the survivors of the future explain the seed that was the tree of evil in folklore?"

I did not see this one coming, "Say what, folklore?"

"You heard me; I want you to pretend it is the far future, well into the backside. What will the folklore about the seed of the tree of evil that has engulfed our nation sound like?"

Now you have me rubbing my jaw, "Well, the seed of the tree of evil that has engulfed our nation is simple. It is the United States Supreme Court. But now you want me to explain why with some kind of future folklore?"

Now your eyes light up, "Exactly. Explain it in future folklore, but if that's too much to ask, let's just skip this one and move on to the next guideline."

This is like we're playing chess and you've just told me that my King is in check, "Folklore huh?" No way am I going to concede this round, "Give me a moment to think about this."

"I'm not going anywhere. Take all the time you need." My, you do look smug and so the game is afoot. There's a long silence as I sort this out, punctuated only by Sheba chewing a bit of biscuit.

"OK, this is folklore as it is told by the survivors to their children well into the backside." With that, I clear my throat and begin the tale.

"In the time before time when America was a mighty nation, the monied and powerful went to the most supreme of all courts in the land and said, 'Hear us, mighty ones who possess power over life. We are your monied kin, and your first allegiance belongs to us, for we plunder the masses of commoners you judge. But as mere citizens, we, your monied kin, are vulnerable and need the rights of royalty so that we may plunder, murder, and despoil without consequence.'

"With regret, the court replied, 'You are our kin, but we cannot make you royalty, for even we have limits. Go and find a way to ask of us that which we can provide, and then we happily will.' So it was that the monied and powerful arrived upon a solution — corporations.

"They returned to the court to gleefully explain their scheme. They explained with great relish, 'corporations are very limited today in what they can do. They must be created to serve a given purpose such as the building of roads and bridges. We have tried to corrupt the leadership to allow more, but they refused us. So we ask you to reinvent corporations as human persons with all the rights thereto, but without the responsibility of flesh and blood. Thus we shall have more than the power of royalty, for it will give us dominion in other countries as well.' The court considered the request of their monied kin of power, and so they did agree to create imaginary human persons from thin air, with ink and seals and sheaves of paper. So, it was done which created great suffering and injustice in its wake for the generations to come.

"The court's monied kin celebrated their royalty status by edict in kind, and it was good for them, but it came at the expense of the suffering and exploitation of the many. Then, years into the future, the monied kin of power came to the knowing of life itself, and of the making and the changing of different forms of life. Then the possibilities of greed became irresistible to the monied kin of power. So they returned to their kin of the court and said, 'We cannot corrupt the leadership so that we may create life to own and to profit there from.' Their pleas were heard with great sympathy, and so it was ruled that the royal corporatocracy of their monied kin would be granted the power of gods, therefore to fashion life and to own it as though slaves with the protections of law. Once again the monied kin of power rejoiced, for they had seen the satisfaction of their selfish demands.

"However, while tolerance can be infinite in a democracy, it can also be short-lived, and this was unforeseen by the court and their monied kin of power. And so a rejection of their conspiracy and the resulting suffering inflicted upon the commoners they ruled with impunity arose. Weighed down by foods of poison and other hideous creations, voices began to be heard from within the many, crying out in anger for the masses to organize.

"Wary of the masses they exploit, the kin of power immediately heard these voices of resentment and began to fear for themselves, for were the commoners to organize in rebellion, they would surely lose their abilities to act as gods. And so they returned to the court with terror in their hearts, 'Hear us, our kin of the court, and givers of power beyond the reach of moderation. There is a growing tide of resentment among those whom you rule and from whom we profit. Before it grows dangerous we must conspire together to subvert the political process so that independent voices of integrity outside of our control are silenced. For our mutual good, give us the power to manipulate the electoral process by flooding it with monies and entitlements to corrupt the leadership of the nation to act in our favor.'

"Moved by the pleas of their kin, and out of a sense of vulnerability for themselves, the supreme of all courts granted unto their monied kin unfettered powers to manipulate the last vestiges of democracy. And thus they ended the hopes of the commoners to find recourse for their grievances through a political system that would now only serve to divide them.

"And so, a mighty nation, once proud and well-regarded, succumbed to its own demise at the hands of those who were given the power of flesh and blood gods, unhindered by consequences, to plunder, murder and despoil. And so it was that when the Earth shook in the grip of the Destroyer, the people turned away from a governance they had once loved. Yet another corrupt empire fell into dust, as did the fruit that had been born of an evil seed that first sprouted in a supposed field of justice. The end."

You clap enthusiastically, "Superb. That was something else." You look over at Sheba, "Well girl, was that a good folk tale?"

"Woof, woof! Woof, woof! Woof, woof!"

I make a slight bow as I wonder to myself once again, "What is it about this dog?" Taking the last sip of root beer in my bottle, I wipe my mouth. "OK, the show's over. Let's move on to the sixth guideline."

"Let all nations rule internally resolving external disputes in a world court." You begin to chuckle, "After that folklore account, it's obvious this is a non-starter."

I chuckle with you, "I must agree, given the many failures of the United Nations and the League of Nations before it. However, it does give us an interesting insight into the thinking process of whoever created this monument."

"And that is?"

"They believe a good empire is possible, despite the fact that history shows us time and again that there are no good empires, just failed ones. It's an immutable law of nature, yet there is this persistent belief that a good empire is possible. Folks come along and say they're more clever than those who came before them and then fail themselves, just like those before them, who likewise felt they were more clever than their predecessors, and who also failed. It's the oldest story in the book. Now read guideline number seven."

"Avoid petty laws and useless officials," you're barely able to finish it before we start laughing hysterically together, "There are no good empires just failed ones."

"Agreed." I look over at the cooler, "We've got two bottles left. What do you say?"

You wink with a cheerful grin. "I say do it while I recite the eighth guideline, 'Balance personal rights with social duties.'"

With the cooler empty I see melted ice water at the bottom, so I pour some of it into Sheba's tin pan. Thirsty from the dry dog biscuits, she begins slowly lapping it up as I open my last bottle. "When I think about the people who gave us this eighth guideline what comes to mind is the old adage, 'Do what I say, not what I do.' That being said, this eighth guideline may be of use in the future and I'll explain that later on. Now read the ninth guideline."

"Prize truth — beauty — love — seeking harmony with the infinite."

"This guideline mentions truth, beauty, love, and harmony. Yet in a tribulation world, there will be a different attribute that is more valuable than those inscribed on this monument. What do you think that attribute is?"

"To be honest, it's beyond me right now to think of what that would be, because I still see the whole tribulation world through an intellectual haze. So rather than making a foolish guess, tell me, because I want to know."

"That's a very wise answer. Whoever built this monument, like the rest of our present society, admires the clever. It's a part of the empire-builder mindset that they feel they are more clever than those who failed before them. Then they fail for the same reasons. Rather than admiring the clever it is wise to admire the kind because in a tribulation world these are the people the survivors will admire — the kind. So had this monument's ninth guideline been inscribed with the word 'kindness,' it would have demonstrated a truly enlightened view of the future. Nonetheless, as with the other two that I pointed out, keep this one in mind because we're going to return to it. Now with that, read the tenth and final guideline."

"Be not a cancer on the earth — Leave room for nature — Leave room for nature."

"This guideline is a critical indicator because it is sending a message. Not necessarily to the common man, because concern for other species and habitats is not what you would call a top-down issue. Rather, it is the outcries of the common man that brings into focus the need to correct destructive behaviors. For example, in South America thousands of good folk have been executed by selfish interests for protesting the manner in which they are laying waste to the Amazon, the very lungs of our planet. And for what, to so they can raise beef and make palm oil for fast food restaurants? And the list goes on and on."

"So what's the point?"

"The point here is that whoever built this monument is a part of an elitist control system, but they clearly are uncomfortable with some of what this control system is doing to our world. Therefore, what we see here is an issue of division between the elites who enslave their minions and us."

You nod your head, "Now I get it. The elites divide us to their advantage, but, 'what's good for the goose is good for the gander.' It goes both ways."

"Yes, indeed. And while they want you to believe that they are all-powerful and that you are without hope, that's just smoke and mirrors. To your credit, you see it. I'm proud of you. Now, with this in mind, we need to revisit the fourth, eighth, and ninth guidelines. We need to examine them not as two people with our own prejudices and opinions, but as faith-based tribulation leaders seeking opportunities."

"We can find opportunities because during the tribulation those who seek to re-enslave us will inevitably do something to their minions that will create small hairline fractures in their solidarity. They will weaken their minions' belief in their promises of a new, good empire."

"Such as breaking promises and abandoning their minions on the surface?" you add.

"Bingo! Given that these very minions will be at the outer circles of the elites' control scheme, we will most likely come into contact with some of them. When we do, there may be opportunities to encourage them to be in service to God and not to the elites they currently serve. To illustrate this point, imagine you've met one such minion and with that in mind, repeat the fourth, eighth, and ninth guidelines."

"Rule passion — faith — tradition — and all things with tempered reason. Balance personal rights with social duties. Prize truth — beauty — love — seeking harmony with the infinite."

"You have just read thirty-two words in three different guidelines. Given the right opportunity, some or all may help you to appeal to a disgruntled minion's inner sense of nobility. They may become inspired to serve God; for as the Bible tells us, no one can serve two masters. They will love one and hate the other. They either serve the elites, or they serve God, and if they begin to serve God, then you will have more in common with them."

Taking a slow drink of root beer, you contemplate that thought, "But how do you know they could be interested in serving God in the first place. The monument builders say nothing about God in their guidelines, so where do you see this interest coming from?"

"It is in the last five words of the ninth guideline, 'seeking harmony with the infinite.' Here, my friend is where even the tiniest schism between the minion and the master presents an opportunity. This is because no matter what age, what planet, or what species is involved, the cycle of Empire is always the same. Empires rise quickly in the beginning because all share in the bounty. But then, those in a monied position will inevitably consolidate the empire's wealth and power into their own hands, and thereby make the vibrancy of the young empire brittle. Then over time, this brittleness will sap the political enthusiasm of those at the bottom which results in a greatly weakened Empire. Consequently, threats which a young empire could have easily overcome will now cause the rapid decline of a brittle empire. At that point it is only a matter of time. An Empire thus weakened will succumb to any number of threats and fail."

"So where is the hope for the future then? Or is humanity just going to keep repeating this endless cycle of failed empires?"

Elbowing you in the side I say, "I'm delighted by your quick grasp of this important issue. There is only one thing that can break the cycle of empire. It has been done on other worlds and at other times; so we know it works."

"What is it?"

"A species must change the very premise upon which its social structure is organized. With empires life is organized around power, acquisition, and exploitation. These are the values that perpetuate the failures of empires time and again."

"And that new foundational premise is?"

"Harmony my friend, harmony within ourselves and with all that is about us. Here is why the last five words of the ninth guideline are important, "seeking harmony with the infinite." Whoever created this monument may not have fully understood the cosmic ramifications of the word harmony. Harmony may nonetheless resonate with a minion who has been misled with broken promises.

"The other word that is equally important is 'infinite.' The choice of this word tells us that whoever constructed this monument may pretend to practice a mainstream faith, but only for the sake of appearances. This is because the terrestrial views of mainstream religion are measured in finite terms such as: me, my church, my nation, and so forth. Expressing belief in the infinite is a more cosmic view which says you are connected to, and thereby part of, all there is. There are no limits to the infinite neither on this world, in this galaxy, or even beyond what the human mind can imagine."

As you turn and stare into my eyes, I can imagine the wheels turning in your mind, "This makes sense in a way. But how can I bridge a minion's belief in the infinite to a desire to serve God?"

"This can be accomplished by persuading them that if they choose to serve God, they will help to usher in something vastly more real and beneficial than a misguided belief in the possibility of a 'good empire.' The 'good empire' is a belief they very likely have private doubts about. We can help them to understand that by serving God they will help bring about an enlightened future for our species and the promise of trusting friendships with other races in the galaxy."

Stretching your arms and shoulders, you take a sip of root beer and say, "Two questions come to my mind. The first is, "How can you be certain that it was low-ranking minions and not higher-level power elites who built this monument?"

"The answer to your first question is that W. C. Christian was a shadow figure, not a real person. Where he got the money to build this monument is unknown. We do know, however, that funding was limited due to where the monument was made and where it was placed. In terms of where to make it, Elberton, Georgia was a no-brainer. It's the granite capital of the world, and the monument came from Pyramid Quarry just ten miles away from where we're sitting now."

I pat the Earth beneath us, "As to this bit of farm land, it was one of the several parcels on the open market which were available at that time. Its greatest virtue was that it was relatively near the quarry. It costs money to haul stone, and to a site farther out would have been more expensive. All in all, the estimated cost of the monument was $300,000 in today's dollars. So, we're not talking about people with unlimited wealth here. Given the financial constraints, this clearly was a minion-level budget project. If this answers your first question, then what's your second?"

You shake your head with a grin, "I knew before I asked that you'd have a slam-dunk answer. So let's move on to the second question. Assuming I find myself presented with the opportunity to have a conversation with a potentially disgruntled minion, how do I persuade him or her to serve God and not the elites?"

Setting down my bottle of root beer, I wave my hands in front of my face, "Whoa, whoa, whoa! It would be presumptuous of me to tell you how to persuade anyone to serve God, let alone a disaffected minion. This you must figure out on your own. However, I can share with you an example of what I might say with the understanding that I'm only presenting my argument as a point of reference. Are you okay with this?"

"Point taken, now a twist for the twist master, let's do a role-play. I'll pretend to be a disaffected minion who has put you under arrest and had you hauled in for questioning. Then, being yourself, see if you can open my mind to a new world of possibilities."

Twist master that makes me laugh, "OK, hot shot, but you may want to rethink your suggestion because if you are to be a convincing minion, you will have to deny the basic tenets of your faith. You will have to enter into the mindset of a Godless, amoral minion who is willing to do any type of terrible evil thing if ordered to do it. If that's a hot potato, you're welcome to drop it." I can see my hot potato answer annoys you.

"So, are you accusing me of being rigid in my thinking?" you shoot back, "So much that I'm incapable of participating in a role-playing exercise?"

"That depends on how much you let doctrine and dogma define your world, and how accurate your imagination of an evil worldview can be. I'm not accusing you of anything by the way. It's just that if you're going to engage in a role-playing exercise with one hand politely tied behind your back to shield that which you hold dear, then nothing useful can come of it."

"Then please explain to me how I would engage you in this role play with one hand politely tied behind my back."

"Look up at the capstone atop these slabs," I point up to a flat, square slab sitting atop the vertical slabs. "What we see on our side is Babylonian Cuneiform which translates to, 'Let these be Guidestones to an Age of Reason.' On the other three sides of this capstone, the same wording appears in Classical Greek, Sanskrit, and Ancient Egyptian Hieroglyphics."

"'Let these be Guidestones to an Age of Reason' is a clear reference to a book, by Thomas Paine published in 1794 and titled, 'Age of Reason.' What Paine is essentially espousing is an early 17th-century philosophy that religious institutions, which use revelation and miracles to prove the existence of God, are tools of the elites, who in turn use them to divide and subjugate believers. In contrast to that Paine argues for a natural religion that proves the existence of God but without revelation or authority."

"But what does Paine believe himself?"

"As to his rejection of organized religion, Paine states it quite succinctly in his book, 'My own mind is my own church.' To be frank, I find his personal view to be most compelling. Therefore, if you are to engage me in this role-playing exercise, you must do so as a minion without any allegiance to any belief or institution that commands otherwise. If you're going to do this, you need to walk out to the edge of your belief system and in other words look over the edge without getting vertigo. So, again I ask; is this a hot potato you'd rather drop?"

"Vertigo? That's a bridge too far, my friend." With a serious expression, you rise up and shake yourself off. "Let me consider this," you say as you begin pacing around the monument. It's obvious that this is a pivotal moment in your immersion into what it will take to be a faith-based tribulation leader. So I sit silently and hold Sheba next to me by bribing her with little bits of biscuit. After several circuits around the monument you finally stop and face me.

"Your question took me all the way back to the moment I began this journey with you, and it reminded me of what was going through my mind at that time. For thousands of years spiritual leaders like me have warned of a coming tribulation with all sincerity. And in a few instances, short-term warnings only proved to be unfounded. But for the most part, leaders could warn believers who would listen time and again, never doubting what they heard. Then again, they never once doubted that this tribulation would happen far into the future, certainly not in their lifetimes or that of their progeny. Bottom line, it was easy to wholeheartedly believe in something which was of no consequence to you."

"Impressive observation," I say, "So what changed?"

"What changed is that as I stood on the front lawn of my house looking up at the sky, I knew in my heart something previous generations never knew. I realized that this is happening on my watch. Many around me still refuse to believe, They have been assured this would be nothing more than an interesting light show. So, unlike those before me, I am faced with a dilemma that demands action and not theological debates. It comes down to choice, and my choice is to do whatever I can to get my flock to safety; so they can live, prevail, and thrive as you say. This is a calling I can neither refuse nor deny."

"You're not alone," I chime in, "There are many others like you who now feel the same calling."

"But are they willing to be flexible in their thinking? This question reminds me of a sermon I gave about Matthew 15 where it tells of the time when the controversy between Jesus and the Pharisees, a group of religious leaders of that time, was growing sharper. The disciples of Jesus came to him asking if he knew that he had offended the Pharisees. Jesus answered them, 'Leave them; they are blind guides. If a blind man leads a blind man, both will fall into a pit.' So then, am I to be blind to the clear and present danger I see in the sky, and resent the challenge you pose to me like a Pharisee? No, I will take up your challenge. This, I will do."

Upon hearing this, I stand up, shake myself off and say, "I applaud your courage, for it is rare." Then walking up to you I place my hand on your shoulder, "However, if we are to do this, it is not about challenging conventional wisdom as Jesus did. Rather, it is about learning to lead like a Moses."

You shake your head, "I didn't see that one coming. Let's sit down and finish our root beer as you explain that to me."

"Works for me," I answer as we return to our spot and once again lean our backs against the cool stone of the Russian slab.

Lead Like a Moses

After a slow swig of root beer I finally say, "What we're about to do now with this role-playing exercise is something that you may look back upon as a pivotal moment in your life because now you really are going to learn what's at stake."

"I'm ready."

"Good, I'm glad to hear you say that. When I say you need to lead like a Moses, I'm not speaking of Moses in the Biblical sense of him being a spiritual leader; even though he was certainly that. Rather, I am talking about Moses as a prince of Egypt and a commanding general. As such, his command of strategy and tactics was brilliant, and yes, he could be utterly ruthless when he needed to be."

"And often times he was," you add.

"As a Prince of Egypt, Moses had access to intelligence that was far beyond the reach of the common man. Ancient wisdom was secreted away in vaults and accessible only to the upper echelons of Egypt's leadership. There he would have learned about what the Egyptians called the Destroyer; what we call Nibiru or the Planet X System today."

"As a strategic thinker, Moses would have understood this military dictum, 'In chaos is opportunity.' Moses also knew that a flyby of the Destroyer through the northern skies above the ecliptic would cause natural global catastrophes. These in turn would put the Egyptian people and their powerful government into chaos."

Now you're curious, "Am I getting a sneak-peek at what I'll learn tomorrow in the Tribulation Carousel Theater?"

"Yes, as a matter of fact, the last flyby of the Planet X System caused the ten plagues of Exodus. Moses not only knew of this when God commanded him to lead his people out of bondage;', he also knew it the very day he fled from Egypt. So while it is not recorded that Moses bided his time awaiting signs of the Destroyer's return, he certainly knew that the chaos it would cause would present him with an opportunity to free his people."

"This is exactly what happened."

"Precisely, and I'm glad you're connecting the dots because now I can tell you in just a few words what is at stake for humanity in this coming tribulation."

"I'm ready."

"Good, here is what's at stake. In this coming tribulation there will be once again an opportunity in the chaos. Though, this time it would not just free a people; it would free our entire species from slavery once and for all. This is why I continually say that I am in it for the species. This is why all that I do, all that I think, and all that I hope is to this end: that our species will be freed to evolve spiritually and we can have the 'Star Trek' future we rightfully deserve. This is a future where we go to the stars as a peaceful and welcomed race; not as the violent slave warriors of a self-serving elitist cabal that rules our home world."

"This is what is at stake, and it is much more than just getting your flock to safety. If you choose to be in it for the species, then you can give your flock something they desperately need, a noble pursuit that gives them hope for the future. No matter where you lead your flock to safety, if you are in it for the species, your community will become a center of hope, a source of enlightened continuity, and comfort."

You shake your head with a mystified look, "Barely staying alive is going to be hard enough. Now you're saying that we must have a noble mission too? How on Earth is this supposed to happen?"

"This is the right question, and you will have your answer when you are ready for it, but not today. Rather, that answer will come over the course of the next few days. It begins tomorrow with our visit to the Planet X World's Fair Tribulation Carousel Theater. The critical lesson today is that a futile sense of hopelessness and despair only serves the interests of those who seek your death. A noble mission makes a life worth living.

"Your lesson today is that you must retake power as an individual and reverse the tactics the elites are using against you. You do this by placing positive, noble, spiritual wedges into the fractures between the Luciferian elites and their disgruntled minions. You must learn this and believe in yourself if you are to lead like a Moses, It will not be due to the tactics you will learn; though they will be useful. It will be the result of you learning the importance of seeing things as they are, and not through the prisms of judgment and prejudice which are easily manipulated by the malevolent. Learn this vital lesson today, and you will know where to find opportunities within the chaos to come and how to leverage them to your advantage."

"Now are we going to do the role-playing exercise?"

The Interrogation

I see you tapping your fingers. You're anxious to get started, "That's right, you will be the minion, and I will be the faith-based tribulation leader you are questioning. Upon your orders I've been arrested for this inquiry, and Sheba, a corporal in your security forces, will escort me to your interrogation room." I look down at Sheba and ask, "Are you ready to be a corporal?"

"Woof, woof!"

With that I cross my hands at the wrists pretending to be bound. "This spot will be the interrogation room. So you stay seated there on the ground while Sheba and I walk around the monument. After we make a full circuit, you will command Sheba, 'Bring in the prisoner,' and with that we'll begin our role-playing exercise."

After moving out of your sight, I begin to walk counterclockwise around the monument. I plan to return to a spot where I can sit on the ground with the English slab to my back. As I do my best to pretend to be a prisoner whose hands are bound, Sheba follows behind me. Instead of wagging her tail as she usually does, this time she has her head down a little bit, and I'm hearing an occasional low, throaty growl. During all this I'm thinking to myself, "My God, she's really getting into the part. What is it with this dog?"

As we come around from behind the English slab, we hear you announce in a stern voice, "Corporal Sheba bring in the prisoner," and she follows me to a spot in front of you, where I sit down on the ground.

"Thank you Corporal," you say to Sheba, and she happily curls up next to her tin with a good view of the two of us as you begin.

Pretending to thumb your way through a thick file folder you say, "I see here that you are the Chief Steward of the Knowledge Mountain Church of Perpetual Genesis. For starters I've never heard of the title, Chief Steward. Who gave you this title?"

"I gave it to myself when I founded the church. As someone who has lived most of his life as a science-minded person, I was not comfortable with the usual titles such as pastor, rabbi, or priest, I did not come to this position through formal religious training. Rather, what brought me to this position was the process of science itself and the transformative nature of my Planet X research. I have learned that science alone only takes you to a place of doubt and despair when contemplating what is to come. Instead of being caught up in all of that, I found my way to God, and through my work I now have a relationship with God that has made all the difference in my life. I'm grateful for it every day."

"Do you understand why you are here today?"

"Yes, your security people came to my house, threw a bag over my head, pushed me into the back of a truck, and well, here I am. I would have come if you had asked, so I'm curious as to why you did that if you don't mind my asking?"

"You are here today because your Knowledge Mountain Church of Perpetual Genesis is suspected of being a combative institution."

"Combative?"

"You heard me. Your church is a front for terrorists who are opposed to our lawful government."

"Ours is a supportive institution. Our church does not advocate or endorse any combative doctrine or philosophy. Why do you say that we do?"

"Because you are not supportive of the government as mainstream churches are, and many of your followers consistently refuse to accept vaccinations and RFID implants."

"We never tell people to accept or reject these things," I nod in the direction of your imaginary file folder, "I'm sure you'll find that fact in your very thick file. All we do is follow the three precepts of our church. We serve others by sharing self-sufficiency knowledge, hope for the future, and the knowledge that they are not alone. This is all we do as a supportive institution, and I challenge you to prove otherwise, that is without resorting to fabrication or false accusations."

"Fabrication and false accusations, you say. Is that what you teach people to think of their lawful government?"

"You are what you do, and we are what we do. Shall we just leave it at that?"

"For the time being, right now I want to understand a few things about your church, or shall I say alleged church. The Knowledge Mountain part I know because your ham radio members are broadcasting self-sufficiency knowledge every day."

"Which you carefully monitor and often jam. Why do you do that? Is learning how to deliver a breech baby a crime against the state?"

"When you raise that baby to be an enemy of the state, it is. But what I'm interested in knowing today is the meaning of this term, Perpetual Genesis. Where does it come from?"

"Earlier I told you I've never had any formal religious training, but I did receive informal spiritual instruction as a young man in my late 20s. During this time I learned the teachings of the Medicine Wheel from a Native American medicine man in preparation for my own vision quest. A vision quest takes a good deal of time to prepare for which in my case was about six months. Once you're ready, you do it entirely on your own because this is the point of a vision quest. You will find your own understanding and connection to Creator without the influence of anyone else. When the medicine man felt I was ready, I embarked upon a journey to a place of my own choosing. My experience was so profound that day; I completely lost my fear of death."

"So, does Perpetual Genesis mean that you're not afraid to die? Are you promoting suicidal thinking?"

"No, we do not promote suicide although your government certainly does. In fact many have found their way to us after losing their resolve to let you fire a pneumatic blade into the base of their skull at your assisted suicide centers. And, by the way we thank you for not murdering them anyway when they turn away."

"That is only because they inevitably come back to finish the process. Don't play games with me. Now tell me about this concept of Perpetual Genesis and what it means. And yes, I've read it in this folder, but I want to hear it from your own lips."

The Philosophy of Perpetual Genesis

"When I had my vision quest, I was shown something very clearly, but I instinctively knew that it would take me half a lifetime to explain it to others. As I said before, my work is transformative, and so I finally found a way to explain what I had seen so many years ago. This was when I created the philosophy of Perpetual Genesis which begins with three simple questions: Where does God live? What is God's mission? And what has all this got to do with me?"

"And I suppose the answers are some kind of new age woo-woo."

"No, and by the way you said that you already knew the answer to this question, so why the prejudice? I thought you wanted to hear this in my own words."

"Fine, strike the woo-woo. So what do this vision quest you talk about and this philosophy of Perpetual Genesis have in common?"

"I will be happy to explain, but first tell me; do you know about the granite monument called the Georgia Guidestones which are located off Georgia Highway 77 in Elbert County about 90 miles East of Atlanta?"

"I know where the monument is."

"So you are a believer in its message?"

"For the most part, but why is this of interest to you?"

"Because you are interested in me, and I am trying to find a common point of reference for our conversation. With this in mind do you believe the guidelines of the monument are based on the 'Age of Reason' by Thomas Paine, and if so, how do you feel about that? Again, I ask only to find a common point of reference for our conversation."

"Most likely so, because Paine does makes a sound case for the philosophy of Deism which rejects the revelation and authority of mainstream religions. Deism asserts that to determine the existence of a single Creator of this universe we must use reason and observation of the natural world instead of religious claptrap."

"Then dear friend, I believe we have found a point in common between your philosophy of Deism and my philosophy of Perpetual Genesis. Would you, by any chance, have a copy of the ten guidelines inscribed in the Georgia Guidestones?"

"Look at the poster on the wall behind you."

I look over my shoulder. "Ah yes, there it is. Excellent, may I call your attention to the ninth guideline, 'Prize truth — beauty — love — seeking harmony with the infinite.'"

"And..."

"May we focus on the last five words of that guideline, as a touchstone, to help explain my philosophy of Perpetual Genesis beginning with the first question? Where does God live? To begin, do you view the phrase 'seeking harmony with the infinite' in the affirmative?"

"Yes, continue."

"Earlier you expressed your favorable view of the Deism philosophy Which is the use of reason and observation. Well, a vision quest is somewhat similar in that it relies upon personal observation through experience which in my case was very profound."

"Now, when we ask mainstream religion to explain where God lives, we can expect some kind of line-of-sight answer. If it is beyond our line-of-sight, it's God. However, during my vision quest, I saw a cosmic view that makes these line-of-sight explanations appear more Earth-centric to me than anything else. Simply put, they were not representative of what I had seen."

"And what did you see?"

"It took me years to understand what I saw, but eventually I did, and it was mostly through science. Keep in mind; most religious line-of-sight explanations are focused on normal matter, which only comprises roughly 5% of our universe. The rest is 'dark matter' and 'dark energy.'"

"So you're saying that science is a religion?"

"No, though it certainly does have its fair share of golden cows. However, it was through science that I arrived at a cosmic understanding of what I had seen half a lifetime earlier during my vision quest."

"So what's the point?"

"The point here is what Diests such as yourself see and what you do not see." That observation leaves you shaking your head.

"The universe as we know it and see all about us and in the night sky represents only 5% of all there is. The other 95% is comprised of dark energy and dark matter, which only scientists can only theorize about. Likewise, they also theorize that we live in an ever-expanding multidimensional universe where each universe can operate under its own unique laws.

Therefore, the multiverse exists within lifelessness of the void which in turn encompasses everything and is endless. This is where God lives. In this endless void. Ergo while God is greater than what God has created, namely us, this endless void is greater that God and us within that which God has created.

As a Diest, your belief system is incapable of grasping this cosmic reality because it grew out of a time when everyone assumed the 5% of the universe we exist in was all there is and that the Earth is flat.

You scratch your head. "I must admit, I've never been called a flat Earth thinker in such a unique way. Continue."

"This brings us to this second question of Perpetual Genesis,'What is God's mission?' This is where flat Earth thinking comes to a screeching halt, because after all we all have a mission. You have a mission; I have a mission; and everyone does. I maintain that if we are created in God's image, it is because we are not a reflection of God's mission; Rather, we are the intended result of it which is life that is perpetually created from the lifelessness of the void. This is what God has always done and always will."

"So you are saying that God can make something from nothing. If so, for a man who says he is science-minded, isn't this just sophistry?"

"No, it is not about making something from nothing. If you cannot use observation then, as a Deist, I urge you to employ reason. Does reason tell you that 'dark matter' and 'dark energy' only exist within a limited part of the infinite as you call it? Or, are 'dark matter' and 'dark energy' the very infinite soup of the infinite itself. In other words the void in which God lives?"

You rub your chin reflectively, "So, theoretically speaking, and I'm beginning to find this a little far-fetched, you're saying that God is playing with the universe as though it were a big box of unlimited tinker toys?"

"Absolutely not, this is serious and nothing could be more so. Nor does God need to create something from nothing, assuming God has that power."

"So is what we know about physics correct? That even God cannot create something from nothing?"

"Frankly, neither of us can say one way or the other. After all physics has also raised the probability that we live in a multiverse where other universes exist, and each has their own unique laws of physics. But as a science-minded person, I would agree with you that God cannot create something from nothing because it is wholly unnecessary for God to do so."

"Continue," you appear to be pleased that I've finally agreed with you about something.

"Rather, the philosophy of Perpetual Genesis tells us that it is through free will and intention that God creates normal matter which is necessary for the creation of life by converting 'dark matter' and 'dark energy' into normal matter through intention."

"Assuming this is so, what is the correlation between the infinite and your philosophy?"

"When you, as a Deist, say 'seeking harmony with the infinite,' what you are admitting is that you see yourself as a part of all of that of which God is a part of, and more, the vast infinite of the void beyond the existence of God."

You wag your finger, "You're clever, but you've only given me the answers to the first two questions that are the basis of your philosophy of Perpetual Genesis which I may add is arguably far-fetched. Nonetheless, the third question is the one of interest to me now, 'What does all this have to do with me?' as in reference to yourself."

"Thank you for asking. As a Deist, is it safe to say that you believe when reason is elevated over fear and myth, only then can we see a better society as a whole?"

"You can assume so for the purpose of this conversation."

"With Perpetual Genesis a better society, as a whole, is likewise the desired end-result. Likewise, we could argue that our beliefs echo many other beliefs in the world. But for the point of this conversation, when I say that I am a Perpetual, what do I mean by it?"

"Well..."

"As a Perpetual, I am not saying anything to you. What I am doing is saying to God, 'I am in perpetual service to your eternal mission. At this moment I am incarnated here on this planet, in this species, and when my job is done here, put me where I can serve you best, regardless of the planet, time, or species.' In other words, my commitment to God is infinite and eternal. Can you say the same?"

"So you're saying that you're doing this to express your love for God and all of mankind, including the ones who would like to kill you?"

"My love for God is unconditional. As for our species, I do love our species, as a whole, for if we do not love our own species, who will? But when it comes to loving mankind, I do it one person at a time."

"Again, this is a little far-fetched for me, but assuming that as a Perpetual you are seeking a better society, or a better species, or whatever, what is the political or social mechanism you must employ to achieve this goal?"

"During the tribulation what will we see? Most of the '-ologies' and '-isms' that we use to order our lives are failing all around us. As a Perpetual, I favor no particular political or social mechanism at all. In a manner of speaking why flog dead and dying horses? Rather, through kindness and compassion we seek to become more like roses. This is our method."

"You've got to be kidding, roses?"

"Think of this for a moment. Roses are beautiful flowers, but they have these sharp thorns that prick our fingers. Yet, when someone dies or we want to express our love for someone, what do we do? We give them roses."

"That's a curious observation. Why?"

"The vibratory rate of the human body is approximately 50 to 80 Hz, depending on your state of mind. On the other hand, a rose has a vibratory rate of 320 Hz. So even when a rose is dying it is still giving off more life energy than we do. This is why we tolerate the thorns. In other words, if we as beings seek to become more like roses, we will not only see better societies, but as a physical species, we will become the worthy and capable hosts of more ascended spirits in service to God. Ascended spirits need higher vibratory rates in a body to be able to successfully live in it. It's just that simple; because as I like to say, the greatest truths are by and of necessity simple."

"So, what you are saying is that you believe the lawful government of this country is inferior to your beliefs because it is not a rose?"

"That is not a statement of fact, but an accusation of passion," I turn and point behind myself, "I asked you to read the fourth guideline, 'Rule passion — faith — tradition — and all things with tempered reason.' Tell me, was what you just accused me of the result of tempered reason? Or was it an accusation of passion?"

RFID Tag Implants

You hold out your hands palms out, "All right, enough of this theoretical claptrap. The reason why you are here today is because almost all of the people who call themselves Perpetuals are refusing RFID tag implants and inoculations."

"As a Deist, do you maintain that they are not within their rights?" Again I point behind me, "The eighth guideline says, 'Balance personal rights with social duties.' So I put it to you, are you accusing Perpetuals of offending the state by virtue of a contrived balance purely of your own self-interested making?"

"You're pushing the line now."

"Fine, then let me back off to just one of the two issues you have raised. Specifically, that of the RFID tag implants."

"Continue."

"What have you been told by your superiors as to why they are necessary?"

"They are simple transponders that help us to ensure safety, allocate scarce resources, and provide necessary services. They also eliminate the need for physical currency and hence the corruption of a black market. But you already know that; so why are you asking?"

"Agreed, all you have told me is what everyone hears every day in public service announcements and speeches. What have you heard that is not being told to the public about these RFID implants?"

"Are you going to launch into some kind of cockamamie conspiracy theorist rant now?"

"No, but I am going to tell you something you can learn for yourself if you have the ambition to do your own homework within your own system."

"Okay, I'll give you enough rope to hang yourself."

"The functionality of these RFID implants goes far beyond what people are being told. What I can tell you, as a science-minded researcher, is they are actually multi-mode devices that can transmit and receive simultaneously on multiple frequencies. They have embedded within them features the government has yet to activate. However, in time your government will begin triggering these hidden features for various purposes such as to calm the public. When this happens, the user's experience will be rather pleasant. In a manner of speaking it will be electronic Prozac."

"However, there are other functions built into these government implants that can be activated. For example, once you launch new satellites into orbit, they can broadcast social programming messages directly into the mind through the implanted RFID implants."

"Do you have any proof of that?"

"You already do provided you have the courage to see it for yourself. However, the feature embedded in these RFID implants that we find most disturbing serves a very unique function. Apparently, your developers have discovered the frequency with which we humans speak with God, or what you refer to as 'the infinite.' It is through this frequency that we feel God's presence. That is until a special-purpose jamming circuit in these RFID implants is activated. Once that happens, it will block that frequency thereby severing the person's sense of connection to God, or what you call 'the infinite." Keep in mind; I am not asking you to acknowledge what I've just said in any way. Rather, you told me you were giving me enough rope to hang myself. Well, let's see if you have what it takes to do your homework, and then let's see if you can honestly tie a hangman's noose for me?"

"Nonsense."

"Of course you need to say that, so let's cut to the bone here and put what really matters on the table."

"Haven't you already done that?"

"No, and it is important because it is why I do all that I do and hope for all that I hope for. Are you not in the least bit interested to know my motivation?"

"Continue."

"Nobody lives forever. One day each and every one of us will stand before our God. When that day comes, I want to know, and I want God to know that warts and all I kept the faith. This brings me to you and your belief in, and I quote from the monument, 'seeking harmony with the infinite.' When your day comes and you stand before your God, or 'the infinite' if you prefer, how will you explain your involvement in this government's aim to isolate citizens who love God from the God they love for the benefit of your superiors? How will you explain that you participated in a program that beamed false messages from God directly into people's minds? What justification will you present to God, and do you really believe God will buy it? Now, may I go home?"

You start chuckling, "Okay you got me. Lesson learned, and yes, it is time to go home. I've got three bottles of root beer in me, and I seriously need to make a rest stop."

"No worries, we can stop at a gas station on the way."

"We can do that? Stop at a gas station on the way home?"

"We're time travelers my friend. Let's gather our stuff and get going."

6

The Tribulation

There is a steady knock on the door of the caretaker's cottage, and I slowly open the door.

You greet me holding a tray in your hands with covered dishes and a mug of hot coffee. "We missed you at breakfast this morning. One of the kids said you ate a small bowl of cereal and then headed off in this direction. I thought you'd like something a bit more substantial than kiddie cereal. Here are your new favorites — buckwheat pancakes with homemade blueberry syrup, scrambled eggs, and sausage."

I gratefully take the tray and walk back to the workbench as you shut the door behind us.

"Something is troubling you."

Nodding in agreement, I uncover the plates and pick up the knife and fork from the tray. "Got up early this morning and couldn't fall back to sleep. So, I figured on getting something at the food court after we get to the Planet X World's Fair. Then again, whatever they're serving at the food court, it's nowhere near as good as this. Thanks for bringing me a real breakfast."

"My pleasure, but when you opened the door I saw a distressed look. What's bothering you?"

"You, I suppose."

"Me?"

I shrug my shoulders, "Not in the way you think. It's just that I know today is going to be harder for you than you could possibly imagine right now. I guess that's what got me up with the sun. So, I came here and made another batch of root beer. It's funny how piddling around in the cottage like this is so relaxing for me."

"I know what you mean. So tell me, are we still going to The Tribulation Carousel Theater today?"

I stuff my mouth full of sausage and pancakes and nod yes, "And one more exhibit, 'The Threat Matrix Exploratorium.'"

"I see." You wait for me to swallow and then ask, "By the way, where is Sheba? We didn't see her at the house, and she's not here with you. Did she just take off and go somewhere?"

"I fed her this morning, and she was here until about 10 minutes ago; then she scratched on the door to go out. She probably had to do her business."

We hear scratching at the door, "Apparently so, enjoy your breakfast. I'll let her in."

"Thanks, and if you would do me a favor, this new batch of root beer needs to go to the back of the refrigerator if you don't mind sorting the bottles around."

"My pleasure," you say as you go to the door, "Enjoy your breakfast. Sheba and I will take care of the root beer." I nod appreciatively and stuff another forkful of those wonderful pancakes into my mouth.

I'm happily munching away as you let Sheba in and she immediately smells what's on my plate. "Share and share alike," I think to myself and pick up the last sausage link. "Here you go, girl," and the little sausage is gone in a few happy chomps. There's still plenty for me to eat as you set about reorganizing the root beer bottles in the refrigerator.

After a bit you come back to the workbench and sit down on a stool and begin petting Sheba as I finish my breakfast. "It's a nice quiet moment," I think to myself as I sip my coffee, "Too bad it can't last."

As I scrape up the last few tidbits on my plate, you venture a question, "You know I never asked you before, and it didn't come to mind until today, but what happens when we're finished with all of this and it's time for me to go back to real time? What happens then?"

Wiping my lips with a napkin I answer, "I'll send you back to the instant just after you first came here. So from your perspective, there will be no loss of time. One second you're here; the next second you're there."

"Will I remember?"

"You'll remember everything; otherwise, what's the point of all this? You can also take things back with you in the time machine."

"Like some root beer."

I chuckle, "Yup."

"Well, I'm glad to hear it. It would be a futile waste of time if I couldn't remember all of this. So when are you going to be ready to send me back?"

"Good question, in fact I've been waiting for you to ask that question because only then would the answer make sense to you. Every journey begins with a first step and ends with a last step, or what I call launch and destination. These you must define for those who follow you and trust to fill in the rest."

"Is launch and destination what I'm going to learn about today?",?"

"No. You know we've all heard the old adage, 'prepare for the worst and hope for the best.' Well, today you're going to learn the worst — death on an unimaginable scale. That's why we went to the Georgia Guidestones yesterday. Do you remember the first guideline?"

"How can I forget it? 'Maintain humanity under 500,000,000 in perpetual balance with nature.'"

"Well, today you're going to learn how the population is going to be reduced during the tribulation. On the one hand this is some pretty freaky stuff. If you're weak, you could just turn into an ostrich trying to bury your head in the sand deep enough to make it all go away, although it never does."

"Or?"

"Or, you can view what you are going to learn today through the eyes of a Moses. In other words yes, there is a dark cloud coming, but every dark cloud has a silver lining. That's what it means to think like a Moses because Moses used the chaos of the last flyby to free his people. He accepted the inevitable truth that with such events come horrific losses of life. That doesn't mean you trivialize these deaths. Life is precious. Rather, it means you accept it so that you can flow through the misery to create a constructive result. Does this make sense to you?"

"What makes sense to me is that this is not going to be a very pleasant day."

I look down at Sheba, "Well girl, do you think it's making sense to him?"

"Woof, woof, woof."

"All I get is a maybe," you complain.

"Woof, woof."

I laugh, "Now she's saying, 'Yes, all you get is a maybe.'"

You rub your jaw thoughtfully, "Okay, let's see if we can get some clarity on this. For starters I get the beginning and end thing, what you call launch and destination. That's pretty straightforward, but here is where I'm a little vague. What am I supposed to be doing if the people I'm leading are figuring out all the steps in between?"

"You're doing a lot of things, but the two most important are that you always keep your eye on the destination, and always see to it that the community gets to that destination. Second, you are always looking for opportunities to promote the Three I's of Invention, Insight, and Initiative."

"Is this what I'm going to learn how to do today, the Three I's?"

"Not today. Today we are going to the Tribulation Carousel Theater and the Threat Matrix Exploratorium at the Planet X World's Fair. If you are to lead like a Moses, you must understand the sequence of events that will occur during the tribulation cycle and the threats that will be facing your community. What you are going to learn today will help you know when to get your flock to safety, and how you keep them as safe as possible during the chaos. Are you ready?"

"Will I need something stronger than root beer when we get back tonight?"

"Woof, woof!" Sheba's timing is perfect, and we both howl with laughter. What is it about this dog?

I point towards the door, "We'll take the tray back to the house when we get back. Now it's time to head out to the time machine."

As we approach the tree line, you ask pensively, "Why do so many people refuse to believe what they see with their own eyes? Why do they think it will just pass by without any problems?"

"We've touched on this before, but the short answer is the collective unconscious. Untold generations of our ancestors have seen death rain on them from the skies while the earth shook, tidal waves raged, and volcanoes blacked the skies and created summers of snow and freezing weather. These memories are dark and foreboding, especially because our ancestors had no idea what was happening. Consequently, most people experience unconscious terror, followed by irrational denial. From the point of view of irrational denial anything that pushes this idea and this terror away is entirely rational."

"So, in other words they become childish about it?"

Your assumption makes me chuckle, "No, children are more perceptive about what they see with their own eyes than adults. They may have delayed trauma later on, but at the moment they'll trust their instincts about what they see and take action. On the other hand adults become more 'adult-ish' if you will excuse the term, and frightened adults must be handled in a very calming way. This happens to be exactly what you'll see in the Tribulation Carousel Theater today."

"Well then, let's get going!" We step up the pace.

Tribulation Carousel Theater

Once again, we're standing at the entrance to the fair beneath the large, colorful arched sign at the entrance which reads, "Welcome to the Planet X World's Fair."

Sheba is standing next to us, and I look down at her and ask, "Well girl, can you lead us to the Tribulation Carousel Theater?"

"Woof, woof."

"Then, lead on." And with that Sheba steps ahead of us at a brisk pace. She occasionally looks back to make sure that we're following.

As we walk you note, "Earlier you said that frightened adults must be handled in a very calming way. That has been spinning through my mind, and I'm curious as to exactly how that works."

"Well, you're going to see how that works shortly, but I can tell you what you're not going to be told. When people are behaving in an 'adult-ish' way, they are filtering everything through their own fears and sense of responsibility. Therefore, if you are to convey any necessary knowledge to them, you must end run these filters by speaking directly to their inner child."

"Fair enough, I know this is going to sound a little odd, but I'm craving a funnel cake with some kind of sweet, delicious icing drizzled all over it."

I begin laughing so hard I have to stop walking, "I think you've had a premonition that you will really, really need some comfort food after this. Let's get to the theater and get this over with."

With Sheba in the lead we continue walking to the far side of the park where we finally reach the theater. It is a massive building with a large circular center surrounded by an outer ring. The entrance leads into a large lobby with two large entrance doors.

An attendant is standing in the middle of the lobby, "Welcome to the Tribulation Carousel Theater. The tribulation program is fifty minutes long. For your convenience there are restrooms on both sides of the lobby. Seating for the program will begin shortly. When the doors open, please enter through either side and find an open seat."

Behind the young man is a large, plastic display that resembles a pie chart. It is divided into six differently colored wedges that represent each of the six theaters in the carousel. Above the pie chart is a large digital countdown clock to the next performance. Each section lights for three seconds with the theater's name in bold, bright white characters.

We take a moment to watch. To the left of the wedge at the nine o'clock position are large brass letters with an arrow pointing to the outside center of the wedge. It reads, "You Are Here." It lights and the title is, "Theater One, Introduction."

Then we see the other five wedges flashing on and off in clockwise order: "Theater Two – Pre-Perihelion Volcanism;" "Theater Three – Pre-Perihelion Impact;" "Theater Four – The Kill Zone;" "Theater Five – Pole Shift Harbingers and Event;" and "Theater Six – Transiting the Tail, Deluge and Backside." After a few minutes the auditorium doors open automatically.

"I'm glad we visited the Planet X Orbitarium first. I know that these wedges are lighting up in a clockwise order because that mimics the orbit of the Planet X system."

I nod appreciatively, "Ah yes, the force is strong with this one." You jab me in the ribs in a good-humored way, and we file into the theater with the rest of the audience.

Theater One — Introduction

You spot a couple of ideal seats in the center, and we slide in and take our seats. In the background, we hear "Concerto No. 1, Spring" from Vivaldi's "The Four Seasons" playing. It sets a serious but soothing tone for what is to come.

There is ample distance between the plush seats and a safety bar that rotates backward into a locked position when the auditorium is in motion between theaters. As with the visit to the Orbitarium, I seat myself and fold down the seat next to me for Sheba. With a nod from me, she eagerly jumps into the chair and curls up. As she settles in, I look at you and notice that you're taking in everything.

The wedge of the auditorium is sharply angled into a small stage that has a semicircular front which faces the audience. A few feet back from the stage front a tall, red velvet curtain sweeps across from top to bottom. However, I notice that you're more interested in the holographic projectors mounted in the ceiling above the stage front, "Now, I wonder how that's going to work out," you mutter aloud.

"You'll see soon enough," I say as the last of the audience members take their seats. "I think you will like it." Moments later the theater lights begin to dim to black and all that is left are the overhead lights focused on the curtain. As the music begins to slowly fade away, all that remains is the lighted curtain.

We feel the audience's anticipation growing as the scene remains static for the longest moment. Then the curtains part just a few feet, and reveal a pitch-black stage though we can just barely make out the shapes of stage props. Slowly the audience's whispers subside as above the stage a holographic projector whirs to life. The form of a tall woman materializes front and center on the stage with her hands by her sides.

She is wearing an embroidered turquoise silk yarmulke on her head. She is also dressed in an aqua blazer with a white blouse, white pants, and a turquoise pendant necklace that compliments her bright silver hair which is styled in an attractive manner. Her presence gives you the impression that whoever she is, she's most likely from the Southwest.

Her distinguished face features strong blue-gray eyes with a twinkle in them and a warm, confident smile of welcome. To look at her is to know that she is accustomed to standing before group's of people. Her demeanor conveys a feeling of peaceful love and inclusiveness.

With subtle, smooth motions she raises her hands with palms out to the audience and with a glowing smile says, "Welcome to the Tribulation Carousel Theater. I am Rabbi Sarah Steiner, and I will be your presenter for this six-part series. I have a quick safety note before we begin. Before the auditorium begins to move, the safety bar in front of you will lower and lock into place. It will rise to the upright position once the auditorium stops moving. Also, for the comfort of others, please turn off all cell phones and electronic devices."

She points to the two exits at the rear of the auditorium, "If you need to leave the auditorium for any reason during the program, please proceed to the exits at the back of the auditorium. These exits will lead you out of the building.

"As a rabbi, I'm obviously not a scientist. However, I did take two semesters of astronomy in college. I've been an avid amateur astronomer ever since then. This is why, when I look up at the sky, I do see a clear and present danger approaching our world. Today I'm not speaking as an amateur astronomer, but rather, like most of you, I am the leader of a faith-based organization." Making a sweeping motion with both hands outward and pulling into the center she continues, "And my instincts tell me the time has come to get my flock to safety."

Pointing her index fingers at the audience, she adds, "No doubt the same holds true for many of you. Whether you lead others to safety or follow someone who has chosen to shoulder this burden, you're here today because you care about what is going to happen during the tribulation. You care enough to be in service to others so they can get through it. With this in mind I'm going to share with you things I've learned from experts and through my own research. Many of you are perhaps already doing the same and relying upon those you trust for information. If so, what you will see today in this program, will likely confirm much of what you already know. And with that, we begin our program here in Theater One – Introduction."

> She slowly sweeps both hands outward with the palms facing the audience and the curtain parts. As her holographic image fades out, the lights illuminate the stage in a soft light, just enough to make the set visible.

The audience sees a re-creation of a 1950s era nuclear fallout shelter. This style was common in the homes that had them built in basements back then. Bunk beds were on one side and shelving on the other. A mother dressed in the style of the day is shown comforting her children while her husband stacks last-minute provisions on the shelves.

> To the left of the stage, a podium materializes, and Rabbi Sarah appears behind it.

"What you are about to see will be the major events that will occur in the first 3 to 4 years of a ten to twelve-year-long tribulation." With a pleasant smile and a confident voice she speaks in soft tones that are as bright and comforting as though she is telling a child a bedtime story.

"I know that many of you now wonder if we can survive; so, let me set your mind at ease. Humanity will survive this tribulation. Of this you can be certain. We will also rebuild, and in the future our species will go to the stars. Of this you can also be certain. So, what then is the point of this presentation? It is to help you and those you lead to survive, prevail, and thrive during and beyond the tribulation. In other words our goal is for enlightened continuity, and comfort, and the long-term success of your community not merely survival."

> Stepping around the podium, she begins slowly walking across the front of the stage to the opposite side, pausing from time to time to turn and face the audience as she speaks. A fourth of the way across she stops and turns.

"The first step you as a leader must take to achieve enlightened continuity and comfort for your community is to understand the full scope of what you are facing, or what we call the threat matrix. These are the threats you must survive. We will explain the risks you will actually face and also the order in which they are most likely to occur. Without this knowledge all of the money in the world can only give you a small advantage. On the other hand this knowledge and a limited amount of money will afford you a huge advantage. That's what we hope to achieve with this six-part program. When you leave, you will have the knowledge you need to lead your community to safety."

> With a sweeping gesture of her left hand, she points to the set behind her as the stage light brightly illuminates the set.

"What you see behind me is a Cold War era underground nuclear fallout shelter which is based on a threat matrix from the last century. Thankfully, this was never put to the test. It was known as 'NBC' for nuclear, biological, and chemical threats. The concept was based in part on the misguided belief that nuclear wars could be survivable - if not winnable. This idea was popularized in a 1951 public service film titled, 'Duck and Cover,' featuring Bert the Turtle. Let's watch the first minute of the movie."

> Until now, the curved wall forming the back of the stage has been pitch black, but now it sparks to life revealing that it is actually a curved panoramic video wall stretching from one end of the stage to the other. The spotlighting on the foreground set dims as the holographic figure of Rabbi Sarah fades to black. The audience sees the first minute of an old film playing in the center panels and the sound fades as Rabbi Sarah reappears while the movie continues silently playing behind her.

Walking to the center of the stage she turns to the audience, "What you see here is an untested strategy which is based on the assumption that people could shelter for short periods of times in confined spaces. The truth is these shelters were less comfortable than World War II submarines."

She points behind her, "Today, we see occasional news reports about the discovery of old Cold War shelters and the relics found in them — and relics is the right word. Yet, this nuclear, biological, and chemical threat matrix still exists today in an updated form.   Now it is the NBC+E threat matrix — nuclear, biological, chemical, plus earthquakes. The assumption is if you prepare for these threats, you can expect to survive whatever happens." Facing the audience squarely, she holds out her hands in front of her, palms down, and as she lowers her hands to her side, the screen and the stage go dark behind her. "To think so, is naïve," she says with a slight smile.

Turning again to her left, she walks half of the way to the other side of the stage and turns to face the audience. Behind her the entire video wall lights up and begins silently playing a recent television advertisement that shows a guided tour of a missile silo complex that has been upgraded with private rooms, wood paneling, and other luxuries.

"The facility you see behind me is a commercial property where, for a considerable sum of money, you can purchase a private sleeping room in a converted missile complex or similar underground military facility. What these entrepreneurs have done is to combine NBC+E with a touch of personal comfort.

"However, a common problem with these commercial shelter sites is that they are often located in areas with very low survivability odds for those on the surface. These will be difficult places, if not impossible places, to start over. And there may not be members of the shelter with the necessary skills to rebuild civilization from scratch once you do emerge to the surface.

"When the time comes for you to enter the shelter, you could be housed with one hundred or more strangers. These will be people you've never met. Their only qualification is that they could afford the price of admission. So, after everyone pats themselves on the back for being smart enough and rich enough to buy a shelter space, there will come a lengthy period of time to get acquainted during the worst of circumstances. In other words, if you have money and want convenience, this is what a money-only solution looks like."

The video wall fades to black, as Rabbi Sarah states, "Personally, I do not see this as a viable long-term solution." She holds her hands out, palms facing out toward the audience, "If you seek a noble way to survive, there is another way, a more spiritual way."

> She slowly drops her hands to her sides as she allows the words to sink in while she walks to the other end of the stage. Upon reaching it she turns to face the audience. Behind her the video wall comes to life with a tapestry of beautiful nature scenes. Green grasses are waving against the blue sky, clear water is running in a gurgling brook, and children are swimming in a pond.

"As a faith-based leader, success for your community should not come at the expense of others, but through a sharing with others. What you see behind me is what we call the backside. This is the time, once the tribulation has passed, that our children and we will see blue skies and taste sweet waters again."

She raises her hands from her side and continues, "Between now and the backside outdated and unproven Cold War strategies are not going to meet your needs. What you need is enlightened continuity and comfort." She begins to close her arms in a large, embracing sweep as though she is hugging the audience, "The first step to community success is that we all walk humbly with our God."

" Because surviving the tribulation is not about…" she slowly makes a fist with both hands, "holding onto things." With that she crosses her hands over her heart, "No, it is about holding onto each other."

She slowly drops her hands to her side, "In a moment this theater will advance in a clockwise motion to the next stage. This is the same way the Planet X system revolves around our sun in a comet-like, clockwise orbit. In Theater Two – Pre-Perihelion Volcanism, we will share with you an early harbinger sign to help you build consensus within your community. This will help you to lead them confidently to safety in the most efficient way at the right time. Please remain seated."

> The curtain closes as the holographic image of Rabbi Sarah disappears, and the entire auditorium ring of the Tribulation Carousel Theater begins to turn slowly in a clockwise motion.

You lean over and in a soft voice say, "I'm impressed. I was really expecting her to go into more of a technical discussion. Instead, she kept it light and as hopeful as possible."

"Now you understand the technique — light and hopeful. People know the worst is coming. Reminding them of that with doomsday pronouncements is not going to inspire confidence in you. Rather, they need to see in you a vision of hope for the future. They will learn the details of how to get through it along the way. That is a given."

I look over at Sheba to see if the movement is bothering her, but she seems completely unaffected.   It's probably no different for her than a ride in the back of a pick-up truck.

Theater Two — Pre-Perihelion Volcanism

As the auditorium rotates to the second theater stage, we see closed curtains like before.   Standing in front of the curtains once again is Rabbi Sarah behind a podium which this time is to the left of the stage.

She looks as though she is waiting for the auditorium floor to come to a stop before she begins.   Even though we know it is a prerecorded presentation, it still seems spontaneous and natural.   The safety bars retract as the audience comes to a gentle stop facing the second stage.

"Welcome to Theater Two, Pre-Perihelion Volcanism. For those of you who have had the opportunity to visit the Planet X Orbitarium, you are already familiar with the concepts we'll present here. For those of you who have not yet had a chance to visit the Orbitarium, we encourage you to do so after this exhibit so that you can add it to what you are about to learn."

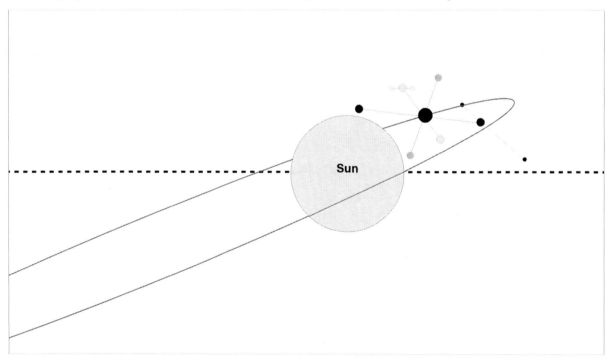

The curtains part as a large circular pedestal rises up from the center of the stage and spotlights begin to focus on a working mechanical model of our solar system. Behind the sun we see the Planet X System with its planets and moons nearing perihelion. A red elliptical wireframe illustrates its inclined orbit around our sun.

"Let me introduce to you the elements of our solar system model." The model begins turning slowly on its pedestal base, "In the center you see our sun. The blue transparent disc emanating outwards from the center of our sun is what we would see as its equator. It is called the ecliptic, the plane of our solar system. It is important for you to remember that the ecliptic of our solar system is not the same as the horizon here on earth. This is because our planet is tilted on its axis.

"However, if you were in a spaceship a far out in space, your view of our sun and the Planet X System orbiting it would be defined not by the horizon on Earth, but by its relationship to the ecliptic. Also, above the blue disk of the ecliptic is an area of space we call the northern skies and below it is the southern skies. What is important for you to understand is that we can expect difficult times here on Earth when the Planet X System is in the northern skies, above the ecliptic.

"We see the Planet X System moving in a clockwise orbit toward its point of perihelion." A bright laser pointer targets the point of perihelion, "The word perihelion defines the point at which the Planet X system comes closest to our Sun during its orbit.

"Also, please take note that this model shows the Planet X System in the pre-perihelion phase of its orbit. This is where it will begin to make itself known to us here on Earth through observable harbinger events.

"What you must understand is that this pre-perihelion phase represents the last opportunity you will have to gain the participation of those in your community who still hope against hope that the tribulation will not come to pass. You must be patient with their doubts which very likely will be reinforced by corporate media that will consistently downplay the public's concerns.

"Nevertheless, events will favor your arguments because what will happen at this stage is our sun, Sol, will be interacting with its brown dwarf twin, Nemesis, which is at the core of the Planet X System. This interaction is already causing significant disturbances here on Earth. Over time these disturbances will be exacerbated. Specifically, expect dramatic increases in the quantity and severity of freakish weather events, earthquakes, volcanic eruptions, and fireballs."

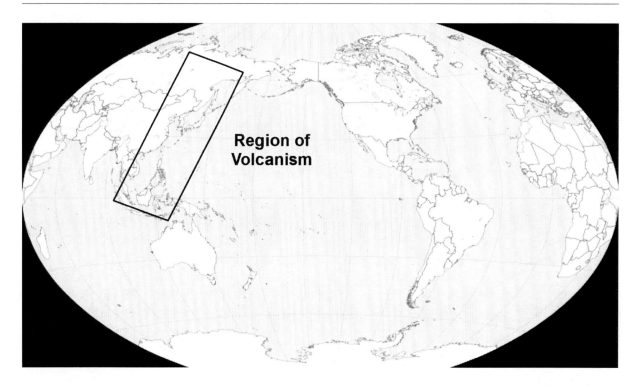

The pedestal with the mechanical model sinks back into the stage floor as a map of the world covers the full width of the video wall with a region of volcanism highlighted.

"Projections show that the most likely area for the greatest number of volcanic eruptions will be along the ring of fire in the Orient and in the Western Pacific. This region of the world plays a critical role in global commerce in the areas of just-in-time manufacturing and food production to name a few.

"At present volcanic eruptions are already closing air traffic on a limited local basis. However, what we can expect to see will be regional shutdowns of air traffic throughout the Western Pacific as volcanism becomes more severe. This disruption in air traffic will have an immediate impact on just-in-time manufacturing that will result in the closing of many manufacturing facilities when they can no longer get parts. This will in turn then create shortages of goods. The ash falls of these volcanic eruptions will also have an immediate impact on regional food production and exports to the United States which will create food shortages and rising prices. So what we will see on the nightly news at this time?

Collages of just-in-time manufacturing videos begin to dot the various panels of the video wall, "The economic consequences will occur because just-in-time manufacturing is a global endeavor that only became possible with the jet age. Component manufacturers in the Orient and other places now manufacture parts on an as-needed basis for assembly lines in other countries across the globe, and then deliver them via cargo liners with very short lead times. No one warehouses extra stock any longer. When volcanic ash blackens the sky, it will ground commercial cargo aircraft traffic. This is when assembly lines will begin shutting down all around the world as we saw with the Japanese earthquake and tsunami in 2011. Immediately following that event, there were nightly news stories about job layoffs, plant closures, and previously viable companies going out of business because the flow of just-in-time parts from Japan had suddenly stopped."

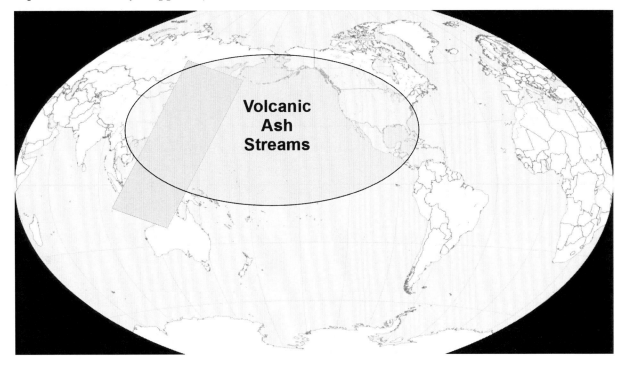

The just-in-time collage on the video wall fades into another global map, noting the pattern of volcanic ash streams moving eastward to the USA.

"We will wake here in America to find thin layers of volcanic ash deposited on our cars and homes. We'll see these stories on the nightly news as well, but this will be more of an annoyance than anything else. However, people will be talking about this and what will be happening in the grocery stores."

A new video collage of shoppers begins to cover the global map. Images of people in stores with empty shelves and stunned looks at the checkout lines; workers receive severance packages and fireballs are in the skies.

"What food shoppers will find are empty shelves where there was once an abundance of products. Worse yet, grocery costs will start to increase and in some cases quite dramatically. This is because the major food-producing regions of the Orient will be covered with ash. Consequently, foods that were once exported to America will now stay in the Orient. And some foods grown here will also go there to help supply those most heavily impacted by the volcanism.

"There will be other signs such as meteors and fireballs lighting up the sky. These will be viewed as isolated incidents until there is a significant impact event. Meanwhile, people will continue to see the ash on their cars and homes, layoffs, plant closures, business bankruptcies, shortages in the stores, and higher prices."

The video wall fades to black, and now a spotlight focuses all attention on Rabbi Sarah as she steps out from behind the podium to walk to the center stage.

She extends her hands slowly outwards toward the audience, "Know this; when these things come to pass, it will be your last, best opportunity to create and launch a viable survival community." Then she pushes her hands, palms out and facing the audience. "Despite all of these troubling events, a great reluctance toward planning and preparation will be evident among a substantial portion of your community." Turning her palms inward, she brings her hands back towards her chest, "However, if you use this opportunity wisely, a sufficient number of community members will join with you in the necessary task of creating a rapid-deployment survival solution."

She walks back to the podium and looks out upon the audience with a sad expression, "And here I must sadly tell you that while we all want to save as many lives as we can, in the final analysis, it is not our jobs as leaders to save everyone. Rather, it is their job to save themselves."

She then adds with strong emphasis, "The lesson here is that you must save those you can save because they choose to join with like-minded others and to take action in service to others. And this you must do so with great alacrity, because what comes next is the beginning of a great dying as you will see next in Theater Three – Pre-Perihelion Impact. Please remain seated."

Theater Three — Pre-Perihelion Impact

As before, the auditorium slowly rotates around to the third theater stage where the curtains are closed. Rabbi Sarah stands behind a podium on the left of the stage.

"In Theater Two – Pre-Perihelion Volcanism I showed you a projected harbinger event that will have a profound impact on the world without taking many lives. As a faith-based leader, I must emphasize to you that before an event of the scale you are about to see occurs, your community needs to be already located in a survivable area."

"What you are going to see now is what we believe will be the most likely, initial, catastrophic event with massive loss of life worldwide. The possible event you'll see next will be of sufficient magnitude to have an impact on every human being on the globe."

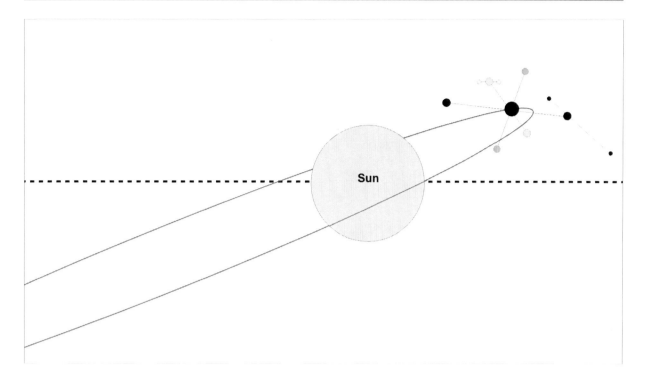

The curtains part as a large circular pedestal rises up from the center of the stage and spotlights begin to focus on a working a version of the same mechanical model shown in theater two, but the Planet X System is now farther along in its orbit toward perihelion.

"We often hear prognostications about asteroid impact events happening hundreds and thousands of years apart. However, with the passage of the Planet X System through the northern skies of our solar system, those calculations will change and herein lies the danger."

A bank of small laser lights paints a dense cluster of small asteroids on the model which are scattered throughout the inner solar system.

"According to astronomers, as of June 6, 2016, there were over seventeen hundred known potentially hazardous asteroids larger than 100 meters in size. They are called Potentially Hazardous Asteroids or PHAs if they can come as close to the Earth as 0.05 AU or less, which is roughly 7,480,000 kilometers or 4,650,000 miles. The term AU stands for astronomical unit which is the average distance of the earth to the sun. These asteroids come as close as 5% or less of the distance between earth and the sun. Under normal circumstances these PHAs are a concern, but typically, they are not imminent threats — that is until the planet X System begins to pass through the northern skies around our sun."

The pedestal with the mechanical model sinks back into the stage's floor. A pool hall fills the full width of the video wall. A player aims his stick at the cue ball and breaks the rack.

"To visualize this, let's imagine a game of billiards, where the Planet X System is a large cosmic cue ball that sends the other balls scattering in all directions. The same holds true here. We expect the Planet X System to act no differently than a cue ball that will scatter PHAs into deadly Earth-crossing orbits. It will only take one major PHA impact event to get our attention. To illustrate the danger, I'm going to step you through a potential impact event."

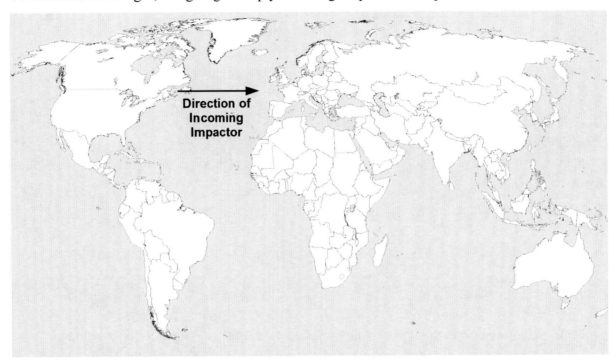

The video wall scene of the pool hall fades to a global map that also notes the direction of the incoming asteroid impactor.

"In this example an asteroid is traveling from west to east in the northern hemisphere as it approaches its point of impact."

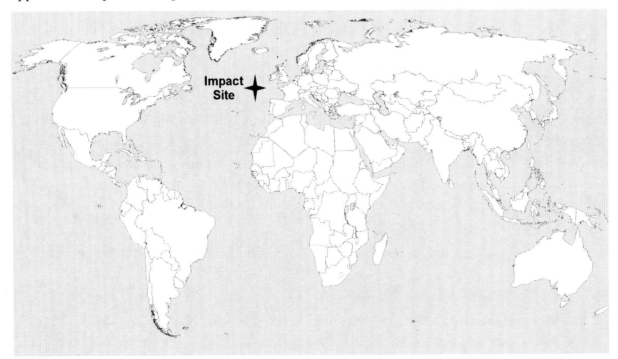

The video wall shows the next slide noting the impact site.

"And here we see the point of impact off the coast of Europe, striking the deep basin of the Atlantic Ocean. One might think that pushing through this much sea water would lessen the effect of the impact, but as you will see, that is a false assumption."

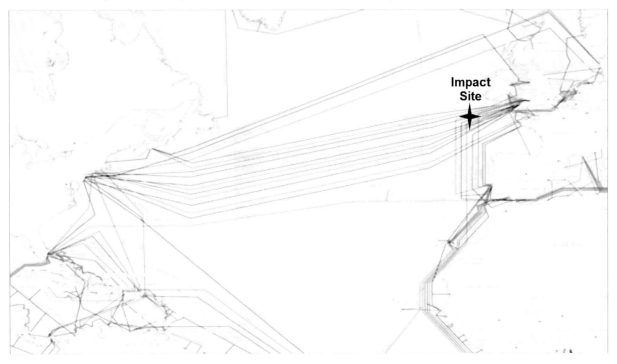

The next slide on the video wall shows the Atlantic Ocean with sub-sea transatlantic cables.

"In this example impact scenario the impactor strikes an area of the Atlantic seabed with a dense nexus of transatlantic, sub-sea, communication fiber-optic lines. Therefore, the first thing that will happen is the conversations between people in the United States, Europe, and Africa will immediately be affected."

"And then come the tsunamis. The impact event will drive tsunamis in two directions. The larger of the two will slam into Europe's western coast with massive walls of water. The smaller of the two will speed across the Atlantic to North America at the speed of a passenger jet. It will wreak havoc all along the Northeastern Atlantic Seaboard of the United States and Canada. That will be bad, but then a greater woe is to come for both continents."

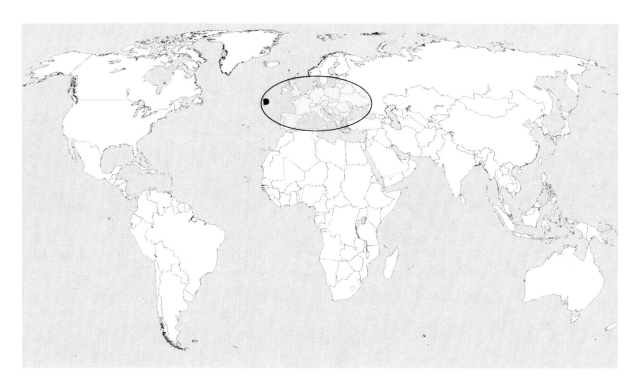

The next slide on the video wall shows a global map noting the ejecta patterns across Europe.

"In Europe burning ejecta from the Atlantic seabed impact event will rain down all across Europe killing people who are out in the open and setting entire cities ablaze."

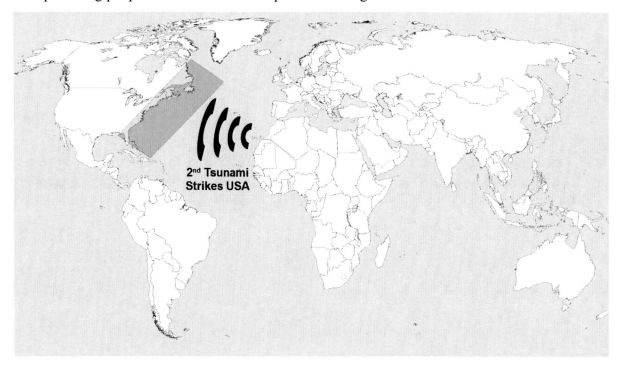

The next global map shows the 2nd tsunami's threat for the USA and Canada.

"However for the United States and Canada the worst will occur when the forces of the impact of the asteroid striking the Atlantic basin shake La Palma in the Canary Islands. This will cause Cumbre Vieja, the younger volcano on the southern end of the island, to erupt and this will result in a collapse of its western flank into the Eastern Atlantic. This will then send a second tsunami towards North America which follows closely behind the first. Unfortunately, this second tsunami will be far larger in scale and will strike before those who survived the first tsunami can reorganize. From Florida to the south to Nova Scotia to the north, the entire eastern seaboard will be devastated. And yet, this will not be the end."

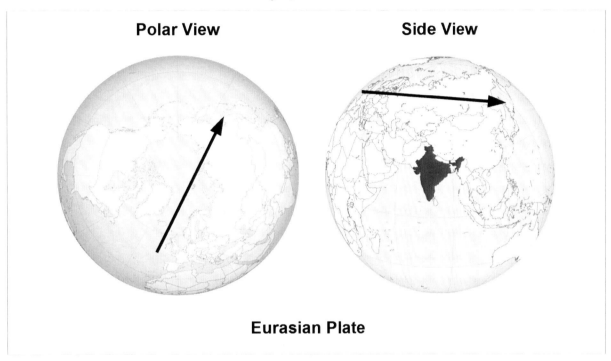

The video fades to black. Now the wall divides into two sections. The left side is a polar-view world map and the right has the equatorial side-view map. Each map has red arrows showing the direction of travel for the same impact energy wave from the two perspectives.

"To the left, you see a polar view of our planet and to the right, a side view of our planet. The red arrows in each view show the direction of the same impact energy moving through the interior of our planet from the western edge of the Eurasian plate to its eastern edge. The energy of this impact will be considerable, and when it reaches the eastern edge of the Eurasian plate, it will set off huge earthquakes and volcanic eruptions in Russia, China, and Japan."

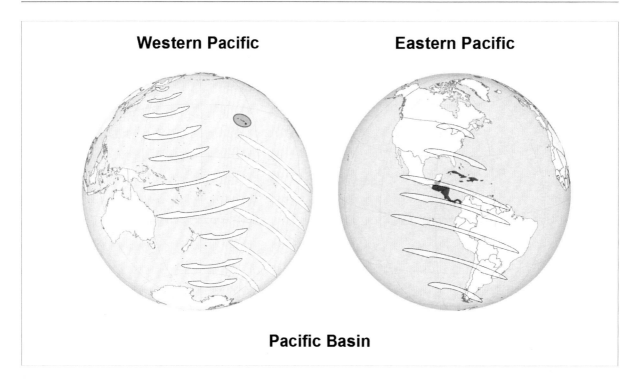

Western Pacific   **Eastern Pacific**

Pacific Basin

The dual globe maps fade to black. Now the left side of the video wall shows an equatorial view of the Western Pacific, and the right shows an equatorial view of the Eastern Pacific. Laser lights create an impression of movement starting from Russian Kamchatka down to Antarctica, then bouncing back up toward the western shores of the Americas. A single red laser highlights the Hawaiian Islands.

"Once this energy wave reaches the basin of the Northwest Pacific in the Russian Kamchatka region it will be redirected by a Pacific sub-sea mountain range southwards toward Antarctica. Along the way, it will cause the liquefaction of sea beds, and many of the beautiful islands we all dream of visiting on vacation will cease to exist."

"Once the energy wave reaches Antarctica it will be redirected northward toward the Eastern Pacific. Along the way, Hawaii will be devastated. When the last of the energy wave reaches the shores of the Americas, there will be great havoc."

The video wall fades to television news coverage of the 2004 Indian Ocean earthquake and tsunami without audio.

"To put this in perspective, the 2004 Indian Ocean earthquake and tsunami event was a regional disaster that claimed nearly a quarter of a million lives. What we see here is the potential for a global catastrophe that could claim 20 to 40 times that number of lives. No doubt this will be a devastating blow for the entire world as entire nations fail, or simply disappear."

The video wall fades to black as the curtains close. A spotlight focuses attention back onto Rabbi Sarah standing behind the podium.

"What was the point of showing you this impact scenario? That's simple if you have not already relocated to a survivable place with enough supplies necessary to begin constructing your own rapid-deployment community, now is the time to do so — right now. Procrastinate and you, along with those who depend on your leadership, could face a very bleak and uncertain future, as we will see next in Theater Four – The Kill Zone. Please remain seated."

Theater Four — The Kill Zone

The auditorium rotates around to the fourth theater stage. The curtains are closed, and Rabbi Sarah is standing behind the podium as the auditorium floor comes to a gentle stop.

"Welcome to Theater Four – The Kill Zone. Unlike the other events you will see in this program, the kill zone is not a single event. Rather, it is a series of events over a span of time in which your community will be beset by a wide range of threats. It is most likely that your community will not be afflicted by all of these different threats, but rather, only a portion of them depending on where your community is physically located; how you've prepared your shelters and frankly, the luck of the draw."

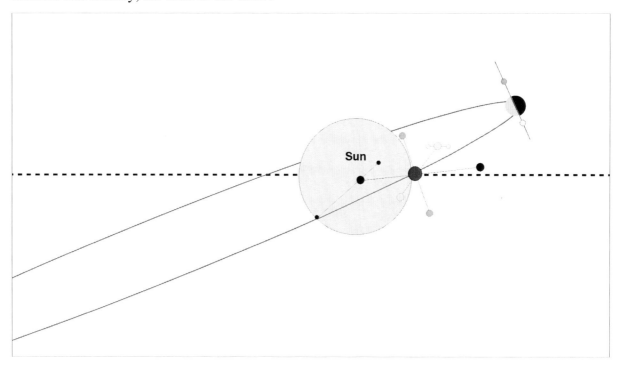

The curtains part as a large circular pedestal rises up from the center of the stage and spotlights begin to focus on a new version of the same mechanical model shown in the previous two theaters. Here the Planet X System is shown at two points in its orbit. First when it is at its point of perihelion, and then when it is at its post-perihelion location at the ecliptic.

"Here we see a solar system model with the Planet X System displayed at two different points in its orbit."

A laser lights up the perihelion position, " Perihelion is the first which is the Planet X System's closest distance to the Sun." The laser moves around the orbit to the ecliptic position, "The second position is at the ecliptic, where the brown dwarf star, Nemesis, at the core of the system will be between the orbits of the planets Mars and Jupiter."

A bank of laser lights uses broad beams to paint the sky around the perihelion and ecliptic points.

"Therefore, the region we call the kill zone extends along the orbit of the Planet X System from its point of perihelion to the ecliptic. This is when we will face many different catastrophic threats."

> The lights on the mechanical model fade to black. As the pedestal lowers back into the floor, a spotlight focuses attention back onto Rabbi Sarah standing behind the podium.

"We call it the kill zone because this is when the electrical interaction between our sun and Nemesis at the core of the Planet X System will reach its greatest levels. In recent years a new theory has gained popularity, the electric universe theory. This theory maintains that we live in an electromagnetic universe and that our two suns, Sol and Nemesis, have been interacting at not one, but two, levels: both gravitational and electrical. Is there a basis in fact for this theory? There are those who believe we have already seen the early signs of it here on earth for some time now. We'll talk more about that later in the program. However, I'm sure the big question on your minds right now is, 'What is the worst possible threat facing us in the kill zone?'"

> The video wall comes to life with a slow, majestic over flight of the Grand Canyon in Northern Arizona.

"To set the stage for that answer, here we see the Grand Canyon National Park in Northern Arizona. A popular tourist site, to be sure. We're told the Grand Canyon was formed by water erosion, although admittedly the explanation seems to defy its visual impact. So with this in mind, let's look at a different canyon."

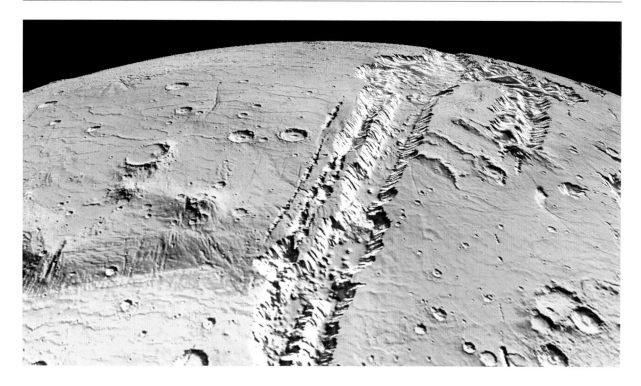

The video wall fades to black, then fades up with a distant establishing shot of the Planet Mars and then moves forward to an over flight of Valles Marineris.

"Or more specifically, a different canyon on a different planet, because here we see Valles Marineris on the planet Mars, and it's much larger than the Grand Canyon. At twenty -five hundred miles long and four miles deep it is the largest canyon in our solar system. Scientists theorize that it was created by a large crustal crack on the surface of Mars. But, like the Grand Canyon water erosion theory, the crustal crack theory also seems to defy the impact of what we actually see. So then, what if Valles Marineris was created by something other than a crustal event, and if so, what could that possibly be?"

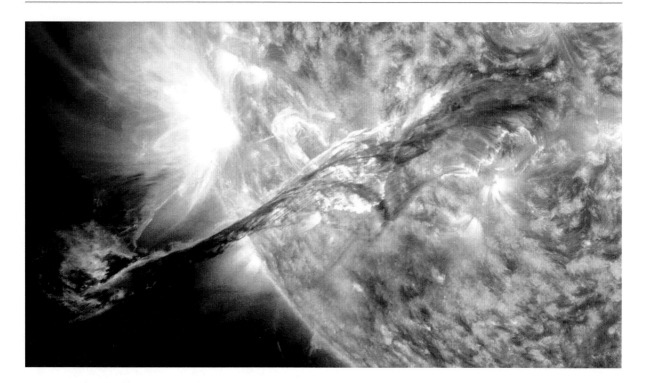

The image of Valles Marineris fades into a view of the sun as seen from space. In the animation the audience sees a massive solar flare erupting outwards into space.

"Others maintain that Valles Marineris was created by a violent interaction between our sun and the planet Mars called a solar sprite or cosmic lightning bolt. What you see on the video wall behind me is a massive solar flare. Events such as these are far less extreme than cosmic lightning bolts. That being said, solar flares will more likely be what we experience as the Planet X System transits the kill zone. Nonetheless, is it possible for a cosmic lightning bolt to strike Earth?"

The video wall fades to black and then fades up with a collage of various images and videos with Major Ed Dames. In the center of the wall, the audience sees an excerpt from Dames' 2004 *The Killshot* video.

"According to popular remote viewing instructor, Major Ed Dames, that's exactly what will happen. He made this prediction in a video he released in 2004 called *The Killshot*. Dames is a retired, well-decorated United States Army intelligence officer and was an original member of the U.S. Army's prototype remote viewing training program. In his 2004 video, he describes how he used remote viewing to foresee a cosmic lightning bolt striking the earth about the same time a large planet is passing between the Earth and the sun."

The video wall fades to black as a spotlight focuses attention on Rabbi Sarah.

"So can it happen? It could, but where will it strike? This is a good question as Nibiru will be in front of Earth and closer to the Sun at this time, and is several times the size of Earth. But assuming a sprite does strike Earth, it would be a very disastrous regional event with global implications. So, what to do?"

"When it comes to any tribulation prophecy or prediction there is a helpful rule, "Always be mindful of prophecy and predictions, but never live in expectation of them." Therefore, living in fear of a kill shot event may not serve us well, but what will serve us well is to be mindful of Dames' kill shot prediction. This allows us to address that possible threat during our planning and preparation. Another thing that we need to do as effective faith-based tribulation community leaders is to base your perceptions on hard facts, not on wishful thinking or hopeful biases."

The video wall fades up from black with a collage of various Mayan Calendar documentaries aired before December 2012.

"A case in point is the Mayan calendar. In the run-up to December 21, 2012, the many predictions and prognostications of numerous cable television documentaries ranged from a day of sudden new age enlightenment on the one hand, to the complete end of life as we know it on the other. So what does the hard data tell us about what happened on December 21, 2012? The data shows us that it was an ordinary day, and many were embarrassed for having been stampeded into gloomy predictions as the cable television industry quietly counted their immense advertising profits."

The video wall fades to black as a spotlight focuses attention again on Rabbi Sarah.

"So was December 21, 2012, just another embarrassing non-event? If you see it through the prism of wishful thinking and hopeful biases that certainly was the case. However, when we view it from the standpoint of empirical data or hard facts, we see an entirely different before-and-after story.

"To put this in perspective, consider this. True prophecies always come in two parts: the harbinger event and the prophecy event. The harbinger event is a sign that the fulfillment of the prophecy is at hand. With this in mind, let's posit a question, 'Were the Mayans looking at December 21, 2012, as a harbinger date, or a prophecy date?' Logic eliminates the prophecy date expectation because after all, what good is a prophetic date if your world is ending that same day?

"Therefore, we must ask, 'Was the Mayan calendar prophecy of December 21, 2012, actually a prophetic harbinger of a near future event?' To answer that question let's use two different sets of empirical data. These are hard facts that are incontrovertible.

"We'll begin with fireballs. Assuming the Planet X System is inbound, what you learned in the previous theater, Pre-Perihelion Impact is that it is likely pushing Potentially Hazardous Asteroids (PHAs) towards us like the one featured in our impact scenario. If so, the first signs of this would be an increasing number of smaller fireballs in our skies which would continue to increase, along with the appearance of larger bolides as well."

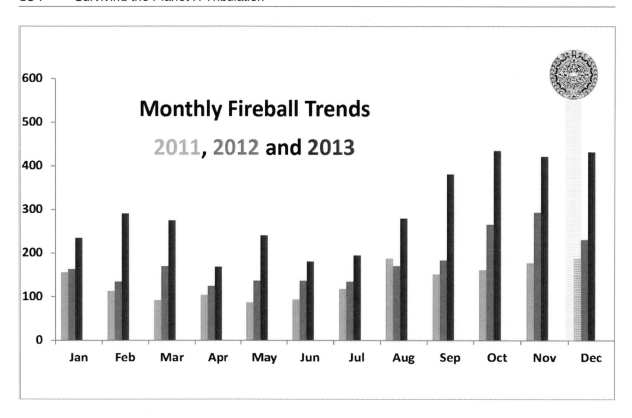

The wall fades up from black and reveals a Monthly Fireball Trends analysis for 2011, 2012 and 2013.

"Here you see a monthly trend analysis of fireballs observations reported by people in the USA and Canada. The year 2011 is shown in green, 2012 is shown in blue, and 2013 is shown in red. What this analysis shows is that during 2011, there was a rough average of between one hundred to one hundred and seventy-five fireballs observed per month. Then in 2012 we see that number increase, especially in the two months preceding December 21, 2012. However, in 2013 we see an average of two hundred to four hundred fireballs being reported by people in the USA and Canada."

"Another question is, assuming our sun is responding to the inbound approach of the Planet X System, would that interaction also effect the Earth and specifically, in regards to earthquake activity?"

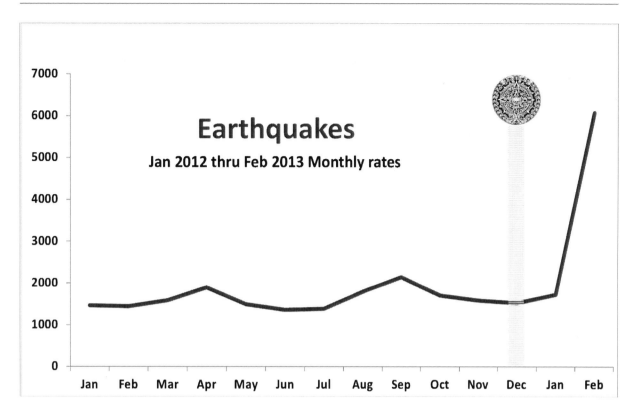

The wall fades to show an earthquake trend line for the period January 2012 to February 2013

"Consider this. For the entire year of 2012 there were, on average, fifteen hundred to two thousand total earthquakes per month for all magnitudes. After December 21, 2012 we saw that figure jump by the end of January 2013 to well over six thousand total earthquakes per month. That is a huge jump!"

The video wall fades to black as a spotlight focuses attention on Rabbi Sarah.

"Therefore, we do see a compelling case that our two suns are interacting on two levels, gravitational and electrical. Furthermore, apparently, the Planet X System is already pushing small space bodies towards us as evidenced by sharp increases in fireball observations."

"In response to those who maintain that December 21, 2012 was nothing more than an embarrassing non-event, we offer this empirical data. These hard facts, not television gimmickry and self-promotion, tell us a very different story than what was portrayed in the media."

"The ancient Mayans were sending a harbinger warning sign via their calendar across the expanse of time to their descendants in the future. They were warning us to watch for a unique celestial alignment; an alignment that would occur on December 21, 2012. Once their decedents observed this alignment, they would know the time was at hand to prepare for the next Planet X System flyby."

She pauses to smile at the audience as the curtain closes behind her.

"Up to now we've considered three threat possibilities: Cosmic lightning bolts, fireballs, and earthquakes. I hope each of you understands that these three only represent the tip of the iceberg so to speak. This is why I urge you to learn about all of the various tribulation threats your community could possibly face in the Threat Matrix Exploratorium. Next up is Theater Five – Pole Shift Harbingers and Events. Please remain seated."

Theater Five – Pole Shift Harbingers and Event

As before, the auditorium rotates around to the fifth theater stage with closed curtains and Rabbi Sarah standing behind a podium.

"In this presentation you will learn about the coming geographical pole shift both in terms of the two harbinger events that precede it, the pole shift event itself and the aftermath possibilities."

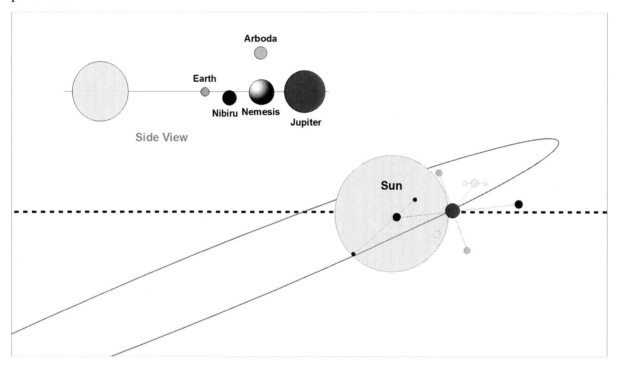

The curtains part and a large circular pedestal rises from center stage and the spotlights focus on a working version of the same mechanical model which was shown in theater four where the Planet X System was passing southward through the ecliptic. At the same time the video wall slowly fades up from black with a side view of the same celestial alignment.

"In this scenario, the pole shift will occur when Earth and the Planet X System are on the same side of the sun. At this time the brown dwarf star at the core of the Planet X System, Nemesis, will be passing southward, crossing the ecliptic between the orbits of Mars and Jupiter, as seen in the side view on the video wall behind me.

"The Planet X System also has its own planets and moons. So let's quickly look at the three largest planets of that system and their moons as they are shown in this scenario." A laser highlights the innermost planet on the stage model. "The innermost planet to Nemesis is Helion, a bright gaseous planet, with a moon, named Harrington, which is approximately the size of our own." The laser moves to the next planet out. "Second out from Nemesis is the planet Arboda, a smaller rocky planet." The laser moves to the outermost planet. "And beyond that is the planet Nibiru with its own moon, Ferrada."

> The pedestal with the mechanical model lowers back down into the stage as Rabbi Sarah continues to speak.

"Of particular concern to us will be the planet Nibiru and its moon Ferrada. This is because the first harbinger sign of an imminent pole shift event could be a collision between a major object in the Planet X System and a planet in our system. In this scenario the likely objects for this collision are the planet Venus and Nibiru's moon, Ferrada."

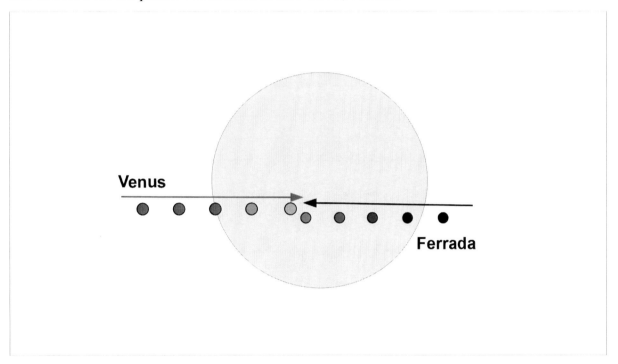

> The video wall fades to a close-up of the sun as Venus and the moon Ferrada approach each other from opposite directions.

"Here we see this possibility playing out between Venus and Ferrada where the northern pole of Ferrada collides with the southern pole of Venus. A collision like this will scatter impact debris into the inner solar system. Most of this debris would eventually fall into the sun, but some would be captured by the Planet X System, and some could become Potentially Hazardous Asteroids (PHAs). Given that Venus is just 0.723 AU from the Sun, we would likely see increased impact events and meteor storms resulting from a Ferrada-Venus impact."

> The wall fades to black, and a spotlight focuses attention on Rabbi Sarah.

"Our ability to view the impact event depicted in this scenario would largely be determined by two things: Earth's location relative to Venus and the Sun, and the condition of our viewing sky which will likely be quite poor. This is because at this point in the tribulation our atmosphere will be filled with a great deal of dust, volcanic ash, and other particulates. Therefore, even if the alignment is favorable to viewing, the tribulation skies will make it very difficult, if not impossible, for amateur astronomers such as me to observe the impact. In which case our only hope would be for our governments to be forthcoming with their own satellite observations."

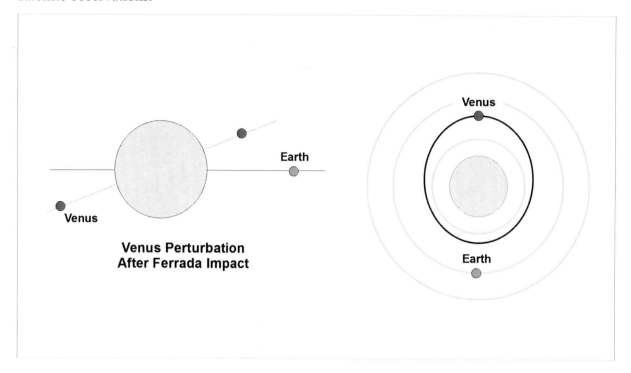

Venus Perturbation After Ferrada Impact

The wall fades up from black with split images. To the left, a side view of a projected post-impact inclination in the orbit of Venus, and to the right a more elliptical shape for the orbit.

"Here on the left you see the orbit of Venus becoming steeply inclined to the ecliptic, and to the right you see its orbit becoming more elliptical in shape. This is something that amateur astronomers would be quick to observe once we reach the backside of the tribulation where we'll see blue skies and taste sweet waters once again. However, the second pole shift harbinger event will not depend on clear skies or a favorable alignment."

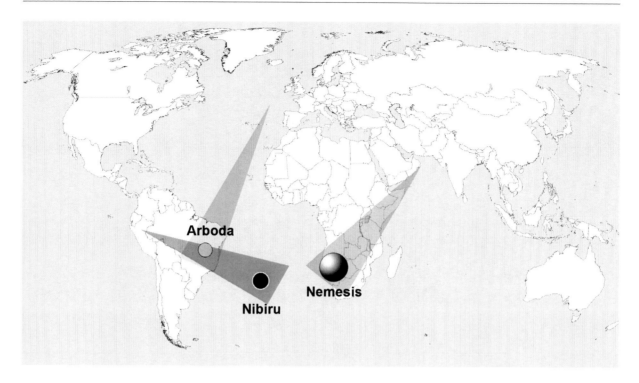

The wall fades to a global world map with three Planet X System gravitational lock-points noted on the Earth.

"The second of the two harbingers will likely be remembered as 'lurch day,' because every living soul on our planet will feel a sudden, powerful lurch as the major objects in the Planet X System combine their tidal gravitational forces upon Earth's lithosphere.

"The lithosphere is the rigid outer layer of our planet which consists of the crust and upper mantle. In this scenario we see three potential lithosphere lock-points where Nibiru locks onto South America, Arboda locks onto the North Atlantic, and Nemesis locks onto the Indian Ocean."

"Following lurch day the pole shift event begins, and it will take several days to be completed. These are days that future generations will remember as the 'Days of Darkness.' If your community is to survive the pole shift, this is when you must all take shelter underground."

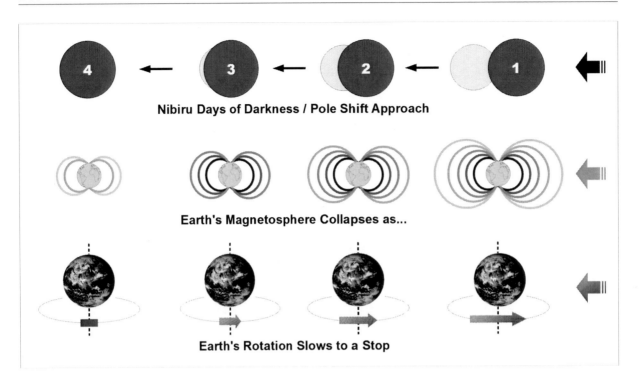

Nibiru Days of Darkness / Pole Shift Approach

Earth's Magnetosphere Collapses as...

Earth's Rotation Slows to a Stop

The video wall fades into a matrix of panels four wide and three columns deep. As the Rabbi speaks, the panels show the passage of Nibiru and its effect on Earth's magnetosphere and spin at each of the four approach stages.

"The pole shift days of darkness will begin as Nibiru passes from right to left between the Earth and Venus. In the first stage of this approach phase the spin of our planet and the magnetosphere that protects it are both stable."

"In stage two Nibiru begins to eclipse our sun. This is when the days of darkness begin and everyone will feel the profound changes happening to our planet as the tidal gravitational forces of the Planet X System begin to slow Earth's rotation. Thiswill cause our magnetosphere to begin a gradual collapse which will expose anyone left on the surface to dangerous radiation from space until Earth begins to rotate again and the magnetosphere rebuilds.

"In stage three only a small crescent of our sun remains as Nibiru approaches and creates a total eclipse. Now, the slowing of Earth's spin causes our magnetosphere to collapse significantly. At this time exposure to extreme solar and space radiation and solar storm threats begin.

"In stage four the planet Nibiru completely eclipses our sun. Unlike in a lunar eclipse, there will be no bright, beautiful, gossamer halo just darkness. This will be darkness such as we cannot imagine, and this is when the spin of our planet will come to a momentary halt, no doubt resulting in horrifying physical experiences. These experiences will cause many people to actually die from fright. But as the old proverb says, 'It's always darkest before the dawn.'"

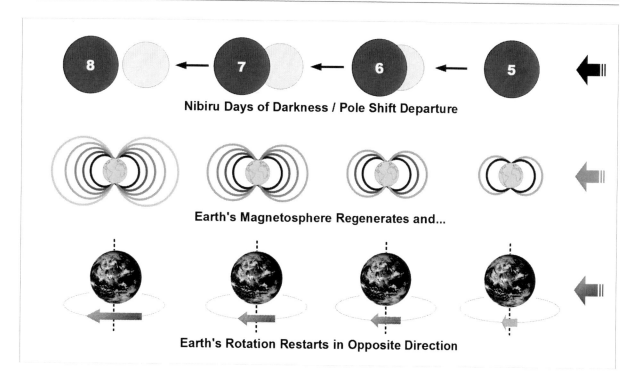

Nibiru Days of Darkness / Pole Shift Departure

Earth's Magnetosphere Regenerates and...

Earth's Rotation Restarts in Opposite Direction

The video wall fades to black. Then large, simple, white text appears, "A New Beginning." The text remains on the screen for five seconds and then fades back to black. Then another matrix of panels like before fade up showing the four departure stages.

"With stage five of the days of darkness Nibiru enters its departure phase. For those who were first horrified by the pause in the Earth's rotation, now Earth will begin to spin in the opposite direction. Again, there will likely be horrifying effects from this change.

"Stage six signals a new beginning for humankind as our sun begins to slip out from behind the dark obstruction of Nibiru. This is when the desire to return to the surface will find new hope as the magnetosphere of our planet begins to regenerate.

"In stage seven Earth's surface is bathed in sunlight once again, and its rotation is increasing in speed. Our magnetosphere is well along in its regeneration. This will be a time of renewed hope for the future and preparations for the celebration will begin."

"In stage eight Nibiru passes and leaves us with a fully regenerated magnetosphere to protect us from the sun and space radiation. Although our planet will be spinning in the opposite direction, survivors will feel the Earth beginning to settle as they celebrate the end of the days of darkness worldwide."

"Ours will not be a perfect world at that time, but it will be a new one. For example we already expect the first major change to be sunrise and sunset. After the days of darkness our sun will rise in the West and set in the East. So, what other possible changes could occur?"

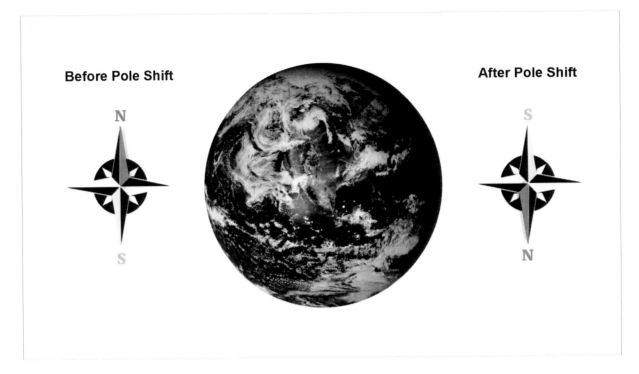

Before Pole Shift

After Pole Shift

The video wall fades into three divided panels. To the left we see a compass; in the center we see the Earth; and in the third panel to the right we see another compass.

"In the aftermath of the days of darkness there are many different possibilities to consider. However, we can certainly expect a geomagnetic reversal, or what is called a magnetic pole shift. In fact we already see the early signs of a shift like this in the South Atlantic. What will that mean for those of us who use a compass? North will become South, and South will become North."

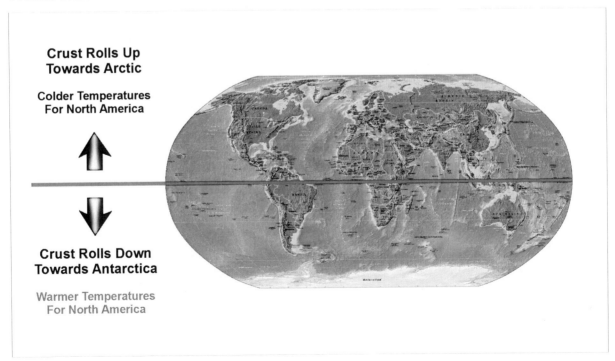

Crust Rolls Up Towards Arctic

Colder Temperatures For North America

Crust Rolls Down Towards Antarctica

Warmer Temperatures For North America

The video wall now fades to a single global image of the Earth spanning the full length of the wall.

"Of greatest concern to all is something known as a crustal pole shift. This is where the crust of our planet moves to a new location, sliding over the core of the earth. The core of the earth continues to orbit our sun in the same way so the crust will be in a different part of the globe from where it was before. Regions of the world that once bordered the equator could now find themselves in the Northern or Southern Hemisphere. However, for those of us living in North America, the big question will be climate change. If our planet's crust rolls upward, we can expect colder temperatures. Conversely, if our planet's crust rolls downward, we can expect warmer temperatures. Either way, there will be winners and losers around the earth."

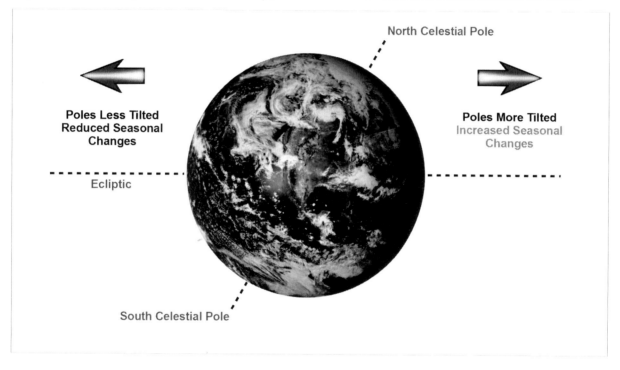

The video wall fades to a single global image of the Earth with its celestial poles.

"Another concern will be the seasons of the year. At present, the Earth's axis is tilted at an angle of 23.5° away from the plane of our solar system's ecliptic. If our planet's tilt changes during the pole shift, so will our seasons. In other words, if the poles become less tilted, we'll see reduced seasonal changes, and if their tilt becomes more extreme, we can expect intensified seasonal changes. Either way these changes will have profound consequences for all life on our planet."

The video wall fades to black as the curtains close and a spotlight focuses attention on Rabbi Sarah.

"Can humanity truly survive the physical adversity of a pole shift? Well, there are those who believe we already have, and that the last pole shift event was Noah's Flood. Instead of a deluge flooding the Earth, they maintain that a pole shift caused the oceans to come out of their basins which resulted in an ebbing tsunami wave that gently lifted the ark off its chocks before pulling it back out to sea.

"This is an intriguing notion to say the least. Especially, since these same people believe that the forty days and forty nights of rain described in the story of Noah's Flood actually occurred but not at the beginning of the pole shift. Rather, they insist it happened afterward. We're going to talk about that in our sixth and final presentation, Transiting the Tail, Deluge, and Backside. Please remain seated."

Theater Six — Transiting the Tail, Deluge and Backside

The auditorium rotates around to the sixth theater stage. The curtains are closed, and Rabbi Sarah is standing behind the podium as the auditorium floor comes to a gentle stop.

"Welcome to the sixth and final presentation, Transiting the Tail, Deluge, and Backside. In the previous theater, we learned about the pole shift and how it will be the worst of all of the catastrophic events during the tribulation. This is because a pole shift can claim billions of lives."

"Of particular concern is that those who do survive the pole shift may unwittingly believe the worst of the tribulation is now over, and they will happily go about the business of rebuilding their lives. But they are unaware that two more major events await them. For the unsuspecting these two events will cause additional death and destruction, and crush the hopes of many for a quick end to the tribulation."

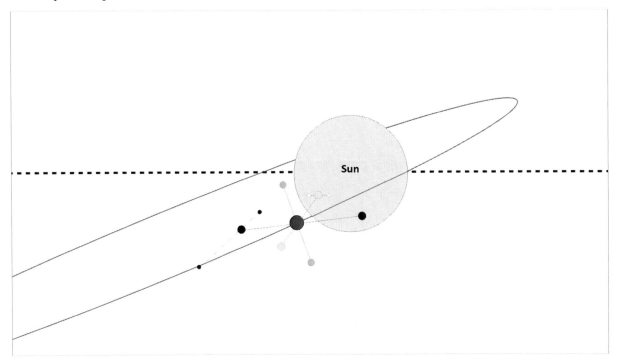

The curtains part as a large circular pedestal rises up from the center of the stage and spotlights begin to focus on a working a version of the same mechanical model shown in theater five. The Planet X System is now shown in the southern skies below the ecliptic.

"The last two major events will occur when the Planet X System is in the southern skies, and well below the ecliptic. It is on its way out to the farthest reaches of our solar system. It will not return for another thirty-six hundred years. This is when the old prophecies warn us that the dragon will return to crack its tail on the earth. No wonder we call it 'transiting the tail.'"

> The pedestal sinks back down into the stage as the video wall fills with a cloud of red dust in space moving from upper left to lower right.

"Although the main body of the Planet X System will be below the ecliptic at this time, there will be another part trailing behind it well above the ecliptic. This is the debris tail of the Nemesis brown dwarf system, and it is very long. This is because brown dwarf stars are very dirty, and they drag behind them a vast debris tail with a potential mix of iron, hydrogen, carbon, phosphorus, nickel, palladium, and many other elements. These elements will fall to earth in the form of dust, and meteors.

"This raises a very important question: Given that our skies will be dirty from volcanic ash, dust, and smoke, how will we know when Earth is about to enter the tail of the Planet X System?"

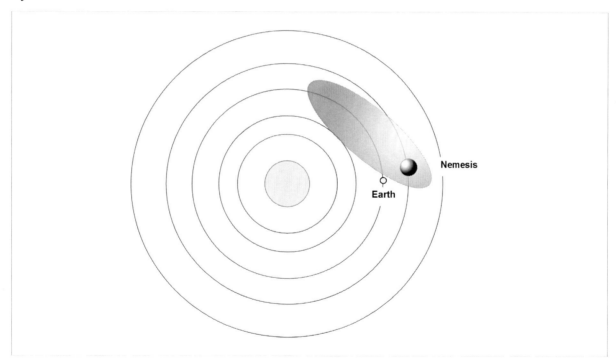

> The video wall fades to black and then divides into four horizontal panels. In the first panel on the left, a polar view of the system with orbits delineated and the Nemesis tail appears.

"Even though we will most likely be unable to see the tail, we'll know our transit through it is about to occur when we smell the iron dust. Here is where the blind can be invaluable. Because of their blindness, their sense of smell will be more attuned, and they will notice this odor before most others do."

"This is when those who return to the surface to plant crops must quickly harvest whatever is possible. As the Earth enters the tail, Earth's entire surface will be blanketed with iron dust. Not only will this kill and contaminate crops on the surface, all surface water will be poisoned as well. Too much iron ingested into the human body is toxic and can be fatal. We will also see the waters turn blood red at this time."

> In the second, third, and fourth panels, video scenes of bricks being made in a brickyard appear.

"To imagine how this works, let's imagine we're visiting a local brickyard to see how they make decorative red bricks. What we'll see is that they use a standard mix and then color it red by adding iron."

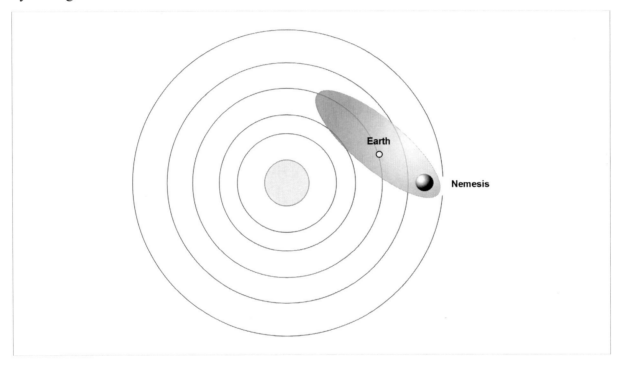

> The first panel fades to show Earth inside the tail showing farms, lakes, and cities blanketed with red iron dust.

"Once Earth begins its transit inside the Nemesis tail, iron dust will settle upon the entire surface of our planet. Sources of fresh surface water will turn blood red and will no longer be fit to drink. Our soils will no longer sustain growth. Even worse, the waters will eventually turn from red to green because of the phosphorus in the tail."

> The images in the second, third, and fourth panels fade to various views of blue-green algae.

"This is because nitrogen and phosphorus support the growth of algae and other aquatic plants. For blue-green algae this massive infusion of phosphorus will become a veritable feast causing vast blooms. These blooms will then cause another plague when the algae generate a very powerful toxin. In sufficient quantities this toxin can kill both man and beast and not just in the water. The airborne fumes generated from the blooms will cause serious respiratory distress. This is why, after the days of darkness have passed, your community must make sure that it has ample supplies of clean water stored in underground cisterns and tanks."

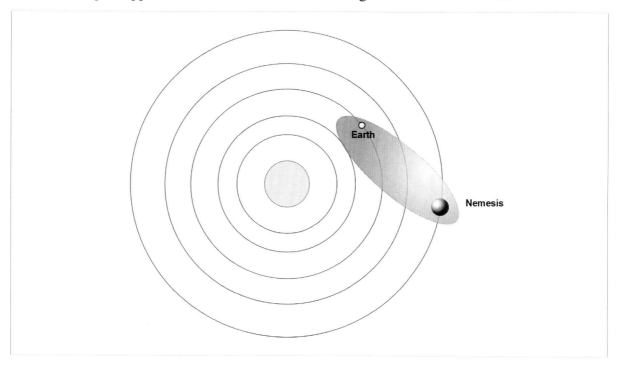

The images in the second, third, and fourth panels, fade into meteor showers falling on the Earth.

"Another problem will be horrific meteor showers. Those caught unawares by the transit of the tail will be pummeled by very demoralizing meteor showers. These showers will come and go like summer rains, and the average size of these impactors will be roughly that of a pig's head. They will destroy above-ground structures such as homes and water tanks and leave the unprepared without fresh water, food, or shelter. Sadly, this is when many pole shift survivors will perish."

The images in the second, third, and fourth panels fade into a single panoramic scene of a blind woman with a cane, standing on a mountain top and giving a thumbs up signal to her friend.

"Eventually, all that will be left will be the smell of iron and no more meteors or large particles. When that happens, it will be safe to come above ground for short periods of time as Earth nears the end of its transit through the tail. While the meteor showers will have ended by then, most of the harm already will have been done, and the land will remain coated with iron dust and other elements of the flyby."

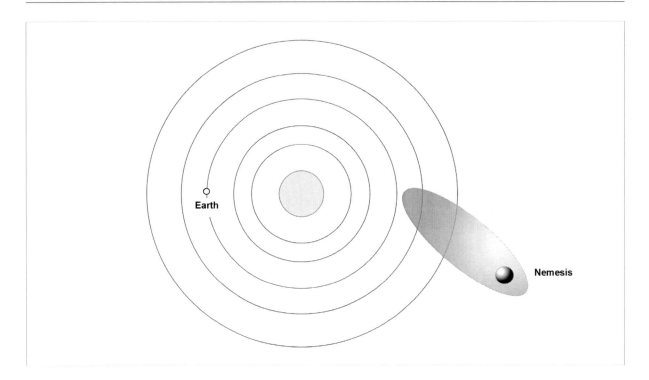

The first panel fades to show Earth on the opposite side of the solar system from the tail. The second, third, and fourth panels show a montage of monsoon-like rains, desert rivers flooding, mudslides, and lahars.

"Sometime on or before Earth and the Planet X System are on opposite sides of the sun in their respective orbits, a global deluge will begin. Yes, there will come a proverbial forty days and forty nights of rain when Mother Earth cleanses herself. This deluge will bring both opportunity and heartbreak as what remains of many homes and cities are flooded and carried away. So be mindful, and do not rebuild or replant until the deluge has passed."

"This is why you must build your shelters as high as possible above the flood plains. Also, during this deluge streams, natural water pathways, and rivers will overflow their banks. Therefore, not only must you build well above the flood plains; you must also do so at safe distances from rivers, lakes, and natural drainage areas as well."

The second, third, and fourth panels fade into a montage of raised sea beds being cleansed of salts, and lakes and rivers being cleansed of iron.

"While the deluge will be horrific for some, for the prepared it will signal a great healing of the planet. Although slow-moving bodies of water such as sloughs and swamps will not recover for a century or more, all other water bodies and pathways where waters can move more quickly will be flushed clean of the residue deposited by the Planet X System tail. Also, during the pole shift as some existing land masses sink; new ones arise from the sea beds. During this deluge these new land masses will be washed clean of their salts, leaving vast new areas of highly fertile soil for cultivation."

The second, third, and fourth panels fade into a montage of vast grasslands set against blue skies and scenes of crystal-clear lakes and streams.

"After the deluge has passed, we'll know that the worst of the tribulation has passed and that we will finally be at the beginning of the backside. We will see blue skies and taste sweet waters once again."

The video wall fades to black as the curtains close. A spotlight focuses attention on Rabbi Sarah.

"At the beginning of this program, I explained to you that we would cover the first three-to-four years of a tribulation that may last as long twelve years. What can we then expect for the remaining eight-to-nine years of the tribulation?

"Our planet's geology and weather changes will be in flux, and it will take time for these changes to settle. So, for the remainder of the tribulation we can expect high levels of volcanic eruptions, earthquakes, earth trumpets, and ongoing severe weather. However, these will lessen in severity and frequency over time. Also, impact events will be ongoing, but will gradually decline in number."

Rabbi Sarah steps out from behind the podium and walks to the center of the stage to face the audience.

"There will come a time, after the tribulation and in your lifetimes, when Earth will once again be serene and beautiful. Many of our forests and trees will have been lost, but they will grow back. In advance of that we'll see vast expanses of grasses and flowering weeds which are the first plants to return after cataclysms. They will be beautiful, green, and lush." She extends her hands outward to the audience from waist level, "As the spiritual leaders of faith-based survival communities, the backside will not be about the end of this civilization."

Turning her palms towards the ceiling, she begins slowly lifting up her hands, "Rather, we must make it a clean slate for the beginning of the next civilization. Our species can enter an age of enlightenment where we no longer idolize the clever but instead admire the kind."

She points her index fingers at the two exits at the back of the auditorium, "In a moment the doors behind you will open, and you can visit the rest of the park. My hope is that you will proceed directly from here to the Threat Matrix Exploratorium."

She drops her arms and makes a slow pushing motion with the palms of her hands, "I strongly urge you to visit the Threat Matrix Exploratorium because what you've seen here is only a high-level overview of the tribulation process which has been provided so you can plan for possible events before they happen."

Turning the palms of her hands inward, she slowly brings her hands together, "But in the Threat Matrix Exploratorium you will be able to access very specific information about the various types of threats your community must anticipate. You will also learn some simple ways to deal with those threats."

"If all of this seems overwhelming at first, let me share with you an old Jewish saying, 'We will do, and we will understand.' This means that action often precedes understanding. In other words just start doing it, and the rest will sort itself out."

Her arms drop slowly to her sides as she closes with, "It has been my honor to serve you today, and I hope to see each and every one of you on the backside. This concludes our Tribulation Carousel Theater Program."

As her holographic image fades out, the audience lights come up and "Concerto No. 1, Spring" from Vivaldi's "The Four Seasons" begins to play.

Instead of suddenly jumping up to leave, the audience members remain seated for a few minutes to listen to the music and to contemplate what they've just learned. Finally, a few begin leaving and the rest follow.

I look over at Sheba and ask, "Well girl, do you need some time on the grass to have a dance with my super-duper poop remover?"

"Woof."

"Well," I say admiringly, "You've got a better bladder than I do."

"Ditto on that one," you chime in, "Let's head for the Exploratorium and find us a pit stop along the way."

"Works for me," I say, "Let's roll."

"Woof, woof!" What is it about this dog?

7

Threat Matrix Exploratorium

The exit from the Tribulation Carousel Theater leads into a small courtyard between the theater and the smaller, dome-shaped Exploratorium building with a long wishing pool in the center. Strolling through the covered walkway to Exploratorium, we see people are tossing coins into the pool and making wishes.

"What do you think they wish for?" you ask quietly.

I look at them more carefully and observe, "Not one of them is under forty-five. So I'd say they wish that their children and grandchildren will survive."

"Oh my God, you're right. There are no children making wishes."

We continue walking silently with Sheba beside us as we enter the main entrance hall of the Threat Matrix Exploratorium. It is a wedge-shaped hall with an information booth in the center. To our left we see people shopping in a well-stocked bookstore and reading in an adjacent cafe. To the right, we see restrooms, a comfortable-looking lounge area for nursing mothers, telephones, and water fountains. Just beyond the information booth, the lobby narrows to a ramp leading to a lower mezzanine level. There is a small booth in the mezzanine, and the entrance is roped off. A sign reads, "Guided Tours Starting Every Five Minutes."

Standing behind the podium is a distinguished-looking African American gentleman doing a head count of the people queuing up for the tour. He looks to be in his sixties and is dressed in a blue oxford shirt with the sleeves rolled up, a fine silver watch, black slacks, and a lanyard with his docent ID attached dangles from his neck. He finishes his count, opens the entrance and says pleasantly, "Please step this way, proceed to the center of the exhibit, and wait for me there." His voice is deep and warm, and his eyes sparkle in a knowing way. We're one of the last to enter, and he gives Sheba a wink as she jaunts by.

Threat Matrix Pyramid

At the center of the exhibit, we find ourselves in a large, circular area with a massive pyramid in the center. Turning slowly on its base, it reaches nearly all the way to the roof. It is a most impressive sight. From its base to its capstone, the pyramid is divided into six different-colored layers. On two sides there is descriptive text for each layer, and on the remaining two sides, single-digit numbers.

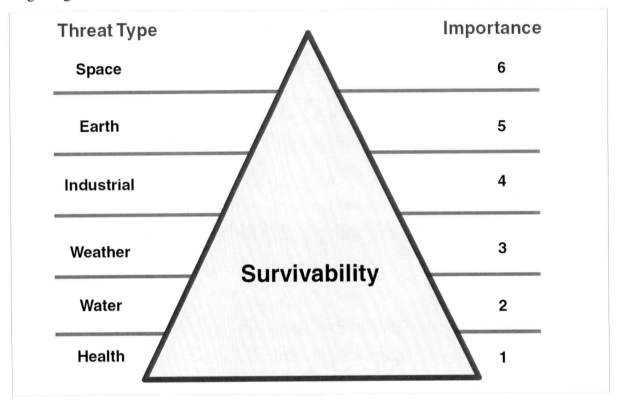

Beginning with the capstone at the top and continuing down we see: Space — 6, Earth — 5, Industrial — 4, Weather — 3, Water — 2 and Health — 1.

Stepping onto a small pull-out pedestal the gentleman says with a sweeping gesture of his arms, "Please gather around," and the group assembles before him. "I see that we have seven adults, three children, and one dog — a manageable group. Hello, everyone and welcome to the Threat Matrix Exploratorium. I'm Charlie Michaels, and I will be your docent for this guided tour which will take approximately 50 minutes."

Charlie is a likable figure of a man with closely-groomed white hair and a full and impressive mustache. With bright eyes and a high forehead, he comes across as a professional who is comfortable making presentations to groups of people. With a deep voice and charming accent he continues, "We're presently on the lower mezzanine with our Threat Matrix Pyramid exhibit, which you can see behind me."

Charlie turns slightly towards the pyramid and points at the upper two levels, "On two sides of the pyramid you see the names of the six different types of threats that form the matrix:

Space, Earth, Industrial, Weather, Water, and Health. On the other two sides, you see the planning and preparation importance rating number for each of these threat types."

"But why are the numbers reversed?" an elderly lady standing towards the back of the group asks, "Assuming that six stands for the sixth least important, it seems counter-intuitive to me that space threats would be the least important threat. Why is this?"

Charlie smiles, "You know ma'am, that was my first impression as well, and here is what I learned. The primary message of the threat matrix pyramid is that survivability is what matters most. If you look at the capstone at the very top, its small size tells us that our ability to survive space threats is very little compared to the base of the pyramid, which is health. So the underlying message of the pyramid is this, 'Focus your greatest attention and efforts on those things you can do the most about surviving.'"

"But if you're not prepared to survive an asteroid impact, what's the point of being healthy?" the lady responds.

"That is an excellent question," Charlie says, "So let me answer it this way. Let's assume that a community has expended most of its resources and time on building a sophisticated underground survival shelter capable of withstanding a medium-size asteroid impact event. As a retired aerospace engineer, that would certainly be an interesting project, but consider this — all it takes is for one community member to ignore the rule to wash their hands after using the restroom, and then they help prepare a community meal. The next thing you know, half of the community in this wonderfully complex survival structure is dying from cholera. Now does it make sense?"

"Well, when you put it that way," the lady admits, "I see your point."

Charlie adds with a smile, "May I also hasten to add that you do need to provide protection from the asteroid impact this kind lady mentioned. While it may not be an elaborate underground facility, you could find shelter in an abandoned train tunnel, or even a natural cave or cavern that could be quickly adapted for use."

"The point here is that there are no perfect solutions. Each and everyday survivors will learn how to do more with less. Likewise, each and every decision will be heavily weighed with what is on hand versus perceived dangers. This is the point of the threat matrix pyramid. The more survivable a threat is, the greater its importance to prepare for."

A young red-haired girl standing next to her mother blurts out, "So if I want to survive I need to wash my hands!"

Her outburst makes Charlie laugh, and he points both index fingers at her, "Now this little girl really does get it," he says proudly to the group, then leans towards her and says, "Dear child, I couldn't have said it any better myself."

He walks to the wall, "Let's see, we've got three courageous young kids here today," and with a smile for Sheba adds, "and one brave puppy."

Stepping off the pedestal, he pushes it back into place and goes to the wall, pulling out a drawer and removing four plastic packages. Inside each is a red bandana folded into a triangular neckerchief with an official Planet X World's Fair neck-slide. He hands three of the packages to the parents of the children and the fourth to me for Sheba.

The parents begin opening their packages to the gleeful excitement of their children. Wagging her tail, Sheba leans up against me as I remove the bandana from the package. "You want your bandana, don't you girl?"

"Woof, woof! Woof, woof!"

As I fasten it around her neck, Charlie continues his presentation, "The Exploratorium is divided into six galleries, one for each of the six threat matrix types. In each of the galleries, I'll give you a brief presentation and then answer your questions. You'll have a short period to familiarize yourself with each of the exhibits. Please remember, when the tour is over you're encouraged to come back and spend as much time as you like visiting all the galleries. Closing time is 10:00 p.m. this evening. Also, please remember to be respectful of the other tour groups coming through."

He pushes the drawer back into the wall and looks around with a smile at the children having great delight with their new bandanas, "On the opposite side of the pyramid is a curved ramp leading up to the Space Gallery on the main floor. If you just walk around the pyramid and up the ramp, we can move to the next part of the tour." With that, the three children run around the pyramid and up the ramp, racing each other to the main floor. Sheba is not far behind, wagging her tail like a happy puppy.

You lean over and whisper to me, "That's the first time she's ever left us that way."

"Are we a bit jealous now?" I joke.

"Smart-Alec," you say as you wrinkle your nose, "I see Charlie is holding back, no doubt to make sure he doesn't lose somebody from the group. Let's walk with him because I have a question or two for him."

"Sure. But only as a courtesy to a fellow smart-Alec."

Chuckling, we step to the back of the group next to Charlie, and you ask, "Charlie, docents are usually volunteers. Are you a volunteer?"

"Yes, I'm proud to say that I am."

"So are you from around here?"

"No, I'm retired, and I live far away. But I have a dear old friend who's letting me use his guest bedroom while I'm here at the fair as a volunteer. He is volunteering too, but in a different exhibit hall."

As the leader of a faith-based organization, you appreciate people who volunteer their time and who will go to great lengths to do so, like Charlie. "Do you mind if I ask why you volunteered and went to all of this trouble to be here?"

"Not at all."

"Well then, why are you here and why did you go to all this trouble?" I'm tickled to see that Charlie has made you ask and that you did.

"I'm a proud father and grandfather and a happily married man, but being a retired aeronautical engineer, I'm the only one in my family with a deep interest in science and I've been in awareness about what is coming for quite some time. The problem is that trying to get the family to even glance at the science is impossible. They're all in denial, and we all live along a coastline."

"It was breaking my heart, and I didn't know what to do about it, or what to think about it until I heard a certain someone on the radio." With that, Charlie winks at me and says, "Marshall, it was something you said that changed my life, and I spotted you coming through the entrance. If you think I was going to let you tour with another docent, no way, no how."

Stunned, you glance at me, then at Charlie, back at me, back again at Charlie and finally back at me, "Okay," you say while pointing the finger at me, "What on earth did you tell this man that changed his life?"

I shrug my shoulders, "I do so many radio interviews, God only knows which one. What was it, Charlie?" With that, we give Charlie an inquisitive look that makes him chuckle.

"It was when Marshall explained why I'm aware, that even before I was born, I made a promise to Creator to do what I'm doing now. He explained that my mission is threefold: to teach, to mentor, and to comfort. Marshall, when I heard you say that on the radio, it was like a bolt of lightning hitting me, and all the frustration that I had about my family being in denial stopped tormenting me. Sure, it still hurts, but now I have a way to live with it. So when I saw the opportunity to come here as a volunteer docent, I also saw a way to keep my promise to Creator. Every minute of every day that I'm here is a blessing in my life."

I'm so touched by what Charlie just said that all I can think to say in return is, "Group hug!" As we hug, out of the corner of my eye I can see some of the other members of our group ahead of us looking back with that, "Now just what's going on there?" look in their eyes, but I couldn't care less. This is one of those magic moments in life that is precious beyond measure.

"Thank you for making my day, Charlie," I say as we finally break the hug.

"And thank you for making mine," he answers, "Now we better get going before that pup of yours, and those three kids wind up three galleries ahead of us." We all laugh and speed-walk up the ramp to the first gallery.

Space Gallery

Stepping up on another pull-out pedestal, Charlie calls the group together doing a quick headcount, "We have some other people who are independently viewing the exhibits here in the space gallery, so please gather round folks and then I can speak more softly." The group congregates with the children and Sheba up front, next to the pedestal. The little red-haired girl is holding tightly to Sheba; the two of them are utterly enamored with each other.

"As you recall, the space threats have the lowest planning and preparation priority because they are unfortunately the least survivable. This does not mean that you are defenseless. Quite the contrary, because Mother Earth can provide you with some of the finest shelter imaginable, and in most cases, it will not cost you a single penny. Sure, you can build complex, deep shelters and many of you will do so as members of communities. But you'll also learn to use the simple things too, like rock overhangs, caves, tunnels, and so forth to protect yourselves and your loved ones. And while space threats can be very dangerous, we live on a big planet, and the odds that you'll be in harm's way is slim. Now let me briefly tell you about the four groups of exhibits here in this gallery."

Pointing to the opposite corner of the room Charlie says, "The first exhibit group is called, 'Impactors.' These fall on us from space, and in the impactor category, we have five different exhibits: Asteroid Airburst, Asteroid Deep Impact, Meteor Showers, Small Impact Events, and Large Bolide Airbursts. A simple rule of thumb with impactors is that you will need earth or rock over your head, twelve feet at a minimum but, of course, the more, the better."

Pointing to the corner of the room he continues, "In the far corner is the second exhibit group, Spaceborne Elements. Here we have three different exhibits: Cosmic Dust, Nemesis Tail Particulates, and Nemesis Tail Gases."

"For those of you who've already enjoyed the Tribulation Carrousel Theater, you know that our passage through the tail of the Planet X System will be a difficult one. Some say it will be no different than the 1910 Halley's Comet scare. There was a panic because there was a possibility that Earth would pass through the comet's tail, which some astronomers said contained a cloud of poisonous gas. In that case, nothing happened other than hucksters making a lot of money on gas masks and placebo comet pills."

"However, this time there is a genuine concern. So be sure to see this exhibit group. You'll see several suggestions about the kinds of gas masks and respirators you can stockpile for your communities for the worst periods, which will be relatively brief. Most of the time light particle masks or the simple cotton bandanas that your children are wearing today will offer protection against common dust and particulates. So hold on to them kids. They'll come in handy one day."

Pointing to the opposite corner of the room he continues, "In the opposite corner is the third exhibit group, Solar Events. Here we have four different exhibits: Solar Flares, Solar CME Plasma, Solar Sprites and Solar Weather.

"The most common solar event is called a CME (Coronal Mass Ejection), and it typically begins with a solar flare which reaches Earth in about eight minutes. The CME is then followed by solar plasma (electrified gas) which can take up to 48 hours to reach the earth. The CMEs we need to be concerned about are the Earth-directed kind. That is, they're coming straight at us. So while CMEs will frequently happen during the tribulation, only a few will strike the Earth, and even then they will just be regional events. As with the impactors, being underground during these events with a minimum of twelve feet of earth or rock over your head is your best bet. Of particular concern will be solar weather during the days of darkness and the pole shift event. This is when the magnetosphere is going to be heavily degraded, so please do not be on the surface at any time during that period, for any reason."

Pointing to the floor he continues, "Here, where we're standing right now, is the fourth exhibit group, Solar Radiation. Here we have eight different exhibits: Gamma, X-Ray, Ultraviolet (UV), EMP, and Radiation Shielding."

"Of all the threats in this room solar radiation is, in my opinion, the worst of the lot and here is why. Gamma radiation causes serious damage when absorbed by living cells. X-rays are destructive to all biological organisms, and exposure to them can cause DNA damage and mutations. During the days of darkness and pole shift, do not go above ground so you can stay safe from these threats."

"Now, while many have heard of gamma radiation and X-ray threats, there's a third one that is nearly as bad. It's ultraviolet radiation, or UV as its known, and prolonged exposure to UV can result in acute and chronic health effects on the skin, eyes, and immune system. So get clothing and eye-wear that offer UV protection."

"For example, check to see if hats and shirts you are considering offer protection such as UPF 50+, and when you buy sunglasses for your tribulation survival kit, make sure they block out 99 to 100 percent of both UV-A and UV-B radiation. There's a lot of information here in this exhibit, and we also have several excellent books available in the gift shop with additional useful information."

"Finally, I do want to mention EMP, which stands for electromagnetic pulse. This can come from the sun, but it also can be the result of an atomic bomb blast or the detonation of an EMP weapon. In any event, EMP is not harmful to the body. However, for those with surgically implanted medical devices such as pacemakers, EMP can cause these devices to fail catastrophically, along with electronic devices of all kinds."

"Regarding protection from solar radiation always remember two things. First, solar radiation is a principal component of all solar events, and it moves in a straight line down from the Sun to you. Second, shielding is your best defense, the more shielding, the better."

"As a retired engineer, shielding is one topic that is near and dear to my heart. So please be sure to take the time to review the shielding exhibit because it will tell you how different types of commonly available materials are offer effective shielding. From most effective to least effective they are: lead, iron, steel and volcanic basalt; bricks and rocks; reinforced concrete; dirt, sand, and clay; ice and permafrost; wood; and snow. As with impactors, the same simple rule applies to solar events; you want to have twelve feet of earth above your head at a minimum."

"We'll spend another five minutes in this gallery so that you all can walk around and quickly familiarize yourself with the various exhibit groups and exhibits. After the tour, you're welcome to come back and spend as much time as you wish in this gallery." With that Charlie steps off the pedestal, pushing it back into place as the group scatters in every direction, with Sheba following the children.

You stand close to me and ask, "Will we have time to come back and spend several hours here?"

"As much time as you want. If you want to come back tomorrow and review all of this information and spend even more time in the exhibits nothing would please me more."

You nod appreciatively, "Good because I got more questions for Charlie." You move closer to Charlie and I follow you.

"How can I be of assistance?"

"Charlie, I'll be coming back through and spending a lot of time on these exhibits. I appreciate the information you're giving, but I have a question for you of a personal nature. Is it OK to ask it?"

"Never hurts to ask."

"Could you tell me more about your family, and what you've done to try and explain all of this to them, and why they just won't open their minds to it? I'm asking because I have people in my congregation that are going to be dealing with these same denial issues."

Charlie smiles, "Well, all of them tell me the same three things, 'It's all nonsense. Nothing's going to happen, and I don't want to hear about it.' None of them have a science background, although I'm not sure that would have made a difference. My wife is a devoted Christian, and that is the driving force of her life. She even leads the church choir. I suppose, for her, imagining how her happy, comfortable life could end and most of the people she knows and cares about could die, is just too unbearable to contemplate. As for my kids, they pat me on the shoulder and say, 'We'll see dad, we will see.' Then there is my middle-born, she's an artist and doing well. The minute I even begin to mention all this, she starts to tell me that I am manifesting negative, disastrous things and that it's an invention of my mind. She only wants to hear happy things about the future, and she believes that will create them."

"Are they any of them leaning in the smallest way toward accepting your message?" you ask.

"Well, yes. The one that is a little different from the others is my youngest because he's getting into politics. He's young and wants to make the world a better place. He's beginning to see some of the things I'm talking about regarding what our government is doing to prepare, and the kind of secrets that are being kept. On the one hand, he cannot deny it, but on the other hand, he simply does not want to know."

"So what do you think it would take to make them listen?"

"I don't know, and to be honest, I've given up on it. They have each made their choices to be ignorant of what is happening to the world around them. Trying to shake them out of their little denial bubbles is only going to upset the boat. So I just do my thing and try to help the ones I can. Meanwhile, I keep asking God for advice. I hope you don't think I sound a bit touched, but I feel like I'm getting it, and it's helping me a lot."

I put my hand on Charlie's shoulder and say, "You have a good bead on it my friend."

He nods his head as the young red-haired child runs up to him. Charlie sees her mother looking on from across the room, "Mr. Charlie, I have a question."

He smiles, "Sure. By the way, what's your name."

"I'm Cynthia, and I was wondering. Will I survive the tribulation?"

Hearing a question like this come from the mouth of a small child stuns all three of us. It puts the purpose of what we're all doing front and center, and in a very personal way.

Touched by her question, Charlie kneels down to see her eye-to-eye, "Cynthia, nobody knows the answer to that, but here's what I can tell you. You are a kind person, and you have a good heart. So don't let anybody change that because these will be your greatest survival strengths for the rest of your life."

"And I can tell you from the bottom of my heart that I hope you do survive the tribulation. This is why I get up each morning and come here to talk to people just like you. I want you to survive, and if there is something that I have said during this tour that does something to help you to save your life, or someone else's, then you have given my life purpose, and I'm grateful to you for that."

Beaming like a bank of floodlights, Cynthia jumps up, gives him a big hug, and says, "I hope you survive too, Charlie." And just as quick as that, she turns around and runs back to her mother, who smiles and holds her hand.

Charlie slowly stands back up. We can see that his knees are a little stiff but he doesn't complain, and his eyes begin to well up. In a choked voice he says, "That little girl has more awareness in her pinky that my whole family has all put together. I would give all that I have and more if each of them could be a Cynthia." Staring down at his watch he clears his throat and says, "Well, it's time to move on to the next gallery."

Walking to the center of the entrance he turns to face the group, "Remember, you can come back here later and spend all the time you like."

People begin filing out, and we join the group walking around the curved hall. To our left is the massive pyramid slowly turning on its pedestal, and to our right, a full-sized mural on the wall between the galleries depicts a survival community. You can see people doing a broad range of tasks and working together.

At the top of the mural we see the text, "The Three E's of Surviving as a Community." Below it is three bullet points: Everyone Works; Everyone Defends; and Everyone Participates. Walking past the mural, we come to the second gallery, Earth, and follow Charlie through the entrance.

Earth Gallery

As before, Charlie stands atop a small pull out pedestal, "Please gather around folks. This is the Earth Gallery, and it is the fifth priority threat type on the threat matrix pyramid. This is because if you're living in a place that is near an ocean like me, you're not going to do very well there. Not well at all. However, mitigating the risks of this threat type is simple. Perhaps all of you have heard of the three rules of premium real estate, which are: location, location, and location. In other words, if you are in a high-risk area, your first and the best way to deal with Earth threats will be to relocate to a safer area."

A gentleman standing in the back, a father of one of the boys wearing a bandanna asks, "Are there some simple guidelines you could recommend?"

"I'd be happy to," Charlie responds, "If you're living along the coastline, you want to look for an area where you are 150 miles or more inland and at an elevation of 2,500 feet to 5,000 feet. Locations above 5,000 feet will put you into a high-altitude farming situation, and this will limit your ability to grow food once things settle down. In general, stay away from the major cities and look for rolling hills, soft earth, and ample water from wells and springs, and tall trees."

"Why tall trees?" the man asks.

"That's a good question," Charlie replies, "I'll get to the answer in just a moment, but first let me tell everyone about the exhibits."

Pointing to the opposite corner of the room Charlies says, "The first exhibit group is called Regional Disasters. We already see these kinds of disasters, but during the tribulation, they will become far more severe and far more frequent. In this group, we have nine different exhibits: Earthquakes, Floods, Sinkholes, Animal Die-Offs, Insect Die-Offs, Defoliation, Desertification, and Earth Trumpeting."

He then looks at the man who asked the question, "You want to find areas with tall trees to be sure that life goes down deep into the soil. During the tribulation, the surface is going to take quite a beating, and in many areas the soil could become dead and lifeless up to 18 inches or more. If you see tall trees you know that life goes deeper than that, so there will still be some capacity left for growing food after the worst of the tribulation."

Pointing to the corner of the room he continues, "In the far corner is the second exhibit group, General Earth Movements. Here we have five different exhibits: Land Mass Separations, Land Masses Rising, Land Masses Sinking, Landslides, and Mountain-Building Earth Movements. Again, the three rules of premium real estate apply here: location, location, and location. In general, you want to avoid being near large fault lines such as the San Andreas, Cascadia, or New Madrid."

"But let's say that circumstances prevent you from relocating to a better area. What do you do? You make the best of it. For example, let's say you live in the San Francisco Bay area. In that case, being to the east of the San Andreas is not going to be a good place. But being to the west of the San Andreas could be a viable option, and here's why. During the tribulation, all of the coastal areas are going to be affected, and I'm sure everyone here has seen the various post tribulation maps on the Internet where entire swaths of the country wind up becoming seabed."

"If you live in California and you are to the west of the San Andreas, you might get lucky and just wind up living on an island, if you arrive there after the tsunamis have passed,; because this is what we expect will happen to California. The western side of the state will become an archipelago of islands after being swept by earthquakes and tsunamis, and the mountainous areas to the east will survive entirely. While there are no absolute guarantees as to the safety of any location on the face of the planet, doing something is better than doing nothing. The smallest things can make the biggest differences."

Pointing to the opposite corner of the room he continues, "In the opposite corner is the third exhibit group, Noxious Gas Emissions. Here we have five different exhibits: Carbon Dioxide, Carbon Monoxide, Hydrogen Sulfide, Methane, and Other Noxious Gasses."

"Just out of curiosity, how many of you here have visited Yellowstone National Park? Please raise your hands," he counts the hands one at a time, "Four of you. I'm impressed. Please keep your hands up for a moment because I'm sure that all four of you were impressed by how awful it smelled when you went to see Yellowstone's geysers and hot springs."

"Now, those of you who have your hands up, if you never heard any of the stories about people being scalded to death at these geysers and hot springs drop your hands." All hands remain up, "Again I'm impressed. Thank you, and you can put your hands down now."

"The point here is that human deaths are well reported, what is not well reported are the deaths of park animals due to noxious gasses. This was first documented back in 1897 when a geologist visited an area of the park called, "Death Gulch," where he found a cluster of eight large bears that had recently died. The geologist attributed their deaths to an accumulation of carbon dioxide or hydrogen sulfide gasses that seeped out of the ground."

"In the years following that more animals have died in Death Gulch. In a recent account in 2004, five bisons died after being exposed to poison gas in a geyser basin at Yellowstone. The point here, ladies and gentlemen, is that you need to locate your survival communities in areas where poison gasses cannot settle in around you."

Pointing to the floor he continues, "And here, where we're standing right now, is the fourth exhibit group, Volcanic Eruptions. Here we have eight different exhibits: Lava Flows, Volcanic Ash Falls, Volcanic Ejecta, Volcanic Gas Emissions, Volcanic Lahars, Volcanic Pyroclastic Flows, and Volcanic Winter."

"Once again, the three rules of premium real estate apply; location, location, and location. If you are living on the flanks of an active volcano, you're not going to do very well in the tribulation. However, you can be far from volcanoes and still suffer impacts."

"Earlier I talked about Yellowstone National Park, and a lot of people are worried that this supervolcano could erupt again because it is overdue. But because it blew its cap in the last eruption, and has been redistributing magma over the last decade or so, there are those who believe that we could see something less disastrous with Yellowstone. Probably a series of

Mount Saint Helens-type eruptions, and the type of walking lava flow eruptions like those we see on the big island of Hawaii."

"However, should Yellowstone blow catastrophically as some fear, the whole northern hemisphere would find itself in a volcanic winter. That would make life tough, to say the least. However, the super-volcano of more concern to me is Long Valley Caldera in California. It has a single magma chamber and a cap, and this volcano is growing. Unlike Yellowstone, it is not spreading its magma outward, but rather its single magma chamber is inflating. Given its relative location to the San Andreas fault line, some believe it presents a worse threat than Yellowstone. So for those of you looking for relocation areas, avoid Southern California, Arizona, Southern Nevada, New Mexico, and western Texas, as these areas will most likely be affected in the event of a catastrophic eruption."

"And now you have approximately five minutes to briefly familiarize yourself with the exhibits in this gallery. Of course, you can return after the tour to spend as much time here as you'd like."

The group breaks up and scatters to explore the exhibits as you and I stay with Charlie.

This time Charlie looks at you and says, "Another question?"

You shrug your shoulders and answer, "Yup. Earlier you were using the word 'awareness,' and you said young Cynthia has more of it in her little finger than your whole family put together. What I'd like to know is when did you come into awareness? And what happened?"

Charlie ponders the answer to that question for a moment, and finally he says, "Well I think it was when I was eleven years old and visiting New York with my father. My father came from New York ,, and he was very proud of the city as he told me all about it. But all the time we were there I just had this premonition or feeling, if you will, that I was in a city that was destined to die. I suppose that's when I first came in to awareness."

"After I got home from that trip, I began having dreams of tsunamis and earthquakes and people dying. So I started drawing pictures with crayons of what I'd seen in my dreams. When I showed my pictures to my parents they became very upset, and my mother was rather close to convincing my father that I had come under some kind of demonic possession."

"That must have been a frightening moment for you," I chime in.

"You bet it was, and to this day I thank God for my Grandfather. When he heard about it, he came straight to our house, looked at all my pictures and then told my parents that I was just fine. He told us that when he was my age he had prophetic dreams of World War II, and sure enough they happened. That cooled my parents down a bit, and my grandfather assured them he would have a serious talk about it with me."

"How did that go?" you ask.

"It was one of the best days of my life. My grandfather and I went to the park where we could have a private talk, and he told me about his prophetic visions of World War II. But then he also told me that he had dreams of tsunamis and earthquakes as well, which mystified him because he knew those things would not happen in his lifetime."

"That was when he said something I've always appreciated. He said that all his life he wondered why he saw events that would not happen in his lifetime, and that only after I started drawing pictures of my dreams that he understood the reason for his dreams. He knew he was supposed to help me because he had seen in his dreams what I had seen in mine so that we could connect and we did. This was when he made me promise never to talk about prophetic dreams with my parents again, and I never did. But up until the day he died we talked about our dreams often, and those talks are some of the most beautiful memories of my childhood."

Pushing the pedestal back into place he looks down at his watch, "Excuse me, but I need to check with the group behind us to see how ours is doing on time. In the meantime, please enjoy the gallery. I'll be right back."

"Tell me something," you ask me, "How often do you hear stories like Charlie's?"

"All the time. What the Charlies of the world don't realize is how many of them there are. The problem for them is that they are typically isolated, whereas because of what I do, I get to see them all the time. That's why every chance I get I tell them that they're not alone."

"Is that what really bothers them? They think they're lonely oddballs?"

"Yes, and I'm glad to help them because it is a miserable place to be."

"Is this why Charlie is revealing so much of his own life to us?"

I nod with approval, "It's because he sees that we honestly care and that we want to know. As you can imagine, that does not happen very often. So while Charlie is helping you, you're helping him in return. Both of you are going to look back on this as a very special day, and I'm happy for both of you."

"You're right, it is a very special day." After that we quietly look at a few exhibits and before long Charlie is standing at the entrance to the gallery.

"Folks, we need to push on so that the other group behind us can come in, so please follow me to the next gallery."

The group starts moving to the entrance with the children skipping ahead and Sheba alongside. Walking through the corridor we pass another large mural on our right. This one depicts men and women working together to clear a space in a cavern. The text along the top reads, "Survival is less about individual threats but more about how we work together to face all threats."

Industrial Gallery

Unlike the previous two galleries, the Industrial Gallery is nearly half the size, yet the ominous feeling of the room makes it seem larger. Charlie pulls out a small pedestal and stands upon it, "Here, ladies and gentlemen, is the Industrial Gallery, and it puts a whole new twist on the threat matrix. In the previous two galleries, we saw natural threats. However, the threats you'll see here are all the result of irresponsible greed. This is why we docents like to call this gallery the 'Hall of Shame.' In the next two galleries, Water and Health, you'll see why."

Pointing to the corner of the room he says, "In the opposite corner is the first exhibit group, Manufacturing. Here we have three different exhibits: Heavy Metals, Industrial Waste, and Water Pollution."

Pointing to the far corner of the room he says, "In the far corner is the second exhibit group, Fossil Fuels. Here we have three different exhibitions: Fracking, Dead Zones, Mining Leaks and Runoff, and Uncontrolled Oil Spills."

Pointing down to the floor, he says, "All along this side of the gallery we have the third exhibit group, Nuclear. Here we have five different exhibits: Fukushima-Type Events, China Syndrome, Airborne Radiation, Nuclear Dead Zones, and Ocean Radiation."

When we think of nuclear threats, the first thing that comes to mind are missiles raining down on us with powerful warheads. What's more likely will be disasters involving the nuclear reactors already on the ground and operational. A specific concern to me is the GE Mark I type, such as the reactors that failed at Fukushima."

"According to Nuclear Regulatory Commission record, there are twenty-three similar reactors installed in America, and this design was inherently flawed from the beginning. These twenty-three reactors, along with those in Japan, should have been decommissioned when the flaw was discovered. However, for financial reasons a makeshift upgrade was designed. This 'upgrade' is more for show than to fix anything, and the reactors were grandfathered in by our nuclear regulatory agency with the full knowledge that they are inherently unsafe by design. Consequently, there are those who believe we're just not facing twenty-three possible Fukushimas, but one hundred twenty-three possible Fukushimas or more, all across this country, and all around the world."

Pointing to a small theater alcove at the back of the room he adds, "Over in the Nuclear exhibit group at the back of the room is the Fukushima Events exhibit. It features a special video presentation by Arnie Gundersen of Fairewinds Energy. With a running time of twenty-eight minutes, it is the longest-running media exhibit in the Exploratorium. You will not have a chance to watch it during the tour, but please, when you come back to spend more time with the exhibits, try to set aside time for Arnie's presentation. You'll find it most illuminating."

"So is there a general rule of thumb when it comes to dealing with industrial threats? Yes, there is, and it is the very same one you learned in the Earth Gallery. The three laws of premium real estate: location, location, and location. When it comes to nuclear reactors, a simple rule of thumb is to locate your communities at least fifty miles upwind and one hundred miles downwind of these plants. Of course, the further the better, because prevailing wind patterns will change after the crust of the earth moves in the pole shift, and after the rotation of the earth changes direction."

Pointing to the far corner of the room he continues, "Over in the Fossil Fuels Exhibit I suggest that you pay particular attention to the Fracking Dead Zones, especially if you come from Pennsylvania. No doubt, those who survive the tribulation will remember former Pennsylvania Governor and Homeland Security Director, Tom Ridge, as the fracking 'angel of death' for what he did to his state and others. As a result of his efforts and those of others, more potential tribulation safe areas have been lost to fracking than to any other single cause."

"This is because a fracking well casing is designed for a thirty-year lifespan under normal conditions, although a few do fail on the very first day of operation. However, when major fault lines such as the San Andreas and the New Madrid produce mega-quakes, the horizontal ground waves generated by these events will fracture fracking well casings all across the country. The result will be that geographic areas which were once safe become uninhabitable because of poisoned water and topsoil. So, when selecting a site for your community, be sure to give a wide berth to areas with fracking wells. Similar to nuclear threats, the further away you can locate, the better."

"We have about five minutes for you to familiarize yourself with the exhibits in this gallery before we move on to the Weather Gallery, where you'll have a little more time." He steps down from the pedestal, and as the group begins to wander amongst the exhibits, he pushes the pedestal back into the wall.

This time instead of us going to Charlie he approaches us with a somber face and asks me, "Marshall, I've got a question for you. Do you mind?"

"Not at all, Charlie. You know what they say, 'The only stupid question is the one that is not asked.'"

There is a little sparkle in Charlie's eyes as he chuckles, "Tell me, just between the three of us, how much of a difference do you think I'm making here?"

"You know Charlie, I probably ask myself that question more times than I care to imagine, so here's what I can tell you. Everything that I do, I do with this one thought in mind. One day I'll be standing before Creator, and when that day comes, I want to be able to say that, warts and all, I kept the faith. I did what I could whenever I had the opportunity." I place my hand on Charlie's shoulder, "What you are doing here, brother, is that you are keeping the faith, and it just doesn't get any better than that."

"Marshall's right Charlie," you chime in, "You are keeping the faith, and I thank you for that. I want you to know that you and your family will be in my prayers. I'll pray that they come into awareness while there is still time left for them to act. And if that is not possible due to their free-will choices, I will pray that their final days and hours are filled with God's peace and comfort."

Charlie brightens, as though a load is lifted off his shoulders, "I'm sure glad I met two of you today. This is a good day."

As though on cue, you and I both answer the same way, "Amen to that!" With that we spend the remaining time talking about Arnie Gundersen, learning that he is one of Charlie's personal heroes. That makes sense because Arnie is a personal hero for many folks.

Finally, Charlie checks his watch and calls the group together at the entrance, "I hope you will find time to return to this gallery because it is very important, but for now, please follow me to the Weather Gallery."

As before, he leads us to the curved hall with the massive threat matrix pyramid to our left. To our right, another large mural is on the wall between the galleries. It depicts a group of survivors walking with shovels and picks. At the top, the text reads, "The Three C's of Survival Teamwork." Below that is a bullet list, "Communicate — Know what others are doing; Cooperate — Work together to achieve common goals, and Command — Lead by example."

Weather Gallery

The Weather Gallery is somewhat smaller than the others. Charlie steps up on a pedestal, calls the group together, and does a quick head count. He looks for Sheba among the kids, "Well puppy," he says to her, "I lost track of you back there, and I wondered if you wandered off. Nice to see you're still with us."

"Woof, woof!"

Charlie smiles back at her, "Folks, during the tribulation we'll experience every imaginable kind of weather, and it will become worse than anything we have seen before. In fact, we'll see new weather extremes plus new kinds of extreme weather threats that will boggle the mind. The result is that traditional farming methods will become increasingly vulnerable to weather threats. That's why survival communities need to employ indoor farming techniques such as hydroponics and aquaponics. You can learn more about those vital techniques at the Survival Village Imaginarium. But for now, our focus is on tribulation weather."

Pointing to a corner of the room he says, "In the opposite corner is the first exhibit group, Severe Regional Events. Here we have six different exhibits: Cyclones, Hurricanes, Droughts, Floods, Megacryometeors, and Snow Hurricanes."

Pointing to another corner of the room he says, "In the far corner is the second exhibit group, Extreme Weather. Here we have seven different exhibits: Cold Snaps, Ground Lightning, Heat Waves, Rainstorms, Snowstorms, Tornado Clusters, and Unseasonal Snow."

Pointing down to the floor, he says, "All along this side of the gallery we have the third exhibit group, Supercell Storms. Here we have seven different exhibits: Flash Flooding, Hailstorms and Sleet, Mega Hail, Hypervelocity Winds, Thunder and Lightning Storms, Sudden Plasma Inversions, and Violent Tornadoes."

"Regarding new types of weather, be sure to check out the Megacryometeors exhibit in the Severe Regional Events exhibit group. Megacryometeors are very large chunks of ice that fall from the sky like hailstones, but when there is no storm happening. They can cause considerable damage and death."

"Another old, but new in our times, severe weather threat will be Sudden Plasma Inversions. The public got to see how destructive they can be in the 2004 blockbuster, '*The Day After Tomorrow*.' This rare weather phenomenon was responsible for the sudden deaths of wooly mammoths in Siberia thousands of years ago. As a matter of fact, these ancient, flash-frozen beasts are still being dug up today with fresh grasses in their mouths and in their stomachs. Again, as we learned in the Space Gallery, one simple rule applies — you want to have twelve feet of earth above your head at a minimum."

"What's equally important to remember is that no matter where you live, north or south, warm or cold, dry or wet climate, you must have adequate clothing for the widest range of environmental conditions. Some simple rules of thumb to follow are, always dress in layers, prepare for both hot and cold weather, and be prepared for rain."

"If you already have suitable survival clothing you're ahead of the game. If not, you may have to scrounge it up along the way. So always remember that hot-weather clothing needs to breathe and allow perspiration to dissipate, which reduces chafing and aids cooling of the body. Cold-weather clothing needs layers, including an inner layer that wicks moisture away from your body. Otherwise, hypothermia may set in when you get hot from exertion, then damp, then cold. So please take a few minutes to familiarize yourself with the exhibits in this gallery, then we'll continue on to the Water Gallery."

Before the group begins to scatter, Sheba takes off, making a beeline for the Megacryometeors exhibit with all three children running after her. You, Charlie, and I watch this with fascination.

Charlie rubs his chin thoughtfully, "Your dog reminds me of when I was a kid and how I loved to watch Lassie reruns on TV. It always amazed me how Lassie could be so smart, and how she always seemed to know what to do."

"Like when Timmy fell into the well," you add.

"Actually, it was Lassie who fell into the well," Charlie says, "Timmy never did fall down a well, but he always managed to get trapped in a mine or some such thing. The point here is that she's different from other dogs, and I've had dogs all my life."

You and I look at each other with a knowing grin, "Maybe she was a service dog?" I suggest.

"Nope," Charlie says, "I've seen plenty of service dogs such as guide dogs for the blind, and they are impressive thanks to their training. By the way, what's the dog's name?"

"Sheba," we answer simultaneously.

"Hmm. Well, Sheba is smart, but not in a trained way. I can't put my finger on it exactly, but it's like she was born smart."

I cannot help but laugh, "I know what you're talking about. You can't imagine how many times I ask myself, 'What is it about that dog?'"

Now you and Charlie laugh as well.

"Say, Marshall, I have an idea," Charlie volunteers, "You know this place as well as I do, if not better. But how about I give your friend here," he nods towards the Megacryometeors exhibit, "and Sheba a private tour of the Exploratorium this afternoon? We can start with lunch in the staff cafeteria and trust me, the food there is great. Sometimes I think it's the only reason some volunteers keep coming back. Besides, the other docents would be delighted to meet Sheba. What do you think?"

"Sounds like a great invitation," I glance over at you, "and I've got something else I want to do this afternoon, so this would be perfect for me. I'm sure Charlie is going to give you and Sheba a world-class VIP tour."

You extend your hand to Charlie, "I accept, and I thank you very much."

As you shake hands, Charlie says, "While I'm at it, I think the cook will be happy to whip up a little something special for Sheba. So if you two don't mind, I'm going to make some quick calls and get this all set up."

We nod in agreement and Charlie goes off to get things organized. You turn and look at me, "I know all of this is somewhere in time, and in a place, you have created in ways I cannot begin to understand I've just got to know, is Charlie real?"

"He is as real as you or me, my friend," I answer. "But here's a better way of looking at what's happening here. Remember the Tribulation Carousel Theater, and at the end, Rabbi Sarah told us about that old Jewish saying, 'We will do, and we will understand.' Well, you are already doing it, so be patient. The rest will sort itself out."

"Fair enough," you reply, "But I'm sure Charlie is going to have a lot of questions about Sheba. Are there things that I can and cannot talk about?"

We see Charlie return to the gallery, "You can talk with Charlie about everything that has happened since you first arrived at the lake house. He'll understand."

Standing in the center of the entrance, Charlie announces loudly, "Folks, it's time for us to move on to the Water Gallery." Then, looking over at us, he gives us a thumbs up sign and a big smile.

"Looks like you and Sheba are going to have an enjoyable afternoon," I observe as we walk out the gallery into the curved hall. To our right is another large mural on the wall between the galleries.

This mural depicts a scene of a small group of people hiking through hill country, carrying knapsacks on their backs. In the mural, we see an old woman with a walking stick. In front of her is a teenage boy with his own pack on his back and he is holding another pack in his hand.

The old woman is not wearing a pack, so it is obviously hers and the boy looks back at her as she smiles gratefully at him. Across the top, the letters read, "Survival is less about doing for ourselves, and more about doing for others."

Water Gallery

The Water Gallery is a somewhat smaller than the others, but more than spacious enough for its exhibits. Standing up on a pedestal, Charlie explains the gallery to the group, "Water is life, which is why this is the second most important category in the threat matrix pyramid.

Pointing to a corner of the room he says, "In the opposite corner is the first exhibit group, Biological Threats. Here we have five different exhibits: Algae Blooms, Human and Animal Carcass Decay, Human and Animal Waste, Fish Die Offs, and Natural Poisons and Toxins."

Pointing to another corner of the room he says, "In the far corner is the second exhibit group, Man-Made Threats. Here we have four different exhibits: Chemical Spills, Heavy Metal Pollution, Malicious Poisoning, and Radiation."

Pointing down to the floor, he says, "All along this side of the gallery we have the third exhibit group, Potability. Here we have six different exhibits: PH Balance, Diseases, Gases, Parasites, Particulates, Safe Water Sources, and Filtering and Disinfecting Water."

"During the coming tribulation many sources of water will become polluted due to natural, and man-made causes and others will simply go dry. Ergo, finding potable water during the tribulation will become a daily chore for many, as it presently is in many third world nations where it can take half a day to find and transport a day's worth of water back to the home."

"Therefore, the best solution is to plan ahead when searching for a good survival community location. The best strategy is to go deep for water. Shallow water tables close to the surface can vary with the season and may become polluted and unreliable. That's why you want to locate on land that sits over a large primary aquifer. Sure, you'll have to drill deep, but the water will be available in abundance throughout the tribulation, and it will always be sweet and safe."

One of the mothers standing with her young son asks, "And what if we can't drill deep as you say. What do we do if we're limited in terms of resources?"

"Madam, that's a brilliant question," Charlie responds with a twinkle in his eye. "In the lobby, we have an excellent book store with a wonderful little cafe. The book store is stocked with top-notch survival-related books and media. When it comes to water for those with limited resources, I suggest 'The Preppers Water Survival Guide' by Daisy Luther. It's a small book with big ideas on how to gather water, purify water, drill wells, and much more. After the tour, please take some time to check out the book store and to peruse the wonderful survival how-to and reference books you'll find there."

The woman takes a small notebook out of her purse and writes down the name of the book, "Thank you, Charlie, I'll do that."

"Now folks, please take some time to familiarize yourself with the exhibits in this gallery and then we're going to move on to the sixth and final gallery, Health."

Stepping off the pedestal, Charlie pushes it back into the wall and walks over to join us. "Well, it's all arranged. First, we're going to the staff cafeteria for what I am sure will be a wonderful lunch, especially now that they know I have a guest of honor plus one coming. Then I'm yours for the remainder of the day. The fair is open till 9:00 p.m. so I'm good all the way to closing if you like."

"Thank you so much," you happily reply, "I wouldn't want you to go home too late. After all, you do have a life."

"Never you mind. If we go to 10:00 p.m, that is assuming it's OK with Marshall, all I'll miss is a pinochle game, and between us, I'm usually the one writing a check after that game."

"You two take as long as you like. Trust me, I've got plenty to do. The later you two hang out, the better for me. When you need to find me, just call the administration office. They'll always know where I am."

"Well, then we're good to go. And what about Sheba?" Charlie scans the room to find Sheba. She's with Cynthia over at the Algae Blooms exhibit, "Does Sheba have any special diet needs?"

On cue, Sheba comes trotting across the galley to where we're standing, with Cynthia following close behind and looks up at Charlie with wide eyes. We start to chuckle, and you ask him, "So Charlie, are you having a Lassie moment?"

Charlie looks at you out of the corner of his eye, "Yeah, I kind of am."

"Now here's her vocabulary, Charlie," you explain, "One bark for no, two barks for yes, three barks for maybe, and if she does two barks twice it is a very emphatic, 'yes!' So, give her the options, and she'll tell you what she wants."

Cynthia starts jumping up and down, "I got it. I got it. Let me do it. Let me do it."

"Okay, Cynthia you do it," Charlie answers and leaning towards me says in a whisper, "This I've got to see." He then waves for Cynthia to come near. She does, and he bends down and whispers the options into her ear."

The girl nods happily and turns to Sheba, "OK Sheba, you have three choices. You tell me which one you want most. Do you want fish?"

"Woof."

"Do you want chicken?"

"Woof, woof, woof."

"Do you want beef?"

"Woof, woof! Woof, woof!"

With a bright, beaming smile Cynthia announces, "Sheba wants beef. Lots and lots of juicy, delicious beef."

Charlie says, "Great! I'll let the kitchen know." With that, he checks his watch and points towards the entrance. Calling the group together we leave the Water Gallery for the last gallery on the tour, the Health Gallery.

The large mural to our right in the curved hall has a more somber message than before. In it we see a group of men and women gathered in a small shelter with books scattered about them. To one side we see children listening attentively as the adults discuss a hand-drawn shelter design on an old chalk board.

The text reads, "Preparation is not a place or a time. It is a state of mind, and only fools wait for others to keep them safe or to take action first." Of all the murals the group has passed by on the tour, this is the first one where the group members actually stop to study it and to contemplate its message.

Health Gallery

To everyone's amazement, the Health Gallery is the largest of all six galleries. Now it makes sense with some of the others being smaller. Charlie steps up on a pedestal and begins his introduction, "As we learned earlier, the most survivable type of threat is health. Therefore it has the highest importance of all threats. This is also why this is the largest of all six galleries, and why it is organized differently. There are two major exhibit groups and then the others in the center. But let's talk about the two major groups first."

Pointing to the side of the room he says, "On the opposite side of the gallery is the first major exhibit group, Violent Death. Here we have seven different exhibits: Accidents and Aggressive Animals, Attacks by Animals and Humans, Attacks by Warlords and Governments, Cave-ins and Building Collapses, Cannibalism and Rabies Biters, Gang Violence, and Rape and Murder."

Pointing first at his feet and then to the back of the gallery he says, "On this side of the gallery is the second major exhibit group, Tribulation Threats. Here we have nine different exhibits: Asphyxiation, Exposure and Dehydration, Concussions and Flying Debris, Infections and Burns, Traumatic Bleeding and Fractures, Radiation Cancers and Sickness, Ash and Other Skin Ailments, Poor Diet and Starvation, Food Poisoning, and Adrenal Fatigue."

"Before I introduce the other three exhibit groups, let's talk about these two first. When it comes to violent deaths, a common-sense approach to safety can prevent a significant number of violent deaths during the tribulation. For example, plan surface outings carefully in advance, and always travel in groups. Now, let's talk for a moment about community defense."

"On the mural wall between the Space and Earth Galleries we saw, 'The Three E's of Surviving as a Community,' which are: 'Everyone Works, Everyone Defends and Everyone Participates.' Here we need to focus more closely on the second E, 'Everyone Defends,' which in a survival sense has only one real meaning, 'Everyone fights. No one runs.' But this does not mean that everyone has to fight all the time. Communities will naturally have groups of individuals within them who will serve as security responders, and they will be able to handle a large proportion of the incidents. Rather, there will only be rare incidents that will require everyone to respond."

"For this reason, everyone, including boys and girls above the age of twelve, will need to become proficient with firearms and train regularly as part of a reserve security force. It will also be common especially during the early years of the tribulation for all adults to be armed at all times."

"This is just saber-rattling," one of the women in the group blurts out, "Give me one good reason why women and children should be armed. Why can't we just trust our soldiers and police to carry the guns for us?"

Now the room grows quiet. You could hear a pin drop as all eyes turned from the woman to Charlie in expectation of his answer.

He looks at the woman and considers her demeanor. She looks angry and self-righteous. After a long, hesitant pause he answers, "So let me see if I understand this question correctly. What I think your asking is why must women and children be armed when soldiers or police can carry the guns for them. Is that correct?"

"Yes," she says.

Charlie smiles calmly at her. By this time the tension in the room is thick enough to cut with a knife.

"Well ma'am, in answer to your question, we need to go back to December 29, 1890. While we hear about all kinds of mass shootings today, the largest in the history of our country actually took place on that day at Wounded Knee Creek on the Pine Ridge Indian Reservation in South Dakota. On that day, federal agents and soldiers of the 7th Cavalry went to the reservation to confiscate firearms. They told the 297 Sioux Indians there at the time that surrendering their firearms was necessary for, and I quote, 'their own safety and protection.' After the Sioux Indians had complied and peacefully turned in their firearms, the slaughter began. Every one of the 297 unarmed Sioux Indians was shot to death; 200 of them were women and children. Ma'am, does that answer your question?"

The woman looks completely stunned. For the first time during the tour, one of the older gentlemen in the group speaks up, "I'm one-quarter Sioux, and I say, 'never again.' Did this answer your question, or not? I want to know."

The woman stares at him, still trying to wrap her mind around what she just heard, then she just starts to walk off. Halfway to the entrance Charlie calls out to her, "Ma'am, please come back," she turns and looks at him, unsure of what to do. "You don't have to answer any questions ma'am, but please do come back."

Hesitating for a moment, she quietly walks to the back of the group.

Charlie smiles at her and holds up his outstretched arms to the group, "Folks, what you have seen here is something that's going to happen very often during the tribulation. People who are passionate about what they believe in will find their passions coming into conflict with the passions of others."

"The problem with that is that the strong will prevail in those circumstances, and then the community will suffer for it because survival requires everyone's participation. So what we really need here, and also during the tribulation, is something I call loving CPR: Courtesy, Politeness, and Respect."

Pointing along his side of the room he continues, "Now let's take a quick look at the other major exhibit group along our side of the gallery: Tribulation Threats. Again, a little bit of common sense goes a long way and while it may seem a little cumbersome at first, it's always best to wear protective gear such as hard hats, leather gloves, and impact-resistant eye wear. Then whatever you're going to do that day, be sure to communicate continuously with the other members of your party, without being loud."

"Here is where developing hand signals is useful and better yet, helping everyone in the community to learn a single dialect of a sign language. Whenever you're on the surface, always make sure to carry along a pair of binoculars, and someone in your party will always be assigned as a lookout. Biters, humans infected with rabies, and cannibals will be a severe problem during the early years of the tribulation. The best way to deal with these dangers is to spot them first, then give them a wide berth."

Pointing again to the far wall, he continues, "Going back for a moment to the Violent Deaths exhibit group, one thing you'll see in the Cannibalism and Rabies Biters exhibit is human depravity. There is no negotiating with cannibals or those infected with rabies. They're just going to come at you, and when they do, you need to avoid them. If you cannot, then do not hesitate to terminate them. So, in addition to a pair of binoculars, a good sharpshooter will be handy to have in your group when you're above ground. Now, let's talk about the exhibits in the center."

"We normally think of the big threats, and sometimes we just forget that we can die from rather ordinary causes just as often. So the three exhibit groups in the center of the gallery are just as important as the two major groups along the walls."

Pointing to the third exhibit group in the center near the entrance Charlie continues, "The third exhibit group in the center of the gallery near the entrance is Common Causes. It has the following six exhibits: Communicable Diseases, Sexually Transmitted Diseases, Dental Disease, Strokes and Cardiopulmonary Issues, Aging and Diabetes, and Childbirth and Infant Mortality."

Pointing to the fourth exhibit group in the center of the gallery he continues, "In the center of the gallery is the fourth exhibit group, GMO Poisoning. It has the following four exhibits: Bowel Disorders, Impaired Immune Systems, Impaired Mental Processes and Lethargy, and Poor Balance."

Pointing to the fifth exhibit group just beyond the GMO Poisoning exhibit group, he continues, "And finally, at the rear and center of the gallery is the fifth exhibit group Mental Disorders. , It has the following five exhibits: Melancholia, Severe Depression, Severe Psychotic Episodes, Sociopathic Behavior, and Suicide. Let's talk briefly about each one, beginning with Common Causes."

"People get sick on a regular basis even during good times. During the tribulation, they'll do so more frequently, and with greater severity. Here is where common-sense and natural alternatives such as chiropractic, essential oils, herbal medicine and homeopathy can make all the difference for a survival community. This is because modern healthcare has a three-to-five-day lifespan. That's how many days of diesel fuel are going to be stored and available for the emergency generators at hospitals. Once the generators stop working, the hospitals will go dark. And that's when modern medicine as we know it will cease to be available."

Likewise, diseases that were far more common in the past will become common once again. For example, in ancient times dental disease was a big killer. An infection from an abscessed tooth can cause death if it spreads to the brain or heart, or when swelling cuts off the airway. However, if the community plans ahead and stockpiles the right supplies, there is a simple Ayurvedic solution that is very effective in helping to maintain dental health. It is called oil pulling."

"A few times a week you put about one tablespoon of oil in your mouth and pull it through your teeth as you swish it around for twenty minutes. Then you spit out and discard the oil, which has also pulled toxins out of your body. Oil pulling is best done before the first meal of the day, and it works best with organic, cold-pressed coconut, sesame, olive, or sunflower oils. Combined with regular brushing and flossing, oil pulling can significantly increase your chances of avoiding death by dental disease. For this reason, I really recommend that your community stockpiles a healthy reserve of these oils. You can also store seeds for growing these oils, of which black oil sunflowers are the easiest to grow, plus acquire a durable, non-electric expeller press."

Pointing at the center of the room Charlie continues, "The newest exhibit in this gallery is GMO Poisoning. In my opinion, companies like Monsanto have set us up to fail. Proof of this is when you see pictures of preppers' food shelves stocked to the ceiling with inexpensive GMO foods: GMO wheat, GMO corn, GMO rice, and so forth. In almost every case, these preppers have never gone beyond simplistic maximum-calories-for-the-dollar calculations to actually try out and experience what happens when you live exclusively on packaged and canned GMO processed foods."

"A few will have cast-iron stomachs, and they will be okay for the most part. However, for most people, especially folks my age, their gastrointestinal tracts will become stricken with common GMO ailments such as irritable bowel syndrome, and that's when the misery begins."

"A diet based solely on GMO foods will eventually cause rampant bouts of constipation and diarrhea. Worse yet, approximately seventy percent of the human immune system depends on the good bacteria and microbes in the lower gastrointestinal tract which GMO foods will wreak havoc on, thus lowering immunity. Consequently, those who live exclusively on GMO processed foods for any length of time will not only be debilitated by lower GI disorders, but their immune systems will be drastically impaired making them more susceptible to disease."

"For this reason, communities should only stockpile non-GMO foods, and organic if able, to preserve their immune systems. If you're on a budget, start a garden and can or dehydrate your own. Whether you stockpile GMO or organic, a diet rich in fresh foods is the best way to ensure the long-term health of your community. Ergo, the sooner you can grow own fresh, organic food the better."

Pointing to the back center of the gallery, he continues,"And finally, Mental Disorders will be a very serious health risk during the tribulation. Today we have a broad range of modern medicines to treat these conditions, but there was a time before modern psychiatry when families kept mentally deranged family members locked up in their own homes."

"Folks, during the tribulation survival communities will not even be able to do that much. So here is where very emotional conflicts within the community will arise about this issue. Community concerns will mount over obvious signs of impaired judgment or irrational, potentially dangerous behaviors in an unstable individual. Ultimately these behaviors will threaten the community with random shootings or unprovoked physical attacks."

"This is why a proactive mental health strategy must be an integral part of your community health and wellness planning. Mental and emotional stresses during the tribulation will reach extreme levels, and folks will additionally need to live closely together as a community for many years. The American lifestyle of social isolation and individualism will be replaced by an older, agrarian community style of intensive daily interaction, "community first" thinking, and interdependence. Those who currently depend on television, electronics, and alcohol or other substances to manage their stress and emotional states will no longer have access to those options, and withdrawal can lead to emotional instability and crisis."

"Many communities will be forced to filter out mentally or emotionally unstable individuals sooner rather than later to ensure the survival of the community as a whole. Sociopaths, especially, will present a clear and present danger to any community."

"If a trained mental health professional is not a part of your community, one thing to keep in mind is that ego-driven people (as opposed to spiritually-driven people) will get people killed. Thankfully, they are easy to spot. They will be the ones who say, 'I don't know what I'm doing, but I've got to be the boss.' With this in mind, here is one good rule of thumb for survival, 'Not all ego-driven people are sociopaths, but all sociopaths are ego-driven.'" And on that note, we conclude our tour. Please feel free to explore the exhibits in this and the previous galleries at this time, and also to return later."

Pointing toward the lobby Charlie continues, "Out in the lobby you'll find a wonderful bookstore stocked with a wide selection of top-notch survival, how-to, and reference books. I strongly urge each and every one of you to spend some time there. If you are short on time, the clerk will be happy to give you a printed list of all the titles we offer so you can acquire them elsewhere later on."

"Personally speaking, the one book that is most near and dear to my heart is '*The Baby Book*' by Dr. William Sears. When it comes to setting health and wellness priorities, successful natural childbirth and reducing infant mortality, have got to be at the top of the list. Without continuity of progeny, a community will ultimately fail. '*The Baby Book*' explains the traditional society method of parenting, which Dr. Sears calls 'attachment parenting.' The babies and mothers stay close together, and nursing continues longer than for most Americans these days. This results in a healthier, more calm, and well-adjusted baby, and those benefits continue throughout that baby's life. It's just that simple, and that's why we're proud of our comfortable lounge area for nursing mothers, whom we support wholeheartedly."

Charlie begins passing out a paper to each member of the group, "This form is a docent critique. We'd like to know what you liked and didn't like about your tour experience, along with any ideas and suggestions you may have. Again, I'm Charlie Michaels, your docent for this tour, and it has been my great honor and pleasure to be in service to each of you. Thank you for touring today."

Stepping down from the pedestal for the last time, Charlie comes over to where were standing and says in a quiet voice, "I hope my Wounded Knee story reached out to that participant successfully and that it doesn't result in a poison pen critique."

"I thought you handled it very well," I quickly answer, "I might have said something like, 'How many times would you have to be raped before you'd be willing to pick up a gun? — provided you survived the rape in the first place.' That's a pretty similar message to the one you gave, and sometimes it does reach women who are reluctant to take responsibility for defending themselves."

The others nod their heads, "So Charlie, what's the plan?"

"Well, I've got to go do some paperwork, but I'll be finished with that by noon." He looks at you and says, "How about I meet you and Sheba in the bookstore cafe at noon, and then we'll go straight from there to the staff cafeteria. I can guarantee every available docent will enjoy meeting Sheba. Then I am all yours until 10:00 p.m. tonight."

"Works for me," I chime in.

"Works for me, too," you add, "We'll see you at noon in the bookstore cafe, Charlie." With that we all leave the gallery, smiling as we wave goodbye, everyone heading in different directions.

"I feel like I hit pay dirt," you happily chirp, "That private tour with Charlie is going to be the cat's whiskers!"

"Yes, you surely did! Before I leave, let's both stop off at the bookstore. It's time you stocked up on a few vital reference books."

"Lead the way."

The Bookstore

The threat matrix exploratory in the bookstore is certainly one-of-a-kind. It's not like the bookstores you find in airports or train stations, with all the murder novels at the front and sports magazines and business books at the back. This bookstore is about survival and everything related to it, and the shelves are well-stocked.

I point to the small shopping carts next to the door, "Get yourself one."

You raise an eyebrow and push a cart over to where I'm standing.

"You'll need a cart unless you want to lug a ton of books around."

"Uh, okay," you mutter, "I didn't realize I would need that many books."

"All right, let's start with some general reference stuff." I start scanning the shelves and spot two big thick books, "Here are a couple of big reference texts that I really like, '*The Encyclopedia of Country Living*' by Carla Emery and '*When Technology Fails*' by Matthew Stein." I toss them into the cart.

"Follow me," I say as we head for the agriculture section. Along the way, we pass a center aisle display, and I stop for a moment to see what's featured, "Hmmm, here are a couple of old favorites, '*98.6 Degrees: The Art of Keeping Your Ass Alive*' by Cody Lundin. That's an oldie, but goodie, and here is another, '*Adrenal Fatigue*' by James L. Wilson. Both good finds. OK, let's move on."

As we continue walking towards the agriculture section you ask, "I remember back in the Health Gallery Charlie was talking about adrenal fatigue, but he didn't really get into an explanation of it. What is it? And how is it survival-related?"

Adrenal Fatigue

"Adrenal fatigue is certainly an important health consideration for survival. Let me start this way. When our ancestors were walking across the savannas of Africa and found themselves being stalked by a predator like a lion, their adrenal glands would kick in big-time, and they would take off running for all they were worth, thinking, 'Feet don't fail me now!' At some point, they would either make it to safety or become dinner. If they made it to safety, their bodies would relax and stand down from the massive adrenaline explosion that got them out of harm's way."

"However, in our modern world, we no longer have lions chasing us. What we have is our eighty-hours-a-week jobs, smartphones, tablets and other such slavetronics, and absolutely no peace of mind. So what modern life is really doing to us in terms of our adrenal glands is that we are always running away from that proverbial lion, but our bodies never get to ramp down from that constant need to produce adrenalin. As a result of this unending, chronic stress, adrenal fatigue has become a classic 21st-century health syndrome. It reduces immunity, causes chronic fatigue, impairs mental clarity, and reduces resistance to stress itself."

"So, how does this apply during the tribulation?"

"Simple. During the first few years of the tribulation, when things are at their worst, we're not going to be dealing with slavetronics that take over our lives, nor have to work for companies that will fire us if we dare to use all of our vacation days. No, that's gone. Forget that."

"What we'll have every day for the first few years is stress: stress about finding water, stress about having enough food, stress about adequate shelter, stress about staying alive, stress about being attacked, and don't forget stress from living in a completely different type of community. In other words, we will have stress, stress, stress, and more stress. We will also be cooped up underground for long periods of time and will have difficulty getting enough exercise to stand down our adrenal systems so they can rest and recharge. This is why I like this book. It explains the syndrome and has some good tips and even a simple soup recipe to help you recover from adrenal fatigue."

"Gosh, this survival business is very complex," you say with a sigh, "There is just so much to know and to deal with."

"Ah, don't worry about it. Just keep plugging away, and one day you'll be at the top of your game. That's what survival is, a process of learning what hurts and what works." I put my hand on your shoulder, "The goal is not to be omniscient. The goal is to learn what works before what hurts has a chance to kill you." I nod towards the agriculture section, "Off we go."

Growing Enough Food

As we walk toward the back of the store, I explain, "If you're going to have a truly successful community you not only have to grow enough food for yourselves, you need to grow ten times as much food as you need. This will allow you to share food with your neighboring communities. This way your neighbors become your strong allies, and then you are going to be able to create mutual defense pacts with them. These mutual defense alliances will become even more important than the food you share."

"So it all begins when you're looking to acquire your community property. For starters, you need to find a place that's well-suited to permaculture. This idea was created by a couple of Australian fellows, and is really brilliant. Some people also call it, 'forests that feed,' because the general idea is that you want to set up an integrated natural system that essentially runs itself and produces tremendous quantities of food and herbs for your community."

"Now keep in mind, you're not going to be able to do this in the beginning because the tribulation is going to cause great destruction on the surface. At first, you'll need to do indoor gardening, aquaponics, and hydroponics until you're able to come back to the surface and begin your permaculture system. After that, you can add in traditional organic farming if you would like to."

"That makes sense. Buy land that is suitable for permaculture after the worst of the tribulation, but during the tribulation rely on indoor gardening. Then switch over to permaculture as soon as possible."

"Why switch over? Run both together. Both systems are highly productive, and if you run them together, you're going to have what I like to call fail-over farming. You always have a Plan B, and you always have a surplus."

You nod appreciatively as we reach the agriculture section, "That sounds like a wise strategy. So, what are your recommendations on books?"

Scanning the shelves I see some of my favorite books and start pulling them out, "*Here is 'How to Grow More Vegetables*' by John Jeavons. This guy is an urban farmer who thinks outside the box. People love him, great ideas!" I drop the book in the cart as I scan the shelf for the next book, "You can never get enough books on aquaponics and hydroponics, but a good book to start with is '*Aquaponic Gardening*' by Sylvia Bernstein." I drop it in the cart and continue to scan the shelves, pulling out two large, thick books. "Aha. Found you. These two books are on rainwater harvesting by Brad Lancaster. After the pole shift growing food is going to be a whole different animal, because you won't know what your growing environment and weather patterns are going to be like until you come up to the surface. If you wind up in desert-like conditions, rainwater harvesting will be very necessary."

"Great. I really appreciate your helping me with this."

"My pleasure. Let's go up to the checkout stand." You follow me with the cart up to the checkout station where I'm greeted by the clerk.

"Hello, Marshall. It's a pleasure to see you again."

"Thank you. My friend here is off to a good start with a few titles, but I know you can really help with additional, helpful survival library titles. Please charge these books and any others to the lake house account and have all the books delivered there."

"Certainly. I can see your friend is off to a good start, and it will be my pleasure to help in any way I can."

I look at you with a big grin, "You're in good hands now. When you're finished with Charlie, ask him for directions to the Doctor Feelgood's Mud Baths and Health Spa. You'll find me there." With that, I wave and head out to the lobby.

8

Survival Village
Imaginarium

Having had an amazing mud bath, steam bath, a full body massage, a nice swim in the hot and cold mineral pools, and one of the most amazing organic, vegan meals of my life at Doctor Feelgood's Mud Baths and Health Spa the day before, I slept like a baby all night. For the first time in days, I can say that I am fully rested, and it feels great! Bounding upstairs to the kitchen for an early morning breakfast I find you at your usual station in front of the pancake griddle. However, this morning you're not cheerfully tossing the pancakes high into the air. You're just lazily flipping them over, and you seem to be in a pensive mood.

Everyone greets me, including you, and I answer "Top of the morning to one and all!" I look directly at you and ask, "Did you sleep well?"

"Well enough," you answer, "I just have a lot on my mind this morning."

"Then how about wrestling me up a stack of those fantastic gluten-free pancakes you're making? I'm so hungry I could eat a hobby horse."

"Coming right up," your voice is nonplussed, and everyone at the table is aware of it. We exchange looks at each other, and it appears the consensus is to leave you to your thoughts. So I join the social morning chatter and chow down on a breakfast fit for a king.

After the table has been cleared and all the plates are stacked, you and I head out to the cottage at a slow pace. Halfway there, Sheba dashes out of the woods and runs up to us. You kneel down and pet her, and she licks your face. Even she can sense your tinge of sadness and grief.

"You look like you could use a bottle of root beer," I say trying to break the ice.

"Yeah, I suppose so. A taste of some backside magic would hit the spot right about now."

We do not say much after that because I know you're really not ready to talk yet. After entering the cottage in silence, I fish a cold bottle of root beer out of the refrigerator and open it for you. You take a deep swig and wipe your lips with satisfaction.

"So, are you overwhelmed by all of the threats that you saw during the VIP tour with Charlie yesterday?"

You rock your head from side to side, "It wasn't pleasant, but that's not what has me down. Besides, Charlie is a real godsend, and he's made arrangements to give us a personal VIP tour of the Survival Village Imaginarium." You look at your wristwatch, "And I'm afraid we're going to run late for that."

Your observation makes me chuckle, "You don't get it yet. It's impossible for us to be late to anything unless we choose to be. We are time travelers, after all." For the first time all morning you break a weak smile. "That's the spirit," I say, "Now it is just the two of us, and nothing leaves this cottage. What's got you so down this morning?"

"Money, it doesn't take a rocket scientist to figure out that building a survival village, or whatever you want to call it, is a very expensive proposition. That kind of money comes with long strings attached to it. Strings tied to humiliation, hypocrisy, and greed."

"Does this have anything to do with that new school and library for your church?" I say with sympathy, "I never sensed that you were delighted with it, so I never pressed the issue."

"That's what is on my mind. A man by the name of Jim Daggot who donated the money, with lots of strings attached. The elders of my church pushed me to do my 'necessary duty,' as they called it, and it was easy for them to say. All they had a do was to make a decision to pressure me into doing what they felt was my necessary duty. So I had to praise Daggot and his wife from the pulpit, and it didn't end there. His wife micromanaged everything including all of the brass plaques, the selection of the book titles themselves, which was awful, the color scheme for the library, and the big gala ribbon-cutting ceremony. They wanted everybody to fawn all over them. So for months it was one necessary duty after another. I am not even sure it was all worth it to get our library. Some of the book titles I wanted to share with our congregation were not even included."

"Sounds unpleasant, but is this what bothers you right now?"

"Do I have your discretion?"

"Like I've always said, nothing leaves this cottage."

"I think what hurt me the most was the hypocrisy. Daggot made his fortune the old-fashioned way. He stuck his hands in other people's pockets, and he didn't care who got hurt along the way. Who knows, maybe he was feeling his mortality and decided to do something to make merit with God."

"Even so, instead of just walking into my office and writing a check he turned it into a hero-worship showboat. I suppose he thought he could then stand in front of God on Judgment day, point to it all and say, 'look what I did!'"

I shake my head sadly, "He's been so successful at being clever he forgot that while he's good at pulling the wool over everyone's eyes, God sees all, and God knows all. And God knows the true intentions of our hearts and takes them into consideration. It's sad that the man can be so arrogant as to think he can fool his Creator."

"Exactly, And all I could think about last night when I went to bed and this morning, was that to secure the funding to create this survival village, I'm going to have to kowtow to a bunch of egotistical Daggots. The rest of it I can deal with I suppose, but trying to survive by being at the whim of people who like to beat you over the head with a checkbook mortifies me. And then what will it be like during the Tribulation, when they want to run everything? Pure hell, I'm afraid."

"Well, there's that," I agree, "Truth be told, ego-driven people are the worst amateurs in the world. As with all amateurs, they feel they have a God-given right to make stupid mistakes at everyone else's expense."

Your jaw drops and your eyes light up, "That's it! That's what's bugging me — all of these selfish people with their checkbooks and no spiritual vision of what needs to happen. For them it will be their way or the highway, and others are going to suffer for it either way."

"So instead of having an effective survival village leadership, you see yourself running around playing a perpetual game of Whack-A-Mole, trying to clean up after their ego-driven disasters, some of which will have System." and lasting consequences."

You nod in agreement, gulp down the last of your root beer and set the bottle in an open slot in the case of empties, "You know, I can put up with the humiliation and the hypocrisy, but here's what's eating at me. How do I explain this to a family who has lost a loved one because some idiot with a checkbook is blaming everyone else for his or her stupidity? How do I explain it?"

"You don't," I say, "and I'll explain why on the way to the time machine, so let's get going." I look down at Sheba, "What do you say, Girl."

"Woof, woof!"

We're about half way to the time machine when I finally decide to say my piece, "There's an expression in business: 'catch the market.' If you bring a product to market before people realize they have a need or desire for it, you're faced with a hard-sell situation. Likewise, if you come to market after people have figured out their need or desire, you're competing with everyone else who was smart enough to catch the market.

"The point here is that you had to put up with nonsense to get this money for your church's school and library because this fellow Daggot was the market, and he knew it. So did your elders. So who cares if he wanted to pull a spiritual bait-and-switch on Creator? That will fail, and your elders were just practical. If it was necessary for you to lavish Daggot with attention, as far as they were concerned that came under, 'and all other duties,' on your employment contract.

"But let's not forget that, to your credit, you got the job done and now your church has a magnificent school and library. After all, is said and done, what will people remember? Not that Daggot was doing it for God because they all know he was doing it for his own ego-gratification. What they'll remember is what you did for them and their families. So let's turn this lemon into lemonade."

"Okay."

"As miserable as this whole thing was, your congregation knows you are in service to them. That's worth something. So with that in mind, I'm going to share with you a look ahead. The last lesson is what I call the launch. It is how you will organize your flock and get them engaged in active planning and preparation for the creation of a viable survival village. When the time comes, the majority of them will be ready for it, and they will want to participate, and I do mean participate — they won't just want to dabble and talk out both sides of their mouths.

"Likewise, this is when Daggots will come to you with their checkbooks, and their terms, and their meddling ways. It's simple, people who have a lot of money may be dumb, but they're not stupid. What they understand is the risk. Trust me, when they're watching the nightly news, they're not going to cling to hope like mice clutching at straws in a flood. They'll know they're being lied to because they'll be looking up at the sky and their gut instincts will be telling them the same thing your gut instinct is telling you right now — a clear and present danger is coming our way."

You shrug your shoulders, "So, they'll just go and buy one of those fancy commercial survival bunkers."

"Some yes, but others no. They'll know it's a convenience store survival solution, and that in the long run, it's not going to work for one simple reason. When the day comes that their checkbooks are only good for kindling, they'll be nobodies. And the people they hired for security and staff, if they don't have good moral compasses, who will own the goodies and run the show now? Will the formerly wealthy people even survive this change in leadership? Will they wish they hadn't survived it? Wakey, wakey, my friend, they'll know these risks, though they'll be loath to admit it, and you can take that to the bank. Why? It's because your community will have integrity and moral standards."

"So how do I manage these negotiations?"

"When you talk to these people and their checkbooks, always have one foot out the door. Remember, most of them did not earn their wealth. They're either trust fund babies, or they got it by sticking their hands in someone else's pocket. This is not to say that people do get rich while doing good things for people. Some do, and these folks deserve your kind respect and attention. But as for the rest, like I said, always have one foot out the door."

This is getting your attention, "So how does it play out?"

"In a lot of different ways, but most likely they'll come to you with tough-call offers. They'll want you to you include them or their progeny in the community, and the funding will come with terms, such as special considerations and payments in steps so they can keep the strings attached. Then, to sweeten the deal, they'll offer you enough to subsidize one or two other families besides themselves."

I stop, turn, and point my finger at you, "Hear me now. If you take deals like these, your community will fail, because there will never be enough for what needs to be done. Worse yet, these jokers will hamstring your leadership, and before you know it, you'll be so embroiled in one penny-pinching fiasco after another that everything will start coming apart at the seams.

"Simply put, you're better off without this type of strings-attached funding, no matter how difficult your situation is. So here's what you do. Tell them to submit a proposal to you in writing, and that you will consider it at your earliest convenience. Then walk away and don't look back. Of course, they're going to pressure you to take what they've offered. But having one foot out the door means that you dictate the terms, and likewise, you will tell them what their contribution needs to be."

"So won't they just go somewhere else?"

"The first one who talks money loses. The reason why they'll come to you with their cockamamie offers is that they've already looked at their other options, and here is what they'll know. If they're going to keep themselves and their progeny alive, their chances of doing it will be considerably greater with a congregation of people who honestly walk with God, keep their promises, and understand that it's one-for-all and all-for-one. Never forget that. Likewise, never forget that the pressure is on them, because they know their currency is on a crash course with failure, and once it becomes worthless, they'll be completely at the mercy of fate."

"Sounds like some pretty mean-spirited arm-twisting to me."

"No, it's about being a successful faith-based tribulation leader who gets his or her flock to safety," I lean towards you sharply, "Never forget. It is better to eat beans out of your own bowl than to eat steak out of another man's hand."

You put your hands up, "Okay, I get it, I get it. Now, can we get ourselves to the fair?"

"Woof, woof! Woof, woof!"

Thankfully Sheba breaks the tension, "That makes two in favor, and one abstention. It's pedal-to-the-metal time." What is it about that dog?

Survival Village Imaginarium

We find Charlie waiting for us in front of the Survival Village Imaginarium, and we're early. You chuckle, "It's good to be time travelers."

"Yes, it sure is," I smile as we shake Charlie's hand.

"Folks, the introduction show is running a little early this morning," Charlie says, "So I'm glad you got here a little early. We have to step out quickly, so just follow me, and I'll explain on the way.

"We got a lot of good feedback on the Imaginarium from visitors, and a lovely, little old grandmother from Poughkeepsie had a fabulous idea. She said what we needed was a brief theater presentation before people went into the main exhibit hall. So now there is a small theater at the front where we'll see an introduction program. It's the exact kind of stage set-up that you saw at The Tribulation Carousel. We even got Rabbi Sarah to come back and give us a whole new presentation for it."

Passing through the main gate and into the lobby, Charlie waves at the other docents, and they wave back with big cheerful smiles. We enter the small theater just before the doors are closed, "Whew," Charlie exclaims wiping his brow, "That was a hustle. Let's find some seats and get settled."

The auditorium is half the size of the one at The Tribulation Carousel Theater, but the stage is the same. We find an available section of seats in the middle and Sheba settles into a chair next to me. Charlie is on the other side with you.

"Say, Charlie," you ask, "If this is new, what was here before this?"

"A cafe and gift shop," he answers in a hushed voice, "Both were moved to a new add-on next to this building. The new open-air cafe there is beautiful. Trust me; they serve the best Panini sandwich you ever tasted. How about we do lunch there?"

Overhearing all this, I ask, "Sounds great to me, but do they have something tasty for Sheba?" Sheba raises her head, and her ears perk up.

"I'll text them with a heads-up. I'm sure they'll have something to please. Dogs are omnivores, after all," Charlie says with a warm smile.

You look back and forth between us then say, "Sounds great. I'm in," as we all nod with approval.

After a few minutes, the rest of the audience is seated and the room lights fade to black. Now all we see are a few spotlights on the center of the stage curtain.

Why Domes Make the Best Shelters

The holographic projectors above the stage whir to life and Rabbi Sarah appears at center stage with a pleasant smile, appearing just the same as she did in The Tribulation Carousel Theater.

"Welcome to the Survival Village Imaginarium. I am Rabbi Sarah Steiner, and I will be your presenter. In this brief overview I'm going to speak primarily to faith-based tribulation leaders who are organizing survival villages for their communities, utilizing rapid-deployment strategies. To help you in your efforts I'm going to explain why you want to build domes, the three basic types of dome construction methods, and then I'll offer suggestions on how to work with your technical building experts."

"So then, what is a rapid-deployment strategy? As the name implies, it is about getting things done quickly, but without sacrificing survivability and effectiveness. Therefore, the first part of a rapid-deployment strategy is location. When looking for relocation sites, focus on finding rolling hills, soft earth, and ample water supplies underground.

"These sites also need to be as far away as possible from major metropolitan areas and coastlines. We recommend at least 150 miles inland with an elevation of 2,000 to 4,000 feet. The area should be free of fracking wells. Likewise, you want to be as far away from nuclear power plants as possible. You should be at least 50 miles upwind of the plant, and 100 miles downwind of the plant at a minimum. The further away, the better, because prevailing winds will change after the pole shift.

"When doing your reconnaissance of possible locations you need to look closely at nearby communities. As a rule of thumb, an ideal figure is 10,000 to 30,000 inhabitants, located in areas surrounded with plenty of agriculture.

"One thing you can look for with Google Maps is how crops in the area are being irrigated. You want to see squares and rectangles which indicate flood irrigation or the long line-based spray apparatus. Avoid areas where you see the big circles that are the result of pivot irrigation, which is being pumped up out of a well. These areas are usually distant from water sources, or depend on energy to provide water access.

"Also see what's happening with the local school systems. Make a point of being where you can observe a local high school when classes let out for the day. If you see wary students dressed mainly in the gang-neutral colors of black and gray, then beware. During the tribulation gangs will be a serious security threat for all. For this reason what you want to see are relaxed students dressed in colorful clothing and plenty of it.

"Also, check the quality of the schools. Are they pursuing academic excellence? Or are they just warehousing the children? If the community is investing in the future of their children instead of warehousing them, then you'll know they believe in the future.

"Above all else, make a point of getting to know the locals because they will become your tribulation neighbors. Next, let's talk about why you want to build with domes."

> A podium appears on the right of the stage while the curtains draw open. As Rabbi Sarah walks to the podium to continue her presentation spotlights focus on a large model of the Communal Village Dome, revolving slowly on its base. Then another spotlight focuses on the Rabbi.

Pointing to the model she continues, "As you know, the Imaginarium is a building within a building. At the center of the larger building is a smaller building, yet it is sizable in its own right. At 117 feet in diameter, it is what we call the Communal Village Dome exhibit. It is an actual, full-sized dome designed for the tribulation. So why is it we do not call it a survival shelter? That is simple.

"The concept of a survival shelter is built on an outdated Cold War strategy, and that will not be effective for us in the tribulation. That old strategy focuses only on surviving the end of this civilization with the assumption that we're all ingenious people, and that we will somehow mysteriously find a way to rebuild our lives and our society afterward. Thankfully, that approach has never been tested, and it never should be.

"In contrast, the whole purpose of this magnificent Imaginarium is what the name implies — imagination. We do not imagine the difficulties that will be set us, but rather, we are imagining a future worth surviving for, an uplifting and beautiful future.

"On a personal level, I would like to share with you something that touches my imagination for the future in such a way. It is when the actress Anna May Wong sings the song, 'Happy Talk,' from the 1958 cinema classic, '*South Pacific*.' So now I would like to just share a few lyrics from the song. These are the lyrics that always float through my mind when I'm standing in the middle of the Communal Village Dome."

> The spotlights on the Rabbi and the dome model fade to black as the model lowers down into the stage floor. The curved video wall covering the back of the stage then sparks to life with a film clip from the movie, South Pacific (1958). It covers the full video wall.

"Happy Talk" from South Pacific (1949) - Rodgers and Hammerstein (Partial Lyrics)

> Happy talk, keep talking happy talk,
> Talk about things you'd like to do,
> You gotta have a dream if you don't have a dream,
> How you gonna have a dream come true?
>
> Talk about a moon floating in the sky looking like a lily on a lake,
> Talk about a bird learning how to fly. Making all the music he can make
> Happy talk, keep talking' happy talk, Talk about things you'd like to do,
> You gotta have a dream, if you don't have a dream,
> How you gonna have a dream come true?

> As the film fades to black, a spotlight refocuses attention on Rabbi Sarah.

"Sometimes this topic weighs heavily on me, as I'm sure it does on you at times. When those moments come, it always cheers me up to hear Anna May Wong singing, 'You gotta have a dream, if you don't have a dream, how you gonna have a dream come true?'

"Without a dream for the future there is no hope for the future, and so where do these dreams begin? Not with the end of this civilization, but they begin in the passion for creating a clean slate for the beginning of the next civilization. This must be a future based on building villages as centers of hope, where the defining strategy is enlightened continuity and comfort. So where will we find this passion? In the domes, we build to survive the tribulation and to thrive in the backside.

"Simply put, no other type of structure can match the strength and durability of a dome. A dome is incredibly strong, more stable, and when you make it out of concrete, it will last and last."

The video wall splits into eight panels. The four to the left begin displaying various scenes of tornado destruction.

"Did you know that a concrete dome can withstand a force five tornado? It may be damaged, but it will protect the inhabitants. Many small communities in tornado-prone areas are building domes as part of their high schools or community centers, and they are using them to shelter community members during tornado warnings."

The four panels on the right side of the video wall begin displaying various scenes of earthquake destruction.

"In the FEMA Handbook, 'Rapid Visual Screening of Buildings for Potential Seismic Hazards,' there are several types of buildings mentioned, such as type W1 for light wood frame family dwellings, and type S3 for light metal buildings. Regarding earthquakes, FEMA has determined these are the two most survival types of structures. The two least likely to survive are type URM, or buildings with unreinforced masonry load-bearing walls, and type MH, or manufactured housing, which includes mobile homes.

"In all of these FEMA building type safety evaluations, there is no mention of domes. This is because any engineer will tell you that there is nothing better than concrete domes for surviving tornadoes and earthquakes. In fact, this is why FEMA is subsidizing the construction the large concrete dome structures in tornado-prone areas, as I mentioned before, to serve as community survival shelters. With this in mind, let's take a quick look at the three most commonly used methods to build a dome."

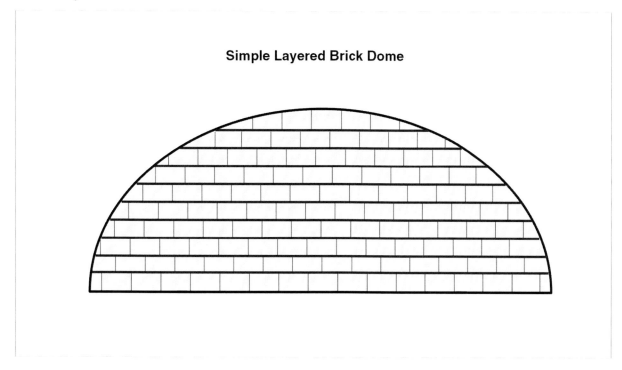

Simple Layered Brick Dome

The video wall fades to black and this time divides itself down the center. On the left side, an illustration of a layered brick design appears.

Rabbi Sarah points to the illustration, "To your left you see an illustration of the most commonly known constructed dome methods. Bricks can be made of commonly available materials to build a dome in rings, from the bottom up."

On the right side of the video wall, a picture of an Inuit igloo appears.

"Perhaps the most famous way to build a simple dome is the igloo, and most of us are fascinated with the practicality of this design. Inuit people build them during the coldest of times of the year to protect themselves from exposure to freezing temperatures and howling arctic winds. But the durability of these domes is subject to the seasons, as they will melt with the spring thaw. So you may ask can domes survive the test of time?"

On the right side of the video wall, the igloo picture cross-fades to composite image of the Pantheon in Rome.

"Yes, and an excellent example of the layered brick dome is the Pantheon in Rome. It dates back to 118 C.E., and it was constructed long before the age of steel. No doubt, long after our steel and glass high-rises have collapsed into heaps, the Pantheon will still be standing.

"By today's standards, there is nothing exotic about the materials used, though for its time it was very advanced. This is because the materials used in the concrete of the dome vary from top to bottom.

"Once we reach the backside, layered brick domes will likely be what we'll build on the surface. For this reason, I want you to pay particular attention to the Oculus, or opening, at the top of the dome. It not only lets the light in, but it is also where a dome structure of this type is weakest.

"In a very clever bit of engineering by the Romans, the oculus not only lights the interior, but it also lightens the weight-bearing load at that critical point, thereby making the structure less vulnerable to collapse. Now let's look at the second way domes are made."

The complete video wall fades to black. Then on the left side, an illustration of an interior dirt mound form appears.

"A different way to build a dome is with an interior dirt mound form. With this modern low-tech method of construction, a dirt mound in the shape of a dome is built up from the ground. Then rebar and support beams are built on and around it. Concrete is then poured in successive layers from the bottom to the top. Once the concrete sets, the dirt is removed. At that point, the dome is ready for finishing."

On the right side of the video wall, an image of a dome at **Arcosanti in Arizona appears.**

"Sixty-five miles North of Phoenix, Arizona, on I-17 near Cordes Junction is a remarkable place called Arcosanti. Built in harmony with the land, it is a city of the future. The brain-child of architect Paolo Soleri, interior dirt mound forms were used for the construction of its dome structures. I strongly urge each and every one of you to visit this beautiful place, for it will inspire you with a picture of what can, and should be, the future of humanity.

"That being said, while this construction method does produce a reinforced concrete dome structure, as opposed to a dome with concentric rings of bricks, it does have its drawbacks. It is time and labor intensive, and these will always be in short supply, especially in the lead-up to the worst of the tribulation. That is why I'm glad to say that there is a newer method of dome construction that is perfect for building survival domes for the tribulation."

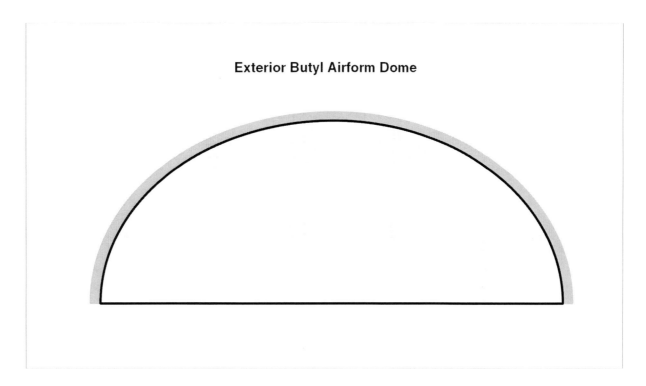

The complete video wall fades to black, and in the left side, an illustration of an exterior butyl air-form appears.

"A whole new way of building domes was developed a few decades ago by David B. South, co-founder of Monolithic Domes of Italy, Texas, which is south of Dallas."

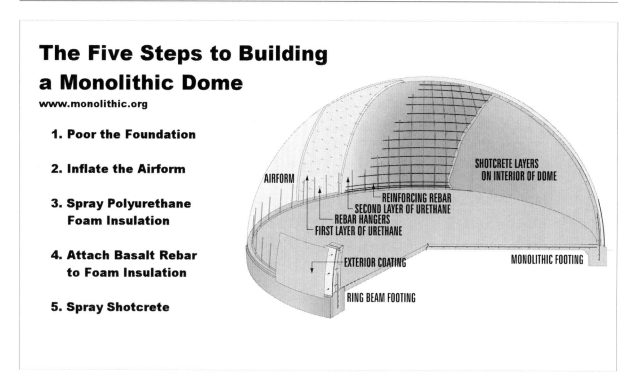

The Five Steps to Building a Monolithic Dome

www.monolithic.org

1. Poor the Foundation

2. Inflate the Airform

3. Spray Polyurethane Foam Insulation

4. Attach Basalt Rebar to Foam Insulation

5. Spray Shotcrete

In the right side of the video wall, an illustration of a monolithic dome cutaway appears.

"David's method has turned the interior dirt mound form method, as we saw at Arcosanti inside out. Instead of pouring concrete over rebar sticking out of a dirt mound, David's method uses a butyl air-form so the concrete can be sprayed onto the rebar from the inside. Of course, this raises a question. Is a dome that is made of concrete that was sprayed on, as opposed to one that has been poured, strong enough to survive the many threats of the coming tribulation?"

The complete video wall fades to black and in the left side a composite of David B. South and a large Monolithic dome appear.

"To your left, you see a picture of David with one of the large dome structures his organization built, and yes, it's a church. But David also builds homes for all kinds of purposes all around the world. This is why I want you to listen to an excerpt of an interview he gave in 2015 about a dome he constructed in Iraq."

The spotlight on Rabbi Sarah fades, and on the right side of the video wall, we see the text: David B. South, September 27, 2015. Interview with Marshall Masters on Cut to the Chase. The text remains on the video wall for approximately five seconds, and then fades to black. As the audio clip plays, a series of animations are shown in step with the audio.

"In 1989 I built thirty domes in Iraq that were for grain storage, and I built one that was for a mosque for our good friend, the president over there. When they started shooting the Iraqis and everybody else, the US government went in and put a 2,000 pound JDAM (Joint Direct Attack Munition – Guided Bomb) down through the center of that mosque, but not inside to the bottom. It blew the doors off.

"What it did is it popped a hole in the top and went off inside. It literally blew up everything of any value, but it did not damage the dome. Now it did dock a little hole where the 2,000-pound missile went through but not inside. It blew the doors off, blew the windows out, but there weren't very many windows.

The British were given that area for their headquarters during that Iraq war, and they put a new skylight over the hole. Then they cleaned up the mess, and it was their headquarters for the many years while they were in charge of that part of Iraq

"The dome was 117 foot in diameter, and I think it was 58 foot tall. The shell was approximately 6 inches thick, the lower areas eight inches. Reinforcement was just steel rebar every 12 inches with the bottom of it being number six rebar in the bottom, which is half-inch, about 3/8 of an inch through the main part, every foot. Considering the size of the building is not compared to what we do if you made a square building if I were building you a new church it would be identically the same."

The video wall fades to black as a spotlight focuses on Rabbi Sarah.

"This 2015 interview with David inspired the design of the Communal Village Dome exhibit in this building, which also happens to be 117 feet in diameter. So this is a monolithic dome absolutely tough enough for the tribulation. Not only that, the monolithic method offers the fastest way to build a survivable community. How fast? Use the Monolithic system and months will become weeks.

"In the exhibit hall around the Communal Village Dome exhibit, you will see tabletop models showing how easy it is to build these domes, and of equal importance, where to place them for the greatest amount of safety. Please note, if you want to learn more, David freely provides thousands of pages of information about his system online at his Web site, monolithic.org."

The model of the Communal Village Dome rises up from the stage floor and begins revolving slowly on its base as spotlight focus on it.

"In closing, I want to take a moment to talk to you as a tribulation faith-based leader about the men and women in your community who will oversee the construction of your domes. What you can expect is that many of them will have little or no direct experience with this method of construction, nor will they have ever lived inside a dome. Consequently, you may get some push-back from them, along with suggestions to use what they know how to build. After all, the familiar feels safest.

"But, as you can see in this presentation, no other structure imaginable will be safer for your flock during the tribulation than a concrete dome. So, in the event you do get push-back from your experts, you are going to have to make your case.

"This is the very reason we created the Communal Village Dome exhibit. When you visit that exhibit, you will feel its spacious, quiet comfort. In fact, there is a peaceful, spiritual quality to being in a dome. Perhaps that is the reason why the Romans built the Pantheon to honor their gods in a dome shape. So I want to leave you with one last bit of advice about how to deal with experts who may disagree with your vision of the future.

"Always remember this: expertise is the catalyst, but consensus and resources will determine the results. As the leader, you are the consensus builder, and you are also the one who allocates the resources. When creating consensus, compromise will be necessary. So what kind of solution are you looking for? One that will get everyone's buy-in so that they will participate. Yes, they may say it is not the way they'd prefer to do it. On the other hand, they'll also see that the consensus approach will work to get something practical built out, and so they will willingly participate."

The spotlights on the model fade to black as the curtains close.

Rabbi Sarah points to an exit door at the front of the auditorium on her side, "This exit will take you to the exhibit hall around the Communal Village Dome with several wonderful table-top models. Beyond that is an escalator that will take you down to the lower floor where you can experience dome living for yourself in the Communal Village Dome exhibit. Then taking the escalator back up to this level, there will be several more table-top models demonstrating how you can use domes for all of your survival village needs.

"But most importantly, what we want you to find here in the Imaginarium is a dream for the future. This is a dream so strong it draws you through the worst of times, because, after all, if you don't have a dream, how you gonna have a dream come true? This concludes my presentation."

The spotlight on Rabbi Sarah fades while her holographic image standing at the podium dissolves. The auditorium lights come on.

As we leave the auditorium, Charlie explains, "We'll start with the table-top exhibits on this side, which are organized into three groups: The Monolithic System, Building Your Dome, and Placing Your Dome. You two are going to be amazed at how fast we'll get through all that, because frankly, it's just simple stuff. But here is what I want to do, if it's alright with you both. As I told you before, I'm staying with an old friend. His name is Lou Spenser, and he's an old ham radio guy who just loves radio communications.

"Marshall, I suggest we move through the exhibits quickly enough to get your friend familiarized with the big picture. Then, how about we all go to the cafe for lunch? I'll have Lou meet us there. He'll bring drawings and give us a great briefing on the types of amateur radios you'll want for your survival villages. That way you can go off and do other things while I return with your friend to the Imaginarium to spend more time with the exhibits."

I turn to you, "I think Charlie has a great idea there if it's OK with you?"

"You have in mind another visit to Doctor Feelgood's Mud Baths and Health Spa?"

I shake my head no, "Actually, I need to organize your next lesson. Or, if you want me to stay here with you and go through the exhibits, I'll be happy to do that as well."

"No need for you to stay. Charlie takes good care of me, and besides, Charlie, you're really a cool guy to hang out with."

Charlie chimes in, "Thank you. I can work in a really great dinner in the staff cafeteria with some great treats for Sheba," he smiles at Sheba, "Would you like that?"

"Woof, woof!"

"Well then, there it is," I say, "Lead on, Charlie."

The Monolithic System

Before starting with the exhibits in The Monolithic System group, we stand at the long rail going around the Communal Village Dome. Roughly five feet above our heads is the top of the dome. Looking down into the lower floor of the Imaginarium, we can see that this structure is enormous.

"What we see here is the very top of the Communal Village Dome," Charlie explains, "The highest five feet or so of the second floor where the bedrooms are located."

"Wow, it's massive!" you exclaim.

"And even though it is so large, it was still created in five easy steps," Charlie says as he nods in the direction of The Monolithic System exhibit, "Follow me. You're going to love this."

All five of The Monolithic System table-top model exhibits are in a row, close to the wall. Behind each model is a metal wall plaque.

"Right now we're just going to focus on the five simple steps necessary to build a monolithic dome. This does not include other preparation and location placement aspects, which we will talk about later. For now, what you need to know is how straightforward and simple the basic construction process is."

Step 1: Poor the Foundation

The plaque for the first table-top model reads, "Step 1: Pour the Foundation."

"As with any structure, you start with a foundation. With domes, the foundation is often referred to as the 'pad.' As to the floor, it is poured over the pad after completion of the dome. Now, here I want to emphasize two important things. The foundation and the shell of the dome must be reinforced with basalt rebar. Rebar, by the way, is short for 'reinforcing bar,'"

"But I thought rebar is always made of steel?" you ask.

Charlie nods his head, "That's the most common type of rebar in use, but basalt rebar is twice as strong as steel and is only 1/5 as heavy. It was invented by the Russians after WWII. Given our tribulation requirements, one huge advantage is that while steel rebar rusts away, basalt rebar never does. Regarding costs, both are about the same, so it makes sense to use the stronger and more durable basalt rebar.

"If you want to increase the strength of the dome while saving yourself some money, here's a handy tip. When you order or mix your concrete, you want a mix of 75% standard Portland cement, and 25% fly ash from oil or coal. The fly ash costs less than other available components, it eliminates air holes, combines with the other chemical components, and makes a better concrete. Now follow me to the next table."

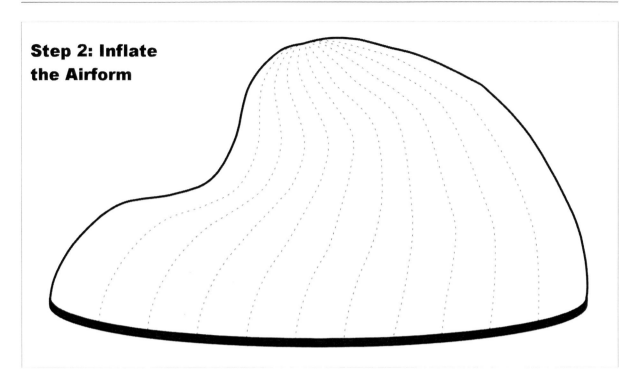

Step 2: Inflate the Airform

The plaque for the second table-top model reads, "Step 2: Inflate the air-form."

"The beauty of the monolithic system is that you use an inflatable air-form which takes shape quickly, as opposed to all the time needed to build a dirt mound as an internal form.

"I've spoken with builders who have experience with this technology, and I learned something rather interesting from them. For domes up to approximately 50 to 60 feet in diameter, the butyl air-form is reusable. However, with larger diameter domes you cannot reuse the air-form; rather it becomes a permanent part of the structure.

"On the other hand, with smaller domes, you can reuse the air-form up to one hundred times as long as you're careful. In which case, you will apply a sealant as the primary water barrier, like the sealants used for basement waterproofing, which obviously cost a lot less than an air-form. Now we'll see how to reinforce the dome while insulating it."

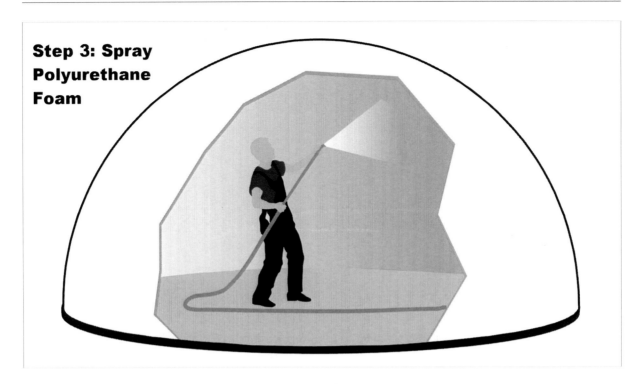

Step 3: Spray Polyurethane Foam

The plaque for the third table-top model reads, "Step 3: Spray Polyurethane Foam."

"To keep positive air pressure inside the dome, you enter the air-form through a double-door airlock so that the air pressure inside stays at a constant level. Then you spray approximately a 1.5-inch layer of polyurethane foam onto the air-form. Rebar hangers are pressed into this first layer of foam, which you'll use to attach the rest of the rebar. Once this is done, you'll spray another 1.5-inch layer of polyurethane over that. Now you have insulation for the dome plus a way to mount your rebar."

"So how efficient is a dome versus traditional wood frame house?" you ask.

"That is one of my favorite questions," Charlie beams, "These domes are amazingly energy efficient. If you're going to use an 80-ton air conditioner for a conventional building, for example, a dome with the same amount of interior space will only need a 20-ton unit. Likewise, if you're using under floor radiant heating, you'll use one-fourth as many panels with the dome as you would for a conventional home. Or, let's say you're using a Franklin stove. If with a normal house you would need four cords of wood to get through the winter, with a dome of the same interior size, you'll only need one cord of wood."

"Wow, that is amazing efficiency!" you exclaim.

"Yes, it is, and here's another huge advantage. During the tribulation, we're not going to be connected to a power grid, which means we'll have found other ways to power our domes. Thanks to the incredible efficiency of these domes, your power demands will be significantly less, and that will make a difference. Now, let's move on to the next model and hang the rest of the rebar."

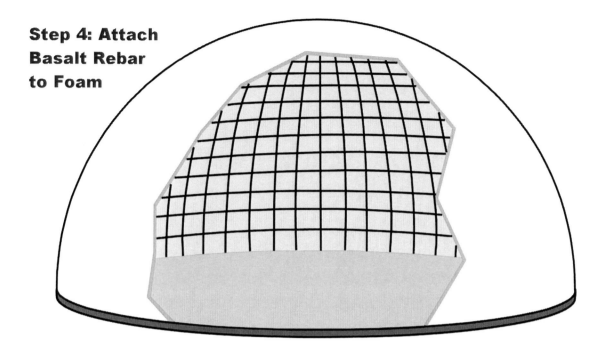

Step 4: Attach Basalt Rebar to Foam

The plaque for the fourth table-top model reads, "Step 3: Attach Basalt Rebar to Foam."

"Here is where decades of building these domes have really paid off for the monolithic designers. Over time they have learned what works best when it comes to reinforcing rebar, and for domes, there is a very big difference between small domes and big domes.

"For starters, both small and large domes are going to use the same layout, horizontal hoops, and vertical ribs. However, the difference comes with rebar diameter and spacing. With the smaller domes, you use a larger diameter rebar with wide spacing.

"Conversely, with large domes you use smaller diameter rebar with closer spacing. When you order your air-forms from Monolithic, they'll explain that to you. Again, remember that basalt rebar does not rust and that it weights one-fifth as much as steel rebar, but is twice as strong. Now let's go to the next model for the fifth and final step."

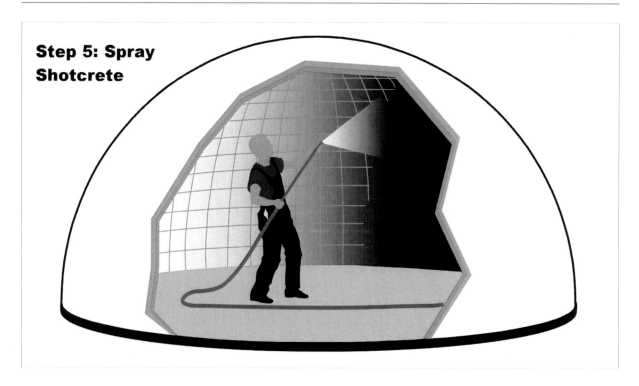

Step 5: Spray Shotcrete

The plaque for the fifth table-top model reads, "Step 5: Spray Shotcrete."

"In the fifth and final step you spray Shotcrete to form the actual rigid structure of the dome around the rebar. The term Shotcrete refers to a process where you use compressed air to force the concrete through a hose and nozzle so that you can spray it on the dome interior at high velocity.

"As with the foundation or pad as it's sometimes called, you use the same mix: 75% standard Portland cement, and 25% fly ash from oil or coal. The thickness of the Shotcrete is 3 inches or more depending on dome size, and for subterranean domes, you add an additional inch to whatever is the structural norm for an above-ground dome.

"When you do this you can cover the dome with up to 30 feet of dirt. Given that we're only recommending 12 feet of dirt and/or aggregate rock, this is more than suitable for our needs. However, what I would recommend is that before you order your air-form is to have them give you the specifications for both the standard subterranean thickness and the maximum subterranean thickness for the diameter of your dome.

"Another thing that I really like about David South is that this man wants to share his knowledge with the world. So send your own crew to Italy, Texas where his training center is, and he'll teach you how to do this yourself. Then all you really need to do is to buy the air-forms, Shotcrete spraying equipment, and other dome-construction-related equipment. Talk about have your cake and eat it too.

"So there it is, my friends, in five easy steps. This is how you build a dome. Now let's go on over to the Building Your Dome exhibit group to talk about how you're going to build your own domes."

Building Your Dome

As with the previous exhibit group, all fourteen of the Building Your Dome table-top model exhibits are in a row close to the wall. Behind each model is a metal wall plaque. Charlie continues the short tour with you, me, and Sheba in tow.

"When building your dome, you need to keep the following in mind, radiation and impacts from above, and earthquakes and water from below. First, we'll start with water.

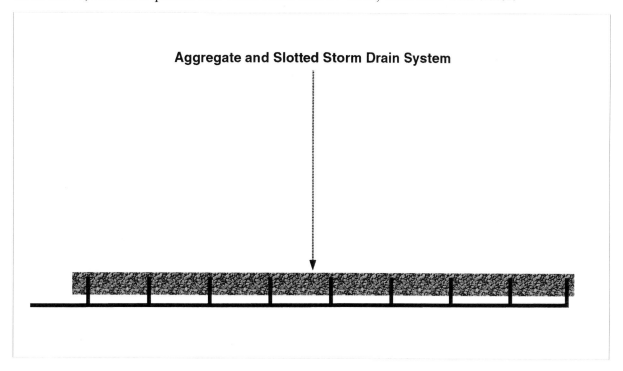

Aggregate and Slotted Storm Drain System

The plaque for the first table-top model reads, "Aggregate and Slotted Storm Drain System."

"The last major event of the tribulation will be the deluge when Mother Earth is washing her surface clean. In other words, expect water and plenty of it. So the first thing you need to do is to lay down an aggregate and slotted storm drain system. What you want is about 2 feet of aggregate with slotted drains. These are standing pipes with slits in them in the upper parts and become solid pipes at the bottom.

"The slotted drain pipes feed into a storm drain system which will take the water away from the dome. This will also handle normal amounts of ground water incursion as well. This system is going to be useful water especially for permaculture, so when you design it, be sure to put your runoff to good use.

"If you're looking to save a little money, instead of buying sized aggregate, ask for tailings. Tailings are not uniform in size, but for this application, they'll do nicely, and they are a lot cheaper. Next, let's look at what you're going to do for earthquakes."

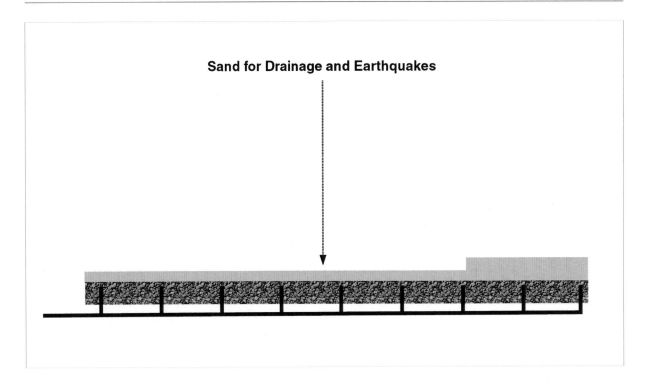

Sand for Drainage and Earthquakes

The plaque for the second table-top model reads, "Sand for Drainage and Earthquakes"

"No other above-ground structure is more able to survive an earthquake than a dome, and when the dome is underground, that's even more so. When a subterranean structure is completely surrounded by earth, it doesn't matter if it is a dome, or a square, or a rectangular structure. Bury it well, and it will be more structurally sound during an earthquake. This is because earthquakes generate ground waves in two directions, sideways and upwards.

"When it comes to upward ground waves, structures are already designed to withstand gravity pressing down on them, so vertical forces are not an issue. It's the ground waves coming at structures from the sides that matter. When a structure is properly embedded in the earth, those lateral-force ground waves will go around and through the structure without destroying it. For above-ground structures it's a whole different story, and we all know how that one plays out from seeing footage of earthquake damage.

"However, there is something better than just earth and rock to embed your domes into. Using sand around your domes to protect from earthquakes will be helpful because you are going to have connecting tunnels and structures. Sand will allow for some movement without things being jarred completely loose or broken. And this brings us to an additional feature you will need for underground structures, protection from water invasion."

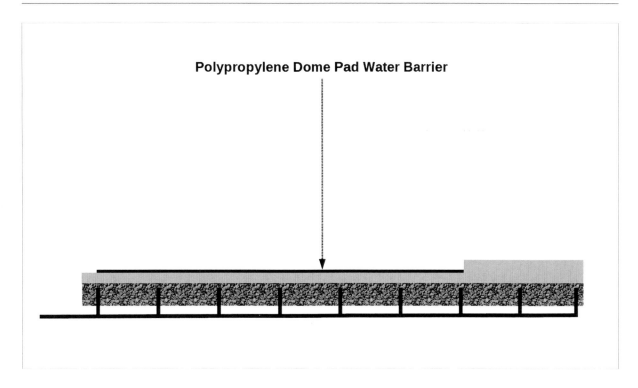

The plaque for the third table-top model reads, "Polypropylene Dome Water Barrier."

""Before you pour the foundation, or what is called the pad, it's a good idea to lay down a polypropylene water barrier layer first. This will help to keep moisture from coming up from the ground, or from a rising water table during flooding, into the foundation. This is especially important because, as you'll learn later on, you will be using under-the-floor radiant heat panels to warm your domes. But for now, we're ready to pour the foundation pad."

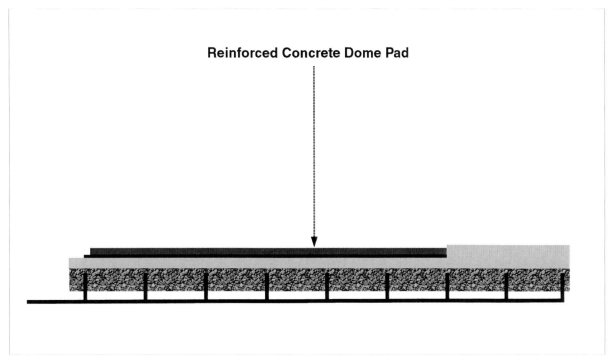

The plaque for the fourth table-top model reads, "Reinforced Concrete Dome Pad."

"This brings us to step one of the Monolithic system, pouring the foundation. As with the rest of the dome, you're going to use basalt rebar to reinforce the concrete. This is especially helpful when pouring the pad because basalt rebar does not rust even if some water penetrates the cement at some point.

"When you order your butyl air-form, be sure to ask the engineers at Monolithic about the proper foundation thickness for your planned structure. Given that we are going to go through immense earth stresses and earth movements during the pole shift, including sinkholes forming in unexpected areas, the thicker the foundation, the better, within reason. So be sure to find out what they recommend as a maximum amount of reinforcement and thickness before you pour the pad. Now it's time for the big show."

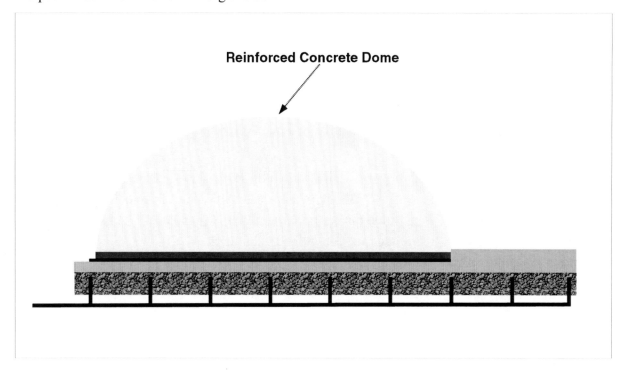

Reinforced Concrete Dome

The plaque for the fifth table-top model reads, "Reinforced Concrete Dome."

"This brings us to step one of the Monolithic system, inflating the air-form. I have to tell you that this process reminds me of when I was a kid and the circus came to town. One of the things I loved most was to watch them raise the big tent. I get the same thrill each time I see an air-form being inflated."

"Just out of curiosity Charlie," I ask, "Do you think this inspired you to become an engineer?"

The question gets the surprised look from Charlie. We can see him thinking it through. "I never thought of it that way," Charlie finally answers, "But you know; you may have a point there."

"Now, when you are inflating the air-form remember that you want to have a good seal. That will keep a positive air pressure inside so the air-form can maintain its inflated shape.

This means you are going to be installing a double-door entry system, basically an airlock. Before going inside that dome, you also need to make sure you're wearing complete protective gear, including a very good quality respirator because you will be dealing with some toxic components and some substances you just don't want in your lungs. Speaking of getting in and out of a dome, this brings us to the next step in the building process."

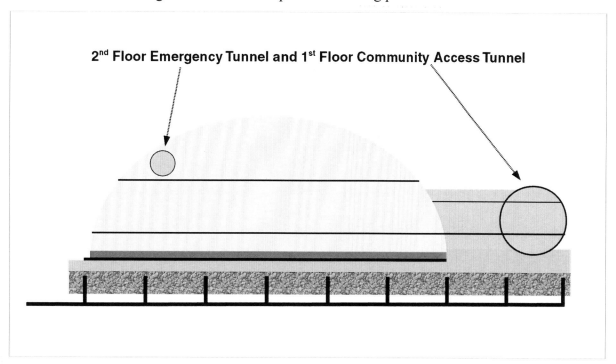

The plaque for the sixth table-top model reads, "2nd Floor Emergency Tunnel and 1st Floor Community Access Tunnel."

"I've seen a lot of people build various types of shelters with large, corrugated steel "I've seen a lot of people build various types of shelters with large, corrugated steel pipes the same type that is used for culverts. While they're strong and they are designed to be buried underground, I do feel sorry those who will live in them as shelters. I don't care how you paint them or dress them up; they're going to be as cramped and uncomfortable as World War II submarines. That may be acceptable for a few days, or a few weeks, but this tribulation will last for years. I hate to think about it because people will go stir-crazy wanting to get out of them. And if the interior structures are built with particle board or plywood, people will also be getting sick from exposure to formaldehyde and other toxic gasses.

"Now with subterranean domes you're probably going to build a few of them in a series, which is the most efficient way for a small community of 100 or so people to build. In this model you see a two-story dome. Assuming this is a standard size used for all the communal apartment domes, you'll likely connect them all together with a community access tunnel.

"To demonstrate the possible materials, this model uses a large concrete pipe for the community access tunnel and corrugated steel pipes for the emergency tunnels. Most likely you'll wind up using whatever strong tunnel materials you can get your hands on. And now it's time to see how we will warm things up in the cold subterranean areas we will create."

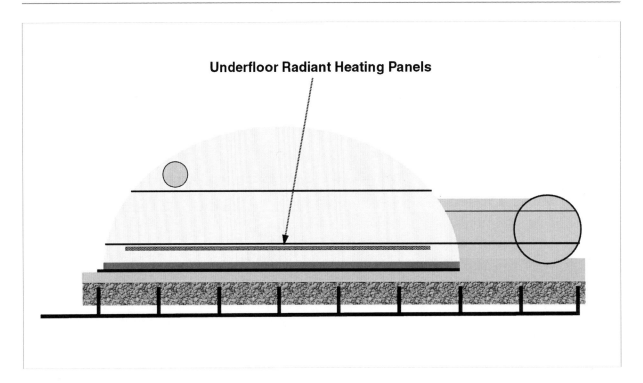

The plaque for the seventh table-top model reads, "Under floor Radiant Heating Panels."

"When it comes to under floor radiant heating you can use water-based or electricity-based solutions. With electricity you are going to have to generate the power. With water-based systems there are numbers of ways to heat the water. While the skies are not going to be very clear, solar hot water panels on the surface could still do the job. They would still need protection from meteor impacts and other disasters on the surface though.

"Whether you use water or electric for your radiant heat, the inherent thermal efficiency of the dome will require less energy to heat than conventional above-ground structures. With a dome whether it is subterranean or above ground, you only need one-fourth as much energy to heat it as you would need for a typical wood frame house."

"Keep in mind that subterranean domes are going to hold heat exceptionally well. Your dome kitchen will heat the dome by retaining the heat you create by cooking. So don't forget to include cooling ventilation of some kind, as well. A cool air chamber of some type in the sand or earth outside your dome could be very helpful in an area with a community kitchen.

"As to actual air-conditioning, you'll never need it for a subterranean dome. Depending on elevation and other factors, you can expect a constant temperature of between 50 to 60° inside the dome without heating or cooling. One of the big benefits of under floor heating is that you do not need a humidifier like you would with a forced air system. This means that you can stay comfortable without risking Legionnaires' disease. Next up, let's look at some of the goodies we have come to expect as civilized beings."

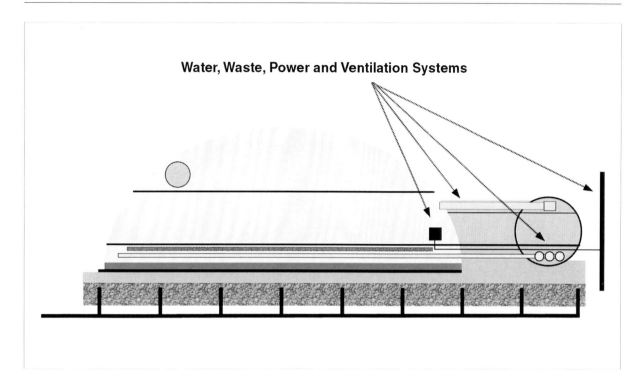

Water, Waste, Power and Ventilation Systems

The plaque for the eighth table-top model reads, "Water, Waste, Power and Ventilation Systems."

"Regarding making your domes truly livable, you'll need systems for water, waste, power, and ventilation. Of particular interest to me are the power systems, beginning with a dedicated copper grounding rod. In modern homes we all use 110 and 220 AC, and that works great because we're tied to the grid. But that won't last long once the tribulation is in full swing.

"So I like to think of a dome as a land ark. This means you can think in naval terms. When you're on a ship, your main power sources are DC not AC. For example you'll have 12, 24 and 48 volts of DC power available to you. Yes, there will be times you'll need AC power for special equipment such as a refrigerator or stove. In these cases you can use an inverter to create the AC from your DC power source. Otherwise, everything is DC and as low voltage as possible, especially your lighting. This is because you can use a bank of car batteries as a standby power system to keep your lights on if the generator fails.

"As for tap water, please, no lead pipes. Use CPVC (chlorinated polyvinyl chloride) pipes for both hot and cold water. It's been used for years, and it's approved for drinking water. Just one tip though, try and source it from somewhere other than China!

"For your waste water there will be two types: brown and black. Brown water is something that's reusable for purposes such as shower water, and it needs its own separate system, away from clean, potable water. Brown water can be used for toilets, permaculture, and other purposes to conserve your clean drinking and cooking water which will become precious during the tribulation as surface water becomes contaminated and toxic. Black water is sewage, and that must go to a septic system with a large septic field.

"One thing you'll see in the Communal Village Dome exhibit is French-style bidets next to the toilets along with dispensers for wiping cloths that can be washed and reused. Toilet paper might be something that you'll carry with you when you're above ground as a convenience. But when you're down in the dome, you'll want to clean yourself with a bidet, especially before and after sex.

"Bidets are more sanitary than paper, provided you dry yourself. Best of all, you're not flushing paper products down into the septic system. As for me, fixing a black water system is the last thing I'll want to do during the days of darkness. Next, we'll see how to keep your dome safe from ground water."

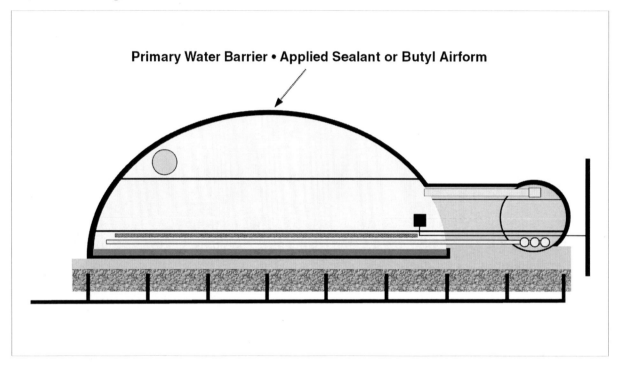

The plaque for the ninth table-top model reads, "Primary Water Barrier - Applied Sealant or Butyl Air-Form."

"Back over at the Monolithic system exhibit group we talked about using the air-form as a subterranean water barrier. With the large domes you will be required to leave the air-form on, so this step is essentially covered during the large dome fabrication process. However, if you're building smaller domes you can reuse the air-form. With that let me acquaint you with a fascinating little term, positive pressure side.

"For those of you who have basements, or your home is built into the side of the hill, you're counting on slump block to keep you dry because on the other side of it is groundwater. That is what is called the positive pressure side, where the water is trying to press into your house through the slump block. Conversely, the negative pressure side is inside your house, and if you only seal your basement on the negative pressure side, you're likely to learn an unpleasant lesson, especially after an earthquake.

"This brings us back to the positive pressure side. Because an air-form is made of butyl, it is a wonderful water barrier. But if you're reusing an air-form instead of leaving it in place, you will need to find a commercially-available product that offers ample positive pressure side protection.

"Here you need to choose wisely. Be sure that whoever is making this call has real life experience and is not just reading a lot of advertising on the Internet. Whether you're using an air-form or sealant as the primary water barrier, just remember the old saying, if one is good, two are better. So let's go to the next exhibit."

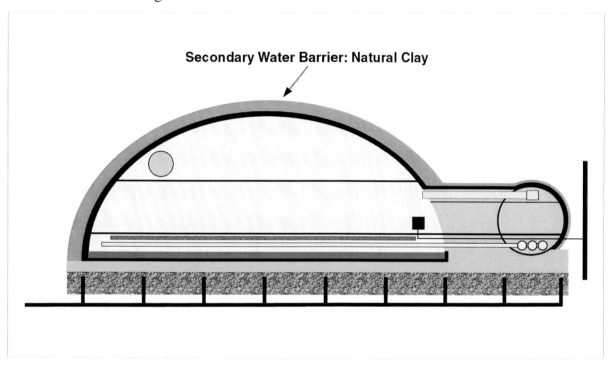

The plaque for the tenth table-top model reads, "Secondary Water Barrier – Natural Clay."

"A thick layer of natural Clay is an ideal secondary water barrier. The great thing about clay is that it is easy to find, and it requires no special processing.

"Proof of its effectiveness as a water barrier is obvious, as folks have used it to seal their ponds for centuries. Why is it that clay can last as a pond liner for centuries? This is due to the inorganic mineral content of clay that survives through long periods of time, much like the parent rock mineral material. Now let's go to the last exhibit for this group."

Complete Habitable Shelter Dome

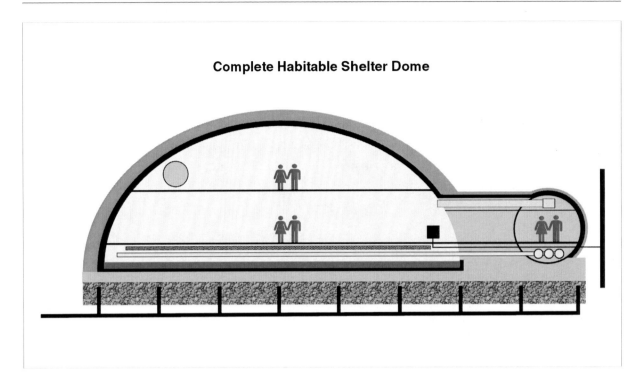

The plaque for the eleventh table-top model reads, "Habitable Shelter Dome."

"Once the secondary water barrier is in place, you have the beginnings of a habitable subterranean dome. At this stage what you really have is what we call a 'green dome.' Now it is time to build out the interior and furnish the dome.

"Here I want to make a very specific point. During the pole shift event, the planet is going to be going through unimaginable contortions. The last thing you need is injuries from people being thrown against walls or crushed by furniture. Remember the saying about, 'a loose cannon' on-board a ship?' Don't let that be your dome's interior furnishings. So when designing dome interiors, remember that you are in a land ark, and you will be going through some very choppy waters so to speak.

"Beds and furnishings should be bolted to the floor and to walls. Shelves and cabinets should likewise be floor-mounted and wall-mounted, with closing and lockable doors for safe storage so that nothing can fly out of them. While some may complain that your dome will look like a nursing home, you will also want to mount handrails everywhere, especially in the bathrooms.

"There will come a time during the long-lasting earthquakes of the pole shift when the only safe place to hunker down will be your bed, and nobody wants to be awakened from their sleep by being thrown against a wall. So make sure your beds all have padded side-rails and safety straps. Also, airline-style seat belts for your common-area chairs and sofas would be a smart addition.

"For the floors, I recommend high quality, three-quarter inch bamboo flooring with safety lighting strips such as those you see in the main cabins of commercial airliners or movie theaters. Powered by your main electrical system, these strips should also have their own dedicated fail-over backup batteries.

"With that let's move on to the next exhibit group, Situating Your Dome. This is a small exhibit, but what you're going to learn here will make or break the survivability of your subterranean dome."

Situating Your Dome

Charlie leads us to the Situating Your Dome exhibit group, "So far, you've learned how easy it is to build the dome with the Monolithic system, and how you can build a subterranean dome for your survival village. However, now it is absolutely critical that you properly situate your survival village, by which I mean, deciding where exactly, you are going to build it.

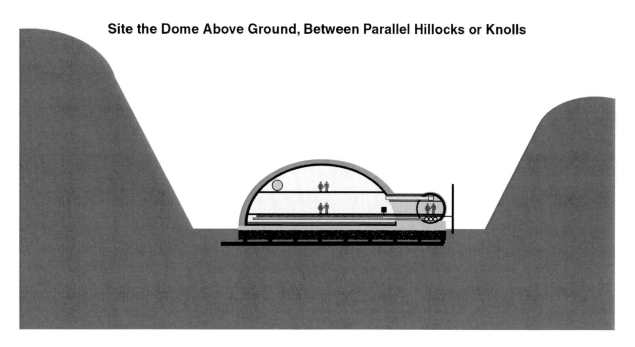

The plaque for the first table-top model reads, "Site the Dome Above Ground – Between Parallel Hillocks or Knolls."

"As you learned earlier, when doing your reconnaissance for survival village location three things you need to look for are soft earth, rolling hills, and good access to subterranean water. With this in mind let's take a closer look at water with this first exhibit."

"Simply put, water is life. No matter how fancy your beans, bullets, and bunkers are, you're not going to last long at all without clean, drinkable water. Did you know you can survive for about three weeks without food, but only about three days without water? This means you're going to want to have access to good, sweet, clean groundwater both in water tables near the surface and in deep, underground aquifers. When it comes to building your subterranean domes, deep aquifers are not a real safety issue, but water tables near the surface are.

"This is why you want to look for properties where you have parallel hills or knolls where you can build a dome between them, above the ground, then backfill over and around your dome. You see; we believe that it is unwise to excavate and dig down into the ground to create an area for your dome. This is for the same reason that water tables become real problems for architects and engineers who design and build high-rise buildings.

"Once they start digging into the earth to create the necessary foundation and sub-floors for their high-rises, they often find themselves having to deal with major amounts of ground water, and that is not easy. So, if you are going to build a rapid deployment survival community, how do you get around this high-rise problem? For that, we go to the next exhibit."

Above Ground = Above the Water Table

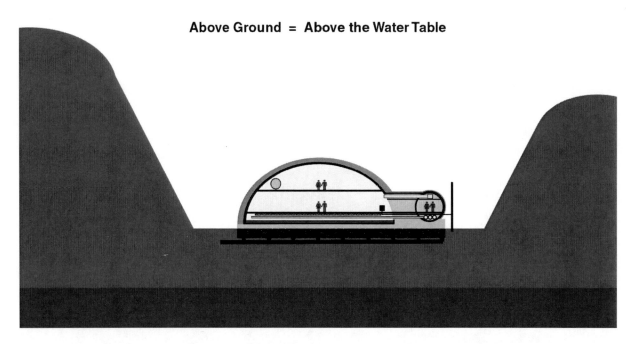

The plaque for the second table-top model reads, "Above Ground = Above the Water Table."

"You can completely and easily avoid having water problems by simply building above ground. Why? Because by building above ground you are also building above the water table. This is precisely why we tell you to look for relocation areas with rolling hills and soft earth. There are several other advantages for rolling hills and soft earth as well. For example rolling hills help reduce the risk of prairie fires and tornadoes.

"After the deluge and the worst of the tribulation have passed, this is the time to begin working on your above-ground permaculture system. To do this you'll going to want to work with well-defined ridge lines, catch basins, ponds, and pastures."

"Once you have your natural system working, it will take very little effort on your part to keep it going. Even so, your 'edible forest' will continue producing wonderful foods to keep you going. You will need to think about this when you choose the sites for your domes."

"Remember, you're going to have storm drain run-off and brown water. Make sure that this water is not lost to poor planning, but rather, that it eventually becomes an invaluable resource for your permaculture system. With this in mind let's talk about backfill."

EMP and Radiation Shield – 8' of Soil Backfill From Adjacent Hillock or Knoll

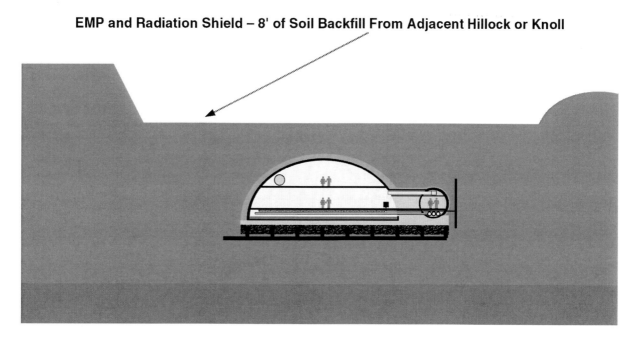

The third table-top model reads, "EMP and Radiation Shield – Eight Feet of Soil Backfill from Adjacent Hill or Knoll."

"How do you turn a dome that has been built above ground into a subterranean dome," Charlie asks us.

You point to the model and say, "It says it right there — backfill."

Exactly," Charlie says with a big smile, "But what you're seeing in this third exhibit is just the first backfill layer over the dome. This needs to be about eight feet thick on the top of the dome. We call it the EMP and radiation shield, although you only really need about five feet of dirt for EMP protection. However, solar radiation will be coming in from incredibly violent solar storms when the Planet X System is in the kill zone. So the more dirt there is the better."

"Also, remember that by adding an extra inch of Shotcrete to the dome wall when constructing your domes, you build a dome strong enough to bear up to thirty feet of earth, which is much more than we are showing with these models."

"So, is just eight feet of dirt all that's necessary for an acceptable level of solar radiation shielding? Not in our opinion, and I will explain this in the fourth, and last, exhibit in this group."

Impact and Radiation Shield – 2' of Basalt Aggregate with a 2' Backfill Cap

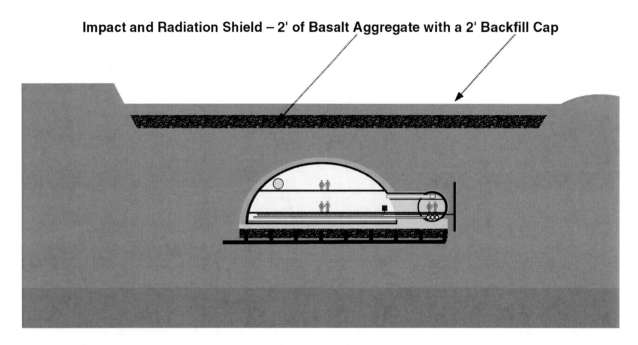

The plaque for the fourth table-top model reads, "Impact and Radiation Shields –
Two Feet of Basalt Aggregate with Two Feet of Backfill Cap."

"What we see here are two more layers of protection on top of the one we saw previously.
We call these the impact and radiation shields, and they come in two layers. The first layer is
two feet of basalt aggregate, but you can use basalt tailings instead and save yourself a lot of
money without sacrificing any shielding capability.

"Keep in mind that natural volcanic basalt offers a really effective solar radiation shield.
According to some experts, it is just as effective as steel inch for inch and for a fraction of the
price.

"On top of the aggregate layer is a two-foot cap of earth backfill. If you design these two
layers correctly, after the tribulation has passed, you can plant gardens on the cap because it is
essentially topsoil, or you can just let nature have its way with natural grasses and flowering
weeds. In the meantime you will have an effective radiation shield for the bulk of the threats
we'll face when the Planet X System is transiting the kill zone.

"When Earth is transiting through the tail, we expect ongoing meteor storms with impactors
on average approximately the size of a boar's head. If one strikes above your dome, a good
deal of its impact energy will be absorbed by the earth cap, and more will be redirected
horizontally by the basalt aggregate before it reaches your dome structure. Then again, if some
huge rock like a small asteroid makes a direct hit on you, none of this will matter because you'll
be dead before you know what hit you."

"That's a cheerful thought, Charlie," you quip.

"Just being honest folks because there is no perfect defense. All you can do is statistically improve your odds, as much as is realistically possible, with the resources and materials that you have available. The name of the game is risk reduction not risk elimination.

"After all, nothing ever goes to according to plan. In fact there is a new concern haunting the elites with their deep underground bases. It is something they did not anticipate when they first started building — sinkholes.

"I don't care how deep or how elaborate your underground base is, if a sinkhole opens up underneath it, you're going to go down like the Titanic. Now, we're ready to visit the Communal Village Dome Exhibit. Please follow me to the escalator."

Communal Village Dome Exhibit

From the top floor with all of the exhibits the escalator goes straight down to the front entrance of the communal village dome. On the way down everyone is breathless with awe. It is one thing to see the top of the dome while walking around it, but it is quite another to approach the massive structure in this manner.

"Oh my, I feel like Jonah going into the whale," you say under your breath.

I nod my head in agreement, "You know that's exactly the way I felt the first time I rode this escalator down. And to be truthful, it still feels a little that way every time."

Standing behind me, Charlie puts his hand on my shoulder, "Amen to that brother."

You're the first one off the escalator, and you do not wait for anyone else. You walk straight ahead to the center of the dome and stare directly up at the ceiling.

As we file in around you, still looking up you say, "The last time I had an experience like this was at The Hermitage in St. Petersburg, Russia. There was such beautiful art on the ceilings; you just couldn't take your eyes off it. I wound up spending half that night with an ice pack on my neck."

Charlie looks up, "This design was created to give you this very sense of openness because the last thing you need to experience when you are in a subterranean dome is claustrophobia. With the large size of these structures when they are compared to the usual submarine-style, 'suicide tube' shelters, claustrophobia is the last thing we would expect anyone to experience."

I suddenly remember my experience with claustrophobia, "Been there, done that. Some years back I had to go for an MRI, and it was one of those tube like machines. You know the ones that make you feel like they're stuffing you inside a water heater. They offered me some Valium before running the test, but being overly sure of myself, I told them I didn't need it. Once they locked me down and slid me into that little tube with all that whirring, clicking, and clattering, I totally freaked out. Next thing I knew; I was screaming, 'Get me out of here!' like a banshee. Thankfully, the technicians got me out of there pronto."

"So, did you go back in?" you ask.

"Yes, but only after ingesting the 20 milligrams of Valium they gave me.'"

"With 20 milligrams of Valium you can get used to most things," Charlie chuckles.

"After that while the machine was whirring, clicking, and making noises, I was singing, 'Come Josephine In My Flying Machine,' at the top of my lungs."

"This is the very reason," Charlie says soberly, "That you want to survive the tribulation in a spacious-feeling subterranean dome. When I think of those people who will be stuffed into those awful corrugated pipe shelters, all I can think is there will be no way to keep from going completely insane after several weeks in there. And there will still be plenty of tribulation left beyond that point."

Now I join in, "On the other hand those who survive the tribulation in subterranean domes are not going to experience claustrophobia, fear, or panic because domes are spacious. To emphasize this point, we know the private bedrooms are all on the second floor, along with bathrooms. But down here on the main floor, standing in the center of the dome we have this immense open-air space that feels simply wonderful. With that in mind I propose we all sit in these comfortable-looking couches and chairs and do nothing. We'll just sit with no talking and feeling the space."

The idea resonates with everyone, and in short order we're all comfortably seated and silent. This continues for about five minutes until you finally speak up, "I had no idea how peaceful-feeling a dome could be until this moment."

"That's right," Charlie says, "And to give you an example of how peaceful and quiet a dome really can be, let's assume that we're not below ground here, but actually above ground about one hundred feet away from an eight-lane freeway. Assuming that this is the case, what do you folks think we would be hearing at this moment?"

You venture an opinion, "An occasional honk maybe, or air brakes on semi trucks?"

Charlie shakes his head, "What you would hear is what you're hearing right here and right now — nothing. That's how soundproof a dome is." With that he checks the time on his wristwatch and tells us, "We've got about thirty minutes until lunch. Lou Spenser has just texted that he'll meet us at the cafe with his ham radio stuff. Since we still need to see the other dome applications on the other side of the exhibit hall upstairs, we'll want to get going soon."

"Charlie, can I ask you for a favor?" you say.

"Sure."

"What I'm feeling now are comforting senses of spaciousness and spiritual relaxation, and I want more. So let's just stay here for half an hour and maybe you could tell us a little bit about those dome applications exhibits upstairs before we leave to have lunch with Lou. After that, we can come back and spend more time in the Imaginarium. Would that be OK?"

"Well, let's see here," Charlie says with a twinkle in his eye, "What you want me to do is to keep sitting in this wonderfully comfortable chair while I talk about something I love to talk about. Well, that's a hard sell; isn't it?" he winks at us, "But I can manage if it's okay with Sheba."

"Woof, woof! Woof, woof!"

"You got her blessing, Charlie, so please go ahead and tell us about those application dome exhibits we've yet to see upstairs."

"I'd be happy to," Charlie replies, "The wonderful thing about domes is their versatility. You can use them for most anything you could think of. For example in the exhibits on the floor above, you're going to see below-ground water cisterns which are going to be essential to store clean water when we transit the tail of the Planet X System. Not only can domes work to store water, they can also be used to store other things like diesel fuel, dried grains and foods, and even to make a cold root cellar or a walk-in freezer.

"You know everyone is going to need to stockpile fuels for the tribulation. So diesel is something you want to have on hand. Some think the best way to go about doing that is to buy an old tanker truck, fill it up with fuel, and then just park it on your property. Well, that's a naïve way to go about it because most of the diesel fuel produced in this country is used within weeks after it's been refined. So, if you're going to want to store it for a few years, you're looking at an entirely different proposition.

"If you store the fuel where it is cool and dry, it can be stored for about 6 to 12 months. Here, the operative word is cool, and given that a subterranean dome is going to be at a constant temperature of 50 to 60 degrees, you have a perfect environment for storing diesel fuel. So once you have it in your dome, you can extend it beyond that shelf life by treating it with fuel stabilizers and biocides."

"Charlie, what other applications for domes do you know offhand?" you ask.

"My friend, I have only scratched the surface; let me give you some more examples. When you are looking to choose a site your community, whoever in your leadership is in charge of security is going to make darn sure that they have the high ground. They're not going to want bad guys looking down on you. So, not only do you need to find a piece of property where you have the high ground, you need to take it a step further. Build a small observation dome on the top of a ridge-line, so your security people have a fortified position with a 360° view. Do that and they will sing your praises."

"Another thing you can do is build a dome for an indoor farm. The dome we're in currently has a diameter of 117 feet. Upstairs you're going to see an indoor farming model of a 300-foot dome that has a height from floor to ceiling of 150 feet.

"Granted, this is the most elaborate of the models, but this is an Imaginarium where you begin by saying, 'money is no object.' You start with the assumption that you have everything you need to build whatever you want, even a 300-foot diameter indoor farming dome like the one upstairs.

"That model has two commercial freight elevators, and beginning ground level and going up there are the six floors: wormery, germination and propagation, indoor orchard and grow beds, hydroponic beds, aquaponic grow beds, and the aquaponics fishery."

"Wow, that would take a lot of power to operate!" you exclaim.

"Yes, it would," Charlie agrees, "So maybe it's not going to happen early on but what about the future? What happens when somebody comes up with the zero point energy device that can reliably produce all the electricity you could ever need, twenty-four seven?

"You know that once the energy companies, special interests, and crooked politicians are no longer stomping all over creative minds in order to line their own pockets, something like this will happen sooner or later. That's when a 300-foot diameter indoor farming dome becomes possible — when Nikola Teslas of the future are free to invent and suppressed."

"You see; I believe in the future. We are not going to have an insane Mad Max world, but as promised in the Bible, the meek truly will inherit the earth. Our lives will be all the better for it."

You light up with a bright smile. Leaning forward, you pat Charlie on the knee, "I want to thank you for that, Charlie. You have no idea how important it has been for me to hear you say those words. Up to now I have struggled to imagine how hope for the future could be possible given what we're facing. But now I'm sitting here in this beautiful, quiet, serene, and spiritual dome, hearing these words. You've just turned it all around for me Charlie. I feel real hope now. So, may I ask for one more favor?"

"You've got it."

"I so love this dome experience that I just want to immerse myself in it for a while longer. Can we just hang out here until it's time to go join Lou for lunch at the cafe?"

Charlie glances over at me with a big smile on his face and nods happily at you, "You betcha my friend. We'll all just sit here and savor the moment until it's time to go meet Lou."

9

Communications
for Civil Rule

Charlie and I are delighted to hear you talking about the Communal Village Dome Exhibit as we exit the Survival Village Imaginarium. You are actually glowing with enthusiasm about your experience. This is important because, for the first time, I can tell it's all starting to make sense to you and you are seeing that the community experience during the tribulation can be a positive one. You are seeing that for a survival village to be successful it must employ a strategy of enlightened comfort and continuity, and that subterranean concrete domes offer a positive living experience that no other underground structure ever could.

Rounding the corner we come to the gift shop and cafe that were added to the side of the Survival Village Imaginarium to make room for the small theater where we saw Rabbi Sarah's presentation. The cafe features a wide patio with ample seating which is bordered by a beautiful garden with small bubbling waterfalls and picturesque flowerbeds. "There is our Elmer," Charlie says pointing to his friend, Lou Spenser, sitting under a colorful Cinzano umbrella with a large cardboard box in front of him on the table.

Lou sees us and waves. We smile and wave back. In his late 60s, Lou is wearing a putty-colored cap with large embroidered letters, "HAM." Under that is "www.arrl.org," the Web address for the American Radio and Relay League, the national ham radio club. A few wisps of curly, silver hair sneak out from underneath his cap, and his bright, tanned face seems to be built around his large, toothy smile.

As we approach he rises and shakes each of our hands with a firm grip. At just over six feet tall, his modestly-trim appearance tells us he is active, an outdoor type. He also kneels down to shake Sheba's paw. Sheba extends her foreleg and Lou says, "So you are the famous Sheba. I have so looked forward to meeting you. I asked the cook to make you up a nice bowl of beef. I hope that is what you will enjoy today."

"Woof, woof!"

Lou laughs and then pets her on the head, "All the docents knows your lexicon now, and I am so glad to hear that you do want beef today."

The waitress comes to our table, greets everyone, and bends to pet Sheba, "I've got a treat for you," she says with a smile. Sheba wags her tail like a puppy.

As she passes out the menus you say to Charlie, "Hey, how about a round of those panini sandwiches and root beer for us humans?" Lou and I give Charlie the thumbs up sign.

"No need for menus today," Charlie tells her. "We're all going to have the *O Sole Mio* special with thick-cut fries and a pitcher of root beer."

"An excellent choice," the waitress says as she scoops up the menus, "plus a chef's special for Sheba."

"I assume your cap has something to do with radio," you say to Charlie, "So what does 'HAM' mean anyway?"

"Lou removes his cap, revealing a full head of hair, and points to the patch, "The only explanation we have is in a book published in 1917 titled, '*The Telegraph Instructor,*' by G. M. Dodge. As the story goes, the radios of these early telegraph operators were very powerful and often disrupted commercial systems. So the early amateurs were called 'hams' by the commercial operators for causing clumsy interference. It was not really a flattering term, but it still became popular with early amateur radio operators, and it has stuck ever since.

"As to the domain www.arrl.org, that's for the American Radio Relay League, of which I am proud to be a member. The ARRL motto is, 'When all else fails…Amateur Radio.' And I can tell you one thing for sure, during the tribulation all other forms of communication absolutely will fail. That's when hams will become truly vital to your survival."

"You got that right," Charlie adds, "Lou, why don't you tell us about what you and the other ARES hams did in Katrina back in 2005."

"Sure. Well, for starters, ARES stands for 'Amateur Radio Emergency Service.' It is an ARRL-affiliated non-governmental organization that works with *Homeland Security when disaster strikes. That's when* hams like me pack up our gear, go set up where we are needed, and start relaying messages to help get vital information flowing again. Back in 2005 with Katrina we were the only available mode of communication for everyone at first, even police radio systems were completely down." Lou shakes his head side to side, "Oh, my Lord, what a mess that was. Everything went down. Cell phones, land lines, Internet, all the radio repeaters in the area, emergency services radio systems, you name it, it was down. Those poor people were in the middle of a disaster and didn't have any way to communicate."

"So did the government ask you all to get involved and help out?" you ask.

"Not at first, but we were not about to wait for a bunch of bureaucrats to figure out that we could help. So a bunch of us ARES folks loaded our trucks and mobile homes with gear and drove there on our own. We went all over the disaster area and got communications going again. In short order we were relaying messages about what was needed and where, reconnecting all the agencies so they could work more effectively, and passing on messages for folks to their loved ones that they were okay. We all worked hard for very long hours, but it was one of the greatest experiences of my life."

Lou then removes his cardboard box from the table top and sets it on the ground next to his chair, "So when Charlie told me you needed some help setting up communications for your survival villages, it really tickled me. That's because I could put some of the things I learned in Katrina and through ARES to use, along with some other ideas I've cooked up for you."

"Heads-up, Lou," I admit, "We are all newbies and on the beginning end of that steep ham learning curve."

Before Lou can answer, Charlie jumps in, "Don't worry. I briefed Lou on what you need, and that is what is known as an 'Elmer' in amateur radio parlance. A seasoned ham operator who volunteers to be a personal mentor to newbies. The goal is to give you personal guidance and assistance in getting started."

"That's right," Lou chimes in, "It is my honor and my pleasure to be your Elmer and help you get started. With that in mind, I've come prepared to talk to you in terms of what you need to know about amateur radio as a faith-based tribulation leader."

"Now, if you're worried that I'm going to throw a lot of technical jargon at you today, rest easy. I'm just going to focus on the basic concepts and terms you will need to know so you will be able to tell a seasoned ham like myself what you need. That will help us to set things up the right way, right off the bat."

I see you nod your head appreciatively, "Well then, Elmer, the truth is I've never had a chance to get to know any ham radio operators. There is one guy at the end of my block with a bunch of antennas on top of his house. I didn't get to know him, but I know he sure got some nasty complaints from busybodies around the neighborhood."

"Oh yes, there's that," Lou chuckles, "But then again, there are a lot of interesting ways to hide those antennas so you don't get picked on by homeowners associations and block committees. It's a shame they never take the time to get to know hams better, or to find out that the interference isn't normally related to radio operation at all! So let me tell you about hams in general."

"For starters, thanks to the ubiquitous cell phones and smart phones these days, most of the hams are old silverbacks like me and Charlie here." That comment gets a raised eyebrow from Charlie. Lou continues, "Young people, and I'm talking mostly about those in their 30s, are not coming in like they were when I was that age, because they just don't see the value of running radios. Sometimes it seems like we hams spend more time going to funerals than attending club meetings and operating our radios."

"That's a sad thing, because hams are some of the nicest people you'll ever meet. We're hobbyists with a passion for what we do. It's not so much what were talking about on our radios, but how far away from each other we are when we do, and we also experiment with different technologies and techniques."

"This is mainly a male-dominated field of interest, but ladies are most welcome. Yeah sure, there are the gals that just come along to do something with their husbands. The ladies we are delighted to see are those who are 'bit.' For them, we tend to roll out the red carpet."

"'Bit'?"

"That's right. Once you get the bite, or are 'bit,' you are a committed ham radio operator. So, if you have to get up at 4:00 a.m. to make DX contacts overseas when the propagation is good, you just do it, and happily so. That's being 'bit!' That's why newbies who have the bite are really appreciated."

"If you ever get a chance to go to an amateur radio swap meet, go with an Elmer like me. He or she will be happy to help you find some really great bargains on used equipment to get you started. Plus, the folks at the swap meet who are selling their gear are good people, and they'll want to help a newbie get started with some good deals. Hams are always excited to have new people joining our hobby."

"I'm glad to hear that Lou," you say appreciatively, "Assuming we were going to go to one of these swap meets to shop for radios for my survival village, what kind of radios would you say we need?"

"Not at first, but we were not about to wait for a bunch of bureaucrats to figure out that we could help. So a bunch of us *ARES* folks loaded our trucks and mobile homes with gear and drove there on our own. We went all over the disaster area and got communications going again. In short order we were relaying messages about what was needed and where, reconnecting all the agencies so they could work more effectively, and passing on messages for folks to their loved ones that they were okay. We all worked hard for very long hours, but it was one of the greatest experiences of my life."

Lou then removes his cardboard box from the table top and sets it on the ground next to his chair, "So when Charlie told me you needed some help setting up communications for your survival villages, it really tickled me. That's because I could put some of the things I learned in Katrina and through *ARES* to use, along with some other ideas I've cooked up for you."

"Heads-up, Lou," I admit, "We are all newbies and on the beginning end of that steep ham learning curve."

Before Lou can answer, Charlie jumps in, "Don't worry. I briefed Lou on what you need, and that is what is known as an 'Elmer' in amateur radio parlance. A seasoned ham operator who volunteers to be a personal mentor to newbies. The goal is to give you personal guidance and assistance in getting started."

"That's right," Lou chimes in, "It is my honor and my pleasure to be your Elmer and help you get started. With that in mind, I've come prepared to talk to you in terms of what you need to know about amateur radio as a faith-based tribulation leader."

"Now, if you're worried that I'm going to throw a lot of technical jargon at you today, rest easy. I'm just going to focus on the basic concepts and terms you will need to know so you will be able to tell a seasoned ham like myself what you need. That will help us to set things up the right way, right off the bat."

I see you nod your head appreciatively, "Well then, Elmer, the truth is I've never had a chance to get to know any ham radio operators. There is one guy at the end of my block with a bunch of antennas on top of his house. I didn't get to know him, but I know he sure got some nasty complaints from busybodies around the neighborhood."

"Oh yes, there's that," Lou chuckles, "But then again, there are a lot of interesting ways to hide those antennas so you don't get picked on by homeowners associations and block committees. It's a shame they never take the time to get to know hams better, or to find out that the interference isn't normally related to radio operation at all! So let me tell you about hams in general."

"For starters, thanks to the ubiquitous cell phones and smart phones these days, most of the hams are old silverbacks like me and Charlie here." That comment gets a raised eyebrow from Charlie. Lou continues, "Young people, and I'm talking mostly about those in their 30s, are not coming in like they were when I was that age, because they just don't see the value of running radios. Sometimes it seems like we hams spend more time going to funerals than attending club meetings and operating our radios."

"That's a sad thing, because hams are some of the nicest people you'll ever meet. We're hobbyists with a passion for what we do. It's not so much what were talking about on our radios, but how far away from each other we are when we do, and we also experiment with different technologies and techniques."

"This is mainly a male-dominated field of interest, but ladies are most welcome. Yeah sure, there are the gals that just come along to do something with their husbands. The ladies we are delighted to see are those who are 'bit.' For them, we tend to roll out the red carpet."

"'Bit'?"

"That's right. Once you get the bite, or are 'bit,' you are a committed ham radio operator. So, if you have to get up at 4:00 a.m. to make DX contacts overseas when the propagation is good, you just do it, and happily so. That's being 'bit!' That's why newbies who have the bite are really appreciated."

"If you ever get a chance to go to an amateur radio swap meet, go with an Elmer like me. He or she will be happy to help you find some really great bargains on used equipment to get you started. Plus, the folks at the swap meet who are selling their gear are good people, and they'll want to help a newbie get started with some good deals. Hams are always excited to have new people joining our hobby."

"I'm glad to hear that Lou," you say appreciatively, "Assuming we were going to go to one of these swap meets to shop for radios for my survival village, what kind of radios would you say we need?"

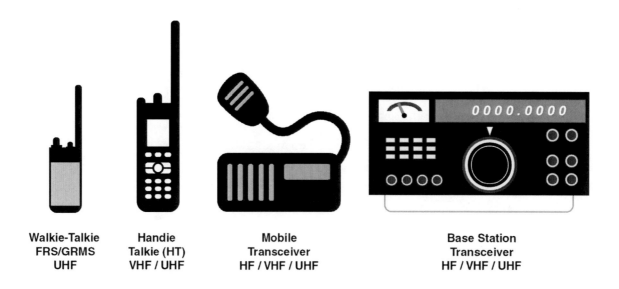

| Walkie-Talkie FRS/GRMS UHF | Handie Talkie (HT) VHF / UHF | Mobile Transceiver HF / VHF / UHF | Base Station Transceiver HF / VHF / UHF |

Lou smiles as he reaches down to open his box, "Glad you asked. I brought a few radios today so you could see what they look like." With that he pulls out the first radio. It is a small hand-held radio, "This is called a walkie-talkie, but it's not technically a ham radio at all. Walkie-talkies operate in completely separate frequency bands from ham radio. This one has two bands, FRS and GMRS. These are popular with families, hunters, active outdoors folks, people driving on a road trip in caravans, and so forth. You also see them used a lot by businesses, especially warehouses."

"We call them 'bubble-pack radios' because folks often buy them in packs, usually two to twelve radios to a pack. FRS is the lower band on this walkie-talkie, which stands for Family Radio Service. In terms of watts, FRS has the lowest transmit power of anything I'll show you today."

"As we'll be using the term watts a lot today, let me put this into perspective. A cell phone or smartphone transmits with between 0.6 to 3 watts of power. With the FRS band, no license is needed because the FCC only allows 2 watts. This is because FRS frequencies are in the Public Service Band used by Police, Fire, Medical, BLM, Forest Service, etc. By limiting FRS to 2 watts the FCC can minimize interference with these other services."

However, the upper band on this walkie-talkie is GMRS, which stands for General Mobile Radio Service. This band requires a simple license because you can transmit with up to 5 watts. No test is required to get a GMRS license from the FCC which includes privileges for your family. But, sad to say, many don't even bother to get the license, which is why we call them 'bubble-pack radio pirates.'"

"How would we use these walkie-talkies in our survival village?" you ask.

"For most everything local and close-by," Lou answers, "The virtue of these radios is that they are very simple to operate compared to ham radios. Go to a department store and you'll see the security people using them. If you work in a warehouse you could be using one yourself, and Community Emergency Response Teams (CERT) often issue them to team members during a deployment. You can show folks how to use them in only a few minutes, and GMRS band radios that can transmit a good distance. That being said, many manufacturers claim that their GMRS radios can transmit up to 25 or 30 miles. This means they are assuming you're standing on a mountain-top, and you're talking to someone in a valley — not very realistic! It's an advertising reach, as far as I'm concerned."

Charlie then reaches down into his box and lifts out another hand-held radio. This one is a little bigger than the walkie-talkie and has lots of buttons and a sophisticated LED display. "This is what we hams call a handy-talkie, or HT for short, and it can transmit with 5 watts of power."

"So if they both transmit with five watts of power, what's the difference?" you ask.

"A lot," Lou replies, "Walkie-talkies work in a very narrow portion of the UHF, or ultra-high frequency band, with only a handful of channels. In contrast, an HT gives you thousands of channels to work with in both the VHF, very-high frequency, and UHF bands. While you do not need a license to simply listen with any radio, you cannot transmit on an HT without an amateur radio license from the FCC. You will have to study for that license, and pay a fee for the test, but passing that test is much easier now than in years past because Morse code is no longer required!"

Lou reaches again into his box and pulls out a small, rectangular radio about four times the size of the HT and sets it on the table, "Now this is what we call a mobile transceiver, and these are the type of radios that you will want to install in your vehicle. By the way, a transceiver is a radio that can both transmit and receive. In the old days you didn't have radios that could do both. Back then, you had radios used only to receive, and radios used only to transmit. But those were the old days. Today we all have transceivers that perform both functions with a much smaller unit. These mobile radios can be used in both your car and your house."

"As a rule of thumb, mobile radios can transmit with 50 to 75 W of power, depending on the model. Most of them are what we call dual-band transceivers. Like the HT, most work on the VHF and UHF bands. But some will also operate in the high-frequency, or HF band, which requires passing two FCC license tests to use. Keep that in mind as we'll get back to that later on as well."

Reaching again into the box, this time Lou uses both hands to gently lift out a large, boxy radio, "This is what we call a base station transceiver, which is intended to be used in a fixed base station, or ham shack. Again, it can be just a dual-band transceiver for VHF and UHF, but it also can do HF. In many cases people will also buy a dedicated HF base station transceiver. It all depends on what you want to do with your ham radio station."

"The bottom line with these base station radios is that they give you a tremendous number of features and they typically broadcast with 100 watts of power. This 100 watts can then be amplified for an even greater transmission power. Just be sure to follow FCC regulations on what power is allowed for what bands."

"While a mobile radio will work fine in your car running off the 12 volt DC battery in your engine compartment, a base station transceiver like this really needs to be in a fixed location with access to a lot of power. However, in ARES we sometimes see large, mobile base station vans equipped with these more power radios."

"These are the four kinds of radios I would be looking to help you by at a ham swap meet if you wanted used, or through a reputable dealer if you want to get brand new equipment."

You nod appreciatively, "Then assuming you are helping me to select radios to buy, are there any brands you would be looking for in particular? And what about special deals?"

"Excellent question," Lou answers, "Let me start with the last part of your question first, namely special deals. If a manufacturer is offering a special short-term discount, that's great. If they have something you want, get it. On the other hand, whenever you see a specific model with dramatic markdowns on a regular basis, or if you see that there are a lot of used units of a particular model on the market, give it a pass."

"Always remember, people cut deals on a specific model because they want to get rid of it. This is why you want to look for radios that hold their price and are not flooding the market used, everywhere. When hams find a good radio they tend to hold on to it, and they usually won't sell it unless they want to upgrade to the latest and greatest. Also, keep in mind this is not a brand issue, because every manufacturer, even the best ones, have their 'ugly child,' so to speak. So if you see them offering an incredible bargain on a specific model, it's likely to be an ugly child. The bottom line here is to stick with tried-and-true reliable models that hold their value and don't get sold as used that often."

"That piece of logic has served me well, so don't forget it," I chime in.

Charlie nods in agreement, "Same for me, and forget the Chinese radios. Sure, they're always cheap, but they tend to be difficult to operate and have high component failure rates. I learned that the hard way. I thought I'd be clever and save myself some money with one. All I did was to buy myself some needless grief."

"Yup, cheap is grief," Lou says with a wistful smile, "Now as for FRS/GMRS walkie-talkie radios, there are a lot of good brands but you need radios that are repeater-capable."

"What you need to know right now about repeaters is that they are essential to extended range communications. Unfortunately, this really limits the field when it comes to FRS/GMRS walkie-talkies. In my opinion the only two brands worth considering are Motorola and Olympia. It's also interesting that the same OEM company manufacturers repeater-capable radios for these same two brands. They're good radios for sure, but just remember, you need to buy a GMRS license from the FCC if you're going to use repeaters."

Lou points at the walkie-talkie on the table, "This walkie-talkie is the one we use here for the fair. It's what you'll see our security and staff using. It's a Motorola MS355R Talkabout, and these work really well for us. However, I strongly urge you get to work with your hams in your group on selecting this, or any other radio, for that matter."

"If you think you'll need 100 radios for your community, double that figure so you have enough to get you through the tribulation. Remember, you're going to use these walkie-talkies more than anything else, so you want the right combination of range, features, usability and reliability."

"Who chose these Motorola MS355R Talkabout walkie-talkies for the park?" you ask.

Lou and Charlie crack a grin and simultaneously point at me, "Marshall did," says Lou, "So why don't you tell him why, Marshall?"

"Thanks for putting me on the spot, fellas. OK, here goes. For starters, I wanted a strong brand and I did a lot of research. For me, power usage is a big issue. With this Talkabout model we can use rechargeable batteries, a NiMH battery pack, or standard AA alkaline batteries."

"Being able to use AA was a big thing for us. Radios that use AAA alkaline batteries go through them a lot faster than AA batteries. Here in the park we mostly use the NiMH battery packs, but the AA battery packs can last up to 23 hours which is good. These Talkabouts also have an LCD battery level meter and a built-in flashlight, which are both very handy."

"All walkie-talkies have a built-in microphone and speaker, but there is a good choice of plug-in accessories for Talkabouts, like hand held push-to-talk (PTT) speaker microphones. We use the PTT speaker mics for our security and maintenance workers for the same reasons the police do. They can clip the speaker mic to a shoulder epaulet on their uniforms, and then they can hear what's going on in a noisy environment without have to use an ear bud."

"However, a specific feature I wanted for the fair was VOX, which stands for voice-activated hands-free communication. We have a lot of things to fix around here. This is where VOX is a very useful feature. It lets a technician or repairman keep both hands on what they're fixing while carrying on a conversation with someone who can walk them through the repair."

With a glint in his eye Charlie asks, "Marshall, is there a time when you might not want your radio set to VOX mode?"

I look up with a groan, "You're in rare form today Charlie," I look at you and wink, "Any time you're not completely focused on what you're transmitting out on the radio you need to switch from VOX to PTT. You wouldn't want to be broadcasting music from your teenager who just cranked up a stereo without permission. It's actually illegal to broadcast music on ham radio, unless you're talking to the International Space Station and they are playing music incidentally in their background. They are the only ones allowed to do that."

"Another thing to think about with radios is dust and moisture. There is something called an IP rating which stands for 'ingress protection.' For example, the IP rating of the Motorola MS355R is IP67, which is well-suited to our general needs. Reading the IP code is easy. The first number tells you the level of particulate protection, and the second number tells you the level of water protection."

"In this case, IP67 means that the radio is fully protected from dust ingress, is waterproof up to one meter, and this radio also floats in water. With all the fountains and pools we have around here, that's a huge plus for us. There were other important and necessary features as well, but these are the ones that drove the final purchase decision for me. So, back to you, Lou."

Before Lou can speak, the waitress arrives with our orders on a large serving platter. She is followed by a second waitress with another serving platter. "Saved by the bell," Lou grins as he takes the radios off the table and gently sets them back into the box while the servers set out our food and drinks.

The second waitress has two large while bowls on her platter, one has water and other holds heaping chunks of beef covered in a thick, brown sauce for Sheba. The waitress takes the bowls to a nice patch of cool grass just off the patio and sets them down. Sheba loses no time in starting her lunch. "She's such a beautiful dog," the second waitress smiles as she returns to the table.

"Enjoy your lunch," the first waitress says, "And let us know if there's anything else you want. Just so you know, we have some very tasty desserts for afterward." Everyone at the table thanks them and we dig in, complementing Charlie on his recommendation. The panini sandwiches are simply amazing.

After a few bites Lou sets his sandwich down and continues, "When it comes to handy-talkies, or HT radios, I agree with Marshall. You want both rechargeable and AA alkaline power packs." He wipes his hands with the napkin, then reaches down into the box and picks up the HT.

"When it comes to HT, mobile, or base station radios, there are only three brands you really need to consider: Kenwood, Yaesu, and ICOM. There used to be a lot of other brands years ago, but these three survived the transition from analog to digital, and all three are excellent brands. As for the Chinese brands, remember that cheap equals grief. Enough said about that."

He points to the handy-talkie, "This particular HT is my own. It is a two-band Yaesu FT-60R and I bought it because it is popular with the other ARES hams in my area. It's affordable, durable, and easy to operate. It also has an Emergency Automatic Identification, or EAI feature, for search-and-rescue work. But most of all, I have large hands and I just like how it fits my hand and is easy to use. Here's a tip, once you're holding it in your hand, you'll know."

"Likewise, an HT is a very personal thing, so remember there are a lot of good models out there from these three manufacturers. Look before you leap. In terms of your community, the people most likely to use an HT will be those doing reconnaissance and security work at, and beyond, the boundaries of your community."

"You're not going to need as many of these HTs as you are walkie-talkies, which cost a lot less and are are just as powerful as an HT at 5 Watts. But like the walkie-talkies, once you figure out how many you'll need, buy twice that many. So, for now, let's enjoy our lunch and then we'll get back into it."

"By all means," you agree and we all enjoy our lunch and each other's company. Having finished her meal, Sheba curls up next to me on the ground and licks her jowls and paws.

As we finish the last of our meal, the waitress returns with a fresh mug of root beer, "Anyone up for cheesecake? Or on the lighter side, we have a wonderful homemade tapioca pudding. We make it here from scratch. Our pastry chef uses old family recipes that he refuses to share with anyone."

"That sounds intriguingly good to me," I say, "Check back with us in a bit." The waitress clears the table and leaves with a smile.

Lou then reaches down into the side of his box and pulls out a large presentation folder. He sets it on the table and folds out the bottom so it will stand upright, "In preparation for today I put together a series of sketches to illustrate the simple things I think are important for a newbie tribulation leader to know. This is not to say I will be boggling you with specific frequencies, or types of antennas, or any type of techno-babble. Rather, let's focus on the essential things you'll need to know when you are asking your hams to set up your survival village communication system. First off is range."

He flips the first page over, "Here you see rough estimates for maximum range for the four different types of radios I showed you earlier. Keep in mind that there are a lot of variables such as the band, frequency, and antenna, so these figures are just to give you a general idea for reference only. Also, these are what we call simplex range. Simplex is radio-to-radio with nothing in between."

"In the innermost red ring you see a maximum range of one fifth of a mile to five miles for both 5 watt GMRS walkie-talkies, and UHF / VHF handy talkies. You're going to use these around the community for general work, and along the periphery of your community for observation purposes."

"In the second blue ring you see mobile radios which have a maximum range of 10 to 50 miles. As I understand it, your community goal is to become a center of hope for the other small survival villages surrounding your community. Obviously, you are going to need to work with these people for mutual defense and other survival issues. In this case, you'll need mobile radios to stay in contact with them. Also, you'll need mobile units for any vehicles traveling to and from these satellite communities."

"Finally in the outermost green ring you see base station radios with a maximum range of 100 to 1,000 miles. During the tribulation you're not going to be able to do much in terms of high frequency (HF) long-haul communications because of atmospheric issues. It will be a pretty messy sky, to say the least, and HF signals won't be able to reliably get through until things clear up."

"However, after the worst of the tribulation has passed, you are going to use your base station long-haul radios quite a bit. In fact, the good news is that bouncing signals off the ionosphere as we do today for long-haul communications will be much easier after the tribulation than it is now."

"This is because solar interaction between the Planet X System and our sun seems to coincide with the difficulties we hams began experiencing with bouncing signals off the ionosphere, which has gotten progressively worse since the late 1940s. So once the Planet X System leaves our area, we should see ionospheric bounce as good as it was a hundred years ago. Then we'll have a new golden age of long-haul radio, and that will be a huge benefit to us all after the tribulation."

"That's when we'll be able to reconnect families and communities over vast distances to share knowledge, news, and to relay messages for loved ones. We especially want to share the kind of knowledge that gives people hope for the future. Now, let's talk about your strategy for buying your mobile and base station radios."

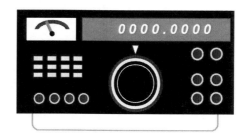

**Mobile
Transceiver
HF / VHF / UHF**

**Base Station
Transceiver
HF / VHF / UHF**

All Bands
All Modes

vs.

Single or Dual
Band Radios

Lou flips to the next page, "There are two schools of thought when it comes to mobile and base station radios. You can get one radio that does it all. As you see in the illustration, that would be all bands and all modes. Or you can get different radios for different bands. For example, years ago ICOM made the ICOM 706 MKII G. It's an all band, all mode mobile radio, and though it's a bit of a power hog, it's still an extremely popular with hams, so much so that they're still darn expensive even on the used market. The current replacement for the 706 is the IC-7100, but it will cost you twice as much. I guess the bottom line is how much cash do you have burning a hole in your pocket?"

"I own a big, old truck, so unlike smaller sedans, I have plenty of room for multiple radios. That's why I prefer single or dual band mobile radios. Besides, for the cost of one do-it-all, all bands, all modes mobile radio, I can buy an HF mobile plus another UHF / VHF mobile to do all the same things. That way, I have different radios running for different purposes. That being said, there may be times when you need a special purpose all bands, all modes radio, so knowing the difference is important especially when configuring your overall communication system."

"Now, the next thing I want to talk about is something that is a bit technical for a newbie, but as the leader of a faith-based tribulation survival village, you absolutely must understand what repeaters are and how they are used."

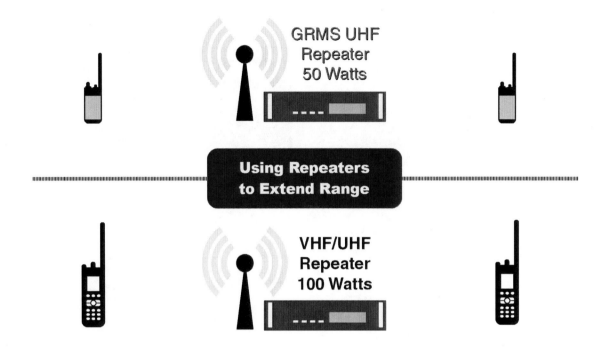

He flips to the next page, "A repeater is simply a radio that repeats a transmission. Earlier I showed you that we use a Motorola MS355R radio here for security and general staff." He points to a tower, "Everyone look up at that tower," Lou instructs, "At the top of that tower you'll see an antenna, well, actually several antennas. But one of those up there is used for our own, unlisted, GMRS repeaters. In fact, we have four of them installed around the fair."

"Now while we say these radios could go up to 5 miles or more, and manufacturers will tell you even more miles, the simple truth is that radios and large structures do not work well together. That's the reason why we use GMRS repeaters."

"It is important for you to remember that the FCC limits GMRS repeaters to 50 watts, which, for your community, is still a considerable amount of power. It is more than you'll need locally, no doubt."

"Unfortunately, the vast majority of GMRS radios on the market today are not repeater capable, so be careful. This is a big reason why we went with the Motorola Talkabout MS350R, although if you want, the Olympia R500 is made by the same company that manufactures the Motorola, and it uses Motorola accessories. It is worth checking out."

"Your communities' VHF and UHF repeaters can transmit at 100 Watts for even greater range. Obviously, this will give you a lot more options for your communication needs with forward observation stations and the satellite villages surrounding your center of hope community."

Lou pauses to take a sip, "In other words, repeaters will be absolutely essential to your mutual defense goals. With this in mind, I want to explain to you five terms you will need to understand when talking about repeaters with your ham operators. These terms are: simplex, duplex, shift, offset and PL tone. Also, there are some differences between GMRS repeaters and VHF and UHF ham repeaters, so I'll be talking about VHF and UHF ham repeaters here. However, the same concepts apply to both types, so let's begin with simplex repeaters."

Using Repeaters

Lou flips to the next page, "With any repeater you're going to have two radios involved, plus the repeater itself. One radio transmits, which is designated as 'TX.' The other radio receives, which is designated as 'RX.' As I told you earlier, a transceiver can both send and receive. Ergo, when you are using a single radio to both send and receive, you are sometimes in TX mode, and sometimes in RX mode."

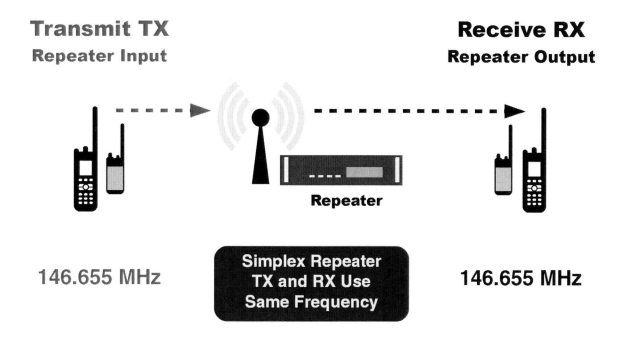

Transmit TX
Repeater Input

Receive RX
Repeater Output

Repeater

146.655 MHz

Simplex Repeater TX and RX Use Same Frequency

146.655 MHz

"A simplex repeater receives and records the signal from the transmitting radio until it stops transmitting. Once that happens the simplex repeater automatically switches from the receive mode to the transmit mode, and it then transmits the recorded message back out."

"Once the simplex repeater finishes sending out the recorded message, it switches back to the receive mode and erases the recording. Now it is ready to record and then re-transmit the next transmission it receives."

"What is impressive about simplex repeaters is that everything happens on the same frequency, using only one radio. The point of a simplex repeater is to re-transmit a recording and increase the distance that the transmission can reach. It overcomes line-of-sight and distance barriers of the VHF/UHF bands that the transmission would otherwise be limited by."

You would use simplex repeaters when you have folks operating in the field who need a fast way to extend their operational range, for instance to transmit over into the next valley. They're easy to design and can be built in the field without test equipment using a single radio.

But keep in mind that simplex repeaters are a bit quirky to use because of the transmission delays from repeating the recording out, and then the reply also must be recorded and re-transmitted. So for everyday use, a different kind of repeater called a duplex repeater is more popular with ham radio operators."

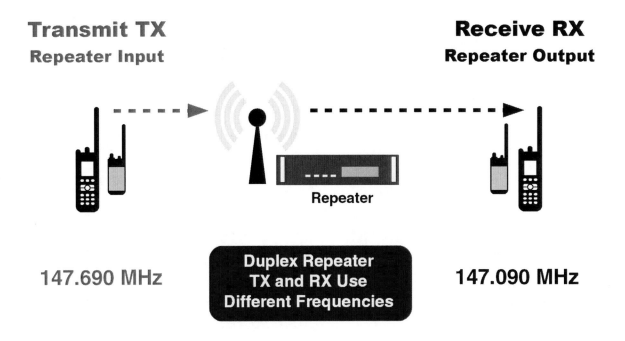

Lou flips to the next page, "What you see here is what we call a duplex repeater. Unlike a simplex repeater, a duplex repeater needs three times as much equipment to build, sophisticated test equipment to set it up successfully, and a lot more power. Even so, duplex repeaters are the most common repeaters that hams use these days. Duplex repeaters are what allow most hams to use the very popular low-powered HTs. These HT radios rely on local duplex repeaters to give them the range that makes them useful and practical. Without duplex repeaters HTs would not be as effective for communications due to their low power and reach."

"As the name suggests, a duplex repeater uses two different radio frequencies. The repeater input frequency is the transmitting frequency, or TX for short. The repeater output frequency is the receiving frequency, or RX for short."

"In this example, the frequency used to transmit to the input side of the repeater is 147.690 MHz. Conversely, the frequency used to receive the repeater output is 147.090 MHz."

"Unlike a simplex repeater, duplex repeaters do not use a recording system. Transmissions received on the input side are immediately transmitted on the output side in real time. In other words, duplex repeaters work in the 'live rebroadcasting' mode".

"This brings us to a new term: Offset."

Lou flips to the next page, "All duplex repeaters use a pair of frequencies, one for input and one for output. The offset is the numerical difference between the input and output frequencies of the pair."

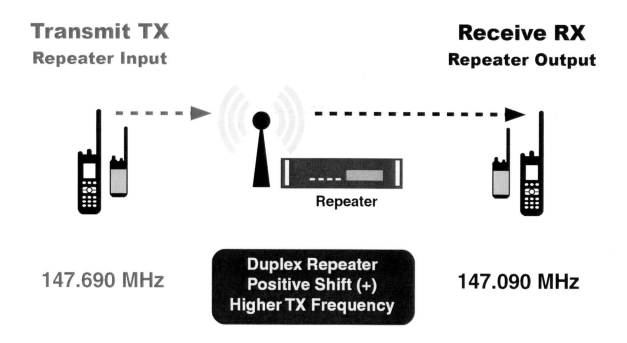

"What we see here is what is called a positive shift. The repeater input frequency here is 147.690 MHz, and the repeater output frequency is 147.090 MHz. So in this case the input frequency is higher than the output frequency, so this repeater has a positive shift. This can also work the other way around."

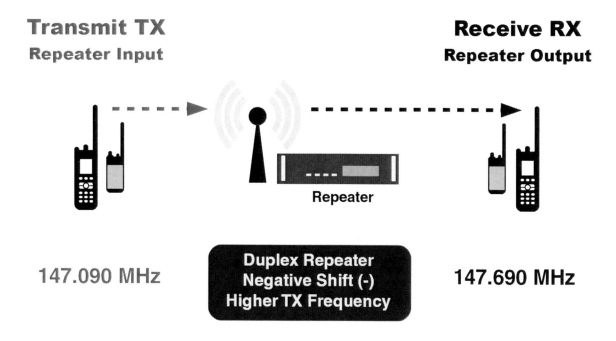

He flips to the next page, "What this illustration shows is the reverse situation. Now, the repeater input frequency is 147.090 MHz, and the repeater output frequency is 147.690 MHz. Therefore, what we have here is a negative shift."

"Technically speaking, is it preferable to have a negative shift or positive shift? Either way the functional results are the same. What is important is that everyone agrees to organize the frequencies the same way so that they will know how to set their radios to use that particular repeater. This brings us to another key concept when working with duplex repeaters."

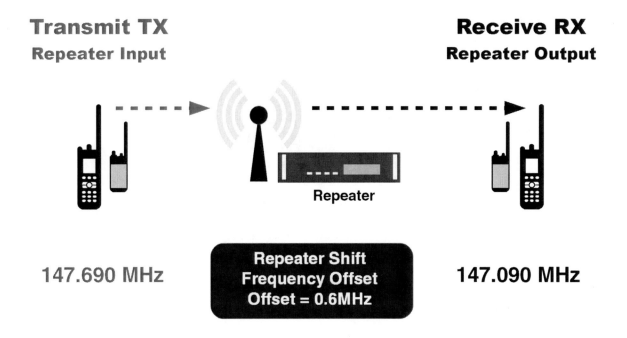

He flips to the next page, "We call this the frequency offset. It tells us how close or distant the two frequencies assigned to a duplex repeater are. In this case, we see the repeater input frequency is 147.690 MHz and the repeater output frequency is 147.090 MHz. So in this case, the offset equals 0.6MHz, which is a fairly standard offset in this frequency band."

"At this point you may be wondering why it is important for you to understand frequency offset? Well, here is why. During the tribulation, various natural disasters will play havoc with radio frequencies in very unpredictable ways. There is no way to know in advance exactly what to expect. Instead, we must all be prepared to respond, work with the varying conditions, and improvise solutions to keep communications working."

"That being said, if your community is in the middle of nowhere you and your satellite survival villages will be monitoring repeaters that you own and control. This way your hams will have a free hand to experiment with different combinations of frequency and offset to adapt to changing conditions."

"And this is not to say you cannot be creative. In fact, you will need to be."

Transmit TX
Repeater Input

Receive RX
Repeater Output

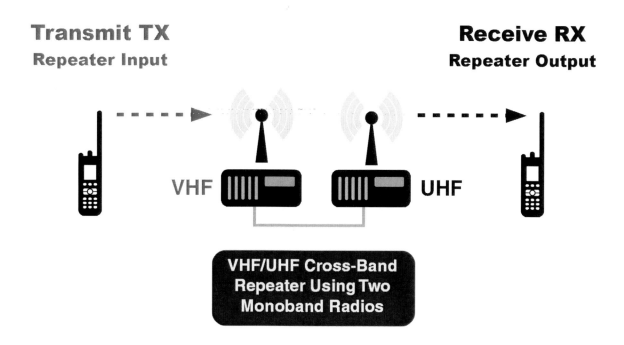

VHF   UHF

VHF/UHF Cross-Band Repeater Using Two Monoband Radios

"For example, you could use a special purpose repeater that uses a VHF radio for the input frequency, and a second UHF radio for the repeater output frequency. These are called cross-band repeaters, and right now they are seldom used. However, ARES hams will occasionally use them in an emergency deployment environment. All you need are two inexpensive monoband radios, two antennas, and best of all, no test equipment is required to set up one of these cross-band repeaters."

"Now let's talk about the one aspect of duplex repeaters that is absolutely essential when selecting any radio for any purpose."

Transmit TX
Repeater Input

Private Line Tone (PL Tone)

a.k.a Continuous Tone-Coded Squelch System (CTCSS)

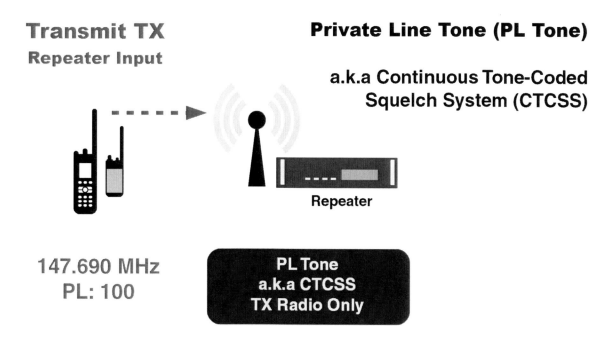

Repeater

147.690 MHz
PL: 100

PL Tone a.k.a CTCSS TX Radio Only

Lou flips to the next page, "No matter what kind of ham radio you are using, it must support what is known as a private line tone, or PL tone, for short. This is also known as a continuous tone-coded squelch system, or CTCSS, but every ham will understand the term PL tone. A repeater that requires a PL tone will not repeat a radio transmission unless it hears the correct PL tone to activate it. You will need to wait about two seconds after pressing your PTT button before speaking to allow the repeater time to process the PL tone and start re-transmitting your message. There is also a rough equivalent with FRS/GMRS walkie-talkies called a privacy code, but these work differently from the PL tones for repeaters on ham radios."

"The reason hams use PL tones is to eliminate the interference of unwanted repeater key-ups in areas where multiple repeaters are physically co-located. So do you always need a PL tone? In the case of a survival village where you're operating a small handful of repeaters, and there are no other repeaters in the area, a PL tone will not be necessary. However, if your repeaters are physically co-located on a mountain-top with those of neighboring communities, then a PL tone will be necessary if you want to avoid interference."

"That being said, up to now we've been talking about two radios. One radio is transmitting to the repeater input and another radio is receiving the repeater output. So if you're using a PL tone, do both radios need to use a PL tone? No. The PL tone is only required on the repeater input side."

"In this illustration we see that we have a radio transmitting to the repeater input on 147.690 MHz and sending a PL tone with the value 100. When the repeater receives the correct PL tone for it's input frequency, it will rebroadcast the transmission on the output frequency."

"So what happens if I don't use the right PL tone?" you ask.

"If you use the wrong PL tone the duplex repeater will ignore your transmission and it won't go anywhere, even if you've set your radio to the correct repeater input frequency. For this reason, every ham radio you buy for your community needs to offer a robust PL tone feature."

"Now that you understand repeaters and how to use them to greatly extend the range of your survival village communications, let's move on to the next topic, three things you'll expect to see in a base station."

**Telegraph Key
For Morse Code**

**Terminal Node
Controller (TNC)
For Data**

**Microphone
For Voice**

He flips to the next page, "When it comes communications with your walkie-talkies, handy talkies, and mobile radios, you are principally going to be doing voice communications. However, with your base station radios there will be other valuable ways to communicate. Here are three things you'll typically see: a telegraph key for Morse code, a good microphone for voice, and finally, a terminal node controller or TNC for digital communications. A TNC is used to connect computers through your radios so that you can transmit data files such as text messages or photographs. This is a kind of Internet on the slow-as-sludge side, so to speak. It is a little bit like the old dial-up service."

"Keep in mind that during the tribulation you will use both station transceivers and mobile radios in your base station, but these can also be used in combination with handy talkies via some form of adapter. Trust me, if there is one thing hams love to do is to make dissimilar equipment work together. So never hesitate to ask if something can be done. They'll love you for the challenge. But for now, what I want to really focus on is the telegraph key."

Telegraph Key
For Morse Code

Base Station
HF / CW
Transceiver

QRP CW
Emergency
Kit Radios

He flips to the next page, "As you know, high-frequency (HF) is the band that will be used to reach out to somebody up to 1,000 miles away or more, once the ionosphere improves after the tribulation is over. The point here is that during the difficult radio transmission conditions during the tribulation, Morse code is going to be essential to your survival as a community. For example, do you remember the 1996 blockbuster movie, 'Independence Day'?"

"Are you kidding?" Charlie exclaims, "Who could forget that scene when General Gray says 'Get on the wire, tell them how to bring those sons of bitches down.'"

"Yup, that's what I'm talking about. In that movie what we saw was that once they figured out how to attack the aliens, they had to get the word out. The problem was that the aliens had commandeered all of our communication satellites, worldwide. So the leaders transmitted their plans using good, old-fashioned Morse code, and it worked beautifully!"

"Another interesting thing is that back in the old days when I first got started, if you wanted to get a ham radio license from the FCC, you had to pass a Morse code test. The test is longer required these days, but Morse code will be absolutely essential during and beyond the tribulation. For this reason, every member of your community must learn Morse code and be proficient with it. Ideally, during the tribulation kids should learn Morse code at the same time they're learning to read and write."

"Another thing you see in this illustration is a QRP CW emergency radio kit. This is critical, so let me break down those two acronyms. QRP is actually an example of what we call a Q code. This particular code lets others know you are transmitting with reduced power. QRP radios are HF radios that transmit on less than five watts of power."

"The other term, CW, stands for 'continuous wave,' which is the manner in which the short and long tones of Morse code are transmitted. CW is as old as the hills, and just as reliable."

"This is why you want to have small emergency QRP CW radio kits on hand that can be assembled as needed. Be sure to store them in EMP-proof, shielded storage containers. That way, should the very worst happen, you will have something that can transmit Morse code at a low power level. I call these QRP CW radios your 'day after' radios."

"This is why you will need to store up a large quantity of these QRP CW kits, along with everything else need to build them and to make them work. Then stash them away for the day after the worst imaginable disaster happens, and everything goes dark. Meanwhile, you can do more powerful things as well."

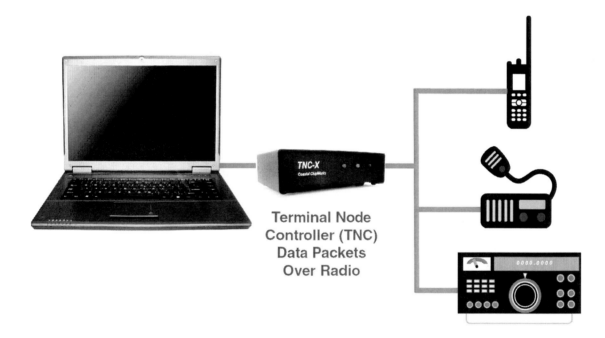

Terminal Node
Controller (TNC)
Data Packets
Over Radio

Lou flips to the next page, "When working with your satellite villages for mutual defense, a picture is worth 1,000 words. For example, imagine being able to send and receive pictures of the warlord operative who is spying on you for attack intelligence. Likewise, what about sending lengthy text messages about how to do medical procedures such as dealing with a breech birth? Being able to transmit text is a lot faster than talking to someone, and a lot more reliable and accurate."

"For these reasons you really want to have the ability to do what we call packet radio to connect computers. To do this you need use a device that is called a terminal node controller, or TNC, for your radios and computers, installed with packet radio software."

"Without getting into a lot of specifics, suffice it to say that any file that can be stored on a hard drive can be sent from one computer to another via radios equipped with TNCs. It's not blazing fast, mind you, but it works, and it works well."

"Now, here is where I want to give you a very strict and specific instruction. The computers you are going to use for your packet radio cannot, and must never, run any version of any Microsoft operating system. What I've learned in my own personal research is that Microsoft installs backdoors into each of its operating systems. So as far as I'm concerned, there is no such a thing as a secure, or a truly reliable, Microsoft system."

"Another problem with Microsoft is licensing, particularly with the latest additions. If, for any reason, the license key is lost your computer will become an unrepairable and unusable tribulation boat anchor. For this reason, you must only use the Linux operating system. It is faster, vastly more reliable, and what I like best about it is that it is open source software. As to which Linux distribution to use, the three I personally recommend for packet radio applications are: Debian Linux, Linux Mint, or Ubuntu Linux. An older computer or laptop with less processing capacity and memory will also function faster and more efficiently than it did with Microsoft systems once it has been converted to Linux."

"Once you start using Linux with ham radios you are going to find an amazing new world. There is one piece of software you must begin with, which is called FLDIGI. This is what you will use to control every aspect of transmitting and receiving digital data packets. And here is something really cool about it, you can encrypt your messages. So yes, anyone can listen in, but if they do not have an encryption key on their end to decrypt the message, all they'll hear is useless static. You can also change the types of digital transmissions and the type of encryption on a rotating schedule to make deciphering your transmissions even more difficult. Now, let's talk about making sure that you have a continuous supply of radios during the tribulation."

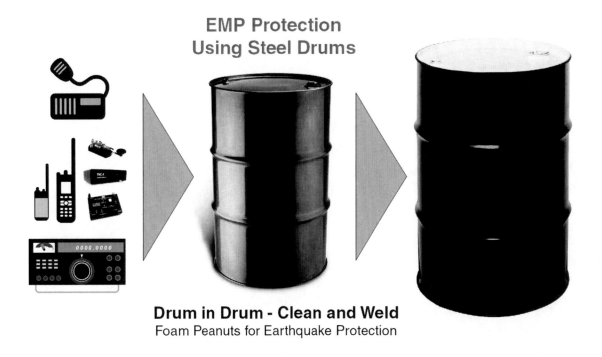

**EMP Protection
Using Steel Drums**

Drum in Drum - Clean and Weld
Foam Peanuts for Earthquake Protection

Lou flips to the next page, "Earlier I told you that if you estimate that you need a certain number of a particular model of radio, you should always double that number to make sure you maintain that capability through, and beyond, the tribulation."

"So, does this mean that if you have 200 radios available and that you're only are using 100, is it necessary to expose your other 100 reserve radios to solar radiation and EMP? No way! Keep them safe and preserved in shielded containers. By the way, EMP stands for electromagnetic pulse, and EMP can be created by either man-made weapons or the activities of sun, for that matter. This is why protecting your reserve radios and computers from EMP is so very, very important."

"I've heard a lot people say that old microwave ovens are good for EMP protection," Charlie says, "Have you looked into that, Lou?"

"Sure did. I ran actual tests, and using old microwave ovens for EMP protection is an urban legend as far as I'm concerned. Granted, a microwave oven will give you some protection, but the best you can hope for with a microwave oven is between 30 to 50% protection. That is just not enough as far as I'm concerned. Besides, there are there other ways to protect your electronics."

"Some are expensive, like specially-made Faraday cage containers, or suitcases expressly designed for EMP protection. If you can afford a lot of them, then by all means use them. However, there is a low tech way to get the same level of EMP protection for a lot less money. With this in mind let me share with you a relatively inexpensive way to protect your reserve electronics during the tribulation."

"You can create very effective EMP protection using steel drums. What you're doing here is protecting your electronics with a drum-inside-a-drum strategy. In this illustration you see a 30 gallon steel drum, like those typically used for oil or hydraulic fluid, and then a larger, traditional 55 gallon steel oil drum. Here's how this works."

"The first thing to do is to clean and grind off the contact edges between the drums and the lids, because there is usually some kind of thin plastic film at this point of contact to prevent leakage. That plastic film has to be sanded off so you will have a clean, metal-to-metal, conductive contact which is required to create the EMP shielding effect. You will need to do this for both drums."

"Next, before packing your radios disconnect all components and accessories from each other. If the antennas can be unscrewed, remove them. Also remove the power packs, external speakers and microphones, and any other connections. Be sure the device power is switched to the 'off' position. Then wrap everything up separately and put it all into stiff cardboard boxes."

"The next step is to put a bed of plastic peanuts on the bottom of the small steel drum. Then, as you stack your equipment boxes, fill in with plastic peanuts between the boxes and along the walls of the drum. Once you've filled the drum, top it off with more plastic peanuts. You do this because the plastic peanuts will help with both the EMP protection and to prevent damage from the strong earthquakes of the tribulation. Remember, during the pole shift the entire earth will be getting a horrendous and long-lasting shaking."

"The next step is seal the top of the small drum, making sure the lid and the drum have pure metal-to-metal contact. Then weld the lid to the small drum to ensure a tight EMP seal."

"The final step is to once again lay peanuts in the bottom of the larger drum before setting the smaller drum inside it. Then surround the smaller drum with peanuts all the way to the top of the bigger drum."

"As before, seal the top of the large drum, making sure the lid and the drum have pure metal-to-metal contact, then weld the lid to the large drum."

"Now you will have an EMP-hardened double-wall steel enclosure that will protect your valuable electronics during the worst of the tribulation. You can actually prepare kits containing assorted types of electronics that can be opened one-by-one, as needed, during the tribulation. Rather than keeping all laptops in a single steel drum, for instance, group kits with the radios, laptops, TMCs, and whatever else you might need to work together as a complete system. If you get hit with an EMP strike that wipes those electronics out, you can still have a complete replacement kit ready to go in another steel drum."

"That being said, there is one more communication system I want to talk about, one I believe will be vital for your communities. It is simple, durable, and best of all, it is EMP proof all the time!"

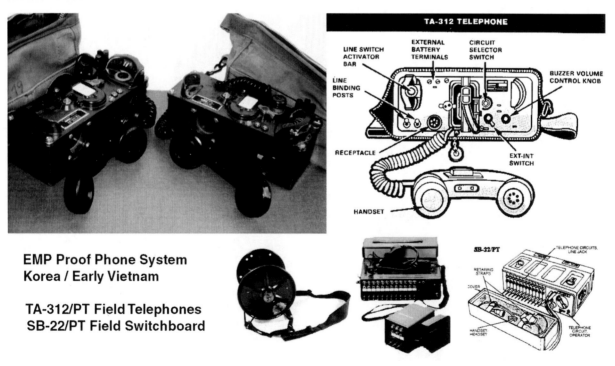

**EMP Proof Phone System
Korea / Early Vietnam**

**TA-312/PT Field Telephones
SB-22/PT Field Switchboard**

Lou flips to the next page, "Radio is always my first love, but during the tribulation communication is going to be absolutely essential for survival. For instance, since you're going to need to have observers in strategic positions where they can see trouble coming from a long way off, you need to have a reliable way for them to communicate back what they are seeing. Obviously, they're going to have radios, but you always want to have a Plan B. Here is where you will need an old-school, proven military-style field telephone system, as you see in the illustration here."

"This is an EMP-proof phone system that is extremely rugged. It was used by the United States Army during the Korean War and early in the Vietnam War. What you're seeing here are TA-312/PT Field Telephones, and an SB-22/PT Field Switchboard."

"Now this equipment is available on the market, and while it is obviously all used you can find telephones and switchboards that are in very good shape and functional. All you need to power these radios are D-cell flashlight batteries, which you can stockpile in quantity. You could also use rechargeable D-cell batteries, for that matter. They could be recharged with solar power, your community's electrical power system, or you could rig up hand-crank chargers to exercise bikes and have people exercise while they charge up some batteries."

"Above all, what you need to remember about this equipment is that it is 'mil spec,' which is short for military specification. Mil spec gear is designed to work in adverse conditions and to keep working even after a lot of abuse. You can also find other mechanical analog phone systems as well, but the operative term here is 'mechanical analog.' The minute you use something with a microprocessor digital chip, it's pointless. An EMP event of any type will destroy it."

"These phones use simple twisted-pair wire for land-line connections. In this illustration you see a wire spool such as those soldiers used to lay down communication wire when they were out in the field. You will need shielded copper wire for these phone systems, and while a soldier would often lay the cable along the ground to be used temporarily, I strongly suggest you bury your cables in the ground."

"There are two different kinds of wires you can use, 18 gauge twisted-pair wire can give you up to 25 miles of range. Smaller, less expensive, 22 gauge wire will go up to 15 miles. Keep in mind that not only do you want to run communication wire to your forward observation posts, you also want to run wire out to your satellite villages so that everyone in your defense network has a Plan B communication system as well. With this in mind, I suggest the 18 gauge wire if you can afford it."

"Another thing you might want to consider doing as you're laying down and burying this wire is to run a fiber-optic cable right alongside it. Sure, you're not going to be able to use that fiber optic cable immediately, but if you lay the two side-by-side, you'll be making a profound statement of hope for the future. You'll be getting ready for when things settle down on the backside. At that time folks can look forward to enjoying the same level of connectivity we have today by way of the fiber-optic cables that are already in place. And that folks, wraps up my radio technology presentation."

We are so impressed with Lou's presentation that we all start clapping, which puts a nice glow on his face. After the applause fades a little, I congratulate him, "Lou, that was brilliant!. Simply brilliant! If you don't mind, there's one last thing I'd like for you to cover that I think would be helpful for a faith-based tribulation leader to understand. Would you mind explaining the difference between the three types of ham radio licenses in terms of the expertise that the individual will bring to the community given each type of license?"

"It would be my pleasure," Lou answers, "If you want to be a licensed operator for handy-talkie, mobile, and base station transceivers, there are three levels of license certifications offered by the FCC: Technician, General and Extra. As a leader of the community, let's say someone comes to you and says they have a ham radio license. This is when you need to find out which licenses they hold, because as a general rule of thumb, the license they hold will determine the skills they can offer you. Let me explain."

"The Technician license is the first license every ham radio operator gets. It's the easiest of the three to obtain, although you do have to seriously study for it. When you get a Technician license, you will be capable of transmitting on most authorized UHF and VHF bands, and on a very limited portion of the HF band."

"People who have a Technician license usually own a handy-talkie, or perhaps a VHF / UHF mobile, and they use local repeaters to talk to other hams in the area. For most hams the Technician license is enough for them, although it is only limited to communication within the United States. Interestingly, it also includes the right to talk to astronauts on the International Space Station, which I think is kinda cool."

"However, if you want full access to the HF band and ability to communicate with people in foreign countries, you need a General license. For all intents and purposes, the General license gives hams access to virtually every frequency they'll want to use."

"Then there is the Extra class. With Extra comes access to the full spectrum of every available ham radio band, with no restrictions. Many hams see the Extra license as something you get just for bragging rights. Here is where I differ sharply from that notion, and there is key aspect of this that is of particular concern for you as a tribulation faith-based leader, as well."

"In a manner of speaking, you could say that someone who holds a Technician class license is an operator, and that someone who holds a General class license is a super-operator. But someone who holds an Extra class license must master a tremendous amount of highly technical information about radio operations and, most importantly, antennas. The Extra license test has twice as many questions in its pool than the previous tests did, and the Extra license holder will know much more about ham radio technology and engineering concepts than the other two types of license holders will."

"With this in mind, let's frame these three licenses in the context of your tribulation needs. For the local radio work around your community and forward observation posts, hams with a technician license will be just fine. For long-haul HF communications with distant communities or those in other countries, you will want hams with a General license in your communication center. However, for designing and building your communication systems, you want to recruit hams with an Extra license, because they will know things like how to make antennas from scratch. This, and other radio-engineering skills, are going to be essential for your long-term success. Or at the very least, they'll know how to recruit and manage hams who can get the job done, regardless of what license they hold."

"You see, I don't care how much power you pump out of a radio. If you're not using the right kind of antenna, and if it is not tuned correctly, you're just wasting power. In fact, you could be transmitting with 100 watts and using the wrong kind of antenna and there I am, transmitting at 5 watts with the right kind of antenna, and doing just as well as you are. In fact, here is an interesting tidbit. There are hams who love to communicate with people on the other side of the planet using just a few watts of power, because they have the ham radio engineering skills to make that work, and they love the challenge."

"Now this does bring to my mind a suggestion for you that I think you should take to heart. As I understand it, there's going to be all kinds of high winds, tornadoes, crazy weather, and so forth during the tribulation. These will be the very kinds of events that will just rip antennas apart and scatter them in all directions. So what can you do about this?"

"Instead of buying a lot of retail antennas, what you need are a few hams on your staff who are proficient in making antennas from scratch. Then just stockpile huge quantities of the raw materials and the tools they'll need to build antennas as they're needed. Given how crazy the atmospherics are going to be in the tribulation, I think this is the best way to handle it." Lou looks at me and asks, "Does that cover everything for you?"

"Absolutely, my friend, that was stellar," I answer, "Now I would like to add something that is not related to any technology issue you've mentioned, but is about communication at a more fundamentally human level."

Staying off the Radar

"Right now there is a tendency for many folks to view our entire government in very negative terms. That is unfortunate, because the vast majority of people working in government are doing it for the right reasons — to be in service to, and to protect, others. Yes, there are those who abuse the system for power, ego, and a whole host of other horrible motives. These destructive players are typically people who've been installed in key positions by the elites to do their dirty work for them during the coming tribulation. That being said, I do not believe that their plans will work as expected, and here is why."

"Right now these evil-installed minions of the elites are able to twist and control those with good hearts and good intentions by means of a banking and financial system which gives them leveraging power. Once that system collapses, these minions are going to have high positions but no real credibility with their subordinates, who by then will know them for who they are. Consequently, these minions will lose their principal force of power and become pariahs. Not at first, but in time this will happen."

"In the meantime, we need to be smart and practical about how we use our radios. Let's use our radios in ways where we are not targeting ourselves for some kind of baseless, evil minion preemptive strike or enforcement issue."

"This is important, because radios are not secure. When you talk on a radio, whatever you are saying is fair game for everyone else on the planet with the ability to monitor your transmission to listen in on. So here are five simple on-air guidelines to help keep your community from being unnecessarily targeted."

"First off, do not be in any way confrontational or negative about the government. Rants will only draw the wrong kind of interest. Broadcasts of this nature will not be helpful, anyway."

"Second, using your radios for local reconnaissance to protect yourselves from warlords and gangs will be viewed as an acceptable local security issue. Just remember to keep it local."

"Third, the more secretively you behave, are the more attention you will call to yourself. Secretive, odd behavior is what the government will be looking for. The point is here is that you are not doing anything problematic in the first place, so there is no need for secrecy. Embrace being the goldfish in the bowl."

"Fourth, avoid any form of religiosity. You must be absolutely and completely secular on the airwaves. Remember, during the tribulation if yours is not an official religion, so to speak, your community will be hunted down as heretics or terrorists. Don't go there."

"Fifth, follow the already established guidelines restricting foul language and personal attacks on the radio. When on the air be professional, courteous, and concise at all times."

"So there it is. Do these five things and you will greatly reduce the threat of drawing negative attention to your communities from those in positions of power who are seeking to justify their existence with unwarranted and malicious police or military actions."

"As I said before, in time these minions will become pariahs as control reverts to local governments and the people themselves. Until then, be smart and keep your community off the radar. Don't let your peaceful, constructive community be mistakenly lumped in with troublemakers or revolutionaries. With that, I'm done. Charlie, Lou, either of you have anything to add?"

"Not me," says Charlie.

Lou agrees, folds up his presentation folder and hands it to you, "I think you can put this presentation folder to good use. In the back is a data DVD with all the files on it."

You look like someone who has been handed a treasure, and it makes the rest of us feel good as you say, "Wow, I want to thank everyone for all of this wonderful information about communications. I was really worried about handling radio communications, because it took me a long time just to figure out how to download an app to my smart phone. I feel much more confident now."

"Speaking of smartphones," Lou says, "Once you get your Technician license, you can use your Smartphone like a ham radio using Echolink. All you have to do is to get set up on Echolink, download an app to your Smartphone, and you're in business. Of course, these technologies will only last as long as the power grid, Internet, and cell towers are operational."

"That's cool, though," you gleefully say as a the waitress catches your attention. You signal her to come over, "It's time for that dessert tray for my friends here. As for me, a plain piece of cheesecake and a cup of coffee would be just perfect."

"Make that two," Lou says.

"Make that three," Charlie says.

"Aw heck, who am I to break a winning streak?" I say, "Make that four."

"I'd be happy to bring out the desert tray to show you all the options," the waitress says.

"Plain cheesecake and coffee," we all say in unison.

"Coming right up," she says, leaving with a pleasant smile.

As she leaves, I see you rubbing your chin and thinking to yourself again. You tend to be doing that frequently these days. Finally you say, "Charlie, Marshall, after desert, I want to go back to the Survival Village Imaginarium to spend more time with Charlie and look at the exhibits. But for now, can I ask you all for a big favor? I'd like to spend the night sleeping in the Communal Village Dome, just to see how it feels."

Charlie smiles with surprise, "That's the first I have ever heard anybody ask for that before, but on the other hand, why not? In fact, I think it's a grand idea. I've never tried it, myself, so I'll join you."

"If it's okay with Charlie, then it's okay with me," I say, "I can pick you up tomorrow morning and get you back to the lake house in plenty of time to make pancakes."

"Yes, that will work," Charlie adds, "And there's a store not far from here where you and I can pick up a toothbrush and whatnot for the night."

"Can I come too?" Lou asks.

"The more the merrier," you answer as Charlie and I nod our approval, "By the way," you add in a sly way, "Do you think we can get up a game of three-handed pinochle tonight?"

"Sure," Lou answers happily. "I'll bring the cards. You bring the checkbook."

"And you bring your checkbook as well, Lou," you quickly answer with a competitive smile.

I lean over and look down at Sheba, "So girl, do you think Lou is going to get a real run for his money tonight?"

"Woof, woof, woof." We all laugh.

What is it about that dog?

10

Incident Command System

It's the first light of day at the lake house, and I know that for an hour or so everyone will be rubbing the sleep out of their eyes and starting the day. As for me, I've stayed up late in the cottage working on something special for my Incident Command System lesson. Even so, I worked in enough sleep time, and I'm feeling pretty good as I enter the coordinates into the time machine to pick you up. Moments later the machine materializes in front of the Communal Village Dome Exhibit in the lower level of the Survival Village Imaginarium. It's now two hours before the fair opens, and the place is dark and quiet.

I step out of the time machine and walk straight into the dome. There I find Charlie on the first floor, sipping coffee from a Styrofoam cup. Next to him is Sheba curled up on a couch and sleeping soundly. On the table in front of him is a large thermos and extra cups. In a hushed voice, Charlie says, "I made some hot Joe this morning for us in the employee lounge. Grab a cup and help yourself."

"Thanks, don't mind if I do," I softly reply as I open the top of the thermos, "So where is our shining star this morning?"

"Up on the second floor, third sleeping compartment to the right."

"How much of this coffee did you drink this morning, Charlie?"

"Not nearly enough."

I just shake my head and head up the stairs to knock on your door. I start with a normal knock and call your name. No answer. So I knock a little louder and call your name again with still no answer. By this time Sheba has awakened and comes upstairs to see what's going on.

This time I pound loudly on the door and shout, "Hey, sleeping beauty, shake a leg! We've got a schedule to keep."

Finally, you come to life, and I hear a groggy, "Oh, what time is it? Is it morning?"

I look down at Sheba, "Can you keep barking at the door here until sleeping beauty comes out?"

"Woof, woof!"

I pat Sheba on the head and walk back down the stairs to drink coffee with Charlie.

"I don't know which is worse," Charlie complains as I settle in with my cup of coffee, "Hearing you pound on the door or Sheba's barking."

"Well, we've got to get our friend up and moving, one way or another."

"Sure. I see you used the coordinates I created for you yesterday. How's the machine working this morning?"

"It's parked outside, Charlie. I've got to admit, it's one amazing piece of machinery. It reminds me of my Dad's old Timex watch, 'it takes a lickin' and keeps on tickin.'"

We quietly sip our coffees for a few minutes and Sheba stops barking. Shortly after that, you're padding down the stairs dressed, but still half asleep. Sheba runs ahead of you and comes to sit beside me as you go straight for the coffee. Pouring yourself a cup you plop down on a stuffed chair.

"What do you mean, calling me Sleeping Beauty?" you grumble. Then you give Sheba a cool look, "And what loud barking!"

Charlie and I chuckle a bit, "Well, it was Sheba barking or drag out the old foghorn from the Queen Mary and give it a few toots."

"Ha. Ha. Ha"

"So how was it last night? Did you enjoy sleeping in a dome?"

You sip your coffee and kick your feet up, "An amazing experience. I just haven't been sleeping well lately, and I went into a very deep sleep, and I'm a little groggy. But it was a good, restful sleep." Thankfully, your mood seems to be improving.

You stretch than say, "Anyway, only had to get up once to use the facilities last night. When I went back to bed, Sheba had one eye open but stayed curled up. So I sat on a corner of the bed and something marvelous happened. I wasn't thinking about anything. I just sat there, completely relaxed and at peace. It was so nice. Then I was out the minute my head hit the pillow, and the next thing I know you're banging at the door like Tarzan on steroids."

"So what are you thinking about right now?"

"What I'm thinking now is how folks are going to feel during the tribulation when they're living in a subterranean dome. They'll know that outside, and far away, other people will be bearing the brunt of those difficult times, but inside the domes, they'll feel safe and secure. That's what I'm thinking right now, and its why I'm glad for this overnight opportunity. When it comes time to organize the construction of our shelters this experience has put a lot of steel in my back to stick to subterranean dome construction, which I know will work and will be the most comfortable solution. No matter how much push-back I get from those who think they know better, this is the way we'll do it, and that's the long and the short of it."

This is the kind of moment that tells us that we've made a difference, and Charlie and I look at each other with gratified smiles. Then Charlie glances at his watch, "We've got about 15 minutes until the cleaning staff comes to change the sheets and so forth. I organized all of that yesterday. So pour yourselves a little more coffee and let's put the time to use."

I wink at Charlie and then look at you, "Yesterday you went back to look at the exhibits upstairs after lunch. What impressed you the most in the exhibit area on the other side where various concrete dome uses were displayed?"

"Hands down, it had to be the indoor farming dome exhibit. There was this amazing model of a huge, 300-foot diameter dome that was 150 feet tall and it had seven levels. Going from the bottom of the dome up to the top here is what I saw. The aquaponics fish tanks were on the first floor, which makes sense since that's the heaviest load. Then the next two floors above that were aquaponics grow beds. Altogether, these first three floors comprised a complete and very efficient system.

"On the fourth floor were the hydroponics grow beds. Hydroponics do not have the same recycling advantages as aquaponics, but this level has its uses. The fifth floor was fascinating because it was twice as high as any other floor. Also, running straight up through the center of the dome was this huge elevator shaft with two commercial freight elevators in it. But on the fifth level, the shaft had this circular observation platform with small offices that reminded me of a tree house. On one side of the fifth floor was an indoor orchard, and on the other side there were mezzanine-like dirt grow beds for root stock vegetables like carrots, beets, parsnips, and potatoes.

"Then on the sixth level there is the starter room where small seedlings were grown for transplanting to the lower floors.   Finally, on the seventh level is the wormery with all those little red wigglers. There is a cool way of collecting worm tea, which is nothing more than worm pee for use in the starter room below. It's a bucket system where the worms keep working their way up through the holes in the bucket above them for fresh food. Once they've done that, the contents of the old bucket with all the shed worm skins are sent to the lower levels. As for the extra worms, they are sent to the first level to feed the fish in the aquaponics tanks and to another dome to feed the chickens."

"Obviously, a facility like this is ambitious and needless to say it would be a bit beyond reach on day one. However, it sure does give me a lot of good ideas for things that we could do in the future."

"That's why we call this an Imaginarium," I say, "It's a pure 'imagine if you will,' about things you can eventually hope to do."

"But there was one thing I learned at that exhibit that we could put to use immediately," you add.

"And what's that?"

"People who are experts in this field have learned that children are much better at making these closed indoor systems highly productive. It's because they do not have to see things through the fog of experience or education. Rather, children come at it with fresh eyes, and they see things just as they are, and then they do the most amazing things through their 'beginner's minds.' So the best way to do this is to let the children of the community run the indoor growing systems with adults working for them and doing safety oversight."

"In that case, there's something you need to have on hand," Charlie says.

"What's that?" We both asked together.

"You should have lots and lots of drawing paper and colored pencils for the kids, and for later, small slate chalkboards and chalk."

You snap your fingers, "That's a brilliant idea Charlie, thank you!"

After that we talk briefly about some of the other exhibits until it is time for us to go. Walking out to the time machine with Sheba following close behind, we both turn around one last time to look up at the dome, "Honestly; it looks so much bigger on the inside than it does on the outside," you exclaim.

I just smile, and as we get into the time machine, Charlie comes out to wave goodbye, "Will I get to see Charlie again?" you ask as the machine whirs to life.

"Woof, woof, woof," Sheba answers, leaving both of us to look at each other with incredulous stares. What is it about this dog?

In the blink of an eye we're back in the woods, and we quickly set out for the lake house. "The schedule for today starts with pancakes. You have me hooked on those things. After that it's back to the cottage for your next lesson, the Incident Command System, or just ICS for short."

ICS Organization

After another delicious breakfast, we sit around the table and enjoy talking about what's going on at the lake house, and what the children are doing. As always, there are no prying questions about what you and I are doing, but then again, that's the way this has been set up. After a very pleasant morning, we're on our way to the caretaker's cottage, and I mention something I had overheard.

"Are your buckwheat pancakes actually gluten-free? Until this morning, I didn't know that buckwheat pancakes are usually a combination of buckwheat flour and regular wheat flour which does have gluten. So, how can you say they are gluten-free?"

"If I tell you, you might not want to eat my pancakes again," you answer cagily.

"I can take it. What's your secret?"

"Well, if you go to a restaurant or cafe, that's how they'll make them, by combining buckwheat flour and wheat flour. However, we found a truly gluten-free recipe that uses buckwheat flour, white sorghum flour, and tapioca starch. So does that take the pizzazz out of the pancakes for you?"

Opening the door to the cottage, I answer, "Absolutely not. In fact I like them even more now because I know that gluten is going to make life difficult for people during the tribulation. Any way that gets away from gluten is the cat's whiskers in my book."

We turn on the lights and go inside, and I motion you to sit on the bench. Sheba curls up behind us on a nice soft bed that I've made for her so she can be comfortable while keeping an eye on us. On the wall behind the bench is a long pegboard system with hooks and all kinds of tools hanging from them.

"Today I want to introduce you to the incident command system, or what's called ICS. It is the outgrowth of a system first developed in the 1970s by an inter-agency group in Southern California to manage wild land fires. The State of California would adopt the system, and a few years later the U.S. Government also adopted this system with some modifications under its current name, the Incident Command System."

"Every first responder in the county knows ICS, by which I mean every police officer, firefighter, paramedic, and so forth. There are two key reasons why a familiarity with ICS is vital.

"First, you need to be positively engaged with the responders in the area where you've situated your community. This is because in a crisis you'll be one of three things, a victim, a troublemaker, or a part of the solution. We always strive to be a part of the solution with local responders. This means participating in local volunteer disaster-response programs sponsored by local law enforcement agencies and so forth.

"Second, folks in every survival village will fit into one of three categories: doers, responders or leaders. The doers we'll talk about in the next lesson, but in this lesson we're going to focus on your responders. No doubt, you'll have a few active or retired law enforcement officers, firefighters, and other responders in your congregation. Likewise, each of them will understand ICS and how it's used when disaster strikes."

"So, is ICS somewhat bureaucratic?" you ask.

"Yes, it is because city, county, state, regional and federal agencies must work together along with non-governmental agencies like the Red Cross to respond to disasters. For government agencies this bureaucracy is simple and intuitive, and for the rest of us on the outside, it's like trying to find divine inner wisdom with a lava lamp. Even so, it makes perfect sense to them, and if you can understand what makes sense to them, then you can talk to them which in turn means you can work with them. And more importantly, with ICS you can survive with them.

"In the simplest terms, ICS offers a way to organize a response by multiple responders to an incident. An incident can be any occurrence or event, natural or human-caused disasters that require a coordinated response to protect life and or property, such as a meteor shower that pulverizes part of a city.

"Learning the ICS system takes many hours of online instruction, with classroom instruction offered for the higher levels. My goal is to help you get focused on the most important ICS concepts and essential terms so that you can quickly organize with those who understand ICS better than you.

"With this in mind, let's begin with me asking you to hand me some tools from this large pegboard system on the wall. Here's how it works. I'll ask you to give me a tool by name without pointing to it, and this is what you need to do. Are you ready?"

"Okay."

"Claw hammer," You hand me the claw hammer, "3/8 inch ratchet drive with a 9/16" socket." You take the drive down from the pegboard, find the correct socket, put them together and hand it to me, "Now give me a small Phillips screwdriver." Scanning the pegboard area with all the screwdrivers, you find the right one and hand it to me, "So far, so good. Now, give me a thirteen-millimeter fizzelbickle."

"A what?"

"You heard me. Give me a thirteen-millimeter fizzelbickle."

"What on Earth are you talking about? No, check that. Are we even actually on Earth?"

"Yes, we are on Earth. Again I'm asking you to give me a thirteen-millimeter fizzelbickle." I know I'm testing your patience, but this exercise is necessary to make a point.

"There is no such a thing as a thirteen-millimeter fizzelbickle!" Now you're getting a little annoyed.

"All throughout the galaxy ask any extraterrestrial for a thirteen-millimeter fizzelbickle, and they'll know exactly what to give you. How can you not know what a fizzelbickle is?"

At this point you're starting to fume a little with frustration, and I'm biting my lip to keep from laughing, "Well, I am not an extraterrestrial, so what is the point of all this?" you demand, testily.

Now I can't stop myself from laughing, and I pat you on the shoulder, "You're right. There is no such thing as a fizzelbickle on Planet Earth, but," I raise a finger, "This is not to say that fizzelbickles do not exist elsewhere in the galaxy."

I point to the tools you've handed me, "The first thing I want you to understand about ICS is that this system is designed much like this pegboard system, where each tool on the board has its own unique and universally recognized name.

"The same holds true for the ICS system. Whatever your civilian title is, be it Chief of Police, Provost Marshal, or Grand Poobah, when you're managing an incident and giving orders, every responder will know you by one unique and universal name: Incident Commander.

"To further help shape your understanding of ICS; let's use this pegboard tool system with an added twist. We'll substitute the word tools with roles. Got it?"

"Got it."

"Good, so, as we look at this pegboard system on the wall, here's your first question. What do we already know about the roles on the wall?"

"That each one has a proper name that is universally recognizable by everyone."

"Correct. Now, if you initially need just a few of these unique roles for an incident, is it necessary to use all of the roles defined by the ICS system on our pegboard, from the outset?"

"No, I'd probably start with one or two, and then go back to the pegboard for others as needed."

"Right again. Now, look over to your left where we have all of the screwdrivers in one area. Then to the right of them, all of the box-end wrenches, and other groups of tools, and so forth. What does this tell you?"

"That each role is designed for a specific function. That being, if I'm going to unscrew a screw, I do not need a box-end wrench. Rather, I'll need a screwdriver. In that case, I'm going to look at that group of screwdrivers or that group of roles over there, which all serve a similar function."

I rap the bench with my knuckles, "Brilliant. Now, let's talk about all those ratchets and sockets in the center of the pegboard. Tell me what you see in terms of roles."

You rub your chin for a moment and then answer, " Well let's see. There are three different kinds of ratchets. At the very top we have quarter-inch, three-eighths inch, and half-inch ratchets. Below those are extenders. Below the extenders are the regular standard and metric sockets. Then below those are the standard and metric deep sockets."

"You nailed it. Now, let's take it the next step. What is our top-down hierarchy?"

"Top-down hierarchy?"

"Let's think it through. What's the first thing you start with at the top?"

"A ratchet?"

"Correct. Now let's assume you need to get at a bolt that is down deep in an engine."

"I would add an extender to the ratchet."

"Good. What comes next?"

"A socket, of course, and that will depend on whether the bolt is standard or metric, and if I need a regular or deep a socket."

"So, what is the top-down hierarchy?"

"Now I see your point, ratchet, extender, and socket. There are three separate tools that are designed to work together precisely with each other in a specific hierarchical order."

I clap with enthusiasm, "By Jove, I think you've got it."

"Got what?"

"The five simple concepts you need to know about ICS roles as a faith-based tribulation leader. Let's do a quick review of what you've learned." I open a drawer and pull out a pad and pen. "Now write these five things down as I review them for you:

"Each role has a unique, universal name.

"Roles are only used as needed.

"Each role is designed for a specific function.

"Roles are grouped by organizational purpose.

"Roles and groups of roles are organized within top-down hierarchies."

"Now this makes sense. What you're telling me is that there is no difference between ICS organization and how this pegboard system we use for the tools here in the cottage is organized. In other words ICS is just a big tool chest."

"I couldn't have said it better myself, and I say that having been certified with six different ICS training classes offered by FEMA: ICS 100, 200, 300, 400, 700, and 800. I'm sharing this with you because when evaluating responders and volunteer responders, it is useful to know their ICS training certifications. This will help you understand the depth of their ICS training.

"For example yesterday in the cafe Lou was talking about how ARES (Amateur Radio Emergency Services) and the ARRL (American Radio Relay League), both non-governmental organizations, work with Homeland Security when disaster strikes. Like Lou, I am also a certified ARES volunteer, and I hold a General Radio license.

"To become certified ARES volunteers, Lou and I had to certify with four ICS online courses. Each takes about three hours to complete, and they are ICS 100, 200, 700 and 800. In addition to ARES I also became a certified CERT volunteer through my local sheriff's office. CERT stands for Community Emergency Response Team. This program is a part of FEMA and requires certification in only two ICS online courses: ICS 100 and 700."

"So, why the difference?"

"The difference is this, with ARES you will sometimes work with other ARES volunteers all across the country. CERT, on the other hand, is always local, and much like a sheriff's auxiliary for example.

"However, what ARES and CERT have very much in common is that they are comprised of good people. These are citizens who volunteer their time to be in service to their communities during a disaster. Yesterday Lou talked about what he and other ARES volunteers did after Katrina hit. Well, today if a similar disaster were to occur here's what you're likely see. While ARES volunteers are running mobile radio stations, CERT volunteers will be going through neighborhoods to find survivors and help run shelters."

"Will they be compensated for it?"

"There's no compensation for either program; they are pure volunteers. In fact, volunteers often buy their uniforms and whatever equipment is necessary to serve their chosen mission role.

"The point here is that these people volunteer because they want to be in service to their communities, and this desire to serve others comes from the goodness of their hearts. This is why you want to encourage members of your congregation to become involved with volunteer programs like these. Along with active, retired, and former professional responders, the training these volunteers get makes them valuable human resources for the tribulation."

"So how many of them will believe that Planet X is a clear and present danger?"

"That will vary from individual to individual. But let me put it this way. Imagine you are racing along on a bicycle named, Planet X. How many people do you expect to see riding a Planet X bicycle alongside you? Not many, that's for sure. So here is where these folks are really precious. They are riding bicycles too, but when it comes to Planet X, they still have training wheels.

"What are these training wheels? They have a commitment to serving others in the event of a disaster. So, even if they're not taking planet X seriously right now, when the time comes, that will change. That's when the training wheels will come off, and then you'll be riding bikes alongside people who are ready for the challenge."

You nod your head appreciatively, "This is something I need to get working on ASAP, and I need to take this ICS training myself if possible."

"That's easy. Get involved with a local disaster volunteer group like ARES or CERT, and then get a FEMA Student Identification (SID) number to enroll in the online classes which are free. FEMA uses SIDs so that you don't have to keep using your Social Security number. With that in mind, let's quickly break down the six ICS courses for you and see what they mean to you as a faith-based tribulation leader.

"ICS-100 is what you would expect any 100-level course to be. It is a broad-brush introduction to the Incident Command System (ICS). However, ICS-200 is where the rubber meets the road, and this was my favorite online course. ICS-200 is a beginner course that teaches you how the ICS system is organized, and how roles are organized within it in response to an incident.

"After taking ICS-100 and ICS-200, you jump ahead to two other online courses that explain the big picture. With ICS 700 you get an overview of the National Incident Management System (NIMS) for regional incidents. Then with ICS-800 you get some good insights into the National Response Framework (NRF) for dealing with really big, national-scale disasters such as an earthquake on the New Madrid fault line that would devastate an entire region of the country.

"After taking all four of the online courses, you're qualified for ICS-300, a more advanced version of ICS-200. It's a three-day classroom course that takes you to an intermediate level."

"Once you've completed the ICS-300 course you'll have the five prerequisites need to go to the advanced level with ICS 400. 400 is a two-day classroom course that's intended for senior personnel, such as fire chiefs and police chiefs."

"So, as a faith-based leader, which of thee six ICS courses matter most to me?" you ask.

"Precisely the right question. The answer is ICS 200, 300 and 400. These are the courses you want to key in on and here's why. With ICS 200, students are learning the basic concepts we've discussed using our pegboard tool system example, roles, and organization."

"With ICS-300 and ICS-400, you learn how the whole system functions and works together. If we were to use these courses with our pegboard system, we'd be looking at all the tools. But what I really like most about these courses is that you learn how the ICS takes the load off of the leader as the incident expands, so that others can quickly step in and begin working toward a common goal."

By the way, incident commanders are easy to spot. They always put their hands on their wallets before they make a decision because everything costs something, and getting stuck with the bill is no fun."

" Of all the courses, ICS 400 is where you're going to get the most valuable skill-set possible for yourself as a faith-based tribulation leader. This course teaches you how to organize an area command which is what your survival village will need."

"On a personal note my most favorite course of all six was ICS-400. That's when it all clicked for me in terms of what will be needed for the tribulation. I was the only volunteer in the class. Everyone else was actively employed in leadership roles, but there was no snobbery, as some might think. We were a team, and it felt great, because these folks truly do appreciate volunteers who are properly trained, professional, and committed."

"So let's break this down into ICS organizational groupings. What you're going to have is an incident commander who is running the show, and who is directly supported by a command staff. The command staff is comprised of a Public Information Officer, a Safety Officer, and a Liaison Officer."

"The public information officer, or PIO, is the person who is going to be talking to the media on behalf of your organization. Trust me; the last thing you want is some yutz pontificating in front of the media. A good PIO will handle all public contacts, and is invaluable."

"The safety officer is responsible for keeping everyone in your incident command safe. This will be an especially important role during the tribulation."

"Then there is the liaison officer. As the name suggests, this member of your command staff is the one who is going to connect and communicate with other organizations involved in the incident."

"So, do I always start off with a full command staff?" you ask.

"No. Incidents usually start with one responder such as a police officer who shows up at the scene. The first on the scene becomes the first incident commander. Then will come the other responders, and once a more qualified person for the role of incident commander arrives, the initial incident commander transfers authority to that person.

"One of the great things about ICS is that it is a management-by-objective system. In other words an incident commander may not be the highest ranking individual on the scene, but rather the most qualified to manage that particular type of incident. As the incident evolves, the incident commander adds new roles to address expanding or changing needs. For example incident commanders and command staff officers can appoint deputies to assist them.

"Then, beneath the command staff in the top-down ICS hierarchical organization model is the general staff. Here you have four standard sections under the command section in the ICS organizational model: operations, planning, logistics and finance/administration.

"As with the command staff, the incident command only activates sections as needed, and each section will have a leader called the section chief. For example the operation section will be led by an operations section chief.

"In the ICS model the two most influential people will be the incident commander and the operations section chief. This is because the planning, logistics, and finance/administration sections are only activated once they are needed to support the operations section. If you ask me, the planning section chiefs deserve the greatest empathy. While everyone else is getting forty winks, they'll be up through the night tweaking the plan for the next day.

"As a faith-based tribulation leader, you will be interfacing principally with your own incident commander and to a certain extent the operations chief. Here are a couple of terms you'll need to be familiar with, and they will be a part of your operations section: strike teams and task forces.

"A task force is a group of different resources organized for a specific purpose. In terms of our pegboard system, a task force would be like taking a hammer, screwdriver, and pry bar with you to fix a door.

"A strike team is a group of similar resources organized for a specific purpose. Concerning our pegboard system example, let's say you need to remove some wood screws from scrap lumber. In this case your strike team would be like a handful of screwdrivers.

"In either case, whether you're organizing a task force or a strike team, it has to be led using a common communications system. During the tribulation, you can expect to need to organize strike teams and task forces on a frequent basis to accomplish various purposes.

"Before we go downstairs there are a few key concepts I want to pass along to you from the ICS system that I think are immensely useful for any organization. The first is unity of command. What this means simply is that everyone in your organization reports to only one supervisor and only that supervisor gives them their assignments. Whether your ship is small or big makes no difference. It cannot have two captains.

"Another important concept is span of control. The last thing you need during the tribulation is someone trying to build an empire or to manage more than what they can handle as a single individual. Span of control in ICS terminology means that there is a limit the number of people you can supervise, and the ideal number ranges between three and seven. Once you find yourself supervising more than seven people, you immediately expand the organization with another leadership role to bring your span of control back into that workable range of three-to-seven.

"And finally, the one thing that is vital is to ask your incident commander for a briefing on his or her incident action plan, called the IAP. The IAP is essential in helping you to understand the objectives of the plan, what is going to be done to reach those objectives, and how long it is expected to take. An IAP can be written, but during the tribulation, more often than not they will be given by way of verbal briefings. As the leader of the community, be sure that you always get an IAP briefing and updates on the IAP as the incident progresses and changes.

"That's enough on that for today. Now I have something special to show you." I go to the refrigerator and pull out of a couple of cold bottles of Backside Root Beer and nod my head towards the basement door, "Now let's go downstairs because I've created something to help you get a feel for what needs to be in your survival village command center."

ICS Area Command

In the basement, you see where I have pushed the chairs off to the sides of the room. In the middle is a table with a scaled topographical model of a survival village and its surrounding areas. "I built this yesterday afternoon while you were visiting the Imaginarium."

"This is impressive," you exclaim as I hand you a cold bottle of Backside root beer.

"Thank you, and once you get your community relocated; you will need to get a surveyor or somebody with a good drone camera to give you an accurate relief map of the terrain around your community. Then, find someone who's good with making clay models and have him or her turn that map into a scaled topographical model. A model like the one you see here needs to be in the very heart of each survival village's operation center."

"I see this has green lines drawn on it, and it is divided into four parts," you say, "What are these for?"

"Most likely, you already have someone in your congregation with field command leadership experience. Preferably, this will be someone who has urban combat experience and has led a motivated security team. Let that person scope out your situation so that they can set up observation posts, warning lines, and establish areas for enfilade, or what's known as flanking fire. After all, being good with God doesn't mean you need to become a good dinner for some maniac. Preparing for appropriate defense is important.

"So what I've done here is to assume that your warriors have analyzed your position and have chosen to divide it into four sectors as part of an effective defense shield. In this case the best way to use an ICS organization for your community is with an area command.

"ICS area commands are used to cover broad areas where multiple incident commanders are required, and each handles a specific piece of the overall area. An area command starts with an overall area commander who has responsibility for the defense of your entire survival village. Then under the area command, each sector will have its own incident commander, and each of these will have his or her own command staff and operations section.

"The three other sections: planning, logistics, and finance/administration will work out of the overall area command in support of the sector area commands and the incident commanders in each of the four sectors along with their operation section chiefs.

"Also, in this specific application of an area command organization there will be a key role for the overall area command public information officer. Your area command PIO will be responsible for giving information updates to your survival village as a whole and for communications with all of the satellite communities in the surrounding area.

"As I said before, each of the incident commanders in the four sectors will have a full command staff to include a safety officer, a liaison officer, and a PIO. However, the PIOs in the four sectors will be restricted to dealing with satellite communities in their surrounding areas, under the supervision and direction of your area command PIO. In this way you will be providing consistent outbound information to your satellite communities."

"So who chooses the area incident commander and the sector incident commanders?"

"Excellent question. The thing about the incident command system is that it helps responders to work with civilian officials. So, let's say you are a leader; you have a council of elders, and you have a successor designated by you who also sits on the council of elders.

"One way to go about this is you, as the leader, would nominate one or more candidates for area incident commander to your council, which in turn would then ratify the candidate of their choice. Once you have your area incident commander, that person must have full authority to do his or her job.

"Do not, and I repeat, do not micromanage your warriors or responders. The last thing you want to do is to learn military strategy and tactics during the midst of an assault on your community. Rather, your role as a leader is to define the goals of the operation or incident resolution and to allocate whatever resources you can. The rest you need to leave in the hands of your area incident commander who will then be responsible for appointing your four incident commanders."

Now the time has come to wrap things up, "So now, as a faith-based tribulation leader, what are you going to do about the incident command system?"

"Throw me a bone here a very, very simple bone."

You make me chuckle, "Okay, let's make this as easy as 1-2-3. One, what you need to do is to recruit someone from inside or outside your congregation who is an active or retired responder with ICS 200, 300 and 400 certifications. Two, use this responder as an adviser to help you evaluate potential area incident commander candidates for your council of elders. And three, each time you meet an incident commander, request an IAP briefing."

"Thank you," you say as you intently study the scaled topographical model on the table. After a long pause you mumble out loud, "Looking at something like this does kind of make you feel isolated."

Building the Bond

"I hear that, and I want you to know that isolation is death during the tribulation. As a faith-based tribulation leader, you must always seek out opportunities to build bonds with others. In this case let's talk about building bonds with local responders. I'm talking about police and fire, and most every community will also have some kind of volunteer organization. Simply put, you need to be involved in these organizations and not just to ingratiate yourself. That's disingenuous, and people will spot that.

"Rather, you want to honestly participate and contribute to these programs. When things start to pop, you are known to be solidly a part of the solution. The more members you have in your community who follow you on this the better. Nothing is more impressive after all in a crisis than organizing a team of people who will show up at the Sheriff's office and say, 'where do you need us and what you want us to do?'"

"But what about the bad apples?"

"Yesterday I told you how the elites had installed their evil minions into positions of power in the government, but that once there's no longer a banking system to give them leverage over people, they'll eventually become pariahs. Remember, the vast majority of people in public service are there for the right reasons. As a spiritual leader, you need to look inside them for their noble sense of service and honor, and then to reward them for it."

"When others criticize harshly and rudely, you make constructive and helpful comments. Where others assume they are silently deserving of service, you warmly and openly acknowledge that service. Remember, building bonds means you need to become a part of the solution. But not only do you need to build bonds with those outside your community, it is equally important for you to build bonds within in your community, and that is exactly what we're going to talk about after lunch."

11

Enlightened Continuity
and Comfort

For the first time in several days, we've had the opportunity to eat lunch with everyone at the lake house, and we enjoyed it immensely. Tomorrow evening will be the big farewell feast, and everyone is urging us to go fishing again so we can have another wonderful fish fry. You and I agree, and so does Sheba; who definitely will be instrumental in helping us to find the fish.

As the next lesson will be a short one, we decide to sit on lawn chairs and watch the children at play for a while. The laughter of children is good medicine for the soul. I tap you on the shoulder late in the afternoon, "It's time," you nod in agreement and we leave for the caretaker's cottage with Sheba alongside.

Opening the door to the cottage, I ask you, "Grab us a couple of bottles of root beer and meet me downstairs." You give me a thumb up sign, and we head off in a different direction. A few minutes later you walk down the stairs with Sheba and find me disassembling the table-top model we had used earlier that morning.

"I see you've really been busy stockpiling root beer for tomorrow night. It looks like there are at least three bottles for each of us, including all the kids."

I smile softly, "One does what one can. Do me a favor, set those root beers down and help me get the room rearranged. I want to get those chairs back in the center so that we can put our feet up and talk." In short order the room is rearranged, and we are sitting in two plush chairs turned slightly towards each other.

"This afternoon we are going to talk about enlightened continuity and comfort, and this will be your last lesson."

"But I thought you said that the launch would be my last lesson?" you ask with a puzzled look.

"You have been a very capable student and better than most. While I usually need to help others with planning the launch of their programs, this time I have decided to do it differently. Rather than making it a lesson, I have decided that planning the launch will be your final exam."

"So how will this final exam work?"

" You will go back in the time machine to the moment after you first arrived here. You will still have your books, and whatever else you may want to take with you. Your memories of everything that you have seen and learned here will also remain intact. But there is one thing that I want you to take with you that in my heart, is the most important.

"Whatever your plan is, you are going to organize a major relocation effort like when Moses led the Hebrew people out of slavery in Egypt but with a critical difference. The Hebrews were happy to leave Egypt, but you should not expect your congregation to be as enthusiastic. Therefore, you will need to factor this into your plan."

"Yes," you sigh, "This has been on my mind."

"I've seen that; which is why I've chosen to make the launch your test. I think you're worthy of it; so here's how it works. I'm not going to tell you anything more than a few hints and tips. Then, after we finish this lesson today, I want you to think it through yourself. Then tomorrow morning, when we set out early with Sheba to go fishing, I want you to give me a verbal briefing of your plan. Do you feel ready for this?"

"Part of me does not even know where to begin, but another part of me knows I am ready. So, I will ask God to be my friend and to give me guidance. When I have it, you will know it."

"Then I look forward to this with great anticipation," I say appreciatively, "One point I do want to make is that the Judeo-Christian ethic teaches us that we must protect the most vulnerable among us. It greatly saddens me to see how often people and societies have strayed from this core, ethical belief. We know these people by what they do, and what they do is absolutely unconscionable. Yet, harming the most vulnerable is often tolerated by those in power because it either benefits them directly, or they are just unconcerned and only interested in serving themselves.

"This kind of tribulation thinking is often demonstrated in Hollywood movies where women are viewed as possessions and sex toys, and where children are aside or abused. This dark vision of the future cannot stand, nor must it be given the tiniest opportunity to present itself. Such a foul darkness of the soul can only lead to misery and death.

"There is an ancient secular wisdom text called '*The Kolbrin Bible*.' It is actually a compilation of two ancient books; it contains parts of 'The Great Book' written by the Egyptians following the Exodus, and the 'Coelbook' written by the ancient Celts around the time of Jesus.

"In 'The Great Book,' the ancient Egyptians call Planet X 'The Destroyer,' which is also the same term used by the ancient Hebrews." I hand you two photocopy sheets, "To set a foundation for this lesson today, I want to share with you a few passages from the Book of Manuscripts from the Egyptian section. It is the fifth book of the eleven books of *The Kolbrin Bible*, and it was written after the last flyby, which was during the Exodus from Egypt.

"We will begin with Manuscripts 3:8 because all good prophecies and predictions must have a harbinger. In other words there will be something to warn us that the time has come to prepare for the prophecy. So, let's read this passage together, and then we'll focus on a few key passages."

We read together:

Manuscripts 3:8 A nation of soothsayers shall rise and fall, and their tongue shall be the speech learned. A nation of lawgivers shall rule the Earth and pass away into nothingness. One worship will pass into the four quarters of the Earth, talking peace and bringing war. A nation of the seas will be greater than any other, but will be as an apple rotten at the core and will not endure. A nation of traders will destroy men with wonders and it shall have its day. Then shall the high strive with the low, the North with the South, the East with the West, and the light with the darkness. Men shall be divided by their races, and the children will be born as strangers among them. Brother shall strive with brother and husband with wife. Fathers will no longer instruct their sons, and the sons will be wayward. Women will become the common property of men and will no longer be held in regard and respect.

"A lot of these predictions ring a bell," you observe.

"Yes, but I'm only going to talk about three. The first is, 'One worship will pass into the four quarters of the Earth, talking peace and bringing war.' Islam professes to be a religion of peace, and yet radical Islamists truly have brought war to all four quarters of the Earth. Mind you, this was foreseen thousands of years ago by the ancient Egyptians, thousands of years before Islam came into being.

"The next passage is, 'A nation of the seas will be greater than any other, but will be as an apple rotten at the core and will not endure.' Considering when this was written, it is stunningly accurate. Ask any naval historian about the fall of the Soviet Union. Not only did it fall like a rotten apple, they'll tell you that on that day, the Soviet Navy possessed the largest fleet of warships in the world. Yes, their fleet was even larger than America's, and by well over twenty-five percent.

"However the one passage that disturbs me most in Manuscripts 3:8 is, 'Women will become the common property of men and will no longer be held in regard and respect.' This breaks my heart, because the global slave trade of women and children for sex and other ugly purposes is higher now than at any point in history."

"All of these stories are sad. For example, non-Muslim women and girls nine years old and up who are captured by Islamic State fighters are imprisoned as sex slaves, brutally abused, continuously raped, and often sold. So what was the response of Islam? A cleric has issued a fatwah instructing the fighters that when they capture a mother and her daughter together, only one may be raped. This is a tragic thing is, it's happening now and it will continue to happen during the tribulation, at least in the early years."

"The point here is that you cannot tolerate even the tiniest hint of such behavior in your own community or in those with whom you seek allegiances. Never forget, my friend, before a man tries to force a woman or a "However the one passage that disturbs me most in Manuscripts 3:8 is, 'Women will become the common property of men and will no longer be held in regard and respect.' This breaks my heart because the global slave trade of women and children for sex and other ugly purposes is higher now than at any point in history.

"All of these stories are sad. For example, non-Muslim women and girls nine years old and up who are captured by Islamic State fighters are imprisoned as sex slaves, brutally abused, continuously raped, and often sold. So what was the response of Islam? A cleric has issued a fatwah instructing the fighters that when they capture a mother and her daughter together, only one may be raped. This is barbaric, and the tragic thing is, it's happening now, and it will continue to happen during the tribulation, at least in the early years.

"The point here is that you cannot tolerate even the tiniest hint of such behavior in your own community or in those with whom you seek allegiances. Never forget my friend that before a man tries to force a woman or a child to submit to him, he will have first submitted himself to a terrible evil.

"Therefore, make no exceptions and show no tolerance for such behavior. As for those who beg forgiveness, be extremely miserly in the granting of it. Once a man's soul has been tainted with the power of abuse, and he feels entitled to it, only a very few will be able to remove this deeply evil habit from their souls. Most who abuse others will continue to abuse others.

"Now I want us to read Manuscripts 3:9 and 3:10 together, for they speak to what is at hand."

We read together:

Manuscripts 3:9 Then, men will be ill at ease in their hearts; they will seek they know not what, and uncertainty and doubt will trouble them. They will possess great riches but be poor in spirit. Then will the Heavens tremble and the Earth move; men will quake in fear, and while terror walks with them, the Heralds of Doom will appear. They will come softly, as thieves to the tombs; men will not know them for what they are; men will be deceived; the hour of The Destroyer is at hand.

Manuscripts 3:10 In those days, men will have the Great Book before them; wisdom will be revealed; the few will be gathered for the stand; it is the hour of trial. The dauntless ones will survive; the stouthearted will not go down to destruction.

"Throughout our world, there are now tumults, dissensions, wars, and the threat of wars. But the one passage that really resonates with me is, 'They will possess great riches but be poor in spirit.' Consider that, at present, you could count on both hands all those who now hold wealth equal to that of the poorest one-third of the planet.

"However, in Manuscripts 3:10, there is one passage that always reinvigorates my commitment to this mission in a profound and reassuring way. So much so, I printed it in large letters and framed it; so I could hang it over the desk in my home office, 'The dauntless ones will survive; the stouthearted will not go down to destruction.'

"The dictionary defines the word 'dauntless' as showing fearlessness and determination. The word 'stouthearted' is defined as courageous or determined. What the ancient Egyptians are telling us in very clear terms is that if we are to survive the tribulation, we must have courage, be fearless, and above all be determined."

"Yes, this is wise," you agree.

"And there is more. Remember our visit to the Tribulation Carousel Theater and Rabbi Sarah's presentation, along with what you learned from Charlie in the Threat Matrix Exploratorium. With that in mind, I chose four more readings, Manuscripts: 5:1, 5:2, 5:5 and 6:16."

We read together:

Manuscripts 5:1 The Doomshape, called The Destroyer in Egypt, was seen in all the lands thereabouts. In colour, it was bright and fiery; in appearance, changing and unstable. It twisted about itself like a coil, like water bubbling into a pool from an underground supply, and all men agree it was a most fearsome sight. It was not a great comet or a loosened star, being more like a fiery body of flame.

Manuscripts 5:2 Its movements on high were slow; below it swirled in the manner of smoke and it remained close to the sun, whose face it hid. There was a bloody redness about it, which changed as it passed along its course. It caused death and destruction in its rising and setting. It swept the Earth with grey cinder rain and caused many plagues, hunger and other evils. It bit the skin of men and beast until they became mottled with sores.

Manuscripts 5:5 The Doomshape is like a circling ball of flame, which scatters small fiery offspring in its train. It covers about a fifth part of the sky and sends writhing snakelike fingers down to Earth. Before it, the sky appears frightened, and it breaks up and scatters away. Midday is no brighter than night. It spawns a host of terrible things. These are things said of The Destroyer in the old records; read them with solemn heart, knowing that the Doomshape has its appointed time and will return. It would be foolish to let them go unheeded. Now, men say, 'Such things are not destined for our days.' May The Great God above grant that this be so. But come, the day surely will, and in accordance with his nature man will be unprepared.

Manuscripts 6:16 The Earth turned over, as clay spun upon a potter's wheel. The whole land was filled with uproar from the thunder of The Destroyer overhead and the cry of the people. There was the sound of moaning and lamentation on every side. The Earth spewed up its dead, corpses were cast up out of their resting places and the embalmed were revealed to the sight of all men. Pregnant women miscarried and the seed of men was stopped.

You shake your head with sad eyes, "If Rabbi Sarah's presentation had been this brutal I doubt that any of us in the audience would have believed it."

"Worse than that," I add, "Many would have simply walked out for the very reason given in Manuscripts 5:5, 'But come, the day surely will, and in accordance with his nature man will be unprepared.'

"Like I say, never underestimate the power of human denial. People will go into feel-think mode. They will think as they feel and believe that they are completely rational, and yet, it will only be their fears speaking for them. Like a young child waking frightened in the night, they will pull the covers up over their heads and create an entirely false sense of safety and security. But the Destroyer will still be in their bedroom, so to speak, as a clear and present danger.

"One of the things that will break your heart will be seeing families in your congregation divided by this feel-think insanity. Some will deny that there is a threat, and they will be helped along by the mass media who will also deny that there is any threat. Some in the divided family will not want to take action, to move out of harm's way, or to prepare in survival village communities. The danger will be clearly seen in the skies as well as in world events, and yet, many families will be divided."

"And when it does?"

"This part really hurts me," I say with a heavy sigh, "If you bring a divided family into your survival village community, they will bring that which divides them as well, and it will poison the cohesion of your community."

The words seem to knock the breath out of you. Dropping your head into your hands, you shake your head in disbelief saying, "I see the wisdom in it. How awful, yes, but I can see how that would play out in a community."

"It might be presumptuous of me, but perhaps now you know how God must sometimes feel, when we don't see things clearly." I reach over and place my hand softly on your shoulder, "You know; we speak of becoming a center of hope and of believing in the future, and many will embrace that. But there remains the bitter truth that the majority of people will not choose to walk this path. Those who do will be the bearers of light, and they shall be our brothers and sisters, and we will bond together with them in the most magnificent and spiritual ways imaginable. As grand as that will be, there will always be the pain of grieving those left behind, even though they lacked the courage and the determination needed for what is at hand.

"Looking back on Manuscripts 6:16, there was one passage that stunned me with its implications. It reads, 'Pregnant women miscarried and the seed of men was stopped.' If you think about it, in the times when these words were penned common people seldom lived beyond their 40s, and most died in their thirties. Therefore a good percentage of the population was teenagers. This means that what they saw in the sky literally caused healthy young teenage girls to miscarry, and teenage boys to become impotent.

"I'm not making a joke here, what Manuscripts 6:16 is telling us is that what we're going to see will literally scare the sex out of a teenager. What a horrifying thought!"

Your head rises up, and I see the tears welling in your eyes. I have felt such tears myself so many times I dare not count them, as you stare at me with sad and speechless eyes.

"We've all heard the old adage that the darkest hour is just before the dawn. I'm sorry my friend, but what I had to show you was the darkness, and it is a very dark darkness, indeed. But now the time has come for this moment to pass, and next it will be my pleasure to show you the dawn of hope when you're ready."

"I could surely use some hope just now; yes, I'm ready," you mutter, looking up.

Survival Wellness Advocates

"Now that we have seen the darkness, it's time to see the dawn. So now we will talk about something that will be vital to your mission — your strategy of enlightened continuity and comfort.

"So far we have talked about several roles in your community. The doers who will make things work, the leaders such as your council of elders with a knack for strategic vision and solutions, and, of course, your responders. The responders are responsible for keeping your flock safe from natural dangers and predators.

"All these things we have discussed in some fashion or another, but there is one special group of people in your community I have not mentioned thus far. That is because without understanding all the other roles and the dark circumstances we all face, you would not see a need for this special role, and it would not make sense to you.

"This special group of people will be your survival wellness advocates, and they shall ensure the success of your strategy for enlightened continuity and comfort. Most will simply be called 'advocates' and the closest role model I can imagine for the role of an advocate would be the medicine men and women of Native American tribes. Regarding the coming tribulation, the advocate role will be similar to the medicine man role in some regards but different in others.

"Now let me give you another planning suggestion for your launch. Your goal should not be to include as many people as possible in your community, to save each and every person that you can. If you do this, eventually there will be blood on your hands from the actions of some destructive individuals who were mistakenly included. Rather, your goal should be to include only those who are courageous and committed. Without those qualities, they will be unable to endure the tribulation. Remember what the ancient Egyptians told us thousands of years ago in Manuscripts 3:10, 'The dauntless ones will survive; the stouthearted will not go down to destruction.'

"That being said, Manuscripts 3:10 does not imply the need for a survival-of-the-fittest approach, for if a grown man trembles with fear, the child by his side will find courage enough for them both. Who will know to recognize this courage and embrace it with loving kindness? Your survival wellness advocates.

"To assist communities my church, the Knowledge Mountain Church of Perpetual Genesis maintains an enterprise Guild program, and one such Guild is the Survival Wellness Advocacy Guild. From your perspective as a leader, this is an autonomous group and the Advocates within your community may or may not wish to become members of this Guild. The benefit for you if you allow your Advocates to join the Guild if they so choose, is that you will have the benefit of trusted liaisons and communications with other communities such as yours. This is a voluntary program, and your advocates must embrace our mission, provided your core faith allows them to venture beyond its paradigm.

"Whether your Advocates join the Guild or not, they shall not have leadership power or authorities within your community, for these things are granted by the elders of your counsel who will be responsible for matters of leadership and day-to-day operations of the community.

"The attributes that define this survival wellness advocate guild are as follows:

- All members of the guild will be fully committed, first and foremost, to their community.

- Their mandate will be the implementation of your policy for enlightened continuity and comfort.

- Advocates will work among the people in strict confidence. An expectation of discretion must be the inalienable right of all those whom they serve.

- When an advocate observes any manner of violent or aggressive behavior against any member of the community, the advocate must immediately report it to a security officer and remain on the scene until a member of your security force arrives.

- Each day a speaker for the community Advocates will meet with the community leader and provide a briefing on the guild's activities and what the members of your community are saying and feeling, but in general terms, without violating their oath of discretion.

- Community leader will allocate resources for their Advocates as available and needed.

- Your advocates will liaise with every aspect of your civilian government and assist them in support of their efforts wherever needed.

"When working within the community, the highest duty of your advocates will be to ensure health, wellness, and hygiene. Their second priority will be providing comfort and care, and the third will be counseling and family negotiations."

The Three Priorities of Advocacy

"The first priority, health, wellness, and hygiene, is very broad. When you talk about health, it often regards simple things. An advocate might remind someone to put on leather gloves so they do not cut a finger and perhaps die of an infection that could have been easily treated today, but will be a different matter during the tribulation.

"Wellness is tremendously important. If your advocates are doing their job, properly they will mitigate the level of demand on your doctors, nurses, and medical supplies. This is an area where I see conventional preppers fail time and again. They usually take a Band-Aid approach to health and wellness, with just enough supplies to get through a few crisis events. After that, it will be like the old Westerns on television, where some poor cowboy has to bite down on a stick while a friend cauterizes his wound with a red-hot knife blade. Yes, cauterization is effective, but in real life do you want to be that unfortunate cowboy?

"Rather, common sense and a few simple things can make all the difference. Our communities can use time-tested home remedies and effective alternatives to pharma drugs, such as chiropractic adjustments, acupuncture, essential oils, hydrogen peroxide, baking soda, herbal medicines, homeopathy, and so forth. These will go a long way in treating minor maladies.

"The big benefit for you as a leader is that thanks to your advocates, your doctors and nurses will have lighter demands, which means more time to rest, to work on alternatives, and to train others. Of course, your advocates will work with your doctors to make sure that small molehills do not suddenly evolve into mountains of plague. But there is also the issue of mental wellness as well.

"Sometimes, you just sitting and sharing a cup of tea can steer someone who is teetering on the brink away from the edge and into a positive course of action. On the other hand, wellness also means organizing weekly square dances, for example, so that everyone has a chance to experience some joy in life and some positive social activity and interaction.

"As for hygiene, you know my stance on that. If one person neglects to wash their hands before they cook a community meal, they could create a communicable disease disaster. While it may not be a desirable duty for an advocate, enforcing hygiene and sanitation standards will be important. For instance, making sure that everyone properly washes their hands before entering a common eating area will be an important role.

"Another reality of the tribulation is that some people are going to suffer and die. They and their loved ones will need the support of the community. Here is where your advocates will function as much-needed palliative and hospice care givers, as well as providing some grief support.

"Earlier we talked about families that are divided, and will bring that division into your community, and why you must exclude them. This does not mean a fully committed family is not going to experience difficult times. All of us will experience difficult times during the tribulation, and this will be regardless of how well-functioning and well-stocked our survival village communities are. This is why counseling and family negotiations will be helpful for the community at large, provided your advocates are seen as being balanced, fair, caring, and thoughtful.

"Another critical aspect of this family counseling will be continuity of progeny. If we look at the vast history of humankind, there has always been a natural continuity of progeny. In other words the whole range of ages of human beings from babies to the very aged is represented about equally."It was only after World War II when we had the baby boom that generational balance became skewed in America. Look where that led America, to a Social Security system that was sound when it was created, but will collapse under the weight of the baby boom generation. It also led to the youth-oriented culture of the 60s and 70s and the 'Me Generation,' which were not helpful to our culture as a whole. Ergo, if by the end of the tribulation, your community is mostly comprised of ten-year-olds and fifty-year-olds with very few other ages in between your community will fail. You need the full spectrum of ages represented as evenly as possible to avoid the statistical burden mechanism that will collapse the Social Security system.

"This is why women and children must feel safe, secure, and appreciated; they will be the heartbeat of your success as a community. The success of each family and their progeny is vitally important to your community. Treasure and protect them; because when you see the backside, you will enter it with a strong, stable, and vibrant community, which will be ready to thrive and to evolve through enlightened service to God.

"For all of these reasons, your advocate must work closely with you to serve your community. They will continually train together so they can improve though sharing ideas about what works, and what hurts. After all, when you get right down to it, survival is about learning and implementing enough of what works before what hurts has a chance to kill you.

"Then finally, for you as a faith-based tribulation leader, what is the personal advantage of having an advocate in your community?"

You smile, "I would hope that they become my eyes and ears in a caring way, so we can resolve differences and problems peacefully and efficiently before anything gets out of hand. I would hope that the most vulnerable among us would come to know that they have people who care, who are in their corner, and who will always stand for them against subjugation or abuse by anyone. And I would hope that everyone in the community would feel secure in that they always have people they can go to, to talk, to find solutions, and to find comfort. No one will be in this thing alone."

"You've got it! A brilliant answer."

"One last thought on setting up an advocate program for your community, and then we'll call it a day. After all, we both need to get some rest so we'll be bright and chipper when we go fishing in the morning."

"Yes, I will need to find a quiet place to sort this all out and do some prayer and meditation to come back to center. Some of what you have shared from the Kolbrin is extremely disturbing! So, what is this last thought?"

"An oath."

The Need for Oaths

"I strongly suggest you require an oath for every position in your community that is specific to each role. This will ensure that everyone understands the rules up front, and has committed to following them. This includes a new member oath that reinforces three simple requirements: 'everyone works, everyone defends, and everyone participates.'

"Your community will need to figure out these oaths for yourselves. But what I can share with you is an advocate oath I created for our Survival Wellness Advocacy Guild. I have made a copy of it for you as a reference," I hand you another photocopy, "Let's read this oath together.

"As a member of the Survival Wellness Advocate Guild, I shall devote myself to making life worth living for the community through a policy of enlightened continuity and comfort. I therefore pledge:

- To promote the general welfare of my community so that it may thrive and prosper.

- To promote an enlightened continuity of progeny through procreation and adoption so that no child will ever fear becoming an orphan.

- To give my respect and support to the leadership of our community.

- To safeguard privacy through discretion for all members of the community.

- To always stand up for those among us who are the most vulnerable and needy.

As a member of the Survival Wellness Advocate Guild, I swear my commitment to furthering the enlightenment and freedom of our species, and to the pledges I have made above without reservation, exception, or avoidance of obligation. Before Creator and all present, so say I.

"My last piece of advice to you before we end this lesson is that there must be a zero-tolerance policy for those who are violent by nature, sociopathic, ego-driven, habitual liars, or cowards. When you're working on your launch, think of ways to spot these people and how to filter them out before they become embedded within your community; for if they do, they will certainly become divisive and corrosive, and they will also get people killed. And with that my friend, we're done for the day."

Up to now Sheba has been curled up in the corner just watching and listening to us quietly. So I call out to her, "Hey girl, how about we go find a good squeeze toy and have a game of fetch? Would you like that?"

"Woof."

"No? Go figure." What is it about this dog?

12

Launch

The dinner last night was sumptuous, and the conversation sparkled with humor and interesting stories. I expected you to be off somewhere all night with a notebook and a pen or deep in thought, but that wasn't you. Sure, you meditated and prayed for about an hour or so before dinner, but that was all.

We both went to sleep early that evening, well, earlier than usual. This morning I woke up, and you were already waiting for me with some hot coffee and reheated cornbread from last night to dispel the pre-dawn darkness. Our picnic basket was ready for us by the door to take out on the lake.

We assembled our fishing gear, and as we headed out the door, you asked, "Did you get the red wigglers?"

"You betcha," I wink, "And they're nice and plump too."

Walking down the outside stairs and toward the dock, we see Sheba sitting alongside the boat. She's waiting for us, and her tail is wagging because she's excited about going out on the water with us. We're equally happy because she is our mega-super-ultimate fish finder.

I pat her on the head as we start to stow the gear into the boat, "Good to see you, Sheba. We couldn't do this without you."

"Woof, woof!"

"Well, it's nice to see you're modest as well," I joke.

A few minutes later we're all settled. I cast off the lines, and you slowly motor us out into the lake. The first glow of sunlight begins to peek through the tall trees at the far end of the lake. Our timing couldn't be better.

"After we catch what we need for our feast tonight, let's go to that cove we found and enjoy the view while you brief me on your launch plan."

"Sounds like a plan. I like it."

Sheba is now becoming very excited. Her tail is straight up, and her nose is pointed at an area of the lake we haven't fished before. I get your attention and point at it. You see Sheba in the bow and with a simple nod; you bring the boat about to the new heading.

"We'll have to slow down in a bit, and when we do, mum's the word," you say.

"Got it skipper," then a question that's been bugging me since I woke up needs asking, "I expected you to be doing a lot of study and thought last night. So I'm curious as to what to expect later on. That is, in general terms."

"I have one advantage over you," you answer thoughtfully, "You've been at this for so many years; you have to be delicate with people's sensibilities, or at least as delicate as possible."

"You mean like when I say that people who are in denial are as dumb as a sack of hammers?"

"Well, I wouldn't say that's the delicate approach," we both laugh.

"I thought about something you said about the elders of my church when they pushed me to do my 'necessary duty,' as they called it, to play to Jim Daggot's ego, that they were doing the right thing. Well, as they say, what's good for the goose is good for the gander; except this time there are not going to be any Jim Daggot theatrics or ego pandering. At least, that's how I see it.

"Once I decided that I knew exactly what to do, it didn't take me long to sort it all out. You'll hear about it in a bit, but right now, we need to put fish on the table," you throttle back the engine and put a finger to your lips, "Shh."

You deftly maneuver the boat into a good spot, and we check our tackle, bait our hooks, and cast our lines. What happened next is something I will never forget for the rest of my life, like machine gun fire the two of us are saying, "Fish on."

After a pulling in several prize fish, Sheba leads us to another spot. Again, like machine gun fire, the two of us are saying, "Fish on."

In less than an hour, the large cooler we brought for our catch is full to the top with lake water and thrashing fish, far more than enough for the evening's feast. As you reel in the last catch of the day you say, "After we get this one in the boat, let's head for the cove we found the first time, the one with the large rock wall. As I recall, there's a nice little beach there that we can pull the boat up on, and then we'll have something to eat. I did pack some goodies."

"Will there be some nice, tasty dog biscuits in there as well?"

"Might just be," you say with a grin.

"Did you hear that girl? Treats for the hero of the day!"

"Woof, woof! Woof, woof!"

We pack the fishing rods and make ready. You slowly turn the boat towards the center of the lake and throttle the engine all the way up for a quick ride over to the cove.

The Plan

Coasting into the cove towards the small beach, I marvel at how incredibly beautiful it is. I was so focused on what I needed to teach you the last time we were here, that I didn't really have the presence of mind to enjoy this wonderful little place on the lake. Mind you, we couldn't catch fish here if our lives depended on it, but then again, the scenery makes up for that.

The bow of the boat slides up onto the beach with a sandy growl, and Sheba is the first one out. I follow her and pull the boat further up on the bank so it is stable, and you begin handing me gear . First, the picnic basket, then a camp stove, some boxes, and finally come a couple of camp chairs.

We carry everything to a nice, shady spot with a beautiful view of the lake and begin to set everything up. You start with the camp stove. It's the kind with a large griddle and two burners underneath. With a big, toothy grin you announce, "This morning we will have buckwheat pancakes and eggs."

"Hot diggity dog!" I exclaim as I unfold the chairs, "It just doesn't get any better than that."

"We work for tips you know."

"And I'm a big tipper."

You light the camp stove, "Okay big tipper — Sheba, you need a walk in the woods?"

"Woof, woof!"

"Okay girl. I'll get a few dog biscuits, and we'll take a morning constitutional."

Reaching into the picnic basket, you pull out a large plastic container filled with pancake batter, "If you time it right the first ones will be coming off the griddle when you get back."

I give you a thumbs-up sign. After being cramped up in the boat, a good stretch of the legs will do me good as well. I stuff several dog biscuits into my shirt pockets and motion to Sheba, "Come on girl. Let's go check out the woods."

Sheba and I had a fine time. It was a good walk, and we both enjoyed it. When she wasn't nibbling on a biscuit, she was sniffing at everything in sight. By the time we got back to the camp you already had a small stack of pancakes on a plate and eggs cooking on the griddle. "Hail the conquering hero," you call out to us, "There's a large thermos with coffee in the boat. Go grab it and let's start eating."

Minutes later we are both chomping down on an outdoors breakfast. Nothing beats a campfire breakfast, and we both feed Sheba small tidbits from our hands.

"You know; I forgot to tell you last night, but I invited Charlie to come over tonight for the big feast."

"I'm glad you did. I enjoy his company."

"So do I and you're not going to believe this; he's volunteered to clean the fish."

You laugh so hard you spray bits of pancake out of your mouth. Regaining your composure, you wipe your mouth and say, "You should invite him more often." We both laugh, "But don't worry; I'll hang out with Charlie, and we will clean the fish together. That'll be fun because we'll have a chance to kibitz."

"He'll like that," I agree as I set my plate down and pour myself some more hot coffee from the thermos, "So, are you going to hold me in suspense all day, or are you finally going to share your launch plan with me?"

You set your plate down with a mischievous smile and slowly pour yourself some coffee, "I remember something you told me about dealing with wealthy people. How, when you talk with them, always keep one foot out the door. Well, that's how I'm going to come at this thing, beginning with my council of elders."

"Now, this is an interesting twist."

"Marshall, if we are going to do this thing, we must do it with a unanimous consensus, and that means the leadership of my organization must be behind me one hundred percent. So, first thing, I'm going to speak with my elders, and I'll lay out the facts. I'll give them the vision of how we start, and what our community will eventually look like, and answer their questions. After that, I'm going to ask them to put it to a vote and to do their 'necessary duty,' just as they have compelled me to do mine. I will also tell them it needs to be a unanimous vote, so if any elder refuses to vote for the proposition, that person needs to step aside so that his or her position can be filled by someone who will."

"That will go over like a lead balloon, but then again, this is fish or cut bait time. What if they balk and someone asks, 'If we say no, what are you going to do?' "

"Well, I'm not going to say something foolish like, 'Don't wait for a postcard,' but on the other hand, if you're not paying to see my hand I'm not going to show it. I'll just tell them I will do what I always do; I will walk humbly with my God. I'll leave it at that until they return to me with a unanimous vote of support."

"I'd love to be a fly on the wall when they're sorting that one out. We know everyone talks the talk, but this way you'll see who actually walks the walk and go from there. Just between us though, what if they don't have the courage to stand behind you? What will you do?"

"As I said, I will walk humbly with my God as a faith-based tribulation leader. If you are going to be a leader, the very first person you need to lead is yourself. That way, when others follow they'll usually follow for the right reasons. On the other hand I must have the courage to take the first step and to take that first step alone, if need be."

"You are stouthearted, that is for sure. I think the elders will see that in your face and hear it in your words. Your love for God is clearly bound by strength and honor. So let's go the flip side. Assuming you do get their unanimous support, what happens next?"

"At that point we work together to develop an announcement packet and an information packet for the members of our congregation. The announcement packet will announce a weekend survival retreat, and the information packet will be a decision packet. It will include an oath, an explanation of all that will be required, and what to expect in terms of time and financial contributions, which will be substantial. After all, we're not going survive the tribulation with a ten-cents-on-the-dollar proposition."

"Once we have done that, the next step will be to organize the retreat. There's a nice place we can use within a few hours' drive of the city with lots of room. It's far enough away to be apart from the noise of life, but close enough to be convenient. We'll schedule it; so everyone shows up early Friday night. We'll start with a welcome dinner followed by a short prayer meeting. After that I'll give everyone a quick briefing as to what we'll be doing over the weekend, and then it's lights out."

"So what will be in the survival retreat announcement packet?"

"Part of the announcement will be that each family needs to bring sufficient supplies for a five-day relocation deployment including food, water, shelter, sleeping bags, protective clothing and everything else that is necessary to be completely independent in the field."

You tap the camp stove lightly with your toe, "Including some way to keep food and make hot beverages. We have several families who are outdoor enthusiasts, hunters, and so forth. I'll reach out to them for help with putting together a reasonable relocation deployment list, and we'll pass these out after services the week before. On Saturday morning we'll have everyone set up in the parking lot for a big show-and-tell of the supply kits they have put together."

"So why a show-and-tell?"

"I half expect you know the reason, but the point of a show-and-tell is for people to lay out their relocation deployment kits so other members of the church can see how serious their level of commitment is. For example the ones who take their commitment seriously will think it through and show up with plenty of food, the kind that tastes good and keeps you going.

"On the other hand clever dabblers will no doubt turn up with the bare minimum or even less, such as a '72 hour kit' of freeze-dried foods, or high-calorie nutrition bars, 'guaranteed' to keep you going for three days. We both know these are nothing more than advertising gimmicks, and they won't be sufficient in real life conditions.

"That will be the morning. In the afternoon and into the early evening we will focus on team-building events. There are a couple of things that I want them to do that are easy and fun. That is assuming a particular team doesn't have to deal with some ego-driven idiot rocking the boat. At the end of the day we'll have two-man fire extinguisher drills with real fires."

"I have a couple of firemen in my congregation, and I did this with them once before. They'll set out a low, steel box on the ground with gasoline in it. Then in teams of two, we'll ach take turns following the correct CERT protocol for using an extinguisher to put out a fire. The point of this exercise is that I want people to experience working together in teams with the realism of dealing with a real danger while using standard procedures and communication techniques. I know my firemen will be happy to help us with this."

"Don't forget to get signed releases."

"That's for certain."

"You said that you had team-building exercises before the fire extinguisher drills. I'm really curious to hear about those."

"The first one is called 'The Tower' and it is an indoor activity. First, we divide everybody up into teams of about 5 to 7 people. We give each team forty sheets of printer paper and one roll of tape and no scissors. We make sure the teams are well separated and assign an observer to each team.

"Once everybody is situated, I will explain that the team has 20 minutes to build a free-standing, self-supporting, paper tower that must be at least 5 feet tall. They can use any design they would like, and that's it with no more rules than that. I think 20 minutes is good, but that can change.

"Once we tell them to begin, our observers will watch what is going on and how the team members are interacting with each other to solve the problem. If you have someone with an ego-driven personality, this activity will flush them out. They'll be the ones who tend to suppress the ideas of others in favor of their own, regardless of the quality of the other ideas presented.

" More importantly, what you're looking for is how the team together approaches problem-solving. It is not important that they meet the 5-foot criteria or that their tower doesn't fall over. What is important is that they are cooperative and cohesive.

"Once we finish that activity, all of the teams will present their towers and explain what worked for them and what did not work. After that, the observers will comment on what they saw, pointing out things that were effective or counterproductive. Be sure someone is taking notes during this because you are going to hear a lot of valuable information about the people involved in this activity."

"That is a really great idea. What's the second one?"

"The second one is called 'Squares on the Ground.' This is much more challenging. Before you organize the teams, prepare the testing area by using tape or spray paint to create seven squares on the ground about 18 to 24 inches square. The center box will have an X through it, and the others will just be outlines. Also, set this up in an area where no one else can observe a team being tested.

"The next step is to divide everyone up into teams of six members. If you want, you can give give them peel-and-stick name labels with their squad number. After you've done this, an observer escorts the squads to the testing area one at a time.

"Meanwhile, we'll have the firemen explain the proper two-man team procedure for putting out a fire without actually emptying the extinguisher. Some fire departments might even have an electronic simulator, which is helpful. Either way, do not let this be a lecture-only instruction. Divide the people into two-man teams and make sure that they put wear personal safety gear like gloves, goggles, and helmets, and that they walk through the procedure several times.

"Meanwhile, once your first squad reaches the testing area for 'Squares on the Ground,' split them into to two teams of three people.

"Now remember, you have seven squares on the ground, and the one in the center has a big X in it. Nobody should be standing on that square when the exercise begins. Rather, the three-person teams should be standing inside the outlines of their side's three squares, and facing the center square and the other team.

"At this point, your observers will give the instructions. I also recommend at least two observers, even though three will be better. They will explain to the six-person team that the activity goal will be to move each three-person team to the opposite side and that they should still be still facing in the same direction that they started out facing after they cross over. If they do that, they win the challenge. They will have twenty minutes to complete the activity. Now come the rules:

"To begin the activity, everyone must be facing the center square with the X in it. However, once the activity begins, participants can face in any direction as they attempt to cross.

"One person moves at a time. Each team member can only move forward toward the opposite side of the square with the X in it. If anyone moves backward, the team has to start the activity all over again.

"Each team member's feet must stay inside the squares at all times. If anyone steps out of a square, the whole team must start the activity all over again.

"To swap sides, team members can go around one person to an empty square that is immediately behind the person they are passing.

"When one team member goes around another, both must keep their feet in the square without going out of bounds. However, everyone can use their arms and hands to steady each other in any way they wish.

"This is a much more intensive test, but it will show you who the real problem solvers are; as well as, those who come up with interesting ideas and have a good memory. I've done it myself, and our team made it within the time limit, but I'm not going to tell you how.

"Once everyone has completed both activities, it's time to take a break and let everyone relax for a while with drinks and snacks. After that, everyone goes to the fire extinguisher area where each two-man team will put out a real fire. Since we'll be charging for this retreat, building in the cost of the extinguishers will be easy, and besides, this really is an important activity. I want my people to face a real danger with a teammate for an authentic sense of realism."

"Sounds like a really intensive and revealing day. So what's everyone doing that night?"

"Dancing is accepted in our faith, so I'm asking this lady, who's a square dance caller, to bring her equipment and to give everyone a basic course on square dancing for beginners. I also know that some of our seniors are active square dancers; so, they'll love it, and they'll be a big help with getting the newbies started.

"At the outset, I'll explain that during the tribulation, we'll need to have fun as a community. In the old days, when the pioneers were settling the country, the weekly dance was always the high point of their week. It was a time to meet family and friends, to get caught up on things, to pursue courtships, to welcome newcomers, and whatever else happens when a community comes together to celebrate life for an evening. They would often dance late into the night, and the younger children and babies would be bedded down around the edges of the hall."

"So far, so good, and I would love to be there for that Saturday, as well. What about Sunday?"

"Of course you're welcome to come, and I would love to see you there, but Sunday is when we really get serious. We'll start off as we usually do with our retreats. We will begin with light refreshments followed by our usual services. Then we'll enjoy a big buffet lunch, and after we clear the tables, it will be time for my final presentation."

"By this time you should have their undivided attention. I'm curious about one thing though; what will your congregation already know about your survival village program before this presentation?"

"While I will likely have spoken about things in general, no one will know the area we're looking at for the relocation, or how we intend to construct our survival village. Rather, I'm going to keep everyone focused on working with each other and see how well each of them interacts. When I finally stand up with all the elders behind me, I want the congregation to be long on curious and short on details. When I make my speech, it will be a short speech, at least a short speech for me," you add with a grin.

"Have you worked out what you're going to say?"

You reach into the back pocket of your jeans and bring out folded sheets of lined paper, "When I set out to write my speech I remembered Abraham Lincoln and how he gave the, 'Four score and seven years ago,' Gettysburg address. It's probably the best-remembered speech in American history, and it was just a few minutes long.

"Interestingly, Lincoln followed Edward Everett, a famous speaker in those days who gave a two-hour oration. That's a hard act to follow, but nobody remembers what Everett said. However, we all remember Lincoln's Gettysburg address, and historians tell me that Lincoln was in the early stages of smallpox when he delivered it.

"As I contemplated that, one key thing about the Gettysburg address was that it framed a turning point in the Civil War for both sides in the conflict. Today, we're facing an even greater turning point, so, as I see it, now is not the time to coddle and plead. Folks will either get it or they won't; so here goes."

You unfold the papers, review your notes, and clear your throat, "My brothers and sisters, we have gathered together before God to experience a small taste of what it will require to survive the coming tribulation. It is the unanimous intention of the elders and me that we create a tribulation survival village. It will serve God in a very special way, not to mourn the passing of this civilization, but as a center of hope and a clean slate for the beginning of the next civilization.

"As you leave here today, you'll receive one information packet for each family. In that packet you will find an explanation of our vision for what we must do to survive this tribulation.

"Keep in mind, regardless of what happens to each of us, humanity, as a whole, will survive and rebuild. Of this you may be certain. Likewise, humanity will go to the stars because this tribulation will cause us to understand the true fragility of life on our planet and to seek to form colonies elsewhere.

"So, what about us and the center of hope vision I am talking about? Our center of hope will be a place where we will survive, prevail, and then thrive following this tribulation.

"This brings me to each family here, and what will be required of those who chose to participate. In simple terms there are three cardinal rules: everyone works, everyone defends, and everyone participates. That being said; we know that not everyone here today will choose to join in this effort. In that case let me advise you of your chances of survival.

"Please keep in mind that this estimate is not from me, or from the elders who completely support me in this effort. Rather, this is the estimate of the elites who run this world, and who, through their own selfish acts, have seen to it that the better part of humanity will perish in the coming cataclysms. By their calculations, only one in ten who are alive on the earth today will survive. Let me repeat that figure for you. By their calculations, only one in ten will survive.

"Of course as the horror unfolds, the elites will be safe in their underground shelters. They have built huge, elaborate, well-stocked shelters with the money they've taken from the fruits of our labors. This is a fait accompli; so there is no point in complaining about it. When the time comes, they will disappear into their massive underground shelters and leave us on the surface to suffer and to die. If you feel that survival is hopeless and you would prefer to go quietly into that dark night, then it has all been arranged. You only need to let it happen.

"Now, let me talk to those in this room who are hopeful and determined to get through what's coming. If only one in ten of the families here steps forward to join this effort, these are already the odds for survival given to us by the evil one. However, on a personal note I believe we can do better than one in ten. No doubt, many of you are surprised by my direct manner. You've never heard me speak to you before in exactly this way, but we are talking about life and death here. So, this is exactly the way I must speak to you.

"Ask yourselves, what good would come from me holding your hands? Pleading with you? Coddling you in an attempt to sway you with words that flow into your ears like warm honey? What good would that do?

"As I said before, this is a Gettysburg moment, and in the coming week each family here must decide its own path into and through the tribulation. For those who wish to make a totally informed decision, there are information packets at the back of the room. There is one for each family.

"Now, let's get to the bottom line. We are taught that God continually tests us and that there is no convenient, one-time super-test. This is not how it works. Rather, God tests us all the time, and this is one of those times. So before you pick up one of those packets at the back of the room, I challenge you now with these ten tests:"

1. If you feel that your sensibilities have been offended in any way, and you doubt our sincerity, then go home and forget about all of this.

2. "If you look up in the sky at what is coming and you do not see a clear and present danger, then go home and forget about all of this.

3. "If you do not believe that the elites who control this world have planned for us to fail, then go home and forget about all of this.

4. "If you are pretending to be seriously interested, but are actually seeking to keep your options open, then go home and forget about all of this.

5. "If you are only interested in yourself and your own family with a me-and-mine attitude, and are unwilling to survive in service to others, then go home and forget about all of this.

6. "We live in an area that has a low survivability factor, and relocation is mandatory. If there is a 'Lot's wife' in your family who will 'look back' and be unwilling to leave, then go home and forget about all of this.

7. "Divided families will divide our survival village community, and this cannot be tolerated. If any member of your family is opposed for any reason, then go home and forget about all of this.

8. "Your time commitment to the effort will be substantial, and if you are unwilling to give that time when it is needed and asked for, then go home and forget about all of this.

9. "Each family will be asked to make a considerable financial commitment. If you are unwilling to give what is asked of you, then go home and forget about all of this.

10. "And finally, in the packet at the door there is a solemn oath each family member above 11 years of age will be required to take. A week from today after services, that oath will be administered once, and once only. If you are absent or plan to be absent, then go home and forget about all of this.

"I am certain that many of you at this moment are wondering how many families here today will join us in this extraordinary endeavor. You may think that I'm a poor salesperson who is bent on self-sabotage. To such questions I can only say that the elders and I have chosen to do this because we believe that our God has commanded us to survive with a noble purpose and to make this a better world.

"If only a handful of the families present here today join with us, I will rejoice in that. They have chosen to answer a calling that will be difficult and taxing to say the least. Yet, this calling will be spiritually and emotionally rewarding in ways we cannot imagine. In the midst of all of this difficulty those who choose to join us in this effort will bond with one another and with God.

"They will bond with purpose. They will also bond with hope for the future, and together we shall all bond with God. Though our numbers may start out small, our ranks will swell with like-minded others who have chosen to pursue their love for God through service to others along this path. Now the time has come for each family here to make a totally informed decision. Whatever you decide, may you do it seeking God's wisdom.

"In closing, please join with me in reciting the 23rd Psalm.

'The Lord is my shepherd; I shall not want.

He maketh me to lie down in green pastures: he leadeth me beside the still waters.

He restoreth my soul: he leadeth me in the paths of righteousness for his name's sake.

Yea, though I walk through the valley of the shadow of death, I will fear no evil: for thou art with me; thy rod and thy staff they comfort me.

Thou preparest a table before me in the presence of mine enemies: thou anointest my head with oil; my cup runneth over.

Surely goodness and mercy shall follow me all the days of my life: and I will dwell in the house of the Lord forever.'

"To those of you who will choose to join us, I celebrate your courage, your fearlessness, and your commitment. For those who will not, there is nothing to judge. You will always be loved, and you will be missed. This concludes our retreat. I pray that you all have God's protection and a safe journey home. Amen."

Tears are streaming down my face, and it takes all my strength to simply say, "You are ready."

The Sleepers

In all my life I have never seen two people enjoy cleaning fish as much as you and Charlie did that afternoon. Because the two of you laughed so often, I was sometimes scared you'd accidentally cut yourself with those sharp knives you were using. But the two of you managed it perfectly, and that night we all enjoyed the most wonderful farewell dinner anyone could ever imagine. The fried fish was succulent and sweet; everyone ate their fill; and the Backside root beer was a big hit. It doesn't' get any better than that.

Of course, Sheba was the star of the evening. Everyone enjoyed feeding her bits of fish and asking questions which she answered cogently with her barks. As always, she warmed our hearts with her insights and playfulness.

Fortunately, we had an extra guest room that was perfect for Charlie. Of course the children were wound up and stayed up a bit late roasting marshmallows for s'mores in the fire pit on the veranda, and they finished every last drop of my Backside root beer. Because it was the last night there, the rest of us just didn't want to turn in as early as usual either, and so, most of us lingered and chatted till the wee hours of the morning.

In the end we all slept like children deep in our slumbers. It was the perfect end to a perfect day.

The next morning I woke up, and everyone was gone from downstairs except for me. I showered, shaved, dressed, and went upstairs. There you are flipping pancakes and cracking jokes with Charlie.

"It appears it'll just be us three this morning," Charlie announces.

Pouring a fresh batch of pancakes you greet me and say, "When I asked Charlie, he just said that the sleepers had awakened. Oddly enough, that makes sense to me, though I don't know why. So, why am I not crawling the walls right now, and wondering where everyone has gone?"

"Inside you already know that they're safe and at home. Because this is a special place in the space-time continuum, you can come in your actual, physical body as we three have. Or, you can come in your spiritual body as a result of a dream. That is what Charlie is getting at. Like you, we too are light workers, and like God, all light workers must respect free will.

"You see everyone else, who was here, was dreaming. Some may remember parts of what they did here, but most of them will remember a few dreams dotted with a restful night's sleep. Yet, whether they remember all of it, parts of it, or none of it, each of their spirits chose to of their own free will.

"What the sleepers take back with them will be good memories which may be expressed through wise choices in the future. This is why the souls within us choose to come to a place like this. We do not solicit anyone. All we do is to provide the opportunity, and they come with their own free-will choice."

"And this is how it works at the Planet X World's Fair," Charlie chimes in, "Most of the people I meet and talk to are dreamers, and that's fine by me. You never know what they'll take back with them, but there is always the possibility that what they take back will help them with important life-or-death decisions."

"Makes perfect sense to me, Charlie" you quip, "How many pancakes you want?"

"Keep them coming till I say when."

"On the way!" you answer as you flip a pancake so high it almost sticks to the ceiling. At the top of its arc, it begins to descend, and you hold out a plate to catch it like an outfielder at a baseball game."

"I'll take that one," I exclaim and grab the plate, "So, what's the drill today, Charlie?"

"Well, we're going to leave here today as a threesome," Charlie answers, "First I'll take our new faith-based tribulation leader home, and then I'll drop you off at the fair. After that, I have some personal business I will need the time machine for."

"Excellent plan," I say while pouring syrup on my pancake, "Out of curiosity, what are you doing today?"

There's a glint in Charlie's eyes. I suppose he's been waiting for me to ask that question. "Do you remember that day when we were having lunch, and you asked me if watching the big tent being put up at the circus with my father inspired me to become an aeronautical engineer? You know that question really hit me between the eyes. I was sixteen when my father passed away. Life was hard for me and my family. Not long after that I put those memories away."

"Why was that, Charlie?" I ask.

"I would like to say that my father died a natural death, or from an accident, but the truth is that we live in a hateful world, and that's about all I want to say about that. However, I loved him, and when I was a small fellow, we would go early to the circus just to watch them erect the big tent. We also loved to see how they assembled the carnival rides while we talked about all manner of things. Those were such precious moments for me. You see; my father was a working man who never had much, but he knew I loved the rides; so, he always managed to find a few dollars; so I could enjoy the ones I really liked.

"I was fascinated by the hissing hydraulic rams of the machinery, the glaring music, and children squealing with joy even as a young boy. The hissing hydraulic rams, the glaring music, and the children squealing with joy. But most of all it was going around in circles, and each time seeing my father leaning up against the railing and looking at me with joy in his eyes.

"After we lost him, I'd still go to an occasional circus to watch them erect the tent, and watch the children riding the rides, but it was never the same. Instead, it became lonely and somewhat painful; so I stopped doing it. It was like I put all those memories away in an old trunk and stashed it in the attic to collect dust. When I did that, there was one memory; I wish I had held onto.

"Even though I was lonely when I went by myself to the circus, I always sensed my father standing there beside with me with joy in his eyes. But you know how it goes. After I had graduated high school, there was college, family, and career, all of which kept me busy enough to forget.

"That was until that day at the cafe, and that night I couldn't sleep much in the dome. It wasn't that it was uncomfortable, but I just sat there feeling as though I had taken down that old trunk and opened it, and all those wonderful memories came flooding back into my mind."

"You didn't imagine it," you say to him softly, "Charlie, your father really was there. He really was with you. He always has been, and he always will be."

Tears begin to stream down Charlie's cheeks, and you and I come around from both sides of the table to comfort him, and I say softly, "Charlie, you need to find a circus." He nods in agreement, and so do you.

After breakfast we spend the better part of the morning with Charlie telling us his memories. Eventually, the time comes for us to close down the house, after which the three of us look around for Sheba, but she is nowhere to be found. I ask, "Did either of you see Sheba this morning?" Neither of you had.

"Marshall," Charlie says thoughtfully, "I've had dogs all my life. You're Sheba's friend, but you're not her Alpha. Maybe she's just had an adventure with us, and now it's time for her to go home. She's very smart that way, you know."

"I know, but I have to admit that I wish she were coming with me. Who knows; maybe we'll see her again. Well, no need for me to be a sentimental old fool. Let's get going."

"I've got the machine all setup and ready to go," Charlie says as he turns to you, "Your books came in. They're in the machine along with a little something from Marshall."

The Return

As Charlie said, the machine is ready, and your box of books is on the floor behind the seats. Next to the box is a small styrofoam container with some root beer the children missed last night. It's the first thing you investigate, "Well isn't this a treat. Five bottles of Backside root beer. I'm going to enjoy these slowly, like cognac."

We get seated as the hatch closes and the machine begins to whir. We look out the window and Sheba steps out from behind and tree and holds up a paw to say goodbye. We wave back as the machine dematerializes, and an instant later Charlie puts his hand on your shoulder and says, "This is your stop, my good friend. Let me help you with your things."

We move your things out of the time machine to a safe distance, and you look at us with a touch of sadness, "Coming back to this moment feels like falling into an ice cold pool of water. I'm going to miss the fair and the lake house more than you can imagine."

"You made the grade," I say proudly, "When you're ready, your time will come to pay it forward and to mentor others as I have mentored you. When you do, the fair and the lake house will be yours to use any time you need to help a new soul along the path."

"How will I know when that time comes? How will I be able to reach you?"

"Just remember what Rabbi Sarah said, 'We will do, and we will understand.' If you just start doing it and have faith in yourself and in your relationship with God, the rest will sort itself out. Then you will know."

Charlie and I get back into the time machine, and we wave goodbye to each other through the window. As the machine begins to whir beneath our feet, Charlie says, "I think we got us a winner here. What do you think?"

"You betcha, and a best of class."

An instant later we're at the Planet X World's Fair, and it's a quiet day with no visitors. This is the day when the park is closed so the staff and volunteers can enjoy it. As the machine materializes before the entrance, we see many of them waiting for us. As the hatch opens, Charlie says, "Marshall, I didn't get a chance to tell you this before, but Lou has an idea for a new addition to the fair. He calls it, the Connectarium, and it will be devoted to tribulation radio communications. I think you'll like it."

"Sounds like my kind of idea, Charlie. I want to hear more about it; that's for sure," I say as we step out of the time machine to a heartfelt welcome from one and all.

I see Lou standing to one side and signal him to join me as Charlie returns to the time machine, "Hey Charlie," Lou calls out, "Where are you going good buddy?"

Charlie turns with a big smile and says, "I'm going to find a circus, Lou," and disappears back into the machine which leaves Lou with a mystified look on his face. Moments later, we see Charlie inside the time machine, his face beaming with a big smile as he waves goodbye and vanishes.

"Lou, Charlie will have to explain the circus thing to you, but he tells me you have an idea for a new addition to the fair. I'd like to hear about it. How about you meet me at the monorail entrance in about half an hour and bring your presentation with you."

"I'd love to, Marshall, see you there."

"You got it."

It would be a simple thing to use an electric cart to get there in a few minutes, but I really enjoy these quiet days when I can just stroll through the fair without all the hustle and bustle. It's a nice walk to the lobby of the arched terminal building for the overhead monorail, and there I find Lou already waiting for me.

The two-car monorail hangs from rubber-tired power units forty feet above the ground. It gives a spectacular view, and the ride takes about eight minutes, but today I feel like going around several times. Lou is holding his presentation folder under his arm, and I nod in the direction of the open door in the first car, "All aboard."

We get in and sit on one of the long benches facing the fair. After the doors close, the monorail begins to move at a leisurely pace.

"You know; Lou, all of this is based on the 1964 New York World's Fair, and I was actually there as a young lad. It was an intoxicating time for me. I remember going to the AT&T exhibit and using a video phone and a telephone touch tone pad for the first time. This was seriously futuristic stuff in 1964. It would be decades before they would become commonplace.

"But it was the memory of riding this monorail that really sticks with me. I remember the people strolling through the fair, taking pictures with their Kodak cameras, and experiencing something that was completely amazing. And yet, I think it would be impossible for today's children to feel that same sense of awe that we all felt in 1964.

"It was a time when we saw our country doing great things, and it was a time of great change and great hopes. That was the year NASA first launched the Saturn booster that would take our brave astronauts to the moon, and it was the year that the amazing X-15 rocket plane broke the altitude record by soaring 67 miles high. What an amazing time to be alive, and to feel that sense of awe, inspiration, and confidence in the future.

"I was a witness to history, Lou, and every time I ride this monorail, my childhood memories come back, and renew my hope for the future. Are you and I going to make it to the backside with Charlie to see blue skies and taste sweet waters once again? Who knows, but I sure hope that we will because I want to live long enough to see humanity take its rightful place in the stars with a Star Trek future. I want to see us go to space and be welcomed as an enlightened species, peace-loving and respectful of all life."

"I know this would probably sound impossible to the children of today, and most especially to those who will be born into the tribulation. As I sit here with you on this monorail enjoying this magnificent view of inspiration and awe, hope for the future is welling up within me again."

"All of us here feel it too, Marshall. It's why we do what we do, and we wouldn't have it any other way."

I give Lou a warm smile, "If we're going to have a Star Trek future, everyone must know that we're not alone. So Lou, tell me all about your Connectarium idea."

Epilogue

The night is still, and Sheba has curled up on a chair in the corner of the veranda which runs the full length of the house. The brightly-colored patio umbrellas are folded, and the lake house is dark except for a few lights that stay on all the time.

Above Sheba's head there is a clear sky streaked by an occasional meteor falling off to the far horizon. She occasionally looks up to watch a few streaks across the sky. However, the one she's looking for has yet to appear, but she knows it will and soon. So she waits patiently; occasionally glancing at the night sky as she methodically grooms herself. In the meantime she lets the memories of the last week pass through her mind, and she relishes each one of them.

After grooming herself, her patience is finally rewarded. Above her head the brightest meteor of the evening appears and falls off to the far horizon. Instead of disappearing, it reverses direction in an instant without wavering or losing speed. Sheba knows this is the one. She lifts her head and follows it through the night sky as it comes overhead and begins a gentle descent.

She hears the familiar hum of a type-two scout craft in landing approach mode, and her tail begins to wag because she knows her Alpha coming. She watches intently as the craft descends closer and closer to the ground, where it touches down on the broad flat area, between the lake house and the caretaker's cottage.

Jumping to her feet, Sheba scrambles down the stairs with yelps of excitement. As she reaches the base of the stairs, she hears the landing struts of the craft settling onto the ground. Halfway between the house and the craft, she pauses, and waits for the right moment.

A ramp lowers from the side of the ship, and the glow of the interior lights spills out upon the dark ground as it comes to a firm rest. Now she is even more excited as two figures walk halfway down the ramp and stop. One of them is her Alpha.

Distinguished in appearance and with shimmering speckles of gray in his brown hair, she can make out the bright blue eyes of his humanoid figure. Next to him is a female with sandy-colored hair and strong, blue eyes. "Come Sheba," her Alpha calls out to her. It is he, and she runs to him with joy in her heart.

He kneels down to embrace her as she runs up the ramp for the warm and loving reunion, "I've missed you," he says tenderly to her as the woman looks on with kindly patience. Sheba licks him on the side of the face; she has missed him too.

Running his hand along the shimmering silver material of his uniform, a pocket opens in response to his touch. Slipping his fingers inside, he removes a handful of small cubes. Each is about the size of a sugar cube, and small aquamarine-blue lines crisscross the salmon-colored, gelatinous glow of the cubes, "Look at what I brought you from your home world!" he says with a smile as he opens his hand.

Sheba gratefully gobbles up the cubes, chomping them down with delight, "So tell me, girl," he says, patting her on the head and rubbing her neck, "What do you think of these beings you've been with? Are they truly worthy of our help? Can we work with them?"

"Woof, woof! Woof, woof!"

"Oh my," he says with a surprised look, "Coming from you this is quite a compliment. I am most encouraged by your assessment." He pats her on the head and points to the open hatch behind them and says, "There are more treats for you in the ship."

He lovingly gives Sheba a little pat as she runs up the ramp. She stops just at the hatchway, and turns and looks at him.

"You did a good job here, Sheba," He waves at her to go in the ship, "You've earned it. Now, go have your treats." She pauses to look at him with loving eyes, then turns and scampers into the ship.

"Commander," the woman says, "I see that Sheba is beginning to shed again."

"Yes, Navigator Ta'al. I know," the commander answers.

"Sir, we all adore Sheba, but do you know how long it is going to take for the maintenance crew to get all that fur out of the air processors?"

"Ta'al, I do appreciate the crew's forbearance with these occasional inconveniences," he answers in a calm and measured voice. "In all my travels to more worlds than I can remember, I have never met a being who is more reliable than Sheba when it comes to being a good judge of character, and honestly, I must include myself in that, too. I am sorry the crew must deal with the fur, but it is necessary for our mission here to be successful. Sheba is the only one who can easily be accepted by these humans to observe and evaluate them as they learn here. Our progress and this most recent report are very encouraging."

Navigator Ta'al studies his face for a moment and smiles, "I know Commander, I know. The things we do for Creator."

Alphabetical Index

Made in United States
North Haven, CT
10 August 2023

40175601R00183